This Land Is Their Land

How Corporate Farms Threaten The World

Evaggelos G. Vallianatos

Common Courage Press   Monroe, Maine

Library of Congress Cataloging-in-Publication Data is available from
publisher on request.
ISBN 1-56751-358-1 paper
ISBN 1-56751-359-x hardcover

ISBN 13 9781567513585 paper
ISBN 13 9781567513592 hardcover

Common Courage Press
121 Red Barn Road
Monroe, ME 04951

207-525-0900
fax: 207-525-3068

www.commoncouragepress.com
info@commoncouragepress.com

First printing
Printed in Canada

Acknowledgements

Writing a book is like giving birth to a baby, except in the case of the book, you hope the baby will last forever. In my case, I took several years in the writing of this book, which is a continuation of the message I left in my other two agrarian books. Yet this book is more than that. It is the culmination of my life experience. In such an arduous and lengthy process of work, study, observation, and reflection I came across scholars, family farmers, peasants, friends, academic colleagues and students, each of whom left an impression on me that, in some instances, found a niche in the pages of this book. I cannot remember all of them, but I am especially grateful to Stahis Panagides, Vanda de Claudino Sales, Bill Devall, Linda Elswick, Nick Maravell, Miguel A. Altieri, Catherine Greene, Mary V. Gold, Jefferson C. Boyer, Christos Evangeliou, Percy Schmeiser, Alanna Hartzok, Jay Feldman, Bill Lambrecht, Nancy Creamer, Ray Weil, Timothy Weiskel, Brent Blackwelder, Michael K. Hansen, Lorette Picciano, Heather Williams, Carol B. Thompson, Albert V. Krebs, Robert L.E. Egger, John Zippert, Eric Kashambuzi, Harland Padfield and Gary Grant. I also remember with affection my late friend Joel Schor who, working for the US Department of Agriculture, never ceased struggling for justice for America's small family farmers, especially black farmers.

**In memory of my father Andreas Vallianatos
and mother Apostolia Vallianatos**

Contents

Preface to This Land Is Their Land

W hat kind of agricultural model is our nation pursuing and exporting to the world? This is the basic question that must be answered before billions more in governmental subsidies are poured into propping it up. E.G. Vallianatos brings to bear his considerable experiences over many decades of being in the midst of agricultural policy decisions running from the green revolution to genetically engineered agriculture and the depopulation of rural America. He is no stranger to agriculture, and he does not approach the topic from an ivory tower but rather from the experience he had growing up on his family farm in Greece.

He carefully works the reader through to the conclusion that a deadly form of agriculture is being practiced in the United States—an agriculture that cannot be sustained environmentally or politically because it compromises healthy ecosystems and undermines the basic foundations of community and democracy.

Vallianatos' message is urgently needed. The decisive contribution of community-based agriculture must be restored for the sake of healthy rural towns and for the underpinnings of a democratic society. Furthermore, if the world fails to move away from the socially and environmentally sterile policies of industrial agriculture, the numerous dead zones at the mouths of rivers worldwide will expand and the earth will keep losing the capacity on both land and sea to support the existing and growing human population.

Dr. Brent Blackwelder, President
Friends of the Earth

Prologue

Something Sweet in the Bitterness of Farming

The Greeks anchored their civilization on the values of the land and very small farms. Platon and Aristoteles considered the small farmers the best citizens of the Greek republics. Xenophon (430-354 BCE), a student of Sokrates, a historian, and a general, was right. He said agriculture was the mother and nurse of Greek civilization. He was also convinced farmers were generous people.

From their agrarian beginnings, the Greeks crafted the values and political institutions that suited their temperament and ethos—piety for the gods, democratic government, peasant citizen armies, the civilian control of the military, private property, art, theater, philosophy, science, literature and very small family farms. These were the ideas that made Greek civilization so powerful and lasting. Agriculture was hard work, however. The overwhelming reality behind everything the Greeks did was their precarious agrarian life—making a living on tiny strips of land at the feet of hills and mountains, rarely on valleys. Menander (c. 341-291 BCE), a comic poet, captured the Greeks' agrarian struggle. He described the Athenian farmer, the Attic man of the land, "working with stony soil, full of thyme and sage, but getting a good deal of pain and no profit." Yet Menander also saw sweetness in the "bitterness of farming." That sweetness was the democratic liberties farmers enjoyed—and the harvest. All agricultural festivals were propitiations to the gods for the blessings of freedom and for increasing the fertility of the land, for a good harvest.

In the month Skirophorion (June), Athenian women celebrated Skirophoria, a festival honoring Demeter, the Greeks' greatest agrarian goddess. The women threw various offerings, including piglets, into pits. During the Thesmophoria agricultural celebration in the month Pyanepsion (October-November), those same women collected the bones of the pigs from the pits and mixed them with their cereal seed sown at this time of the year. The women prayed to goddess Demeter for the fertility of their crops. In the month Anthesterion (February-March) the Athenians broke the isolation and anxiety of winter and prepared themselves for the coming spring with their spectacular three-day wine festival, which they called Anthesteria, the feast of flowers, in honor of god Dionysos.

Summer was harvest season. Hesiodos, a shepherd and an epic poet from Boeotia who thrived 2,700 years ago, says the countryside resounded with feasting, singing, playing the flute, and having fun— men on horseback moving about, others going hunting hares with sharp-toothed dogs, family farmers furrowing the divine earth. The crops would stand tall, the reapers mowing them down, the stalks grain-heavy at the top, this being Demeter's gift of food to the Greeks. Men would toss the grain sheaves on the threshing floor, others, would harvest the vines. Workers carried baskets for the white and black grapes picked from the row of vines. And the vines were full of lush grape clusters. Men were treading grapes; others drew the liquid wine, while still others were having wrestling matches. Summer was also time for leisure in the countryside, a season, Aristoteles says, of thanksgiving for a good harvest, Greeks gathering for sacrifices to honor the gods, offering them the first fruits of their hard labor.

Only when Greece lost its freedom to Rome, large farms began to undermine local democratic institutions and the independence of the small family farmers. With the Romans, large farms and the slavery of the small farmer brought down their republic. Pliny the Elder (23-79), a Roman natural history writer, complained that large estates ruined Italy and the provinces. Yet imperial Rome made large farms the icons of its aggressive policy in the Mediterranean.

It was Christianity, much more than Rome, however, that wrecked the agrarian and religious foundations of Greek culture. It took Christianity and Rome about 800 years of warfare against the Greeks to force them to delete Dionysos from their vine farming and culture. This ethnocide came to an end during the twelfth century. More than 200 years later, George Gemistos Plethon (1355-1452), a Platonic philosopher in Mistras, the provincial capital of Peloponnesos, urged the Roman Emperor to abandon large farms and return to small family farming for the Greeks. In fact Plethon's agrarian proposal—probably the most radical agrarian reform idea in the Western world—would have abolished not merely plantations but farm workers and private ownership of land. Modest-sized farms would be available to families to earn a good living for as long as the members of the family did all work. Once a person or a family stopped working the land, it reverted to the state. Plethon wanted to bring the Greeks to their senses and back to their Hellenic culture. He urged the emperor to discard Christianity and return to the Greek gods. That way Greeks, rather than mercenaries, would fight the Turks who were threatening the empire, and Greece, with extinction. The Roman Emperor did nothing and the Turks swallowed the empire in 1453, a year after Plethon's death.

Despite the harrowing vicissitudes of the Greeks at the hands of the Romans, the Christians, and other barbarians, including the Turks, they never lost their agrarian character and virtues.

I will never forget my pleasure as a teenager in treading on the grapes in the stone lenos or winepress, a small enclosure built right against one of the walls of my house in the mountainous village Valsamata of the Greek Ionian Island of Kephalonia. Linos (spelled with i) was the son of Apollon and the teacher of the great musician Orpheus. Linos was intimately related to the music and enjoyment in the making of Dionysos' sacred wine. It was that essential celebration of life and agrarian culture that Dionysos brought to the Greeks that the Christians suppressed. In fact, Christianity was so brutal towards the gods-venerating Greeks, that after it made them Christians, it imposed on them so many saints' days when they were forbidden to work, they barely had time to raise their food. Yet lenos and the happiness of wine making survived. The lenos in my house was like a small swimming pool with a well sunk in front of it for the grape juice. My cousins and I—and sometimes one or two other men—with bare, clean feet would get in the midst of those small hills of golden and black grapes and start our labor of love. We would march in that mass of soft fruit until all of it was pulp. The feel of the grapes was heaven. The sweet aroma of the flowing juice hung in the air like millions of drops of ambrosia. And for me, the experience was the closest thing I could do to worship Dionysos. The laughter, the games, the food, and the wine made for exquisite labor that connected us intimately to our Greek culture. In the sweet heat of late August, the entire village and island echoed this ancient tradition, celebrating the harvest of grapes and the making of wine.

Treading on my father's grapes was my way of tasting the sweetness of my father's farming, a way of life for most Greeks down to the early 1960s. My father's farming was the ancient Greeks' farming—the same humility on the benevolence and wisdom of nature, the same ten hours a day of work on strips of land that together made no more than 9 acres, the same love for donkeys, mules and horses, the same tools. For wheat we used a wooden plow and hoes for cultivation, sickles for harvesting, circular stone floor for threshing, pitchforks and wooden shovels for winnowing. The sacred olive tree was a symbol of peace for the ancient Greeks. They used small cuttings from the olive tree to award the Olympic champions. The olive tree was food, oil, wood, and fuel for light—to us, and our ancestors. We had a wooden press, similar to the winepress, for the extraction of oil from the crushed olives. However, by the time my father was at his most successful period of farming, in the 1950s and 1960s, a mechanical olive press replaced the traditional methods of getting the oil out of the olives. A mechanical wheat thresher also roamed the village.

My father's farming sustained us during the German and Italian occupation during World War II. My father's farming was defiance, self-reliance, and equality. We raised wheat, barley, lentils, wine, and olive oil. We also had small flocks of goats and sheep. We followed Aristoteles on self-reliance. The main reason my father's agriculture was the farming of the ancient Greeks was that Greece remained a nation of smallholders farming their land all over the country. The few millions of very small farmers were the arteries for the distribution of economic power and democratic institutions in the country. In addition, my father remained faithful to the agrarian nature of Greek civilization. The Greeks built their civilization on agrarian values. Uppermost in their development of democratic states, the Greeks insisted that the size of the average farm be modest (about 9 to 13 acres) and that the largest farm ought rarely to be five times the size of the smallest farm. This Greek farming is now on the verge of extinction. The Americans were successful in converting the Greeks to agribusiness. The second Christianization of the country took the form of agronomy and tractors.

I visit Kephalonia almost every year. With the exception of local olive oil, wine, and fruits and vegetables, the rest of the food comes from other regions of Greece. Villages are nearly empty of small farmers. The island lives or dies on tourism. It has been nearly impossible for me to find some one from the village to work my land. I visit my empty house next to other empty houses and there's no dog, Argos, waiting for me, not even a dying Argos moving his tail to tell me he recognized me. My childhood neighborhood is becoming a ghost neighborhood. My beloved donkeys and mules and horses don't exist anymore. Unforgettable images in my mind from my teenage years are primarily agrarian. They include following a loaded donkey in the heat of August to water the young olive trees; bringing food to my father, sisters, and cousins at harvest time; and, at other joyful occasions, running fast on horseback in the small, beautiful, village valley next to the water wells and the huge, ancient plane trees. Now the very few family farmers in Kephalonia drive small trucks. They work on larger pieces of land with machines and fertilizers and pesticides. They are complaining of the scarcity of traditional seeds. Hundreds of Greek varieties of the life-giving wheat, rye, and barley are lost. Rodakina (peaches), like the breasts of Aphrodite, are gone. The bees of Crete will never make their fragrant honey again. And the Thessalian war-horses that led Alexander in his global conquest and spread of Greek culture are becoming extinct.[1] There's a discontent over Kephalonia and Greece. Rural towns are not yet like America's corporate towns, but they are marching that way. The country is losing its ancient agrarian culture—the sole unbroken root to ancient Greece—for the temporary seductiveness and profit of alien ideas from America and Western Europe. These half-baked doctrines urge the Greeks to convert themselves and their agriculture to genetic engineering and factory-like farms.

Foreword

This book is about the undoing of humanity's first priority for living and civilization, agriculture.

Food is thought of as inexpensive, plentiful, and therefore not a focal point for understanding larger political issues. But the transformation of agriculture from a way of life to a high-tech factory in the field, often a threat to the quality of food, a constant and growing threat to democracy, has become a proven deleterious effect on life on earth.

I write this as a corrective of the usual texts on agriculture, agricultural development, development studies, international affairs, environmental policy, and political science, which ignore the political implications of trashing millennial agrarian systems with agribusiness and make believe, science-based agriculture, the fictional but dangerous "green revolution." In addition to students and researchers, my ideal reader would be the passionate lover of democracy, one who hopes and wants to see the world's countrysides return to small-scale family farming: That form of agriculture is the mother of democracy, healthy nature, pure water, prosperous and healthy rural people and communities, and good food unblemished by toxins or artificial ingredients.

I shall be focusing on a few crucial episodes in the "conversion" of peasants and small family farmers to agribusinessmen, or in their outright annihilation by the science-based agribusiness in the United States and the rest of the world. These special developments are not common knowledge because they have been camouflaged under slogans of fighting hunger, sustainable development, expanding agricultural production, or, even spreading Western civilization to the "underdeveloped" Third world.

I will be exploring the state and fate of the small family farmers and peasants, the former in North America and Europe and the latter in Africa, Latin America and Asia. These agriculturalists, small family farmers and peasants, are the same people, loving the land and working hard to raise food in ways, which leave little if any toxic effects on nature and society. They use tools and, in the case of the small family farmers, appropriate machines to do some of the work in the farm. As I said, my father was a peasant so we used the ancient tools we inherited from our ancestors, and, in the end, even mechanical means for the extraction of olive oil and the threshing of wheat. So, despite my criticism of industrialized farming, I am no Luddite. Machinery has its place, but it should not be designed and used for the domination or destruction of nature and society.

I provide references to both primary and secondary works, so the reader is confident the narrative is sound. I am a historian and a biologist and a passionate student of the Greek democratic tradition and a Greek who likes to know the origin of things. I document my story with scrupulous fairness.

Introduction

I wrote this book for two reasons: First, as I said, I was born and brought up in Greece, the son of a peasant who was self-sufficient in food. This experience made me who I am. My father's farming brought me in intimate contact with my ancient Greek ancestors who practiced agriculture the way they practiced polytheistic religion. In fact Greek farming was Greek culture. Greek peasants, not philosophers, built the polis or state and invented democracy. As a result, they rejected large farms as inimical to their democratic institutions and values: It is this legacy of Greek democratic farming that gave me the inspiration for this book.

I present an analysis of the effects of large and small farms on democracy in the United States in chapter 5.

The second reason for writing has to do with how I spent the best years of my life in the United States: I wrote this book because after working for twenty-seven years on domestic and international agricultural and environmental policy issues, I came to understand the dreadful ecological, agricultural, social and political consequences of spreading America's model of commercial agriculture throughout the world. America's agriculture is known as "agribusiness" or "conventional farming" in North America and Europe and "green revolution" in the Third World—Asia, Latin America, and Africa.

America made its agriculture a factory and then stood behind that industrialization. The tractors and the pesticides and the manipulated seeds were sold to the world as the latest in science and modernization. All things peasant were described as backward and underdeveloped. America, meanwhile, flushed with its World War II victory, advertised to a prostrate Europe its agricultural bounties as the prize of following her "green revolution" in agriculture. The money for the rebuilding of Europe and the emergency for sufficient food did the rest. Western governments bought America's agribusiness idea and lunched their own "green revolution" with subsidies, technical assistance, training their agricultural experts in the United States.

And the Western European peasants, like the peasants of Asia, Africa and Latin America, and the family farmers of North America, plunged into the unknown terrain of making their small farms little factories, first of all, for quick profits and, second, because they were caught by the almost global fever to replace their peasant traditions with what they thought was science. The thoughtless aping of America's factory farming pushed out of global rural culture the seeds, knowledge, and ways of working the land—all that the world had for food security and contact with its ancient traditions.

This industrialized agriculture dates, at the most, from the 1860s. In fact its high tech version, known for its massive tractors and genetic engineering of crops and animals, is bringing about a planetary and political cataclysm that is about fifty years old.

The pre-industrialized farming of the world was agrarian human culture millennial in age and wisdom, the mainstay of the population of the world. It took a myriad of diverse forms, but what form it assumed, nowhere did it transform land into a commodity. Agriculture and living were all part of the whole. Land was Mother Earth, part of the cosmos of production, part of life, religion and death. Everywhere people used their own seed for the next growing season, developing wonderful ways of providing for themselves in years where the elements went against them, keeping food for a time of poor yields.

The first phase in the massive and violent global transformation of traditional agriculture started with the Christianization of Europe and the dropping of Europe from the heights of Greek and Roman civilization to the abysmal ignorance of the Dark Ages. During the millennium of darkness in Europe, peasants lost their freedom to a variety of ecclesiastical authorities, national warlords, and foreign invaders. The Turks conquered Southeastern Europe and reached to the gates of Vienna. They controlled this large region of Europe from the mid-fifteenth century until the beginnings of the nineteenth century. But the Dark Ages (from about the fourth to the fourteenth centuries) gave a great deal of opportunity to the plantation to put deep roots in European soil: It became an agrarian institution of cash cropping and political control.

The second impetus in the making of violent agriculture came from the European invasion of the tropics in the fifteenth century. The Europeans decided they wanted their home farms in Africa, Asia, and the Americas. Anywhere they settled, they took with them their domesticated animals, seeds, flocks, tools, and methods of agriculture. They also wanted to trade with their home country. So they forced the indigenous people of the conquered territory to grow cash crops for them—tobacco, tea, sugar, coffee, cocoa for chocolate, bananas, and cotton. The Europeans put the most productive land of Africa, Asia, and the Americas under cash cropping, caring not in the least about the well being of Africans, Asians and Native Americans. They then exported these luxury crops. In fact in order to facilitate cash cropping in the conquered lands, they expanded the slave trade tremendously. That way, they imported blacks by the millions to the Americas. They did this because Native Americans said no to slavery and plantation work. They resisted the invaders and lost the war and their lives.

The other great push for the destruction of ancient peasant farming came in the early twentieth century with the rise and triumph of communism in Russia, Eastern Europe, and China and Southeast Asia. Communism lasted for most of the twentieth century. The communists said they came to power to abolish the abominable agrarian inequalities of capitalism, doing away with the plantation. Instead, exactly like the capitalists of plantations and giant farms, the communists uprooted peasant agriculture as primitive and backward version of farming and culture. And like the capitalists, the communists created their own plantations, which they made into sterile factories on the conquered land for the production of wheat, corn, cotton, tobacco, and animals. In Russia and China, the largest communists countries in the twentieth century, the communists killed millions of peasants in order to coerce other peasants into plantation workers.

Both communists and capitalists alike killed peasants. So the failure of industrialized agriculture is much more than the poisoning of nature and the ecological devastation it sows in the land. It is a moral and political failure as well. Agribusiness is using genetic engineering to remake the very fabric of life, bringing us that much closer to the terror of the "Brave New World" of Aldous Huxley; and, on the other hand, it is using the state to remake the world. These ambitions converge on the building of animal factories that give birth to mad cow disease, which is as much a malady of animals as it is a pathology of industrialized culture: I will demonstrate that it is simply impossible to base a just society and civilization on an immoral and violent system of agriculture.

Yet despite the wholesale violence against them, peasants still raise food with the wisdom and tradition of ages. They continue to resist the missionaries of giant agriculture and, along with the organic family farmers of the Western world, offer the only hope for the future. Peasants grow several nutritious crops year after year. In addition, these crops thrive without agrotoxins, synthetic fertilizers, machines, or irrigation. Peasants also rely on a variety of domesticated animals for food and work. Peasants do for humanity what no scientists or labs could ever hope to accomplish: They protect the world's genetic diversity without which life would be extremely impoverished or inconceivable. But in addition to this life-saving service, traditional farming gives meaningful work, food, and culture to more than three billion people in Asia, Africa, and Latin America. There's no way to unsettle traditional agriculture, the most ancient of human institutions and the mother of all cultures, without calamitous worldwide effects.

I favor peasants because they are the best farmers. At the same time I denounce their millennial oppression by landlords, who, today, are dressed with the clothes of agribusiness. So my praising of peasant wisdom is not a suggestion to a return to feudalism or slave farm labor, which is a distinct characteristic of agribusiness. Neither I am suggesting we melt down farm machinery. My hope is that we merge the knowledge and traditions of the peasants with those of ecology for an agriculture that is neither brutal to farmers or nature. I would also like to see the international system pay peasants to stay peasants, but without the political disabilities of feudalism. Peasants, like small family farmers, ought to have enough land to make a good living out of farming.

However, as I document in chapters one, seven, eight, and the conclusion, the international system has been rebuilding feudalism in the tropics for about half a century. Under the guise of modernization, and, since the 1990s, "free trade," biotechnology, and globalization, Western Europe and North America have been demanding that tropical countries go on with their colonial cash cropping for export while they open their agriculture to outsiders. When the countries of the tropics succumb to the sirens of "free" trade, they witness a flood of subsidized food imports from the industrialized agricultural giants of Europe and North America. Corn from the United States sells cheaper in Mexico than Mexico's own peasant corn. Mexico also reduced its subsidies to its campesinos growing corn and did away with the Mexican constitution's protection of communal lands for peasants. The results of these policies have been predictable: Genetic engineered corn is contaminating the traditional corn of Oaxaca and Puebla. In addition, a peasant exodus to the cities and privatization of peasant land are undoing the results of the Mexican Revolution of 1910.

Agricultural globalization means the conversion of traditional or peasant farming into industrialized agriculture. Such globalization brings violence—and not merely in the Third World. In India and the Philippines hundreds of peasants producing rice and cotton commit suicide nearly every year. The temptation to become capitalists fast kills them. They borrow money for pesticides and machines, and when they cannot pay back their loans, they take their lives. In Europe and the United States, several hundred thousands small family farmers have been forced out of agriculture. In the United States nearly all black farmers have disappeared.

The countries of the tropics still suffer from the plunder of centuries of colonialism. They have no corporations, giant enough, to compete with those of the countries of the West. They are also endowed with the planet's richest agricultural biodiversity. Consider hungry Africa, which is the theme of chapter seven. Instead of bringing back from colonial obscurity the agricultural richness of Africa, foreign experts and some African politicians are urging Africans to adopt agricultural genetic engineering as their salvation from hunger. Biotechnology or genetic engineering is not food. It is fundamentally the shuffling of genes from one species to another. The primary business idea behind such a hazardous manipulation and colonization of life is that, when successful—adding, for instance, foreign genes to soybeans in order to make them behave in certain desired and profitable manner—it's like the invention of a valuable product. Its owner reaps a harvest of money and power.

I started this book in 1992 with my visit to Brazil. The first chapter is about that journey. Of course, this is not a travel book or a study of Brazil, though I learned a lot from my memorable visit to that vast Amazon country. The purpose of my Brazilian trip, as well as the purpose of everything else I did in writing this book, was to understand the transformation of agriculture in both the United States and the rest of the world. Being in Brazil, gave me a first hand experience with the passions and violence of landlessness and recovering of land for those who have none. In the Brazilian chapter, I tested the idea of agrarian reform and understood the passion of countless millions of human beings for land. In the first chapter, and the rest of the book, I am documenting my key thesis—that, wherever industrialized agriculture takes roots, it poisons more than the land. It sets farmer against farmer, dividing communities, impoverishing rural towns, taking away the economic means to support a democratic form of government and life. That is the logic of the book.

Chapters two and three address primarily the ecological effects of giant agriculture. The term ecology means the study of the relationships between species and nature, our home and that of all non-human species. But ecological effects mean bad consequences for nature (water, birds, fish and wildlife) from employing mechanical and chemical farming to produce food. So ecological effects may cripple and kill wildlife, but they are by no means independent of politics. They are what experts define as anthropogenic or man-made effects. For the most part, humans destroy nature. Chapter four shows the precarious condition of organic farming on the heels of the rising genetic engineering of crops and animals. The presence of biotechnology on the countryside is a constant reminder to organic farming it is growing in its shadow. Some organic farmers are imitating the giants next door that it is difficult to distinguish between them, and not merely in the technologies they use, but in their political footprint as well. Chapters five and six are entirely about the anti-democratic nature of giant farming. In more detail, chapters two through six are about the American agricultural cataclysm: How the American model of industrialized agriculture, with all its ecocidal and democracy-busting effects, transformed rural America from a thriving society of small farms into the world's largest plantation, empty largely of rural people, a biological desert fit for factory production. It happened in the last half century with agribusiness sucking the life out of rural towns.

Industrialized agriculture is also striking nature repeatedly with near ecological paralysis and sporadic death. Now mad cow disease and bioengineered crops are shattering all remaining myths of American farming. Conventional American agriculture is no longer family farming but a factory. That factory is becoming the mad cow disease of America's brave new rural world. BSE or bovine spongiform encephalopathy or mad cow disease is a result of factory greed and bad science. Cattlemen—eager to earn more money from the meat they "produce"—receive the blessings of scientists for adding animal tissue and blood into animal meals, with the result grass-eating animals eating other animals are struck by this most horrible ailment, almost a divine curse, known crudely as mad cow disease. The brain of the afflicted animal becomes porous, like a sponge. The indestructible agents of death, proteins known as prions, drill tunnels in the brain until the animal dies. And humans eating the flesh of such "mad" animals also die from the same excruciating malady.

Mad cow disease is a deadly symptom of a systemic illness in the nature of industrialized agriculture, another cataclysm. This is a global farming system out of control. It denounces autarchy, the self-reliance of my father's farming, and eulogizes trade—converting the most productive land of the poor countries of the tropics to gardens for the rich people of the West. For example, Western "consumers" eat fresh beans from Kenya and Gambia in the middle of winter. Trade also means that the subsidized farmers of the Western countries can go on dumping their excess grains and factory food products all over the tropics. Such dumping benefits the few urban people with cash, but does irreparable damage to the peasants trying to make a living from their cultivation of traditional crops.

Global industrialized agriculture grows soybeans primarily for animals. Fish are turned into powder for pigs. California farmers use more than 5,000 gallons of water to "produce" a pound of edible beef. In fact, livestock farmers in the United States use more than half of the country's water. Every year the United States imports from Central and South America some 300 million pounds of meat. Yet more than 75 percent of children under 5 years old from Central America go hungry. They are undernourished because their parents are extremely poor and have little if any food. Bill Mollison, an Australian defender of family farming, is right saying industrialized agriculture is no longer agriculture but a death system, or, in my opinion, a factory of oppression and death. It uses agrotoxins and giant machinery to maintain its dominions. It is becoming the conduit for the dumping of America's toxic waste on farmers' land.

Industrialized agriculture also uses genetic engineering to postpone the end of agrotoxins and, finally, annex all family farmland. Genetic engineering, however, unsettles life at its most primordial origins—in the cell. Moving genes in and out of that enclosure wrecks normal development. Taking genes from a flounder and putting them into a tomato is teratogenesis, the birth of monstrosity in the tomato. This is because the gene transfer tampers with the organization and workings of life itself.

It is because of the political failure of the United States to protect its greatest ecological and democratic pillar, family farming, that organic agriculture takes on so much meaning and significance. More and more Americans eat organic food because they crave wholesome food uncontaminated by toxins, sludge, waste, and genetically modified organisms. Eating organic food is a political act, however. Many of those who eat organic food dream and see the organic farmer as the "other" family farmer who could possibly reestablish the American rural character so intimately connected with democratic farming. Organic farming is as ancient as Greek agriculture.

Despite the danger of the few large organic farmers, who foolishly are trying the shoes of their enemies, organic farming is a movement. CSA—Community Supported Agriculture, whereby city people pay farmers in advance for food they pick up from them weekly during the entire growing season—is the political message of this movement: Food is too important to be "produced" by giant corporations. City people must, once again, be part of that sacred process of raising food. Organic farmers are our family farmers. They are fighting to reestablish the tattered democratic links in rural America. They are protecting nature. Some of them are the sons and daughters of conventional farmers who are trying to go back to traditional American values and sustainable agriculture. Above all, they don't want anything to do with pesticides. They are just a hope away from the nightmare of giant agriculture. But to be successful in the long run, millions of city people must join CSA and increase the number of organic farmers on the land from thousands to millions. Without enough small family farmers in rural America, all power is in the wrong hands. Without enough smallholders on the land using appropriate tools for the raising of our food, all discussion about democracy becomes academic. Senator Wayne Morse of Oregon was right to say in 1959 that it is impossible to have political democracy without economic democracy: Widespread family farm ownership in the country, no less than private home ownership in the city, is fundamental to the perpetuation of democratic institutions.

We can support democracy by accelerating the settling of rural America with small organic family farmers. We can do that with the use of the $20 billion or so of annual agricultural subsidies that now go to large farmers. That money would assist exclusively the family farmers who agree to abide by the terms of a social and an ecological contract negotiated by their representatives, the leaders of environmental, justice organizations, workers' unions, political parties, and the government. Family farmers—with farms which should probably be between five and forty acres and which they own and work themselves—will agree to raise the country's food and in return the country will guarantee them a middle class income. Most of the food dollar will be going to them and not to intermediaries for "marketing." CSA provides the path. The tiny number of organic farmers shows the way. The purpose of the acreage limitation is to increase substantially the number of family farmers in the United States and settle rural America once again. The social contract will define agriculture as food, democracy, culture, and environmental protection. This means that these family farmers, with the effective implementation of agroecological principles, ought to increase and protect biodiversity, cease water pollution, and produce enough food. The food they raise, however, will be produced without violence against domesticated animals, toxins or genetic manipulation and with minimum hazardous inputs.

For me there's no separating of agriculture from democracy: He who controls the land has a lot to do with the formation of the character of society. That's why the Greeks insisted that small pieces of land be distributed to the largest number of free citizens in their states. That way democracy was the norm, not the exception. The framers of the American constitution incorporated the Greek model of agrarian democracy in the founding of their republic. That was the philosophy behind Jeffersonian democracy of 1800s, the Homestead Act of 1862, and the development of irrigation under the Reclamation Act of 1902. These laws settled on 160 acres being a sufficient and legitimate amount of land for the citizen farmer and, on that limitation, the state promised assistance. The Reclamation Act forbade the government from providing subsidized water to any farmer with more than 160 acres farm. Shifting power in rural America to favor small family farmers would be in accord with these fundamental constitutional principles.

However, agribusiness remade America in the twentieth century: The influence of this America or New Rome was so powerful that it made the Americas, Western Europe, and much of the rest of the world after its own agribusiness image: It's an unbearable sorrow to see English, French, American and Greek villages, or rural towns, becoming bedroom communities for urban people, the peasants or the small family farmers rushing to the cities as the refugees of a local cataclysm.

Chapter seven examines the export of this cataclysm to Africa. I visited Nigeria in 1998, and like my journey to Brazil in 1992, the picture I formed of that vast country and its agriculture, helped me be practical with my theories. I saw the fake and colonial nature of African cities. The skeleton of African villages struck me, half-naked peasants living in a lush countryside and semiarid land, eating not every day, and when eating, their food would often be foreign. Which is to say most African food is a product of an artificial and alien culture of cash cropping that is crucifying the peasants, their refugee brothers and sisters in the urban slums, and the green land. Yes, indeed, cash cropping is as bad as I thought it would be before my travels to the tropics.

Moreover, I spent 1995-1996 at the United Nations Development Programme in New York where—more than anything else, more than writing memoranda or attending meetings, I was amazed by the persistence of colonialism. By this I mean a system of exploitation and oppression, which, like the world's monotheistic religions, has such an extraordinary ability to survive in Africa and in so many other regions of the world. The secret, of course, is, first, that culture's propaganda on the superiority of the colonial order, which, in the "post-colonial" era since the 1960s, is roughly translated into Western progress and development, and, second, the bureaucracy colonialism left behind to keep it alive. At the United Nations Development Programme, some of my African colleagues were as vociferously defending the European cash-cropping legacy in Africa as non-African development bureaucrats.

In addition, I have been down on the ground since at least 1975 when I went to Colombia for research that became *Fear in the Countryside*, my first book about the political and moral economy of agriculture. In the United States I saw the huge mechanized farms and their miserable workers. I felt sorry for their brutalized beasts fatten for slaughter. I studied the violence with which conventional farmers mined the land.

I walked in the ruins of what they did—the disintegrating ecological and human communities around them, here in the United States, in West Africa or Brazil or in the rest of the Third World—Africa, Asia, and Latin America. I have no doubt the deleterious globalization of the industrialized agriculture is a refurbished, armed-to-the-teeth version of the colonial plantation.

I hold such strong views for two reasons. First, there's plenty of evidence supporting the theory that ill fares the earth at the hands of the mechanized plantation, the expanded and up-to-date high tech conventional agriculture, including the genetic engineering of crops. This form of farming has been responsible for deleterious planetary effects, threatening ecosystems and cultures with disintegration and extinction. The second reason I am very critical of industrialized agriculture, putting plenty of responsibility on the United States, my home since 1961, is my experience at the US Environmental Protection Agency (EPA). I spent twenty-five years with EPA, primarily as an analyst of issues relating to pesticides and agriculture. During such long period of time, 1979-2004, I read thousands of memoranda, scientific reports and papers and, otherwise, took part in countless meetings and did many other mundane things one does in a huge bureaucracy—all in the direction of helping in the shaping of policies, which I wanted to believe, were protective of public health and nature. Unfortunately, EPA never lived up to its ideals. Very shortly after coming into being in December 1970, the Agency came under the influence of the regulated industry, its bought and sold Congressmen and Senators, the entire business class turned against a government department, which could, and sometime did, reduce its profits. So by the time I joined EPA in 1979 the game was nearly up. The Office of Pesticide Programs, the largest organization of EPA within which I did most of my government service, is owned by the global chemical-pesticide industry under both Democrat and Republican administrations. "Protecting public health and the environment" is a slogan. I explain EPA, and how I survived in such a hostile place, in another book. But suffice it to say, my time at EPA was uniformly unpleasant. EPA became a testing ground for learning and unlearning, a laboratory of how honest science becomes dishonest risk assessment and cost-benefit analysis, both jargon traps for the uninitiated, putting the government's authority around the cause of the industry.

Cigarette science made billions of dollars for the cigarette companies because the cigarette corporations manipulated science and hid from the government what they knew to be hazardous about cigarettes. The chemical industry adopted such a model of deception to get from the EPA what the cigarette companies got out of the US Food and Drug Administration. EPA, meanwhile, pretended there was good science behind the products of the chemical industry it approved. So with that pretence went all efforts to regulate a goliath intimately connected to members of Congress. EPA, daring not to challenge the corruption of science coming its way, developed its own version of corrupt science to cover up its lack of concern for nature and the health of people. That experience molded my views on science, teaching me that our agricultural problems, why our farmers are hooked on agrotoxins, for example, are far more serious than their appearance suggests.

Conventional American farmers do what they do because they are profoundly connected to a certain view of nature and the world, their problems going well beyond technical issues one can honestly disagree with another. We have a difficult but necessary road to follow in rebuilding our agrarian-democratic foundations. So while this book is not about the EPA, when it sounds that I am overstating a point, and that may be quite often, it is because of my EPA experience. That experience put millions of data at my command, which I cannot cite in footnotes. Remember also I went through an inferno to be in a position to say what I say.

Chapter eight reveals the strategy of the West to keep dumping its hazardous agricultural technologies and goods on the Third World— all under the misleading slogan of sustainable development. Yet no doublethink can hide the invasion of the tropics. The business managers of the plantation system aim to end millennia of agrarian wisdom and practice in the world's villages. Their genetic engineering of seeds, for instance, threatens some three billion peasants who save seeds from their harvest for the next growing season: Biotechnology companies are developing seed genetic technologies designed to destroy traditional agriculture's practice of saving and breeding crop varieties.

These awesome agricultural upheavals that, increasingly, are becoming sophisticated low intensity biological warfare in the countryside—should they ever succeed—are certain to give birth to both global tyranny and a more intense shredding of human cultures.[1]

Unfortunately, the twenty-first century does not bode well for either agrarian reform or business-as-usual resolution of this coming planetary storm. The world population is bound to be 8 billion by 2020, 6.5 billion of which will inhabit Africa, Asia and Latin America. If in the late 1990s with a world population of about 6 billion there were about 900 million hungry people, more than 200 million of whom are still in Africa, one can be certain that by 2020 the number of hungry people will be much larger than that of the late twentieth century.

Industrialized agriculture has never fed, nor can it ever feed, the world's population. Its design as a factory plantation makes that impossible. It is a machine. And machines break down and have none of the knowledge, wisdom or the love of the peasant and the small family farmer for the land and culture of raising food and people on the land. At the same time, the industrial machinery of Japan, North America and Europe, and, slowly, that of the Third World, is deforming and killing the world's wildlife and ecosystems, and even warming the planet, and, therefore, altering its ecology in dramatic and, in the long term, catastrophic ways.

This is why I wrote this book: It is not merely a polite recitation of "facts." I looked at history, I traveled, I interviewed peasants, family farmers, experts, and I also involved myself in what I am writing about. As I said, my experience with EPA nearly destroyed me. I wrote this book to offer my insight, which I gained at great cost. I tried to lessen the powerlessness that comes with study and close observation of the devastation sweeping traditional agriculture in the Third World and family farming and rural life in the United States by putting honesty and truth in this story. I see my friends in the civil society slowly falling apart. These are individuals who are struggling to keep their faith alive in the survival of rural America and prosperous small family agriculture: We don't have much time to continue with our cowardly business-as-usual policies on agriculture and development in general. Civil society must win the struggle for a prosperous and healthy rural America and a better world.

Civil society is a diffuse phenomenon of working people resisting oppression. These citizens are not working for governments or corporations. They have no armies or other organized means of power. They are loosely connected individuals fighting for survival in urban and rural neighborhoods. They campaign against agribusiness, animal factories, and polluters. They are mothers struggling to feed their children, women striving for equality with men, women protecting forests in India, women campaigning against imuno-suppressive chemicals in the environment, estrogen-like poisons in the food they eat and water they drink, and rising female breast cancer in the United States. They are family farmers and peasants standing up to giant corporations trying to steal their land and abolish their ancient rights to save from their harvest the seed for the next growing season. Traditional fishers and indigenous forest people are also defending their fishing grounds and forests that give them life as much as hungry persons are searching for food, environmentalists fighting endless legal battles against corporations, and citizens defending themselves or the human rights of others from arbitrary state power.

Civil society is the singular global hope for putting the brakes on the ecocidal and anthropocidal (man-killing) development strategy of industrialized and industrializing countries. Civil society represents the overwhelming majority of the world's people. Tens of thousands of NGOs—non-governmental organizations—have been emerging all over the North and South in defense of human rights and nature. NGOs are civil society. They are the product of an international political system falling apart.

In the conclusion, I return to the importance of land and small farmers for both democracy and food: Conventional agriculture, the aggressive industrialized form practiced in the devastated rural America, is unsettling both human and ecological communities throughout the world. It must be stopped. It must be abandoned and buried in the archives of an earlier era of war. And its replacement will have to be a seedling out of the marriage of Third World traditional agriculture and ecological farming that is slowly growing in the United States and Europe thanks to the work of small family farmers and a few courageous scientists.

This book provides the theory and the practice for such spiritual and cultural and political and practical transformation. For people to reconnect with the sacredness of the earth and agriculture, they must understand, first, the violence and suffering behind the supermarket and the disappearing family farmer, the decline of democracy that comes with the silent spring of agribusiness, the colonialism breaking the peasant, and, second, the trade policies responsible for the cash cropping road to hunger, food insecurity, and impoverishment in Africa and the Third World.

The Greeks used to say pray to goddess Athena but move your hands and do something about the favor you are asking the goddess: This book is both a prayer to Athena and a political explanation of what humans must do, and why, for their prayer to reach Athena and Olympus.

Chapter 1

In Brazil

International Science under Military Protection

I am flying over the Amazon in the early hours of January 26, 1992. From Belém to Fortaleza in the Northeast of Brazil, the white cloud cover is thin, disappearing but immense. Glimpses of the rain forest and rivers mirror the earth's face in this Brazilian world. The cool whiteness of the upper atmosphere takes a radiance from the soft rays of the hot sun, thus nature sets in one of those eternal processes of life: Sun, trees, water moving upwards, becoming clouds pregnant with rain to revitalize the rivers and clean the environment.

From the sky, Fortaleza, a Brazilian metropolis of the destitute Northeast, appeared like a dream—acres and acres of a Portuguese city built on the edge of the Atlantic Ocean. The red and brown tiles of the countless homes were those of my village and all of Europe. The tiles, the narrow streets, the green tropical trees, the profusion of vegetation, made the city appealing, designed down to human scale. There's poverty in Fortaleza, too many people seeking the shelter of the town and the crumbs of tourists, refugees of the rural violence of the semi-arid Northeast.

By contrast, I stayed in a comfortable room in the luxury Ponta Mar Hotel right on President Kennedy Avenue. That avenue is a main thoroughfare where people perpetually stroll up and down purchasing goods from each other. On one side there are several highrise hotels, and on the other the stormy waters of the ocean. The beach is the commons. The small huts serving cold drinks, food, and company reminded me of my own Greek island's sugar beaches and narrow, market streets.

Dark-skinned and some black, of medium height, the Brazilians of Fortaleza watch TV made by the violent TV culture of Hollywood. Their young people listen to loud rock and, in other ways, worship the same gods of subjugating each other and nature to their own whims and ambitions. I woke up by the sounds of traffic and cocks! In fact I did not use the air-conditioner in the room but the traffic sounds were constant and loud the entire night—exactly like sleeping in my sister Anna's apartment in Nikaia, an Athenian suburb in Greece.

The beach in front of my hotel is a dream place: The sound of the vast white waves crushing on the sand and stones and the sight of that perpetual ocean anger are unforgettable.

At about 11 a.m. on January 27, 1992, Fortaleza's conference center was packed with over 600 scientists from all over the world. In the huge auditorium of the center, decorated for the occasion, the elite of Fortaleza and some federal officials of Brazil—including Fortaleza's archbishop, mayor, the past and present governors of Ceará, the state that hosted the conference—spoke to a full auditorium. They delivered noble orations on the importance of the conference and stressed Brazil's readiness to tackle the dilemma of climate and sustainable development. The archbishop spoke about the victims of hunger and desertification in Ceará. The president of the Brazilian Senate said his colleagues would take seriously the recommendations of the conference. The past and present governors of Ceará said they were ready to make their state a model for sustainable development. Each speaker spent several minutes giving the names and titles of the close-to-twenty guests—all of them addressed as His Excellency. Pomp and ceremony dominated the entire session. When the orchestra played the Brazilian national anthem, the governor of Ceará sang it. Pride and politics found a fertile ground in this ambitious politician's mind.

Just before the arrival of the officials at Fortaleza's modern conference center, a group of the city's underprivileged, the victims of rural violence, marched to protest the attendance at the conference of the state governor and his cronies. The protest took place in front of the Fortaleza conference center. The protesters, men, women and children, were carrying a casket and red and black banners. They would rush, shouting epithets, each time an official would step out of his car. Of course, these officials were protected by countless military police—who, interestingly enough, appeared to be of Indian or mulatto background. They were all young men and dark.

The conference was crawling with cops. Jesse Ribot, a lecturer from the Massachusetts Institute of Technology, and I crossed the line between the cops and the angry protesters, whom a collegue described as communists to us, before striking up a coversation with them. Jesse acted as a translator of sorts in this impromptu exchange.

Three of the protesters, two women and a young man, said that the governor of Ceará, Ciro Ferreira Gomes, and his administration were responsible for much of the hunger and oppression in Fortaleza. The productive land of Ceará was beyond the reach of peasants. The few landlords had grabbed that land from the peasants and used state violence and assassins to keep it. Agrarian reform, the protesters said, was absolutely necessary.

I gave to one of the women protesters my conference paper, which provided theoretical support for agrarian reform. These nice people gathered around Jesse and me and listened attentively. They were so happy we were on their side. I promised them I would try to get permission to have one of them invited to the conference, but my effort was a failure. One of the conference managers turned my request down on the pretense that NGOs (non-governmental organizations) were well represented in the conference. Later on, this administrator introduced me to Vanda de Claudino Sales, a professor of geography at the Federal University of Ceará. Vanda, at twenty-eight, was wild. She looked like Angela Davis of the 1960s. Her Afro hair made her slightly exotic. She is, by her own account, a mixture of French and Indian cultures. The Indian origins come from her father.

Vanda said her group was preparing a lengthy document about the social / ecological problems of Ceará. Vanda and others agreed that agrarian reform does not have a chance in the Northeast. A few experts talked about the Brazilian agrarian reform plan, but the government did nothing. Everaldo Porto, an agronomist who received his Ph.D. at the University of Arizona, explained Brazil's dilemma with agrarian reform in crisp terms. He said the very politicians that run the Northeast are also the absentee ranchers and landlords who own the irrigated and other productive land of the region. Why should these people be willing to part with their property?

The "scientists" at the conference were classic examples of technicians impressing each other with jargon about the climatic condition of the semi-arid regions of the world and especially those of Brazil. But even in their "climatological" monologues they were vacuous—mostly arguing about this or that uncertainty. Because I can no longer put up with pretense, I would listen to some of those "academic" papers and then get out of the conference amphitheater as swiftly as I could. Only Brazilian scientists raised interesting questions about the crisis in the Northeast. A couple of them, in fact, dared mention the unmentionable, *reforma agraria,* that it is needed in Brazil's Northeast for both social and ecological reasons. However, what infuriated me the most was the deliberate planning of the conference organizers—funded lavishly by American and Brazilian money—to cover up the pain of the Northeast under the fancy rhetoric of "impacts of climatic variations and sustainable development in semi-arid regions." Yet the concept of "sustainable development" received no more than superficial attention.

I wrote my paper around some theoretical issues of sustainable development. Yet my paper was buried in the conference's mountains of technical detail. My expectation was I would read my essay to the conference delegates in the hope of generating discussion. But, instead, they put me in a "working group" to come up with a page of recommendations for sustainable development. It turned out that an old professor from Columbia University, an economist who could barely hide his contempt for ecology and sustainable development, chaired this group. Other members of the working group included an expert on technology policy from University of Washington in Seattle, a Canadian professor knowledgeable about environmental impact statements, two Brazilian agronomists, a Brazilian economist, a planner from Ecuador and, of course, me. We spent about an hour and a half in academic gymnastics—arguing definitions, procedural matters, and exchanging hot air. My efforts to persuade the working group to promote agrarian reform was lost on two of the three North Americans. Only the Latins appeared to consider my suggestion. We ended our first round of acrimonious debate with the promise that they would read my paper and reconvene the next day.

I already said that the conference was full of cops, from the *policia militar.* The other characteristic of this international gathering was its intimate local business interests. The industrial organizations of Ceará, including agribusiness, were fully represented by exhibits in the main room of the conference center. The state of Ceará also showed off its products to the international visitors of the scholarly congress. But trying to project the image of prosperous agribusiness ventures sucking the precious water of a water-starving, semi-arid region was in bad taste. This thoughtless siding of the conference with the oppressors of Ceará's people was another indication of how far the organizers of this international gathering are from sustainable development. The protesters were right. Social change and real development in Ceará had and still have a long way to go.

To my surprise, my recommendation on agrarian reform passed nearly unanimously. The four Brazilians on my sustainable development panel enthusiastically endorsed agrarian reform as the chief priority for the Northeast of Brazil. I particularly liked a warm, big fellow, an agronomist from Sergipe, A. Bernardo Lima. He made clear that large farms, *fazendas*, should be done away with. Another collegue, Jose Juliano de Carvalho Filho, a professor of economics at the University of São Paulo, was also very friendly. The only Yankee who went along with me was Philip Bereano of the University of Washington in Seattle.

The teenagers who distributed the reports at the conference told me that many more people at the conference requested the Portuguese or the English version of my paper than any other report. That certainly was gratifying news to me considering that the organizers of the conference practically took me off the agenda.

I knew there was a huge gap between theory and practice in agrarian reform. After all, land and agrarian reform are about power. Land is the very heart of the agrarian culture of Brazil and the rest of the Third World. Agrarian reform, therefore, is by far the most vital ecological and social priority of the earth's people. No pro-peasant development has a chance when land is hoarded by the few in an ocean of landless and hungry human beings. Demetrios Christodoulou, a Cypriot Greek economist who spent twenty years with the United Nations Food and Agriculture Organization in the Third World, says that the global agrarian conflict blights the life of billions of peasants. "The root of agrarian conflict," he says, "lies in the misery, inequality and injustice under which billions of people feel themselves undeservedly condemned to live. Famines are only dramatic manifestations that attract outside attention; endemic grinding poverty and powerlessness are 'normal' features of their lives. In the cause of agrarian reform millions of rural poor have died or suffered torture and imprisonment. Agrarian reform is generally opposed by privileged land-owning interests and their supporters; their hostility and opposition is instinctive and 'natural.' Those close to the land, whose livelihood and welfare depend on it and who are aggrieved by existing agrarian relations, naturally yearn for improvement and change."[1]

Most of the forty million people of Northeast Brazil are certainly aggrieved by existing agrarian relations. In fact the Brazilian economist, Celso Furtado, was right. "The Northeast," he says, "is truly the face of Brazil on which appears, with brutal detail, the suffering of its people."[2] In the 1980s the agrarian inequalities in the Northeast were simply horrendous. The entire region continues to be the private kingdom of a few landlords.

However, any meaningful assessment of ending the misery, hunger, and ecological destruction of the semi-arid Northeast demands that its mega-farms and super-spreads be divided up to very small plots for the landless peasants. It would also be necessary that indigenous people, peasants, and small businessmen be asked to design a development strategy that would also eliminate, once and for all, the persistent hunger of their country. In other words, the key to non-destructive development in the semi-arid Northeast Brazil is the abolition of those relations of production, which create hunger, landlessness, and deleterious control of nature. The huge sugar and cotton plantations and immense land holdings for cattle provide the foundations for transforming this region into a self-reliant and prosperous society of peasants, pastoral nomads, and indigenous people growing their own food and supporting appropriate small-scale rural industries. Northeast should no longer be a colony of the Center-South but a paradigm of environmental and social reconstruction to fit the limits of climate and nature.

If such an experiment in economic development were successful in the impoverished and colonized Northeast of Brazil, not merely Brazil and the Third World but the entire earth would be better for it, particularly, if the big-time polluters who are raising the planet's temperature—North America, Europe and Japan—abandoned their fatal attraction to the fossil fuel technologies and culture threatening all life in this green world.

Land of the Sun

The semi-arid countryside of Ceará is not all dryness and desert. It preserves fragments of the Brazilian Atlantic forest in the mountains of

Baturite. These moist woodlands are full of golden tall trees, marshes teeming with life, bleeding streams carrying away the red soil. Yet perpetual danger follows the trees, plants and animals in this exquisite forest. The loggers who devastated the Atlantic forest for more than 500 years keep coming into Baturite, leaving a trail of plunder after them.

Our journey into the interior of Ceara did not bring us to the Baturite Mountains, but to the dry country. That way, like aliens from outer space, we took a picture of a world whose existence we did not imagine, or, in my case, a world I thought would not have frozen in the dark ages.

Three huge buses rolled off the Fortaleza conference center at about 8:30 in the morning. For the next two-and-a-half hours, the countryside appeared desolate, burnt out, despite its green cover. A typical village along the bus highway was a place called Horozinho. The main street of Horozinho had a few shops displaying chunks of beef hanging in the air. Dark-skinned men with bare chests, small pigs, chickens, and dogs were the other memorable citizens of this landscape. The asphalt road sliced through a flat region of small trees, bushes, goats and cattle grazing ranchland, and immense cashew plantations, producing Ceará's number one cash crop.

From time to time, small, deforested mountains would add to the strange beauty of this green yet semi-arid country. The green vegetation was a result of late January rains. But for most of the year, Ceará is without rains, hence the poverty and desolation. Village women washed their clothes in water holes. And yet here we were, affluent visitors from forty different countries, crossing this land of violence in air-conditioned comfort by means of *expresso de luxo* buses. Huge areas of the Ceará countryside are arid with brown, dead grass skin. Also huge monoliths and low dark clouds seem to close the gap between heaven and earth. In semi-arid Ceará, it's hard to say where one begins and the other ends.

Quixada was the first stop on our field trip. Quixada is like a museum of a surviving old town. There is wealth, water, beautiful homes, hovels, pigs and dogs in the streets, cowboys on horses, dark-skinned peasants, fruit trees and lush green country. Quixada traces its green prosperity to a dam completed in 1906. The Bank of Brazil even has an impressive club for its customers. It was in that cool and airy space of that club that we had a fantastic tasty lunch of meat, rice, salads, tropical fruits, and beer.

Our next stop was in another small town called Canindé. This is

the center of worship of St. Francis of Chagas. People from all over
Brazil visit Canindé to pay their respects to St. Francis. We arrived
in Canindé around 3:30 in the afternoon. And since this is a religious
town, we were expected to attend mass at the impressive seventeenth-
century cathedral honoring St. Francis. Before attending church, I took
a walk in Canindé's main street, dominated by shops selling the patron
saint's picture and other forms and articles of religious art. While I was
admiring the local artifacts, the sky opened its door and the rain came
down like a storm. I was only forty feet away from the cathedral but I
did not dare cross that small distance. The heavy tropical rain turned
everything gray.

Only teenagers added the downpour into their games. Two young
girls played in that stormy water. Meanwhile, I waited in a religious
store looking at countless icons of St. Francis while the store manager,
a middle-aged woman, watched TV while helping a Chinese scientist
from our delegation choose a couple of items. There was also a young
boy who was at most seven years old, without shoes watching us, the
visitors, with great curiosity. He looked at me—a small smile broke on
his face and he took a tiny step closer. I quickly took a note of 1,000
cruzeiros (about a dollar) and handed it to him. His smile got bigger and
disappeared in the rain.

Once the rain let up, I joined my conference colleagues and the
local people attending the beautiful liturgy in honor of St. Francis. My
eyes were immediately glued to banners throughout the cathedral. The
message in these colorful cloth banners was not what one would see in a
church in North America. Here the burning issue was not hell or paradise
or the Ten Commandments but liberation—the liberation of peasants
from oppression. One banner said that the organization of the workers
was terribly important for their emancipation; and another proclaimed
that the concentration of wealth was the root of evil. Clearly, the priest,
a bespectacled, dark-skinned heavy-set man of medium height, was
preaching a theology of liberation, trying to defend the poor by raising
their consciousness. That understanding made the liturgy, in Portuguese,
exceedingly important. I could sense there was a rare intimacy between
the priest and his people. For a change, I said to myself, this part of our
guided tour was appropriate to the spirit of sustainable development, the
struggle of a few people of good will to help the rest understand that the

Earth needs healing, not more ecocidal development. The theology of liberation had a soothing effect on my soul.

Later on we also went to a show, "Missa dos Vaqueiros" ("Cowboy Mass") by the Quinteto Violado. It was the equivalent of an African-American spiritual/festival with all the passion, anger, and love of oppressed people recovering their freedom. Thousands of people enjoyed the passionate performance. You had the impression the entire crowd was becoming a single, huge person dancing and breathing the sounds of that emancipating music. When the concert was over, they drove us to the Praca dos Romeiros (the Amphitheater of the Pilgrims), built during the drought of 1987, where, had it not been for the heavy rain, we would have watched our show. Just before we got into our buses for a return to Fortaleza, I read on a wall, "Viva la reforma agraria." Alberto Uribe, my Colombian friend, took a picture of me next to that message of hope. My field trip could not have had a better ending: Canindé was a city of liberation—or, at least, this was a place where liberation might have a chance.

In the Amazon

Just before I left for the Amazon, Vanda guided me through Fortaleza. This was a city of favelas and narrow streets not visited by tourists. I saw a Fortaleza teeming with destitution. Quiet anger. Children begging, working hard, sleeping on the ground, and homeless. But I also saw a beautiful Fortaleza from the top of an urban hill where the government housed some of the poor. A section of this beautiful city is a copy of a European city. Homes with red-tiled roofs built next to each other, creating an icon of peacefulness and prosperity and community. But this image is shattered when the satisfied eye wanders toward the stormy blue waters of the Atlantic coast, Fortaleza's front yard. The primeval beauty of this coast has been irrevocably lost behind condominiums, hotels, tall office buildings. Fortaleza is not New York but it is in the process of becoming some sort of New York for the South. My hotel room cost $75 per day, and other people paid as much as $130 per day—in 1992. This in a city and region where the per capita income could not be higher than $300 per year.

Vanda took me to the Fortaleza airport and I took a late flight to

Manaus, capital of Amazonas. I was determined to get an intimate view of the rain forest of Amazonia. From my Manaus hotel at midnight, Monday, 3 February 1992, I could see a huge, all encompassing darkness.

Amazonia is a dream, a burning forest, the world's largest, the "lungs" of the earth, the laboratory of narrow-minded scientists, a huge wild frontier for the extraction of gold, timber, rubber and other "resources," the home of feared Indians and despised Brazilians. And, of course, Amazonia is primarily untamed nature for countless species of plants, fish and terrestrial animals. But the Amazon rain forest is also a prize for Brazilians and international environmental politics, nationalism, and violence. It's everything to all people, an unknown place for conquest, love, hate—and passion.

It was my intellectual passion for this great forest that led me into it. I was lucky, first of all, to visit Brazil, and, second, to have found two students from the National Institute for Research on the Amazon (INPA), in Manaus, who invited me to go with them in their research trip into the fabled natural treasure of their country. The students spoke very little English and I spoke no Portuguese but the language difficulties were trivial to our common affection for the rain forest.

Spending a few days in the forest made a difference: The green, overwhelmingly green, nature of the Amazon—the trees reaching for the heavens and light, the fragile sandy soil making all that exuberance of life possible—was burning in my mind. I climbed to the top of an observation point that brought me at the same level with the tallest trees in the reserve and the view of that most fertile part of the forest—usually the home of monkeys and other animals—was awesome. A breeze lighted my sweat and fright from that height. The canopy of the trees, loaded with fruit and nuts, gives the impression of a fecund world covering a quiet but dense green interior between a brown leaf-covered land and the straight tall trunks of those trees, which have captured a space in the sun. But even the quiet green first meters of the forest are a universe of complex biology and exquisite beauty. There are trees that go straight up—nothing spectacular about that, you might say. Other trees send roots all over the land, the air, over and into other trees. In fact the land of the Amazonia I visited is but a complex web of roots and a couple of inches of leaves. Dead trees become the home for other trees, a variety of plants and animals. Nothing of that immense area in the rain forest is empty of life.

The rivers of Amazonia may be the answer to both the mystery and the fecundity of this part of the earth, its overwhelming life, its beauty and taste of fruits, its flowers and, especially, its people and culture. Manaus, for instance, sits on the mouth of the immense Rio Negro whose waters rise every June and July and give another chance to nature. Manaus is 1,000 miles from the ocean and only twelve miles from the mighty Amazon River. During my last day in Brazil, Friday, the 7th of February, I saw the coming together of the Rio Negro and Solimoes outside of Manaus. The two rivers meet but because their waters have different speeds (the Rio Negro moves at three kilometers an hour and Solimoes at seven kilometers an hour) and temperatures and density, the two rivers don't mix for eighteen kilometers. The Rio Negro's dark waters are full of algae and Solimoes is full of silt that makes its water yellowish like mud. Solimoes, by the way, is a nickname for the Amazon River. But my first impression of the coming together of these two huge bodies of water—from the *Verde Paradiso*, a tour boat, in the background of the sprawl of industrial Manaus—is nearly metaphysical. Here nature, in all its perfection and in its utter contempt for the humans who try to control it, is unsettling and regulating at the same time the global environment. The sheer volume of the water of the Amazon River gives life to Amazonia. The fish and wildlife of the entire region, its climate and biodiversity, would probably wither and die without the Amazon River.

We ate *pirarucu*, a boneless fish caught in the Amazon River. This fish can grow up to 240 pounds. We visited two islands in the Rio Negro River, *Teha Nova* and *Xiborena*. They are sparsely populated by people who looked to me like converted Indians or *caboclos*, a mixture of Indians and Portuguese. These people fish and eat corn, casava and tropical fruit. In *Xiborena* there are remnants of rubber and cacao plantations, so we can assume this island's dark-skinned residents must have been, not too long ago, the slaves of white plantation owners. Both islands are now Potemkin villages, places for a constant stream of tourists from Manaus. Their people live like European peasants of the nineteenth century but without any obvious signs of social unrest. Their homes sit on wooden poles to avoid drowning by the rising waters of Rio Negro. Each house has chickens, ducks, and dogs sheltered underneath its raised foundation.

A number of these dark people sell trinkets for tourists with a strong African influence. Rare sloths, parakeets and a boa constrictor were pets for some young people of these islands. In *Xiborena* we saw a beautiful patch of Victoria Regia water lilies.

The Subversion of Ecology

After my memorable trip to the meeting of the river gods in front of Manaus, I went to see this American biologist working for INPA (the National Institute for Research in the Amazon). He is a tall, thin, wiry guy with a huge mustache named Phillip Fearnside. He showed me a book he wrote in 1986 about the "human carrying capacity" of Amazonia. But he had a great deal of difficulty explaining what he, an American citizen, did in a Brazilian government organization for sixteen years. At first, he makes no sense when he says he is the main opponent of the governor of the state of Amazonas who wants to repeal all environmental protection in Amazonia. He said he keeps his American passport but he is a permanent resident in Brazil. Yet behind this man's outward timidity and academic caution, there is a courageous defender of the Amazon rain forest. Being on the scene of ecological devastation, Philip Fearnside has persistently criticized the obscene and Pharaonic development projects throughout Amazonia. He was a friend of the rubber tapper, Chico Mendes, who was murdered in December 1988 for slowing down the destructive work of the ranchers and other exploiters of the rain forest.

Fearnside's careful ecological research has made a difference in the international struggle urging Brazil to consider that the Amazon is much more than a forest for charcoal, pig iron, silver, gold, timber, and cattle ranching. Of course that is not what Brazil wants to hear about the Amazon. In fact, even Fabio Feldmann, one of Brazil's most ecologically conscious Congressmen, whom I met in Fortaleza, is not willing to hear what foreigners say about the global value of the Amazon.

Sustainable development, yes, agrarian reform, no. Theory sounds sweet, even paradoxical to the new converts of the very model of industrialism that is unsettling the earth. Meanwhile, ecology and green thinking, like the idea of sustainable development for the tropics, make for good dinner conversation. Yet the tropics are "the primary heat reservoir for the Earth's climate." In other words, what happens in the Amazon and the other tropical regions of the planet reverberates throughout the world. In addition, half of the earth's surface and three-quarters of the world's population are in the tropics.[3]

The tropics are part of a world of gigantic class inequalities between countries and within countries. According to Tomas Borge, the former Nicaraguan Interior Minister, the social reality in Latin America is terrifying. "More than forty percent of families in our region," he says, "live in a state of poverty, and twenty-five percent in a state of total destitution. At the end of the millennium, it is estimated that the numbers of those in poverty will be 250 million. In our America, one out of every two of our children at the age of six is condemned to live in precarious circumstances or on public charity. More that 100 million Latin Americans show symptoms of malnutrition. Thirty percent of the population of the continent is unemployed or under-employed. The rate of child mortality is more than 100 per 1,000 in certain areas. We depend on agriculture and mining, yet one percent of the landowners own more then sixty percent of the land in which gold is found and seeds germinate. And all this without taking into consideration the annual payment of the external debt which reaches tens of thousands of millions of dollars. To say that the external debt is unpayable and illegal is to mouth a commonplace. It is immoral—a sentence of death."[4] Tomas Borge was not exaggerating. He spoke in 1992. Oscar Arias, former president of Costa Rica and 1987 Nobel Peace laureate, complained in 2005 that more than 50 percent of the families in Central America live below the poverty line and nearly 30 percent of Central Americans "cannot afford to buy the most basic foodstuffs."[5] Meanwhile, the spread of bioengineered crops, corn in particular, in Latin America is undermining the food economy of millions. Agribusiness sells hunger in Latin America. So the debt of Latin America increases hunger and kills children in Latin America in 2005.

At the Fortaleza conference in Northeast Brazil I said it was absolutely necessary for the international community to cancel Brazil's $120 billion debt. The Third World owes its Western creditors the awesome amount of $1.3 trillion. Africa alone owes the West $220 billion. Between 1980 and 1990 Africa's and the Third World's debt doubled. In those ten years Latin America paid out to its creditors more than $375 billion. And in the past fifty years bankers and governments of industrial societies in the North received from the largely peasant societies of the South many more billions than the loans they made to their impoverished clients in the tropics. In the 1990s alone the economic gap between North and South (lending and debtor countries) increased by a factor of six. Oscar Ugarteche, a debt expert at the Catholic University of Peru, said in 1999 it was necessary to cancel both the debt of the Third World and to rewrite the rules of the game—"rules that will ensure that this widening gap is narrowed and finally closed."[6] But, in 1992, like my modest proposal for agrarian reform, the suggestion that the Europeans and North Americans ought to lift their debt sentence of death over Brazil and the rest of the Third World did not go very far. In Brazil alone the terrifying social reality of external and internal colonialism is even murdering children. The Brazilian journalist, Gilberto Dimenstein, published a book in São Paulo in 1990 on Brazil's *War on Children (A Guerra dos Meninos)*. This book was translated into English and published in England in 1991 under the title *Brazil: War on Children*. Dimenstein says that hundreds of cases of violence take place daily in Brazilian cities against children: "violence in the police stations and violence on the street; violence from the security staff employed by private companies, who are under orders to keep street children away from the buildings of their employers. In all cases, the basic aim is to keep juvenile delinquents or potential delinquents as far away as possible. Murder is the inevitable result."

Brazil has a socialist government in 2005. When I was in Brazil in 1992, Lula, the president of Brazil, was a leader of the workers' party. But now that he is in power, Lula is not challenging the class system that manufactures hunger and debt for his country. In fact, under his administration, the Amazon is becoming an immense farm for the export of bioengineered soybeans for the cattle of North America and Europe. Meanwhile, in 2005, the richest industrial countries, the G-8, promised debt forgiveness for the poorest countries of Africa, but not Brazil. International celebrities like Bono put up elaborate and flashy concerts on behalf of the poor, but little changes in the international or country system to alleviate poverty and the horrendous violence that is the sister of poverty.

Violence is also consuming the forest itself, the rain-starved areas of the world. "I have seen death without weeping," says the Brazilian writer Geraldo Vandre. "The destiny of the [Brazilian] Northeast is death. Cattle they kill, but to people they do something worse." But death without weeping? Is that possible? Nancy Scheper-Hughes, a professor of anthropology at the University of California-Berkeley, spent several years studying the Brazilian Northeast and concluded that Geraldo Vandre was right. The Brazilian Northeast, "land of sugar and hunger, thirst and penance, messianism and madness," made death routine—particularly for "the children of poor families."[7]

Scientists are trained to appreciate the planetary effects of serious threats to the integrity of any global ecosystem. But the 600 scientists of the Fortaleza conference did not allow themselves even a breathing spell to contemplate the holocaust, the human sacrifice, underpinning their technical data on the semi-arid regions. And that was the great moral failure of this seemingly international effort to help huge areas of the world and people who need help. Rather than throw light on the factors that diminish life in the semi-arid regions—cash crops, monopoly of water and land, oppressive social and ecological relations in the countryside—the international scientists obscured the drama of the very problem they pretend they know something about. In fact that strange behavior was not strange at all.

Scientists have consistently shown a willingness to side with power and even do its bidding, with some exceptions. In the second chapter I will show that at America's public agricultural colleges (land grant universities), it is the scientists who have been designing the mechanical, chemical, and biotechnological foundations of giant agriculture. And, of course, during the twentieth century of total war, silent springs, and genocides, scientists created the ultimate anthropocidal (man-killing) and ecocidal weapons of all time, the atomic and nuclear bombs. Following that barbarian achievement, and during the cold war, American scientists, in total disregard of human rights and ethical standards, tested plutonium, an exceedingly toxic ingredient of the nuclear bomb, on unaware hospital patients. And in the case of the Amazon, scientists (mostly anthropologists and economists) have been the protagonists in the destruction of the fantastic ecosystems and indigenous societies of that immense forest region of Brazil, Venezuela, Colombia, Peru and Ecuador. The scientists' destruction follows the model of centuries of experience from the European conquest of the Americas. In the 1960s and 1970s, one such a scientist, Napoleon Chagnon, an anthropologist from the University of California, Santa Barbara, "introduced guns, germs, and steel across a wide stretch of Yanomamiland—and on a scale never seen before."[8] The Yanomami are one of the very few indigenous societies in the Amazon that survived the initial holocaust European explorers and Christian missionaries brought to the Americas' non-European people in the fifteenth century.

Patrick Tierney, an American researcher, spent several years in the Amazon documenting the brutal fate of the Yanomami at the hands of Western experts and gold miners in the late twentieth century. His book, *Darkness in El Dorado: How Scientists and Journalists Devastated the Amazon,* paints an ugly picture of ruthless conquistadors parading under the garb of science and economic development for brutal personal ambition and unethical goals. These academic crusaders, American and French anthropologists above all, came across the Yanomami hiding in the inaccessible forest and water wilderness of the Upper Orinoco River in the frontier between Brazil and Venezuela. That fateful encounter in the 1960s triggered another "conversion" against the Yanomami who have been portrayed as fierce people fighting ceaselessly over women. Anthropologists and journalists and economists expanded on that lie and created a fictional Yanomami world so that they could subdue the gentle forest people with guns, diseases, development projects, and civil wars. In addition, these scientists, and their powerful Western patrons, made the Yanomami experimental subjects for the genetic studies of the US Atomic Energy Commission (AEC). These cold war scientists, says Patrick Tierney, mixed their hatreds with science, so that "natural selection became selfish, murderous, cruel, and deceitful. Doctors trained by the AEC gave the Yanomami a radioactive tracer and a vaccine that was potentially fatal for immune-compromised people. Scientists kept on filming and collecting blood in the midst of epidemics. These brave men took a long walk on the dark side, but, in the artificial brilliance of ground zero, they could see no shadows."[9]

The Yanomami had also to deal with the diseases, bullets, and violence of thousands of gold miners and development agents of Brazil, Venezuela and the World Bank who invaded their land. Their society and culture were wrecked. This deadly struggle was going on while I was in Brazil in 1992. All the Amazonian indigenous people are, to some degree, Yanomami. Give them enough land, no more anthropologists, no more miners, no more World Bank economists and no more missionaries, and they can put together sustainability—in both nature and their society. I smile at the thought.

Indians are everywhere in Manaus. But I did not see a single Indian in the Amazon forest close to Manaus. Even well meaning educated Brazilians describe the indigenous people as savage, despite the fact many of them are themselves part Indian. That way they accept the racist and often genocidal effects of their country's policies.

My time in Brazil had come to an end: The driver who picked me up at the hotel in Manaus, a short, dark, muscular man in his forties, Jarusi, complained bitterly about the influence of the Japanese in his city. He also said that the Brazilian government's pronouncements about the Indians are meaningless. He drove me through the city so I saw a slice of this metropolis. Manaus, like Fortaleza, is teeming with poor people, the overwhelming majority of whom are short, thin, and dark. In the hills next to the harbor these poverty-stricken men and women live in favelas, makeshift communities hanging on practically nothing but tenuous shacks they glue to the bare land. Huge piles of garbage could be seen next to the favelas. And I would have to assume that when the massive Rio Negro rises in June and July every year, it washes away all that waste and, most likely, most of the favelas. In fact, the harbor of Manaus was littered with garbage and petroleum. One could also see a petroleum refinery on a hill not far from the heart of downtown Manaus.

I went back to my hotel for dinner and checked out. I had a real late flight to Washington, DC, so I had plenty of free time at the Manaus International Airport. I tried to read but my mind was with the tumultuous events of the past several days: The Fortaleza conference was a public relations gimmick by the government of Ceará, and its Brazilian and international consultants, in order to get loans from the Inter-American Development Bank and the World Bank. In fact no sooner was the conference over than the young governor of Ceará, Ciro Ferreira Gomes, was in Washington, DC, paying his homage to the international bankers, begging them for the necessary gold to fund some more industrial projects in the nearly destroyed semi-arid Ceará.

Meanwhile, Brazil, an immense beautiful Creole country of Amazon rain forest and huge rivers, is seething with unrest and discontent. Rural violence is a dress rehearsal of the coming civil war or, at least, a thermometer of the silent wars fought for land and food all over the country. My travel in the countryside of Ceará revealed Brazil's open ecological and social wounds. Peasant women doing their laundry in water holes is bad enough. But the peasants of Ceará have little they call their own. Nearly all productive land of Ceará is owned by plantations, a system of destructive ecological conditions and explosive social relations. Irrigation water, as precious as good land in semi-arid Ceará, is also in the jurisdiction of plantations. The hungry and oppressive politics of Ceará are forcing more and more peasants to head for cities like Fortaleza that, in 1992, pretend to shelter one-third of the state's six million people. Of course, Fortaleza cannot afford to support so many impoverished Brazilians. Its spreading favelas are a solid evidence of that. Its woefully inadequate sewage facilities, contaminated drinking water, cholera, its rising rates of cancer and other lethal diseases, its homeless children, its militarized security of tourist hotels and the affluent few—are serious symptoms of decay and political failure.

Only the archbishop of Fortaleza acknowledged the sin of Ceará for ignoring the crucifixion of its poor people. He urged the conference delegates and the Brazilians at the conference to listen to the cry of the people and nature. Yet his was a sole protest in a gathering of aggressiveness. His gentle message was drowned in a cacophony of translation, bad science, and even worse, international politics: What with the Earth Summit in Rio de Janeiro in June 1992—perhaps the largest ever conclave of government bureaucrats from nearly 160 nations convened supposedly to address global ecological issues and problems of economic development but, in reality, signed off on a variety of pacts guaranteeing the existing international exploitation of nature and the oppression of the vast population of the earth. This was an agenda for the plunder of the tropics, serving a small but mighty global plutocracy of multinational corporations, university experts, technocrats and "national security" enthusiasts from the ranks of armies, police, and the civil societies of the world.

The same thing happened, and worse, ten years later, August 26 to September 4, 2002, in Johannesburg, South Africa. The United Nations World Summit on Sustainable Development, the Second Earth Summit, became another expensive rhetorical show of governments and corporations. The president of the United States, George W. Bush, who became president in 2001 by stealing the election, saw no reason he should go to Johannesburg. His first international act was to take the United States out of the international negotiations about the warming of the earth. Being honest about who he is, that is, being a president for the protection of corporate plutocracy that elected him, George W. Bush did not bother to go to the World Summit. He sent his Secretary of State, Colin Powell, who was rightly booed by the delegates. After all, those who go to these international meetings are educated people. They know the United States uses the excuse of free trade and global terrorism to abandon its international ecological and social obligations. Colin Powell, the first black Secretary of State speaking in black Africa, was peddling the propaganda of George W. Bush and American corporations, so the delegates jeered him. Thabo Mbeki, president of South Africa, warned the Summit delegates of a solidifying global apartheid between the industrialized North and the agrarian South, but, probably, his message went nowhere. The United States and its allies refused to listen to bad news. They had discovered the free market and they cared less that the global ecosystems were falling apart. What they cared about was how to protect what they had, and what they expected to get through free trade. So they drowned the World Summit with their hysterical free trade agenda and calls against terrorism.

Yet Robert Mugabe, president of Zimbabwe, was a voice of reason in Johannesburg. His policies at home are terrible, including his confiscation of land from white farmers. But his speech at the Johannesburg Summit on September 2, 2002, explained to the delegates why their global conference on environment and development accomplished so much less than Rio, in Brazil, in 1992. He said:

> Ten years ago, we gathered in Rio de Janeiro, in the same numbers and were moved by the same developmental anxieties that many of us have today. We worried about our troubled Earth and its dangerously diminishing flora and fauna. We worried about the variegated poor of our societies, in their swelling numbers and ever deepening, distressful social conditions. We complained about the unequal economic power that existed and still exists between the North and the South...We spoke against unequal terms of trade that made rich and powerful nations enjoy undeserved rewards from world trade. Indeed, we denounced the debt burden by which the rich North continued to take away the impoverished South even that little which they still had. Your Excellencies, we must examine why, 10 years after Rio, the poor remain very much with us, poorer and far more exposed and vulnerable than ever before. Our children suffer from malnutrition,

hunger and diseases, compounded now by the deadly HIV-Aids pandemic. No, the world is not like it was at Rio; it is much worse and much more dangerous. Today Rio stands out in history as a milestone betrayed. The multilateral programme of action we set out for ourselves at Rio has not only been unfulfilled but it has also been ignored, sidelined and replaced by a half-baked unilateral agenda of globalization in the service of big corporate interests of the North. The focus is profit, not the poor; the process is globalization, not sustainable development, while the objective is exploitation, not liberation…10 years after Rio, the time has come for all of us to state quite categorically that the agenda of sustainable development is not compatible with the current dominant market fundamentalism coming from the proponents of globalization. The betrayal of the collective agenda we set at Rio is a compelling manifestation of bad global governance, lack of real political will by the North and a total absence of a just rule of law in international affairs. The unilateralism of the unipolar world has reduced the rest of mankind to collective underdogs, chattels of a rich, the willful few in the North who beat, batter and bully us under the dirty cover of democracy, rule of law and good governance. Otherwise how would they undermine at global level the same values of good governance and rule of law they arrogantly demand from the South?

Mugabe said the things that had to be said. Whether he was sincere or not, it is not for me to say. But he touched on the issues making up the substance of this book. I will return to Mugabe and Zimbabwe later on. Now, however, back to the 1992 Rio World Summit: Brazilian government officials resent any international discussion of the global ecological implications of the rapid despoliation of their fantastic Amazon rain forest. What we do with our "resources" is our business, they say. "You, North Americans and Europeans, what right do you have to defend Amazonia from development? First of all, you chainsaw and clearcut your own forests, which themselves were substantial lungs of the earth and sources of biodiversity at one time. Second, you taught us all we know about development. So how are we to develop if we stop mining the Amazon? And, furthermore, how are we to pay back all the money we borrowed from you without continuing to do the very things you now find objectionable?" Good questions that could not be raised in Rio. In fact they were not even raised in the Fortaleza conference. My quest for putting agrarian reform on that conference's agenda troubled North Americans and Europeans to no end. But the Brazilians said that without agrarian reform sustainable development would not have a chance. Besides, they insisted, Brazil should pull the rug from under the menacing plantation owners and big farmers. These Brazilians know that dividing up the huge farms of Brazil to modest sized-farms would save the Amazon from additional destruction. Landless peasants had to have a piece of land for food; otherwise the Amazon would continue to go up in smoke.

The Fortaleza conference, which took place four months before the Rio Summit, started and ended in confusion. Its sponsors did not have the slightest clue how to blend their industrial-ecocidal bias with the now fashionable rhetoric on sustainable development. They brought from Europe, North America and the Third World old scientists wedded to hazardous ideas and alien pedagogy—muddling a confused colonial ideology under the garb of scientific jargon, "risk assessment" and "uncertainty." These men and women said the world was entirely anthropocentric, and the climatological problems of the semi-arid regions had no direct relation to the anthropogenic (man-made) insults on the global environment. Therefore, and naturally, one was led to believe that "economic" development—not "sustainable" development (meaning development without destructive effects)—was what the semi-arid regions of the world needed: Capital, engineers and economists without any concerns for the future; not development guided by wisdom, ecology and social justice.

Fortunately, I did not end my first visit to Brazil thinking about the fate and dangerous ideas of the capitalist scientists. These people bored me so much I listened to them as little as possible. And then I refreshed my mind in the Amazon rain forest near Manaus. Seeing the immense Solimoes and Negro rivers at their meeting place near Manaus, I thought of the Greek gods Okeanos, the river whose streams ring the Earth, and Poseidon, brother of Zeus and god of the seas and earthquakes. The two river gods glided next to each other for sixteen kilometers before becoming one supergod, the Amazon River. Walking into the country also helped, particularly walking for hours in the solitude of the rain forest, swimming in the crystal clear waters of Acará, a small tributary of Rio Negro, sleeping in the deep darkness of the tall trees, brought me closer to thinking like those trees, those beautiful rivers, Amazonia.

I secretly denounced those who devour magnificent Amazonia. From my airplane, leaving Manaus in the dark, I could only see part of that destruction: Fires consuming my dream looked like tiny sparks 10,000 meters below in the belly of the spreading night.

Chapter 2

Industrialized Farming—Western Culture's Most Aggressive and Colonizing Impulse

Agricultural Wars

My journey to Brazil was much more than a confrontation with the burning of nature and creation. I tried to understand those spending their lives in support of a development model that burns the Amazon and the hopes of a vast number of people for either a good life or mere survival. Brazil was simply the applied version of the agrarian war cooked up in the West, especially in the United States, that gave birth to giant scientific agriculture, factories in the field.

This war is silent. No government, development agency, agribusiness or landlord issues military orders against family farmers, landless people and peasants. When the landless in Brazil, for example, take over a plantation, usually land that is not under cultivation, then the reaction from the absentee landlord can be violent. He may hire security guards and the local military police to expel the landless by force of arms. In the United States we have John Steinbeck's *The Grapes of Wrath* documenting the mechanized violence of the banks, agribusiness, and the landlords against tenants and family farmers in the 1930s.

In chapter six, about the expulsion of the black farmers from the land in the twentieth century, I will discuss the more insidious ways and means agribusiness and government in the United States have been using in their agrarian war. But, in general, the strategy against peasants and traditional family farmers and organic farmers, who reject agrotoxins in their farm practices, is subtle. Its theory is dressed with the vocabulary and technical jargon of science and economics and progress. Like a world religion, this anti-agrarian campaign is global with international research institutions located in food-rich regions of the Third World. Agricultural economists, agronomists, and several other academic experts in agricultural production, teach thousands of students all over the world about the money advantages of scientific agriculture and denigrate any alternatives like peasant and family farming, which they brand as backward. Most of these professors and experts are from the United States and Europe. They justify the monoculture of the United States (planting huge acres with one crop) and the plantations of cash crops and machine food production—not merely in Brazil but throughout the world. The shouting, the machine gun fire, the racism—not the debate—goes like this: It is agribusiness for the affluent North (Europe and North America) but "green revolution" for the poor South (Asia, Latin America and Africa). Yet whatever the name, industrialized agriculture is the most aggressive and colonizing impulse of Western culture. It is a global system of power for the control of the world by the corporate elite of North America and Europe.

The mechanization and industrialization of agriculture started in full force in the nineteenth century. Since then factories in the field have been destroying a way of life (peasant farming and small-size family agriculture) and replacing it with giant business plantations of food production. The results have not been pretty. The Dust Bowls in America's Great Plains in the 1930s, and, to a lesser extent, in the 1950s and 1970s, were strong warnings of the potentially catastrophic ecological and social consequences of treating farmers, land, and crops like they were raw materials for a factory. Yet for countries like the United States and Russia that have had invested so much in being empires, particularly after World War II, agriculture and food were no different from cement factories. What mattered was not democracy in the countryside or wholesome food but immediate production of massive amounts of food that could feed an army. Military strategy had become agricultural policy and fast food. Russia killed off its peasants in the period from 1917 to 1939. Russia then built massive state farms where food production and the factory became one process. The United States did not kill off its peasants because it had none. The murder of the Native Americans (all of them raising or gathering food not very different than peasants) had taken place before the twentieth century. Until World War II small family farmers raised most of the food in the United States. The industrialization of agriculture, however, did not spare family farmers from expulsion from the land. Ploughing up the Great Plains in the United States for the industrial production of cattle, wheat, and corn or destroying the Aral Sea in the 1950s in the Soviet Union (Russia) for the production of irrigated cotton illustrate the application of military strategy in agricultural production. These examples (and numerous others from several countries in the course of this book) show the ecological illiteracy and social backwardness of the technological elites all over the world. In the American case, sodbusting—blasting the fragile prairies of the Great Plains with giant agricultural machinery, ground water from the Ogallala aquifer, pesticides, and cattle factories—continues. In fact, the United Nations Environment Programme (UNEP) described the Dust Bowl as "the worst environmental disaster in the history of the USA."[1]

Yet neither the Great Plains disaster nor other domestic and international calamities (from large projects in the industrialization of agriculture, damming the world's greatest rivers, and other massive alterations of nature) made much of a difference in the course of development in the United States or the rest of the industrial or industrializing world—until 1962.

During that year, a former US government biologist, Rachel Carson, published *Silent Spring*, a book about the chemistry and ecological effects of pesticides. Carson's appeal for better environmental protection policies did have some impact in shaping public policy in the United States—and the world.[2] Her eloquent book is a warning that there's something fundamentally wrong with the science and culture of industrialized agriculture in the United States. Carson's lament was with pesticides, "the chemical barrage" farmers hurl "against the fabric of life—a fabric on the one hand delicate and destructive, on the other miraculously tough and resilient, and capable of striking back in unexpected ways." She was also angry with scientists who talk of controlling nature with pesticides. She said:

> The 'control of nature' is a phrase conceived in arrogance, born of the Neanderthal age of biology and philosophy, when it was supposed that nature exists for the convenience of man. The concepts and practices of applied entomology for the most part date from that Stone Age of science. It is our alarming misfortune that so primitive a science has armed itself with the most modern and terrible weapons, and that in turning them against the insects it has turned them against the earth.[3]

The attempt to "control of nature," unfortunately, is still driving policy all over the world. However, a few things have changed for the better. The US government took Carson seriously for a moment. Congressional hearings in 1963 raised similar issues Carson discussed in her book. In 1966 the US Department of the Interior tried to reassure Americans that "There has been no silent spring—yet. The frogs croak their songs, the wild geese fly north on schedule, and the salmon splash their way upstream into the shallows to spawn. Perhaps Rachel Carson's widely read, widely praised, and sometimes denounced "Silent Spring" helped to keep it from happening."[4]

Three years later, in 1969, the federal government (the US Department of Health, Education, and Welfare) concluded that, yes, pesticides mean trouble—even global trouble. In the most comprehensive study of pesticides ever done in the United States, the US government said pesticides in the environment "may adversely affect processes as fundamental to the biosphere as photosynthesis in the oceans."[5] Almost a year after this report came out, President Richard Nixon who was, some say, our last liberal president, signed an executive order that brought the US Environmental Protection Agency into being. Pesticides and Rachel Carson had something to do with the creation of EPA. The Pesticides Program of EPA is the Agency's largest—and for a good reason. Industrialized agriculture and pesticides continue to present the United States and the world with one of their greatest ecological and social threats.[6]

Two of the most pervasive national ecological problems identified in EPA's 1983 "Regional Environmental Management Reports" had to do with the contamination of ground water by pesticides and their drift in the environment. In 1987 both the US Department of Agriculture (USDA) and the National Academy of Sciences concluded that "Chemical pesticides are responsible for a wide array of unacceptable negative effects on the environment."[7] The National Academy of Sciences also reported in 1989 that conventional agriculture is "the leading nonpoint source of water pollution" in the United States.[8]

Provoking Ravages, Dismantling the Countryside

The social consequences of industrialized farming are also troublesome. Since World War II, US agriculture has been transformed into a giant mechanical and highly specialized factory in the fields. Farmers *produce* crop or animal goods under rigid chemical, business, and contractual regimes. The social effects of such a system have been detrimental to most rural communities—and farmers. Since the 1940s, the rising corporate agricultural economy devoured the family farmers. It forced most of them out of farming. Family farmers could not compete with corporations whose mass production caused the price of corn and soybeans and wheat (and other essential foods) to fall steadily while the price of chemicals, machinery, loans, kept getting higher. In fact family farmers did not, in many instances, have a choice about staying with chemicals. Insurance agents and bankers required them to keep spraying so that they would get a loan. In addition, food processors and grocers would demand that the family farmers' produce would be spotless, thus pressuring them to be vigilant with their spraying regime.[9] If family farmers went bankrupt, the lenders or corporations or large farmers took over their land. Two-thirds of family farmers lost their land between 1940 and mid-1980s. By the mid-1980s five to ten percent of the surviving large farmers and corporations accounted for two-thirds of the net farm income.[10]

The US Department of Agriculture did its own assessment of agriculture and society in the United States in the late 1970s and concluded that the original idea of American agriculture, being primarily small family farming, was no longer true. The 1970s were consumed with efforts to right past wrongs. One of those huge wrongs was the dispossession (funded by the US government with subsidies going to large farmers) of millions of small family farmers by corporate farms. This policy took off since World War II when military priorities of an empire replaced the initial impulse of the United States to be a democratic society. Emptying rural America of family farmers has been having ugly undemocratic consequences and grave ecological effects. I will be describing below that, in the 1970s, the undemocratic nature of giant agriculture—responsible for millions of hungry people—was not so obvious. Millions of displaced farmers and hungry Americans remained invisible. America was fighting a war in Vietnam for reasons of empire. But in the midst of this foreign adventure, the local results of internal colonialism, particularly the killing of nature with toxic sprays used for food production, had created an environmental movement. The US Department of Agriculture was on the side of the sprayers and agribusiness. Environmentalists insisted that the US Department of Agriculture could no longer be trusted to protect human health and the environment from the harmful effects of pesticides. In 1970 President Richard Nixon created the US Environmental Protection Agency (that shifted the responsibility of regulating pesticides from the US Department of Agriculture to EPA) and denounced hunger in America. "That hunger and malnutrition should persist in a land such as ours," he said, "is embarrassing and intolerable."[11]

Bob Bergland, Secretary of Agriculture from 1976 to 1980, was more honest than Nixon. Both men knew why rural America was falling apart and why hunger was increasing in America. Nixon decided to do nothing save for his founding of EPA. Bergland, however, found the decline of family farming embarrassing. As a result, he headed an effort to find out why agriculture in the United States had moved so far away from its family farm purpose. He was born on a farm and lamented that about 15 million men, women, and children had to abandon farming and rural life in the United States between 1950 and 1980. Perhaps he was thinking of the immense rural tragedy John Steinbeck captured so vividly in his 1939 book, *The Grapes of Wrath*. The US government, however, did nothing to head Steinbeck's warning. The US government and agribusiness pretended rural America was fine in the midst of rural devastation and exodus of family farmers and their families to the cities from nearly all over the United States—and California. Bergland had the numbers to prove Steinbeck was right. In the preface to a US Department of Agriculture study, Bergland nearly apologized for what he did and did not do with agricultural policy making while he was a Congressman from Minnesota:

> We thought—we hoped—that if we helped the major commercial farmers, who provided most of our food and fiber (and exerted most of the political pressure), the benefits would filter down to the intermediate-size and then the smallest producers. I was never convinced we were anywhere near the right track. We had symbols, slogans, and superficialities. We seldom had substance.... The success of our agriculture is true, but it is also true that, by 1978, about 7.7 percent of the households in America owned all the farm and ranch land. Of those households, 62,260—the population of a medium-size city—owned three of every 10 acres. How did this come about, in a Nation that came into being with one of its principles being the widespread ownership of property? Ownership of property is still one of America's most cherished dreams, but this was dramatic evidence that few were achieving it, if their dream involved farmland. What is more, about 70 percent of those who owned farmland in 1978 were over 50 years old.[12]

I met with Secretary Bergland in the fall of 1978 when I was working on Capitol Hill. I gave him a copy of my 1976 agricultural policy book, *Fear in the Countryside*. We talked about world hunger and the vital importance of peasants and family farmers for democracy and food. I said to him that my main conclusion from my research in Colombia, and from my study of the agricultural situation in the United States, was that without agrarian reform all would be lost in the world's countrysides. Corporations and landlords had stolen too much land from peasants and family farmers. He nodded his head in agreement. I thought he could reform the US Department of Agriculture and stem the exodus of small family farmers, including black farmers, from rural America. He did nothing, of course. He did not even try. The forces against reform were, and continue to be, formidable.

Secretary Bob Bergland did, however, have the courage and insight to talk about the ownership of farmland, which, in the late 1970s, was illustrative of the rapid concentration of corporate power in the United States. Bergland touched on one key ingredient of what makes agriculture undemocratic and destructive: Too few family farmers, and corporations with too much land and power. Unfortunately, despite Secretary Bergland's good intentions and the outstanding quality of the studies the US Department of Agriculture published under his leadership about the structure of agriculture in 1981, including a report on organic farming it issued in July 1980,[13] nothing happened because the Reagan Administration had different priorities. As a result, the crisis of agriculture in both the United States and the world deepened.

Rural Main Streets are no better off in Europe: A group of professors and members of the Dutch civil society found the agricultural transformation of their villages and countryside so distressing that, in the late 1990s, they formed the Peasant Wedding Foundation to help Holland return to family agriculture. They lament that the agricultural remaking of Holland brought them "so little to be really proud of." They explain:

> Don't we all have mixed feelings about the enormous loans young farmers need to contract to start a business? Don't we all have mixed feelings about the crisis in the pig-breeding sector, with all those suffering animals and people, and with a public sector making a loss of several billions because of swine fever and manure overloads? About abandoned farms where new nature has to be created to compensate for all the natural areas that have disappeared over many decades? About the complex administrative

work farmers and country people have to do to comply with the rules and regulations? Don't we all have mixed feelings about urban youth who no longer have the faintest idea where their food is coming from, their choice being limited to the supermarket and a fast food restaurant? Don't we all have mixed feelings about the large sums spent by the European Union on the countryside? What do we buy there for 45 billion euro per year? About the conflicts between farmers and conservationists in land use projects? About the 'no admittance' notices around nature reserves and farmland? Don't we all have mixed feelings about another road, another (planned) railway, another trading estate and another residential area in a rural zone? About the fact that the manure problem has prevented The Netherlands for decades from complying with the European standards for groundwater, which has to be suitable for consumption?[14]

Don't we all have mixed feelings about conventional agriculture? We should. When young people in the cities of the world—some of which are becoming mega cities resembling gigantic slums—don't know where their food comes from, it is a case of massive global failure and great danger. The Dutch researchers are right. Industrialized agriculture has changed not merely the face but the heart of countrysides and rural culture, in the Americas, Europe, Asia, and Africa.

The crisis of industrialized agriculture is global.[15] DDT is one of the oldest insecticides still in use throughout most of the tropics. It is sprayed for both agricultural purposes and for fighting malaria. It poses unacceptable hazards to global biodiversity and human health. The US Environmental Protection Agency banned DDT in 1972 primarily because it was responsible for thinning of the eggshell, a fatal handicap for the hatching of extremely important birds like eagles and peregrine falcons. By the dawn of the twenty-first century, DDT has even contaminated all wildlife in the high arctic.[16]

In addition to the damage to wildlife, industrialized agriculture is having an impact on global warming. The beef and dairy cattle factories of the countries belonging to the Organization for Economic Cooperation and Development (OECD), the world's most industrialized societies, emit carbon dioxide and methane that account for about eight percent of the greenhouse emissions of OECD.[17]

But carbon dioxide does more than increase the temperature of the planet. It is responsible for the hidden hunger of the world.[18] That hidden hunger—the decline of some of the essential elements in humanity's food crops—started with industrialization of societies, including the industrialization of agriculture, which uses huge amounts of synthetic fertilizers (phosphorus, nitrogen, and potassium) in order to raise the yield of crops. Hidden hunger is the deficiency of micronutrients like iron, iodine, zinc, chromium and selenium in the rice, wheat and corn, which are the main food crops of billions of people in Asia, Latin America and Africa. Carbon dioxide brings down rice's nitrogen by fourteen percent, iron by seventeen percent, zinc by twenty-eight percent; and, in the case of wheat, carbon dioxide is responsible for a lot of the decline of all of wheat's micronutrients save potassium. With increasing carbon dioxide in the global environment, rice, corn, wheat, and other food crops, produce more food, but that food is poor in nutrition. More carbon dioxide seems to have adverse effects on how plants absorb water and nutrients from the land and air. No matter the mechanism of action, the result is that the crops, now bathed by thirty percent more carbon dioxide than the pre-industrial age, take up from the soil less essential nutrients while they produce more carbohydrates that translate into higher yields.

There are about thirty-two elements, which are requirements for all life. No organism can create or decompose or convert these elements into other substances. In humans, elements like chromium, iron, iodine, selenium and zinc make up no more than a hundredth of one percent of body weight. Yet life is impossible without them. Humans and animals replenish these essential elements from eating food crops like rice, wheat, corn and other plants.

While more carbon dioxide in the atmosphere strips food crops of micronutrients, hidden hunger is on the rise, very likely becoming a pandemic in the near future. The hidden hunger of half of the world's people is likely to become the real hunger of all.

The hidden hunger of the industrialized agriculture is invisible. Yet every one can see how this giant farming is changing the face of the world's countrysides. In a policy paper dated July 2000, Ronald Steenblik, an analyst with the OECD Secretariat in Paris, says that modern farming methods led to the ecological impoverishment of Europe. Farmers in that continent, he says,

> tore up or dismantled kilometre after kilometre of hedgerows and stone fences, some of which had been standing for hundreds of years. Changes in cropping practices—e.g., shifting from spring to autumn cereals

and from hay to silage—also had a crucial effect on the ecology of large swathes of farmland.[19]

CRE (Coordination Paysanne Europeenne/European Farmers Coordination), a European civil society organization, is also straightforward about the matter. In a September 2000 press release, it said that Europe's Common Agricultural Policy (CAP) never ceased favoring a very intensive [agricultural] production model, energy-eating, and destructive, which goes on provoking ravages: farms' extinction, water pollution, [and] health hazards.[20]

Rural America has not been faring any better. And neither have rural Africa, Asia, and Latin America, which have been turned up side down. Peasants in Asia, Africa and Latin America are under constant pressure to either *produce* cash crops for export or lose their land or raise some food for their families on tiny strips of land.

The global rural and food crisis is war under a different name. Peasants and small family farmers have been under violent pressure by corporations and large landlords to abandon their land and way of life and move out of the countryside. This silent war against peasants and family farmers is bringing about another enclosure movement of perpetual rural conquest and ever fewer giant farmers and plantations. This global crisis is compounded by the loss of traditional seeds, knowledge, and culture in Africa, Asia, and Latin America. Europe and the United States, meanwhile, lose young people and experienced farmers from agriculture. This leaves their land and agriculture to aging farmers and corporations and also to lay fallow or become urban sprawl. The spread of this industrialized undemocratic giant agriculture throughout the world is unsettling the culture and ecology of the earth.[21]

On a global scale, the impact of industrialized agriculture is severe.[22] Says the United Nations Environment Programme (UNEP) in 1995:

> Overwhelming evidence leads to the conclusion that modern commercial agriculture has had a direct negative impact on biodiversity at all levels: ecosystem, species and genetic; and on both natural and domesticated diversity. Agriculture may be one of the most important causes of pollution, by the production of sediments, by the generation of chemical wastes, or by the use of pesticides, and the runoff of organic wastes and inorganic fertilizers inflicts significant damage on aquatic ecosystems.... At the level of the ecosystems, commercial agriculture has led to considerable homogenization of the landscape. Surface irrigation

schemes, for instance, transform a complex mosaic of micro-habitats into a uniform agricultural landscape, favouring relatively few crop species and varieties. In the process, micro-habitats such as hedgerows, fallow, bushy growth, tree groves and others, which harbour considerable biodiversity, are lost.[23]

A homogenized landscape is symptomatic of either a very narrow base of biodiversity, or no biodiversity at all. A plantation with one or two crops dominating everything on sight is also an invitation to disease and disaster. In 1970 a blight destroyed 15 percent of US corn costing $1 billion.[24] In 1995 gray leaf spot did substantial damage to the corn crop of Missouri, Iowa, Illinois and Indiana. In the United States potatoes were struck in 1995 by the same blight that caused the massive famine in Ireland in the mid-1840s. These corn and potato diseases are manifestations of the striking uniformity of America's food crops. Increasingly, these diseases are the consequences of the genetic erosion of the world's food supply. From about 500,000 plant species, only 150 are cultivated for food, and only four are responsible for some 60 percent of the world's food. In all probability, the loss of agricultural genetic diversity is "the biggest single environmental catastrophe in human history."[25]

This global crisis of food and agriculture gives birth to the idea of sustainable agriculture—slowing down the damage of conventional farming or, at exceptional cases, attempting to raise food in balance with nature.

The 1992 United Nations Conference on Development and the Environment, in Rio, Brazil, was one of the rare moments when humankind thought about nature. Ecology and ecosystems reached the heights of global politics. The world appeared temporarily to appreciate the consequences of its own irresponsible behavior in treating nature like it was another commodity. Rachel Carson's name and books, and her denouncement of those who live with the illusion and danger of controlling nature, were all over the place. Agenda 21, the blueprint of the Earth Summit of what the world ought to do to avert ecosystems collapse and rebellion, had a chapter on agriculture with all kinds of advice on how to minimize the toxic effects of industrialized farming.

There was also a United Nations International Conference on Nutrition in December 1992 in Rome, Italy, the headquarters of the Food and Agriculture Organization of the United Nations (FAO). Plenipotentiaries of 159 countries and the European Economic Community denounced hunger and malnutrition and found them unacceptable. They declared that poverty is responsible for hunger, that nutritional well being is a pre-condition for development, and that food security is of supreme importance.[26]

However, like all other global conferences in the 1990s, not much if anything of value came out of the Earth Summit or the Nutrition Conference. The United Nations simply stayed away from ugly political facts, like those alluded to by Secretary Bob Bergland in the late 1970s. FAO did not even follow up on its own recommendations of badly needed land reform—redistribution of some farm land on a global scale from those who have too much to those who have none, and particularly to those who have been made landless by plantations and large farmers. FAO reached that conclusion after it presided over a World Conference on Agrarian Reform and Rural Development in 1979—the very year Secretary Bergland was shifting through the history of American farming. After all, it would be difficult to argue that the world was serious about "sustainable" farming or development when hundreds of millions of peasants in the South and dozens of millions of very small family farmers in the North had been made landless in the twentieth century.

I remember going in late 1978 to one of the preparatory meetings on Agrarian Reform and Rural Development at the State Department. I represented Congressman Clarence Long (D-Maryland). There must have been at least forty federal bureaucrats around a huge wooden table in a large conference room. I started questioning the coordinators of the meeting from the State Department with what I thought was a very simple proposition. This was to be a global effort to return land to the landless. So I asked the forty men and women at the State Department how many peasants they or the United Nations had invited to address the Agrarian Reform and Rural Development Conference in Rome. After all, who knows more about the pain of the peasants than peasants themselves? The icy silence that followed my question was a reminder that this conference had nothing to do with food and agriculture or agrarian reform. It was rather a forum for the entertainment of men and women from the North and the South who guarded the world's food and agriculture. It was not much later that I became a persona non grata on Capitol Hill.

Enough Family Farms for an Alive Rural World

Sustainable agriculture did not even exist as a slogan in the late 1970s. Congressman Long and State Department officials used to talk about appropriate or light capital technologies, never about agrarian or land reform. As for agrarian reform, only international experts mentioned the concept in order to denounce it. Sustainable agriculture is so ambiguous that it is slightly closer to Americans than agrarian reform. However, like earlier slogans, it remains a pie in the sky. The idea of empowering the landless with some land was a distant goal both in 1979 and 1992. It still is—on the dawn of the twenty-first century.

Nevertheless, the debate on sustainable agriculture, like agriculture itself, continues in the United States and the world. And despite the hesitation to move substantively on any issue relating to agriculture, many people, and policy makers throughout the world, understand that business as usual in farming is no longer acceptable. Klaus Topfer, United Nations Under-Secretary General and Executive Director of the United Nations Environment Programme, says this is the case because "agriculture has a greater impact on natural resources than any other activity."[27]

In addition, that agriculture has a greater impact on a society's democratic institutions than any other activity. In other words, agriculture is vital to sustaining democracy.

William Heffernan, professor of rural sociology at the University of Missouri, has been studying the emergence and consolidation of larger and larger farms and agribusiness in the United States for the past 30 years. In a report he prepared for the National Farmers Union, February 5, 1999, he says, "The centralized food system that continues to emerge was never voted on by the people of this country, or for that matter, the people of the world. It is the product of deliberate decisions made by a very few powerful human actors. This is not the only system that could emerge. Is it not time to ask some critical questions about our food system and about what is in the best interest of this and future generations?"[28]

Heffernan is right. There is a better way to raise food all over the world. By "better" I mean a system that respects democratic institutions and local cultures, one that does not undermine our democracy by giving too much power to "very few powerful human actors." To avoid that danger, we need social and ecological policies that will support peasants and small family farmers to earn a good living while they continue working with traditions of growing food with respect for the land, and maintaining healthy rural villages and towns. At the same time, such policies ought to keep open the option of giving land to the landless willing and capable to farm, reviving homesteading that did so much to build the United States in the nineteenth century. Homesteaders, new farmers, with appropriate training and assistance, could be taught to raise a variety of foods without the hazardous social and ecological costs of conventional agriculture. Another way to express this objective would be to adopt a strategy in the form of an "agricultural green social contract"—similar to the proposal of the researchers in Holland who created in 1998 the Peasant Wedding Foundation like a platform for launching their country into family agriculture. There are lots of people willing to learn.

Such an agricultural social and ecological contract between the government and civil society, including peasants and farmers, would lay down the rules and responsibilities for making ecological farming possible. The Dutch researchers said farmers would be rewarded for preserving tranquility, nature, clean water, air, and *clean* and *living* soil.[29] The OECD's "sustainability objectives for agriculture" were expressed in conventional terms of production primarily, but they were, to some degree, similar to those of the Dutch researchers. They include the preservation of the capacity of the existing agricultural system to always be in a position to satisfy all future demands for "safe and secure food supplies"; maintain the ecological integrity of the land; maintain the capacity of the land for "landscape amenities and recreational opportunities"; and preserve rural culture and healthy rural communities.[30] And the hopes and strategy of the European farmers' civil society organization, European Farmers Coordination, are striving to convince the European Union to adopt policies for "maintaining enough family farms for an alive rural world."[31] Other societies might put other or similar values in their contract, primarily raising food with care for the land and with enough family farmers that the rural world remains alive and full of healthy rural communities.

All this is necessary because the hegemony of the Western industrialized agricultural paradigm—which ceaselessly says it is the only icon of science—is biased in every possible way affecting the growth and development of its antagonist, family farm agriculture. For this reason Jane Lubchenco, former president of the American Association for the Advancement of Science and professor of marine biology and zoology at Oregon State University, is right to suggest "a new Social Contract for science" so that scientists would address "the most urgent needs of society."[32] Few would argue that there is a greater need than that of growing food without wrecking society and the land and poisoning the global ecosystem. In other words, nothing could be of greater policy priority for the United States and the world than to put scientific talent at the service of global family farm and peasant agriculture. What is necessary is to build this agriculture to the point it can produce enough food for all, and repair the social and ecological fabric of the world's countrysides. Yet "scientific" agriculture and agricultural policies ignore or attack the small family farm and peasant alternatives to conventional farming. Those policies, says James Pretty, director of the Sustainable Agriculture Program at the International Institute for Environment and Development in London, "still strongly favour 'modern' approaches to agricultural development and at the same time discriminate against sustainability. They also tend to have an anti-poor and pro-urban bias."[33]

In order to neutralize the bias of conventional agriculture (in both policies and method), I avoid the dominant model's mechanistic and simplistic view of nature and culture. My theory comes from the emerging agroecological science. This science integrates local agricultural knowledge and practice with the latest ecological advances and technical skills and is a prerequisite to reaching solutions in agriculture, which are sensitive to nature and the social conditions of the peasants and family farmers. In contrast to the typical agronomist going to the farm to *produce* certain amounts of bushels of some crop by spreading prescribed packages of uniform technologies, the agroecologist learns what the peasants or the family farmers have done traditionally to grow their food, and, only then, does he bring in his knowledge of biodiversity, recycling of nutrients, and interactions between crops and animals and the land. The family farmer and the peasant remain at the center of agroecology.

Traditional agricultural knowledge is essential. The native Brazilian Kayapo or Mebengokre, "people from the water's source," study their agroecosystems very thoroughly. Says Darrell Addison Posey, an ethnobiologist trained in entomology and anthropology:

> Mebengokre use a precise knowledge of insect behavior to control agricultural pests. For example, they deliberately place nests of 'smelly ants'—*mrum kudja* (of the genus *Azteca*) in gardens and on fruit trees that are infected with leaf-cutting ants (Atta spp.). The pheromones of the 'smelly ants' repel the leaf-cutters. These protective ants are also prized for their medicinal properties. The highly aromatic scents of the crushed insects are inhaled to open up the sinuses. The Kayapo cultivate several plants containing extrafloral nectars, often on the leaves or stems, which attract predatory ants to serve as bodyguards for the plant. Banana trees are planted to form a living wall around the fields, because predatory wasps nest preferentially under the leaves.[34]

Such traditional agrarian knowledge and ecology make up agroecology—a science of agriculture and development. It has the potential to intensify food production without injuring biodiversity while, at the same time, regenerating and protecting the land from erosion. In fact with the accelerating deleterious effects of conventional agriculture,[35] more and more scientists are testing and rediscovering the core of science within traditional farming.[36] For instance, scientists in the Yunnan province of China observed peasants sowing different varieties of rice together for good yield and protection of their grain from disease. The scientists did the same thing in a hugely successful experiment involving hundreds of cooperating peasants in fields covering thousands of hectares of rice in 1998 and 1999. They planted a row of glutinous rice every four rows of hybrid rice, with the result they outperformed the yield of monoculture rice and, in addition, their genetically diverse rice took care of the blast disease. They demonstrated a causal relationship between crop diversity and disease.[37] In other words, these Chinese scientists, in collaboration with an American scientist from Oregon State University, and researchers from the International Rice Research Institute in the Philippines, confirmed, in a nearly classic paradigm of applied agroecology, the wisdom of peasant rice farming. The more rice diversity, the more grain per hectare, the less disease, or no disease at all.

Putting nature on an equal footing with treasured human values should shift our religious, political, and ethical priorities to building economic and social arrangements, which will no longer be inimical to the survival of other species. The knowledge for that great transformation, earth-inspired and earth-venerating, does not exist in industrial societies. In fact, the science of those societies—what Frédérique Apffel Marglin of Smith College calls "epistemic form of knowledge"—is an enormous obstacle in the ecological transformation of those societies. As a result, Marglin says, science endangers "the continuity of our life-environment."[38] She is right. This is particularly true of the science used to prop factory farming. Such science is the child of war.

Industrialized agriculture—especially in its twenty-first century business phase—is a product of the cold war in the United States. It is the food system of an empire, the strategic asset of a state with global hegemony in mind, the science linchpin of a vast corporate development bureaucracy out to convert the "under-developed" regions of the globe into plantations of profitable crops and docile people.

The dense debate about agricultural productivity, modernization, and development, and the racist contempt of Western experts for black family farmers and peasants, and the ceaseless rhetoric about "population control" and "the solution of the world food problem," are all smoke and mirrors: They hide the zealous strategy of industrial societies to pacify the Third World for the export and outright theft of its raw materials, and piracy of its precious genetic resources and wealth. But since peasants are fighting this new colonialism, the West is using its agricultural missionaries to pull the plug on peasant resistance. That is exactly what the "green revolution" and biotech crops are all about.

In practical, political, and metaphysical terms, rebuilding the Third World's agricultural civilization on the Western industrial model is the most sophisticated process of colonization ever conceived. Under the guise of science and under the strict observation of Western scientists, bright Third World young men and women are trained and taught to despise their own traditions.

This means primarily a visceral rejection of everything that the peasant represents—ecological farming, modest ambitions, wisdom, humility. In fact, the Western experts' contempt for the peasant acts as a toxic synergist in the oppressive Third World elite culture. The result is an abusive terminology describing the people of the land, the peasants and all indigenous persons, as "backward," a habit that leads straight to a racist, nearly genocidal policy toward those people. Thus Western agricultural technologies that are depopulating the land of a country like the United States, for example, are becoming lethal weapons in Latin America, Asia, and Africa: They arm the landlords and agribusinessmen with enough power to steal the land from powerless peasants. This means fear and conflict, drawn out civil war, which is ripping the Third World apart from one end to the other.

Chapter 3

There's Going to be Hell to Pay

Tiny Nerve Gas Bubbles in the Honeybee's Pollen Basket

The more money industrial societies spend to "industrialize" Third World agriculture, the more hunger and violence and ecological devastation in Latin America, Asia, and Africa. The peasant was, and continues to be, the master of agroecological knowledge—agrarian ideas and traditional methods of raising food—absolutely essential for the survival of the earth. Which is to say there is no way the peasant could be "backward." If there are "backward" people, they are clearly limited to the industrial societies' agricultural scientists and "development" experts. Their biology is full of weapons but bereft of the principles of life. Theirs is not to learn from nature but to dominate it. And even those Westerners who see the ecocidal path of modern science are terrified of coming to grips with that discovery, and so they do nothing.

Pesticides and Rachel Carson make this theory clear. I already said that Rachel Carson painted a huge canvas of ecocide in the United States in her 1962 book, *Silent Spring*. She castigated her country for deliberately poisoning its food and then policing the result as if, by magic, government oversight would render the millions of tons of agricultural toxins sprayed over land, water, and food harmless, and contaminated drinking water and food itself safe.[1]

By the 1980s and 1990s, industrial agriculture extended the borders of *Silent Spring* to the entire world. It's not only the multinational chemical companies that have been spreading their toxins to the remotest corner of the world. Pesticides on their own move with the winds and water. Wherever they are in nature, they create biological deserts in the land. They kill or deform plants, fish, birds, and wildlife. They speed up the evolution of insects so that an increasing number of them are becoming monster bugs, resistant to most poisons. They hasten the genetic impoverishment of food crops and push animals and plants to extinction.

Honeybees are one of those animals threatened by industrialized agriculture. They are the only insects that for countless centuries have been close to man. They are social animals, so people look at them with curiosity, admiration, even wonder. Besides, bees create honey and pollinate some of the most beautiful and useful plants on earth. In the United States, bees are giving farmers hundreds of thousands of pounds of honey and enormous amounts of pollen every year. Yet industrialized agriculture is crippling honeybees in making honey and pollinating our crops. As a result, the quality and productivity of many crops are not what they could be because there are not enough bees and other pollinating insects to move the pollen from the stamen to the pistil of the blooms. S.E. McGregor, an expert scientist on bees with the Agricultural Research Service of the US Department of Agriculture, reminded the farmers in the mid-1970s that nothing was more important in their work than the work of bees in pollinating their crops. The farmers, he said, "should remember that *no cultural practice will cause fruit or seed to set if its pollination is neglected.*"[2]

Down to the 1960s bees died primarily because of the incredible variety of poisons the farmer sprayed on the land even when his fruit and seed were about to set. I remember the tragic story of a honeybee man I invited to my class to talk about his bees and pollination. This was during the academic year 1988-1989 when I was teaching at Humboldt State University in northern California. The beekeeper, heartbroken from recalling the experience, said he paid a heavy price for pollinating other farmers' crops. Each time he took his pollinating bees to farms in southern California, he would return home without a third of his bees. By the time his bees completed pollinating the crops of the farmer, about a third of them would die in the mists of invisible sprays over the farm and poisons on the blooms. The beekeeper explained it would be useless to complain about the poisoning of his bees because that would deprive him of the little income he earned by putting his bees to do what they do so well—pollinate our crops.

Dee Lusby, president of Arizona Beekeepers Association, complained for years to officials of Arizona and the federal government about the destructive effects of the farmers' sprays on honeybees. She kept reminding those officials, who did nothing on her behalf, that bees pollinate about a third of our food. She said that Arizona once had more than 150,000 hives, which declined to less than 63,000 by 1989. She told me that whenever former presidents of the Arizona Beekeepers Association complained about the poisoning of bees by pesticides, farmers "spray-bombed" their hives, often wiping them out. Thus, the farmers of Arizona enforced silence among beekeepers.[3]

Looking for nectar and pollen in rural America, bees are caught in the crossfire of deadly molecules, invisible deleterious dusts and gases. Even if they make it to their hives, they are different animals. Flying through moving clouds of toxins make some of them freeze to death. Others become aggressive, utterly confused, stupefied, paralyzed; and others still go into the hive carrying with them poison-laced cargoes of pollen and nectar, which devastate the colony in short time. Contaminated pollen remains deleterious for about eight months. Carl Johansen, professor of entomology at Washington State University, Pullman, Washington, says that, in addition to these deadly consequences, the "lethal concentrations" of insecticides worker bees may bring to their hives in their honey stomachs kill the queens. "Severely weakened and queenless colonies do not survive the following season."[4]

This precarious situation deteriorated in the mid-1970s with the appearance in the armory of farmers of parathion trapped into tiny nylon bubbles the size of five to fifty microns, that is as minute particles as those of dust. What made this microencapsulated formulation of parathion more dangerous to bees and other wildlife than the technical material was the very technology of "time-release microcapsule." This acutely toxic insecticide, intimately related to the nerve gases of chemical warfare, would be on the surface of the flower for several days while it continued to escape from its microscopic enclosure. If the foraging bee was alive after her visit to flowers laden with invisible bubbles of asphyxiating gas, babbles exactly the shape and size of pollen particles, she (pollen gathering bees are females) would be bringing back to her home pollen and nectar mixed with parathion. Such nectar, which bees make into honey, and pollen could end up in food stores to be bought and eaten by human beings.

This explains why honey producers are silent while their bees continue to die. They are afraid that their protest will bring the wrath of farmers who will ruin them by suggesting that honey and pollen, valuable health foods, may be full of tiny capsules of nerve gas and numerous other poisons. Moreover, some beekeepers don't throw away the honey, pollen and wax of those colonies destroyed by encapsulated parathion or other insecticides. They melt the wax for new combs. And they sell both honey and pollen to the public.

In addition to killing bees and other beneficial insects, small and large mammals, and terrestrial and aquatic invertebrates, the encapsulated parathion causes various degrees of neurological damage and, quite possibly, death to birds at rates of one pound or more of the poison per acre. The gizzard of most birds grinds down the nerve poison bubbles, thus the poison is free to inflict its crippling or lethal wound. The dangers of the encapsulated parathion have probably declined with the restriction of parathion in the late 1990s. Yet the method of putting other poisons in nylon bubbles is getting more sophisticated so the poisons last longer on the flowers, on the blooms of fruit trees, in nature, thus having more of an opportunity to cause trouble to honeybees and countless other animals.

The Infamous Weather of Horse Heaven Hills

The drift and global travel of most pesticides is one of the invisible threats of these poisons. The winds take more than 99 percent of them far away from where they are sprayed. They rise in the atmosphere and then come down with rain, snow and mist and drop on people in the cities and countryside. They also fall on rivers and lakes, forests, meadows, fruit trees, vegetables, food crops, and wildlife.

In the early 1990s, for example, the air movement of herbicides (weed killers or plant-killing toxins) in the State of Washington brought a forty-year muted unhappiness among farmers to a head. The conflict took place in the Horse Heaven Hills and Badger Canyon, two fertile farm areas in the Benton and Walla Walla counties of southeast Washington State. The drift of herbicide sprays and dusts moved from the higher elevation wheat and potato farms of the Horse Heavens Hills to the downwind farms of alfalfa, grapes, asparagus, apples, pears, berries, cherries, peaches and flowers of the Badger Canyon.

Lane Bray, a politician in the House of Representatives of Washington State, on March 4, 1991, put the blame for the hazardous effects of the drifting toxins on the "infamous weather of Horse Heaven Hills combined with the attributes of the herbicides being applied." The cautious politician did not even mention the poisons by name. By "attributes," however, he meant the extreme power of sulfonylurea herbicides, marketed by DuPont to the wheat and potato farmers of the Horse Heaven Hills since 1984 and to farmers all over the United States.

By 1991, weed killers had been drifting for forty years from the Horse Heavens Hills. Most of them landed on the orchards, vineyards, and fruit trees of Badger Canyon. The farmers of the Badger Canyon were not pleased by the threat the airborne sprays posed to their crops. Yet they tolerated the drifting poisons as part of the cost of accepted farm practices. After all, they too sprayed their crops with toxins. However, when the wheat farmers of the Horse Heaven Hills started using the sulfonylurea weed killers in 1984, the farmers downwind began to protest loudly. They said it was incomprehensible that the government would license the use of herbicides, which could not be identified in the environment. Nevertheless, this time, they were certain those invisible toxins from the Horse Heaven Hills were damaging their crops.

Darwin R. Nealey, a farmer-politician in the House of Representatives of Washington, said on February 13, 1991 that, between 1988 and 1991, about 55 farmers from Badger Canyon and the surrounding areas lost about $40 million from the declining yield of their damaged crops. He urged the bureaucracy of his state to work with the US Environmental Protection Agency to ban the sulfonylurea chemicals until their presence in nature could be documented with certainty. Being able to detect a toxin in the environment, potentially, prepares the authorities to minimize public exposure to the hazards of the toxin; second, once harm registers, legal recourse is possible. So the Washington politician, Nealey, was angry that these drifting toxins could trespass on private property and not only damage crops but even force farmers out of business.

Another Washington State farmer, Ray E. Redman, Jr., sent a letter in November 11, 1991 to a Washington bureaucrat, C. Alan Pettibone, with copies of the letter to several state politicians. Redman said that for about 50 years he raised peaches, nectarines, pears, and apples in the lower Yakima Valley near Wapato, Washington. In 1987 he expanded his farming in Finley near Badger Canyon. He complained that by 1991 drifting herbicides were stunting the growth of his trees. He knew airplanes were spraying the offending chemicals but he did not know what to do. He was a large farmer who used chemicals himself. He felt the wheat farmers had a right to do what they did. In addition, he wanted to avoid warfare among farmers in order to protect themselves from the attacks of "environmentalists and food purists." If anything, Redman was certain it behooved farmers "to form a common front to fight against those people for our own survival." But while he was thinking about the complex and unusual crisis drifting poisons were causing him, he got a clue on what was going on and what he should do from a farmer in his neighborhood. Once he saw this farmer burn his stubble across the valley from him. He wrote to Alan Pettibone:

> It was a very calm day and the smoke from the fire rose straight up in a column until it reached an equal temperature with the air and then started drifting slowly southward. The interesting thing was that the column of smoke stayed fairly well intact and after a distance of several miles it started back down and landed in an area not much larger than the field being burned. Watching this pattern it seemed logical to me that this was the way the spray was being carried. The applicators are using very low volumes of water because of the shortage of water in the wheat country, thus making a very high concentration of herbicide. They also have to break the spray up in very fine droplets in order to make this small amount of water cover the required acreage. This then, is a double-edged sword, less water makes a more concentrated solution and also creates smaller droplets that will drift easier and farther...I'm talking here about herbicides not insecticides. I'm not the least concerned about insecticides, they're designed to kill insects not humans. Herbicides are a different problem. They're designed to kill plants and many of them do not discriminate. Anything they land on will be damaged. It's terribly disconcerting when you realize that a very small amount (like 2/3 [teaspoon] tsp.) will kill all the plants on an acre of ground and the material cannot be detected in the soil once it is applied...These new herbicides are so powerful they're scary...I'm positive that these herbicides are causing damage to what ever they land on. True, it isn't obvious, but the damage is there if you look closely, and I believe it to be cumulative. Sooner or later someone is going to catch on to this and there's going to be hell to pay.

The grave problem with these sulfonylurea herbicides is that they kill plants at minute amounts, usually at a fraction of an ounce per acre. They also survive in the soil for long periods of time, effectively making some land unfit and toxic for growing certain sensitive crops. Ray Redman, however, is right. He is no friend of nature, but his guessing on what the water-poor wheat farmers do to save water in spraying their super toxins is probably right. He is clearly not exaggerating when he says that these new chemicals are very powerful and scary. When glean, a sulfonylurea herbicide and a product of Dupont, is used on cherry trees at the one-hundredth amount of the application rate of the wheat farmers, the effect is dramatic. It destroys the livelihood of the cherry farmer. The sprayed trees bear no cherries. Wheat farmers spray about 2/3 of a teaspoon or 1/3 of an ounce of glean per acre. Minute amounts of glean have crippling reproductive and sterility effects on white or yellow mustard, a minor but extremely useful crop in the United States. They destroy the flowering of the mustard and sterilize the plant so that there are no pollen for fertilization and the growth of seed. They also deform the flower parts of the mustard at the approximate rate of one milligram per acre.

This is awesome power—and very scary. No farmer, or anybody else for that matter, should have access to this or any other milligram of material capable of destroying the food planted on an acre of land. Sulfonylurea weed sprays are chemical and biological warfare, not useful chemicals for farming. One milligram per acre is the equivalent of a part per trillion. In smallness, a part per trillion is like a postage stamp compared to Houston, Texas or roughly equivalent to the thickness of a human hair set side by side to the distance across the continental United States. In addition, available chemical analytical methods fail to detect these poisons in the sprayed field. Thus, the DDT paradigm of "detecting is believing" becomes obsolete in the presence of these super weed killers. In terms of toxicity and ecological harm, they are similar to dioxins in that they can do great harm in fantastically small amounts.

Chemical dioxins are byproducts of pesticide manufacturing, plastics production, municipal and medical waste incinerators and pulp mills. They are dangerous at parts per quadrillion, a thousand times smaller than parts per trillion. The 2,3,7,8-tetrachlorodibenzo-p-dioxin, the most toxic isomer of all dioxins, increases the death rate of young rainbow trout significantly if the fish lives for just one month in water contaminated with 38 parts per quadrillion of the tetra-dioxin. Thirty-eight parts per quadrillion is similar to 38 inches in 85 round trips to the Sun and back. In other words, to understand just how tiny 38 parts per quadrillion is, imagine it in an unfathomable distance: 85 round trips to the Sun. If those trips represent the quadrillion, then the parts would amount to just 38 inches of the journey.

The power of tetra-dioxin to cause cancer is 17 million times greater than that of benzene, 5 million times greater than that of carbon tetrachloride, and 100,000 times greater than polychlorinated biphenyls (PCBs). Tetra-dioxin also concentrates in living things and is very persistent in the environment. The bioaccumulation potential of tetra-dioxin is 20,000 times greater than that of benzene; 6,000 times that of carbon tetrachloride; and 4 times greater than that of PCBs.[5]

Tetra-dioxin is a killer that causes cancer to animals and people. It has caused pancytopenia (a severe blood disorder), anemia, and hemorrhage in rhesus monkeys, animals that are closely related to people. The tetra-dioxin molecule destroys the immune system of fish, rodents, and mammals, including humans.

For all her ringing the alarm, Rachel Carson's work didn't come close to encompassing the total danger. She did not know that tetra-dioxin contaminated 2,4,5-T, a hugely popular herbicide in the United States, which in combination with another immensely popular weed killer, 2,4-D, which made up Agent Orange, America's principal defoliant weapon in the Vietnam War. But 2,4,5-T was sprayed all over the United States for about 20 years before and after *Silent Spring* was published in 1962. Rachel Carson also said nothing about the tendency of agrochemicals to injure people of color more so than white persons because black people eat more of the food of very poor people, which is usually loaded with toxins—processed food and fats, for example. Down to the 1960s, the majority of the black people also worked as farm hands in the cotton, rice, and tobacco plantations of the South that are routinely drenched with poisons. Carson also failed to realize the political role of pesticides in consolidating the position of large farmers.

Deliberately Poisoning Food and Water

Carson stayed away from agribusiness, especially the political implications of the reorganization of rural America by large farmers. This was probably inevitable in the late 1950s when she started her work. At that time the agricultural model of cold war America was a system of factory farming. Which is to say, land, chemicals, animals, crops, water and seeds are material inputs for the *production of commodities*, some of which end up feeding people and others become livestock feed. This system is in essence a global factory, run by corporations that share and trade talent, technology, and grain for maximum power and profit.

Conventional agriculture—agribusiness—does in fact represent the "system" of deliberately poisoning our food and water while federal agencies, including the US Department of Agriculture, the US Food and Drug Administration (FDA), and the US Environmental Protection Agency, attempt to police the results of what can only be described for the most part as a premeditated crime against the environment, the family farmer and the consumer. Agribusiness, however, is an experiment of global consequence. Since 1945 it has degraded an area of more than 2.4 billion acres—a region equivalent in size to India and China combined. Farm run-off from fertilizers, animal waste, and pesticides contaminate water on a massive scale.[6]

Agribusiness run-off also causes a huge deformity in the land. Toxic run-off is only one part of an industrial system that is wasteful and destructive. From 1955 to 1975 conventional agriculture was responsible for the draining and destruction of 87 percent of America's wetlands. The US Prairie Pothole Region (Minnesota, South and North Dakota, Montana, Iowa, Nebraska, and Wyoming), which historically has been a sanctuary for 50 percent of the duck population in the United States, loses at least 33,000 acres of land per year to agribusiness. In the last century or so more than half of the original 8 million hectares of wetlands came under the plough.[7]

Pesticides alone kill "tens of millions of America's birds" every year.[8] Pesticides and fertilizers together kill fish by the millions each year. They end up in surface waters where they contaminate, deform, and kill aquatic life. Frogs and other amphibians, for example, are forced into oblivion. They have been threatened for several decades by mixtures of farm chemicals that foul their water world. Yet it was middle school students, not scientists, who brought to attention of the public the large number of deformed frogs in America's wetlands, parks and forests. This was in the summer of 1995 when a group of teenagers with their teacher went on a field trip in the town of Henderson in northern Minnesota. The students caught frogs and noticed that more than fifty percent of those frogs had missing legs. Soon the news spread and ecologists all over the country and the world confirmed the discovery of the students in Minnesota.

Of the three possible environmental causes for the large number of deformed frogs in nature (UV-B radiation, farm poisons, and parasites),

I side with poisons, especially the toxins farmers spray and incorporate into the soil. Some of those insect and fungus poisons and weed killers are teratogens (monster-forming chemicals in the mother's belly) in their own right. They are sometimes responsible for the birth of human terata—infants with deleterious malformations. If they can do so much damage to human beings, why should they not have similar fatal effects on amphibians? It is also possible that there are synergistic consequences between intensified UV-B radiation reaching the earth, teratogenic poisons from agriculture, and parasites—each weakening the animals' immune system defenses, thus making them more vulnerable to stresses in nature. Joseph Wiesecker, an ecologist with Penn State University, says his studies show that frogs are more likely to end up with severe limp deformities when they are exposed to "acceptable levels" of the weed killer atrazine and the insect poison malathion. Studies show these farm toxins lower or disrupt the immune system of frogs, which then become easier victims to disease.[9]

Pesticides and fertilizers do more than cripple and kill frogs. They enter ground water, where nitrates threaten pregnant women. Nitrates in the drinking water of babies may cause methemoglobinemia or "blue-baby" syndrome. Nitrate from the fertilizers becomes nitrite in the stomach of a human being. When this nitrite comes in contact with the oxygen-carrying molecule, hemoglobin, in red blood cells, they form methemoglobin. This molecule, methemoglobin, unlike hemoglobin, cannot carry enough oxygen to the cells and tissues of the body. That is why methemoglobinemia, a nasty blood disorder, is potentially fatal to infants. In addition, nitrite reacts with many of the natural and synthetic organic molecules in the stomach, creating n-nitroso compounds that are carcinogenic to humans.

Warren Porter, professor of zoology at the University of Wisconsin, conducted experiments with common ground water—water drawn from the ground of farms with typical levels of pesticides and fertilizers. He chose farm water contaminated with the insecticide aldicarb, the herbicide atrazine, and nitrogen fertilizer. He tested that mixture on white mice and deer mice. The concentrations of the fertilizer with each of the pesticides (aldicarb and atrazine) in the ground water were of the order of magnitude government agencies say the chemicals cause "no unreasonable harm to man and the environment." In other words, Porter put to the ultimate test the assurances of the government and the industry about the toxins the government registers and the chemical industry and the government convince the farmer he needs to spray on his crops. Porter discovered the mixture of common ground water and farm chemicals had detrimental effects on the animals' nervous, immune, and endocrine systems. The mice became aggressive and had problems with their thyroid hormones. Their immune system was also compromised in its ability to make antibodies against foreign proteins. The immune system was particularly sensitive to the season and the duration of exposure.

For those who would dismiss these findings because only mice were affected by the toxic water on the farm, Porter reminds them of the thyroid connection between mice and men. Besides, millions of Americans drink the same ground water mixture that Porter used on the mice. Porter says that thyroid "disruption in humans" can have unpleasant consequences with the development of the brain, the growth of our body, and our ability to learn. In addition, harm to the thyroid can have adverse effects on our immune system generating defensive enzymes to protect us from foreign proteins. Thyroid disruption, moreover, can have destructive effects on amphibians—affecting their metamorphosis and survival.[10]

Porter's findings, published in 1999 after five years of experiments, are particularly relevant to children, especially the potential of that contaminated drinking water muddling or slowing down or, in the worst case, destroying the intelligence and learning of children, while making them aggressive. This is not entirely a theoretical concern. Pesticides wound children badly. Another American researcher, professor Elizabeth Guillette of the University of Florida, reached similar conclusions in 1998 about the effects of pesticides on the behavior of Mexican children. Professor Guillette studied Yaqui children, four to five years old, who live in the Yaqui Valley of the Sonora state in northwestern Mexico. Agriculture in the Yaqui Valley is industrialized so the use of pesticides, including the DDT-like organochlorines banned in the United States, is heavy. In such an environment, the exposure of children to dozens of different toxins is a documented fact. Guillette found that those children had weaken stamina; could not catch a ball at a distance of three meters; failed to be fully creative in their play, failed to remember meaningful statements after thirty minutes; roaming aimlessly or swimming in irrigation ditches with very little interaction. In addition, these children were aggressive. They hit their siblings without reason, becoming easily and visibly angry when their parents asked them to correct their behavior. Professor Guillette concluded that her study was a mirror for "identifying communities in which [pesticide] contamination is apparently having deleterious effects on children."[11]

Like pesticides alone, or mixed with pesticides, fertilizers are a massive problem that remains invisible. So much nitrogen fertilizer is fixed every year from the atmosphere for agriculture that the amount is larger than that created by nature. And nature, lightning and microbes, create quite a bit of fertilizer. Lightning and microbes in the soil convert more than 100 million tons of atmospheric nitrogen into food for crops every year. So a considerable amount of this synthetic and natural fertilizer at the farm ends up becoming run-off, nitrogen poison that moves slowly with the rain water into sink holes, creeks, rivers, seas and oceans bringing disaster in its wake. Farming is primarily responsible for such a massive ecological calamity. Between 1960 and 1976, for example, the farmers of Iowa increased the amount of nitrogen they applied to their fields from about 100 thousand tons to over 1 million tons. About 33 to 55 percent of this nitrogen ended in the ground water of Iowa. This means that the farmer dumped on his land much more fertilizer than corn or soybeans could possibly use as nutrients. The Iowa farmer put 50 to 75 pounds of nitrogen fertilizer per acre down the sinkholes and straight to the ground water—a dangerous wasteful practice. In the years 1960s until 1980, in the Big Spring basin in northeastern Iowa, farmers increased the amount of nitrogen fertilizer in their fields by 250 percent. As a result, the nitrate in their ground water jumped approximately 230 percent. So the more nitrogen fertilizer Iowa farmers sprayed on their land, the more poison in their drinking water.[12]

Nitrogen pollution from America's farms helps exotic weeds outgrow native plants, causing blooms of toxic algae Pfiesteria in the Chesapeake Bay, for instance. Nitrogen run-off also kills the beds of sea grass and cripples the home of fish and aquatic wildlife.[13]

Something like 70 percent of crops in North America and Western Europe are grown and harvested so that they be fed to the millions of cattle, hogs and poultry in animal farms. Yet few if any animal factories treat their wastes before they are spread on the land or channeled to the nearest river. The fertilizers, pesticides, animal farm wastes, and other agricultural pollution drained from a huge swath of the United States by the Mississippi River and dumped into the Gulf of Mexico have created a "dead zone" the size of New Jersey in front of Louisiana and Texas and right in the heart of the Gulf of Mexico. Certainly such killing of nature is impervious to borders. It takes place on a massive scale in North America and Europe that camouflage such ecocide with "scientific agriculture." However, killing nature is a planetary evil—and more. It is, without question, the very worst of all crimes and evils. Barbarism, pure and toxic.

Agricultural fertilizers are poisoning the world. They kill the fish and wildlife of rivers and lakes. They make the blue living universe of coastal waters dead zones, which are huge areas in lakes and seas without enough oxygen for life. Agricultural fertilizers are deleterious to biodiversity everywhere, and they destabilize the global climate and ecology.[14] In fact, the overall impact of industrialized agriculture rivals the destructive impact of global warming, which is a result of the burning of petroleum and coal for the industrialization of everything, including farming. In the next 50 years or so an area of the planet larger than the United States is likely to be transformed from wild land to land put under the machinery of farming to produce food for a growing world population. Such monstrous growth of world agriculture will also demand a threefold increase of nitrogen fertilizer and pesticides. More pesticides and fertilizers will mean huge pollution of the world's lakes and rivers. This will decrease the fish, the birds, and biodiversity—with drastic or catastrophic effects on the functioning of the very ecosystems that keep the planet alive. Some American ecologists warn of grave global consequences from this unfolding agricultural disaster unless industrialized farmers move to a "greener revolution," adopting less hazardous methods and cutting down on the poisons they use.[15]

I agree with the ecologists. But I am not sure that industrialized farmers are about to disarm themselves for anybody's agenda. Even if the fate of the earth depended on the farmers' abandoning their toxic practices, I don't think we could count on them. These are hard men determined to win against themselves and others. For political reasons of empire the United States has lavished on them science, machines and huge amounts of money so that they would be invincible in their conquest of society, nature, land, and animals. Unlike their grandfathers, and, to a lesser extent, their fathers, the farmers producing food on the dawn of the twenty-first century are no longer tied to rural America, nature, and the earth. They have no country but the dollar.

The Dead Zone in the Gulf of Mexico

These farmers are powerful enough to remake the country. For example, consider the Gulf of Mexico. The land from Florida to Alabama to Mississippi to Louisiana to Texas to Mexico—measuring in US coastline approximately 1,631 miles—and the almost enclosed sea surrounded by these states and Cuba, make up the Gulf of Mexico. This is a region of the Northern Hemisphere known for both its beauty and extraordinary ecological wealth.

The Gulf of Mexico covers an area larger than 617,000 square miles. Thirty-three major rivers, 207 estuaries, and more than five million acres of wetlands give the Gulf enormous ecological diversity and strength. About 75 percent of the migrating waterfowl in the United States use the Gulf's wetlands as a critical habitat. Other birds, like gulls, terns and shorebirds nest and feed year-round on the numerous mudflats, salt marshes, mangrove swamps and barrier beaches on the Gulf. The waters of Florida, Alabama, Mississippi, Louisiana and Texas harbor endangered whales, the endangered American crocodile, the endangered and threatened loggerhead, green leatherback, hawksbill and Kemps Ridley sea turtles. The waterways and bays of Florida also support the endangered West Indian manatee.

More than 50 percent of the continental United States drains into the Gulf by way of the Mississippi River. This river also created southern Louisiana. Its delta is the home of some 40 percent of the coastal wetlands found in the continental United States. It is in these marshes that genesis is taking place daily: Countless water animals and birds come to life and develop in the Mississippi Delta marshlands. Yet thousands of acres of wetlands are destroyed every year. From the 1950s to the 1970s, that destruction averaged fifty square miles per year just in this region. But the country as a whole during the 1950s and 1970s lost about 9.2 million acres of wetlands, averaging 458,000 acres every year. Giant agriculture used 87 percent of those lost wetlands.[16] Since the 1970s, in the Mississippi Delta, about thirty to thirty-five square miles of wetlands are gone forever every year—an ecological catastrophe, which, either will drown New Orleans outright or, in less than thirty-five years, will make New Orleans, a city less than 100 miles from the Gulf of Mexico, an oceanfront denuded place.

The Mississippi Delta disaster is entirely anthropogenic (man-made). It is three hundred years old. Since the eighteenth century when the Europeans stole Louisiana from Native Americans, the conquerors have been waging a war against nature as well. With levees on both banks of the Mississippi River, people have shackled the mighty river to a regulated stream rushing every year about 130 million tons of sediment and nearly all its precious fresh water to the abyss of the Gulf of Mexico: That way private property owners in southern Louisiana, chemical factories along the Mississippi River, and cities are not drowned in the spring floods of the river. But nature does not exist for the ephemeral pleasures and benefits of a few people. The technologies of control of the Mississippi River—levees and the damming of Mississippi tributaries—are temporary, violent, and destructive. Mississippi's sediment and fresh water were the very roots of creation of the Mississippi Delta. Now that they no longer keep the delta above sea level and they no longer renew the vegetation and life of the coastal marshes, the entire delta, product of a millennial evolution, is inexorably being poisoned by salt water and the massive pollutants of the farmers and the petrochemical industry. It is eaten away by the relentless attack of ocean waves. The Gulf of Mexico is inundated with poisons and hazardous wastes primarily from the industries, cities, and agriculture of the United States and Mexico. One billion gallons of sewage effluents reach the waters of the Gulf every day. More than 100 million tons of hazardous dredged materials are dumped into the Gulf every year. Accidental oil spills add to the huge amounts of wastes from thousands of oil and gas wells right in the nearly closed sea of the Gulf. Several rivers and numerous creeks and streams drain immense industrial and urban areas thus bringing to the Gulf enormous loads of poisons and pollutants. Biocides like the poisons of the farmers kill fish outright and often cripple and kill invertebrate animals as well. The granddaddy of the agrochemical poisons, DDT, is found in oysters and sediment throughout the Gulf. And wherever a major river empties into the Gulf, DDT and its metabolites are certain to be there at high concentrations. In addition to DDT, other organochlorine pesticides like dieldrin, chlordane, nonachlor, and polychlorinated biphenyls are found in parts per billion in the oysters and sediment of the Gulf waters. The mouths of the major rivers have also a heavy load of petroleum and coal refining poisons known as polynuclear aromatic hydrocarbons. Many of these petrochemicals are carcinogenic, teratogenic or mutagenic to the animals that come in contact with them—give them cancer, monstrous deformities and wounds.

Pollution spoils the images we have of the vast coastal area of the Gulf. But pollution is only the external barometer of human behavior. In crude terms, we measure some of the poisons in the environment and say such a pollutant may cause this or that problem on a particular species of an ecosystem. We may even conclude that the man-made, anthropogenic, alterations of the Gulf ecology may bring disease and even death to people themselves.

All these things keep hundreds of bureaucrats busy. They talk to each other, they put together committees, subcommittees, and conferences to discover new data about the workings of nature that, for instance, wetlands are the nursery ground and shelter for an immense number of fish, shellfish, birds, and other endangered animals. We also know that wetlands purify water and check and balance the climatic orgies of nature. In short, wetlands are precious in their own right and, therefore, those who destroy them should be beyond the pale of our culture. They are what the Greeks would call barbarians.

Yet hurricane Katrina, which struck the Gulf Coast during the last week of August 2005, demonstrated that the United States has been following a barbarian policy towards nature. Katrina was the revenge of wetlands and the Mississippi River. Once again, nature lashed violently at those who thought they were its masters. Katrina, picking extra energy from global warming, for all practical purposes, annihilated New Orleans and did immense damage to the coastal communities of Alabama, Mississippi, and Louisiana. This hurricane was like divine punishment of the United States for the hubris of the country or, more precisely, the arrogance of the Republican masters of the country, headed by president George W. Bush, towards nature and the rest of the world. After all, George W. Bush rejected the Kyoto Protocol to reign in industrial pollutants warming the planet while the United States alone emits 25 percent of the greenhouse gasses warming the earth. Katrina also tore through the fragile social contract or secret hatred between classes and races in the United States. Two-thirds of the population of New Orleans is very poor—and black. Katrina drowned New Orleans, the water killing the city becoming a deadly mixture of petroleum, other toxins, wastes, floating human waste and bodies of animals and humans. Many blacks, unable to escape the flood, and trapped in rented apartments without running water, electricity, or food, looted stores, throwing the city into anarchy. The federal government failed to respond to the crisis, giving the impression to the world New Orleans was in Africa. Television presented a spectacle of a drowned American city under martial law where all state and federal agencies failed utterly to help the impoverished and frightened black population stuck waist deep in their ghettos toxic water.

I felt pain for the tragic end of a city I loved. I taught environmental studies at the University of New Orleans during 1991-1992. My students and I studied the politics of environmental corruption in Louisiana. But I also explored wild Louisiana. On March 23, 1992 I flew over the wetlands of southern Louisiana in a tiny hydroplane, spending close to six hours in that beloved nature, so fragile and so resilient. The wetlands I explored belong to the Louisiana Land and Exploration Company (LL and E), a huge multinational corporation of land and oil. Allen Woodard, a young cowboy with blue eyes and blond hair, was the company man who guided me in this unforgettable adventure. LLE owns 650,000 acres of land in southern Louisiana, all wetlands.

We started from Des Allemands Camp, a 3,000-acre reclamation project of LLE in St. Charles Parish in the neighborhood of Paradis, a small town on highway 90 west, about an hour from my apartment in the Lakefront in New Orleans. The pilot was a big man. He and Allen, also a tall, heavy-set man, cramped the front half of the plane completely. I sat comfortably behind them. The hydroplane flew about 100 meters above the wetlands. It bounced in the wind but worked perfectly well. In about 90 minutes of flight time we surveyed the area all the way to the Gulf of Mexico passing over the lakes Salvador, Washington, and the incredibly rich ecosystems of land and water, not far from the Mississippi River.

Yet the icon of beauty bellow the plane, the playful relations of water with land, had all the symptoms of collapse. Oil extraction marred the blue, brown, and green landscape. Deep canals and other permanent symbols of man-made intrusions cut up the already fragmented pieces of land, thousands of islands barely floating above the brown water. The sunken land was still visible from the air, its vegetation drown, its bridge with the rest of the land gone forever. In other areas where the salt water of the Gulf of Mexico had replaced the fresh water, the remnants of dead trees on the land left little doubt that the formerly alive wetland was dying, leaving behind it a cemetery floating in the poisoned environment.

After we landed, Allen took me on a fast ride through the wetlands on a boat powered by a large propeller. I saw several graceful white egrets, pelicans, waterfowl, a few alligators, nutria, snakes and an eagle. Finally, Allen invited me to a tasty lunch of gumbo soup, which I enjoyed immensely. He is proud of his work with the Louisiana Land and Exploration Company. He said the federal government puts obstacles in the path of private development, being the enemy of southern Louisiana.

A few days after my flight over the wetlands of the Louisiana Land and Exploration Company, I met with W.L. (Bill) Berry, the director in charge of the wetlands property of this corporation. He joined LLE in 1987 after 30 years of working for Shell Oil. Berry has a shining forehead with watery blue eyes and white pale face. An engineer by education and experience, Berry is a guardian of LLE's vast 650,000 acres of wetlands, a "resource" for hunting, trapping, oil and gas. Because LLE benefits from wetlands, it is advocating the most radical policy for their protection—leveling the levees of the Mississippi River south of New Orleans. That way the mighty Mississippi will flood southern Louisiana every spring and rebuild its delta and, thereby, revitalize all wetlands. Yet despite this admirable public policy position, LLE is doing nothing to translate its ambitious goal into reality. Berry also said his company saw no trouble with Mississippi carrying loads of toxic run off into the Gulf of Mexico.

Corporate men like Berry like their money and power. They permit nothing to disturb their daily luxury. Pollution is an unfortunate byproduct of what their companies do, but they are certain it won't touch them. That's why they purchase the politicians and academics, securing their position above and beyond the troublesome crises of our time. "You are starting me on a bad mood for the week," Berry said to me while listening to my account of the massive misuse of trust and funds in the damming of the major rivers of the country.

However, the national debate about the rivers or the deteriorating environmental state of the Gulf of Mexico never even hints that there's anything wrong with agribusiness people and others who are destroying wetlands as fast as they can. Louisiana alone loses fifty to sixty square miles of coastal marshland a year. Yet no one feels responsible for such a cataclysmic loss. The catastrophe of hurricane Katrina ought to change that attitude. The Mississippi River dumps into the Gulf of Mexico such a load of poisons, particularly fertilizers and pesticides, that about 4,000 square miles of bottom waters in mid-summer in the Gulf near the coasts of Louisiana and Texas are lifeless; they are a dead zone. This dead zone is the third largest in the world. It is a vast region—the size of the state of New Jersey. It is oxygen-starved ocean bottom right on the Louisiana/ Texas continental shelf very close to the mouths of the Mississippi and Atchafalaya Rivers. Since the 1960s the amount of nitrogen the Mississippi River alone brings to the Gulf has tripled. These fertilizers stimulate the growth of phytoplankton (microscopic plants or algae) in the surface of the waters. When the phytoplankton die they sink to the bottom of the sea and decompose and, in the process, use up the small amounts of oxygen in the depth of the Gulf. Without oxygen the ocean waters suffocate the shrimp, crabs, snails, clams, starfish and worms (all bottom-dwellers) and drive away or kill the fish.[17]

Florida is also stormed by red tides of toxic algae killing millions of fish. Again, the technical people, who publish elegant but often unreadable papers about such ecocidal events, never suggest that anyone in particular is grossly negligent for these murders in nature. And, of course, environmental experts would not dare suggest, as they should, that the government must stop the sewers of poisons that are killing both the Mississippi River and the Gulf of Mexico.

It is reassuring to know that the Gulf still "produces" 2.4 billion pounds of fish and shellfish a year. It is also encouraging that tourism and sports fisheries add billions of dollars to the coffers of Florida, Texas, Mississippi, Alabama, Louisiana, and Mexico. The devastation of hurricane Katrina, however, is certain to disrupt tourism from Louisiana, Alabama and Mississippi. Oil and gas exploration taxes from the waters of the Gulf of Mexico add a respectable sum to the country's treasury and even pay a considerable amount into the Superfund, the money account that supports the cleanup of hazardous waste dumps throughout the United States.

These benefits, however, are only temporary. They are by the grace of nature, which the beneficiaries continue to insult and poison rather than thank and protect. These benefits, furthermore, are a systematic and systemic stress on ecosystems in collapse. Thousands of miles of beaches in the Gulf of Mexico are no longer safe places for swimming. And 3.4 million acres of shellfish-rich areas are closed. Their oysters, clams and mussels are dangerous to eat. Pollution has gutted the beauty of the sand beaches and left garbage, wastes, and disease in the waters and animals of the sea. In 1988 something like two tons of trash covered every mile of beach in Texas. The toxic red tides attacking Florida are merely a symptom of a sick environment. The growing dead zone in front of Louisiana and Texas has the potential to kill the entire Gulf of Mexico.

The Mexican side of the Gulf adds its own load of pollutants to the Gulf waters, particularly untreated human and chemical wastes. More than 65 huge petrochemical plants producing about 15 million tons of products per year are located on the Gulf coast in the Coatzacoalcos region. The Mexicans are also operating their own nuclear power plant in Laguna Verde, north of Veracruz. Thus, the Mexicans are slowly catching up with the Americans' industrial engine right in the Gulf. Their Laguna Verde nuclear electricity compares nicely with that from Florida's Turkey Point nuclear plant. And the Mexicans' exploration, exploitation, processing and transportation of petroleum and petroleum products leaves its own deadly trail of petroleum in the waters of the Gulf—clearly the most persistent, ever-present, and replenished pollutant.

Stopping this pollution, bringing life into the dead zone of Louisiana and Texas, restoring health to the beautiful ecosystems of the Gulf of Mexico, rebuilding New Orleans away from an unshackled Mississippi River may be a task beyond the grasp of an ecologically illiterate and greedy corporate economic system. Not only must Mexico, Cuba, and the United States cease all polluting activities in the Gulf, but the United States must also cease dumping its wastes of fertilizers, pesticides, and other industrial toxins into the Mississippi River and its tributaries. Louisiana, Florida, Texas, and the other Gulf states with wetlands, salt marshes, mangroves must clearly protect and restore the integrity of those life-giving parts of nature. And, if the locals refuse to stop their poisoning practices, then the threatened ecosystems ought to pass under the jurisdiction of a supranational environmental protection authority.

Getting Away with Murder

Such a global ecological agency would have to start with pesticides because they have become part of the deliberate threat of conventional agriculture. The United Nations Food and Agriculture Organization says that "pesticide use has multiplied by a factor of 32 between 1950 and 1986."[18] Each year California alone is "drenched" with hundreds of millions of pounds of agrotoxins spread everywhere—farmland, schools, homes, water, and workplaces.[19] These mountains of poisons endanger farm workers, the rest of us, and nature. In our food alone, in nearly everything we and our children eat, there may be more than 200 cancer-causing pesticides. They are so prevalent in the environment that they come down with rain, snow, and fog.

The consequences of this hazardous agricultural system are already catastrophic. Scientists, agricultural corporations, and government regulatory agencies pretend they are unaware of this slow-moving disaster. But the warning signs are all around us. The prevalence of pesticides in ground and surface water around the country,[20] the incidence of adverse medical consequences for exposed human beings,[21] particularly infants and children,[22] the high cancer rate among farmers as opposed to non-farmers,[23] the frequent killing of fish and other wildlife from the application of agrochemicals,[24] the rapid rise of resistance to pesticides by an increasing number of economically important insects and weeds,[25] and the real danger of toxic sprays to threatened endangered species,[26] are ominous enough to challenge the entire conventional agricultural system and even raise global threats.[27] As early as 1969 the federal government issued a warning on the global toxic reach of pesticides.[28]

That year, 1969, the US Department of Health, Education and Welfare published its comprehensive study: Report of the Secretary's Commission on Pesticides and their Relationship to Environmental Health. On page 337 of this report, there's a figure that gives us a rare glimpse of the deleterious consequences of agricultural racism: race and class in late 1960s rural America. As I already suggested, for blacks and other nonwhite people racism meant a disproportionate environmental violence against them—molecules of agricultural poisons would lodge themselves in the adipose (fat) tissues of their bodies. And racism—and particularly poverty and the habit or necessity of eating primarily processed food and food loaded with fat—determined that the amount of poison getting into black people would often be substantially larger than those moving into white people. In the report's figure on page 337 and its explanation of the impact of DDT, we see that DDT has a cancer-causing isomer known as DDE. It is also important to understand that experts measure the amounts of DDE or DDT in nature or in animal and human tissues in parts per million (ppm), parts per billion (ppb), and parts per trillion (ppt). A part per million is the equivalent of a second in 11.57 days and a part per billion is something like a second in 32 years. A part per trillion is a human hair compared to the length of the continental United States. Poisons like DDT in parts per million, billion or trillion represent fantastically small amounts, but they cause damage nevertheless. In fact, in some instances, smaller amounts of toxins cause more harm to life than larger amounts.

In 1978, Robert van den Bosch, professor of entomology at the University of California, Berkeley, published *The Pesticide Conspiracy*, a book even more powerful than Rachel Carson's *Silent Spring*. In contrast to Carson's tapestry of ecocide, van den Bosch, in forceful prose, documents the corrupt relations of the poison makers with the scientific-biological establishment of American agricultural universities and the entire pest control industry. He speaks about the venality and stupidity of those hooked on poisons, the single-minded Buck Rogers methods of fighting an immoral war against nature, a policy that is causing global ecological and economic impoverishment.[29]

Robert Metcalf, professor of entomology at the University of Illinois and one of the world's greatest experts on pesticides, is also disheartened with America's blindness towards pesticides. In the summer of 1987 he said that: "The short-sighted and irresponsible use of pesticides and antibiotics is producing strains of monster-bugs that are resistant to our chemical weapons. Some strains of insects and microbes have appeared that are resistant to nearly everything in our chemical arsenal. It is difficult to see how anyone can remain intelligently optimistic about the future of chemical control. The outlook is dismal—and getting worse."[30]

Despite the awesome ecological consequences of agricultural toxins, and their equally dreadful effects on human beings, they still reign supreme as an indispensable prop of industrial agricultural production. They are the armor of the plantation, mega-farms and huge ranches. They are the means by which landlords keep and expand their control and ownership of land. In other words, *pesticides are the political elixirs of America's agribusiness empire. They serve no other purpose.* Their bug and weed killing powers are incidental. This is particularly true now that organic farming has shown one need not have spays to raise abundant food. But with pesticides and weed killers, agribusiness, employing a few workers, manages huge plantations and forests, producing so much of crops or wood that they force the family farmers out of business, often hiring those ex-family farmers into their feudal dominions. Thus pesticides become political tools for reorganizing rural America to becoming a colony of agribusiness.

Yet the reach of these poisons is global. Scientists continue to warn us about the threats of the "endocrine-disrupting" chemicals in our environment. They say the danger of these chemicals, some of which come from the farm, is that they "mimic" natural hormones like estrogen (the female hormone) and testosterone or androgen (the male hormone). This brings them in intimate contact with the endocrine system of the body, exerting toxic effects that may result in reproductive and developmental abnormalities and cancer. This is particularly true when the endocrine-disrupting chemicals come in contact with a fetus during the fifth and sixth week of pregnancy. During that early embryonic human development, the gonads of both males and females are identical. Hormones turn a fetus into a boy or a girl. The balance between male and female hormones is paramount in the normal development, growth and functioning of the reproductive system of the boy or the girl. But if during this crucial stage of development of the fetus, foreign chemicals disrupt the balance of the female hormone estrogen and the male hormone androgen, the boy may be more like a girl and the girl may become more like a boy. In addition, the exposed boy or girl may grow into an adult man or woman who will be handicapped by a variety of sex ailments— diminished fertility, changes in the normal male or female personality, and defects in the reproductive organs.[31]

And neither should we follow the siren but deceptive call of our scientific establishment to keep testing chemical after chemical, mixtures of chemicals after mixtures of chemicals, until doomsday. Says Peter Montague, a scientist and director of the Environmental Research Foundation in Annapolis, Maryland:

> Scientists can pretend that they can discern 'safe' levels of hundreds of different chemicals, all acting in combination. They can pretend that they can understand all the ill effects of multiple hormone mimickers on each type of cell, each tissue and each organ at every stage of development from conception to birth, through youth and puberty and into maturity, in each of the thousands of affected species. They can pretend to know these things, but they cannot ever actually know them. They are just pretending.[32]

These chemical-by-chemical scientists also serve the interests of the chemical industry which, like the tobacco industry, has been getting away with murder since its inception in the late nineteenth century.

One example of this recklessness can be seen in the story of Robert Mason, a former mechanic with Rohm and Haas, who barely escaped with his life. He spoke to a couple reporters in 1975 about the work he did since 1955 "in the mechanical gang" in the manufacturing of a highly toxic compound at the Rohm and Haas plant in the Bridenburg neighborhood of Philadelphia. He said:

> I always tried to avoid Building Six, but couldn't. I had to go in to pack pumps. I'd be tearing apart a gear reducer on a kettle agitator on the fifth floor and the siren would go off and what the hell were you supposed to do? You couldn't go down, because that's where it was, so you'd run out the fire escape for 20 minutes or so. If they told you to go into the building, you went in. If one of the glass-lined kettles developed a crack, the foreman would say go down and fix this or that and I'd know that the kettle was supposed to be empty, and they were 25 feet deep. I'd go over the foreman's head, call the safety man and say, 'Dump this kettle.' But I used to get infections, I got sties in my eyes no matter how careful I was. CME left a sweet taste in your mouth, you'd absorb it in your pores and six months later you'd sweat in bed at night and you could still smell Rohm and Haas. Building Six was a kind of punishment building. It was a constant danger. Those operators had no protection. We'd go in Building Six, but we'd cut it short. We figured it wouldn't blow up while we were in there. But those operators were in there eight hours a day or more. They looked like walking zombies.... There was a joke around the plant that there was nothing at Rohm and Haas that would hurt you. It might kill you. But it wouldn't hurt you.[33]

The chemical CME that left a sweet taste in Mason's mouth was chloromethyl ether, a substance the primary purpose of which was to act as a carrier for about 8 percent of BCME or bis-chloromethyl ether, an extremely powerful chemical and a potent carcinogen. The reason Rohm and Haas put CME in the place of pure BCME was that BCME was so caustic that it used to eat through the machinery that gave it birth. You only had to paint the skin of mice with BCME and the mice died of cancer. The Germans and the French thought of using BCME during World War I against each other, but did not because BCME (made from mixing formaldehyde and hydrochloric acid) was very dangerous and unpredictable. Yet Rohm and Haas imported German chemists to create BCME—a poison necessary for the manufacture of ion exchange resins, a $50 million a year business for Rohm and Haas. Without these resins the atomic bombs, the hydrogen bombs, the nuclear power plants and atomic submarines would be unthinkable. The immediate effect of this was that from 1955 on workers at Rohm and Haas began dying of respiratory cancer. Robert Mason quit on time but not before being castrated and losing one of his testicles to cancer.

Another example comes from Dan Ross, a veteran of the Vietnam War, who worked for 23 years in the making of vinyl chloride, the basic material for the manufacture of PVC plastics. He joined Conoco's vinyl chloride plant in Lake Charles, Louisiana in 1967. He lasted until 1990 when he died from brain cancer. But before he died he sued in 1989 and, for 10 years, his lawyer, William Baggett, Jr., and his wife, Elaine Ross, collected more than a million pages of confidential chemical industry papers from vinyl chloride corporations.

Bill Moyers based his television documentary "Trade Secrets"— shown on Public Broadcasting System on March 26, 2001 on these papers. "Trade Secrets" revealed a criminal behavior in the chemical industry worthy of sophisticated gangsters. Like cigarette companies, chemical companies (BF Goodrich, Allied Chemical Corporation, Union Carbide, Dow, and Occidental) had evidence their products would probably cripple or kill the workers that manufactured them after some years of constant exposure. Yet they kept that deadly knowledge close to their chest, telling nothing to workers like Dan Ross who trusted them. Instead, they used their money and power to protect their supreme secret, which was that they were willing to make money by all and every means possible.

In that sense, these chemical companies have been paradigmatic of the carnage hidden behind most modern factories, and of the silent wounds they inflict on everyone else. In the 1950s, young American men were in a terrible state of health. From autopsies of dead soldiers from the Korean War, the following "astounding" fact emerged: 77.3 percent of those young soldiers "had gross pathological evidence of coronary heart disease at the mean age of 22 years." In addition, more than 500,000 Americans per year "sustain silent myocardial infarctions." That is to say, more than half-a-million men and women living in the United States per year go through the life-threatening trauma of some fraction of their heart muscle dying. This was the deadly result of breathing air poisoned with carbon monoxide and other poisons. It is also possible that poor nutrition and eating habits contributed to the disease. In 1974, the government agency responsible for protecting the health of 80,000,000 workers, the National Institute for Occupational Safety and Health, had $2.6 million for research, "equivalent…to one wing of one fighter jet."[34]

Rachel Scott, an American writer, captured the terrible price Americans pay for industrialization. She painted a brutal picture of factory workers trying to make a living. She wrote in the early 1970s:

> As a nation we have worshipped progress and profits, made gods of science and industry, blindly ignoring the evidence around us that they were destroying us—and not just our environment, our resources, but our people. Workers die daily in explosions and fires, are mangled by machinery, deafened by industrial clangor, and driven to the breaking point by harassment and the command to work at a dangerous pace. Hundreds of thousands of men and women—human beings with families and hopes and bodies as sensitive to pain as any person's—are poisoned at work by fumes and solvents and suffocated by lung-filling dusts. Yet, ignorant as primitive tribesmen of the human results of a burgeoning technology, most of them die quietly, their families accepting deceptive diagnoses such as heart disease, cancer, emphysema.[35]

Like Rachel Scott, Paul Brodeur, a science and nature writer, said that during his research, in the years 1967 to 1979, he discovered that the workers had no friends in the factories or the government. He said: "I have never been given a straight answer about industrial disease by anybody in industry. So I learned that industry always lies. I learned that government officials, many of whom are influenced by industry, often fail to tell the truth. And I learned that the Congress, abysmally weakened by timidity and deceit, is being co-opted by industry money."[36]

Bill Moyers' "Trade Secrets" simply confirmed Rachel Scott's findings and Paul Brodeur's suspicions. The carnage continues behind closed doors. In fact, Paul Brodeur's insight explains the carnage. Here's some revealing dialogue from "Trade Secrets":

NARRATION: They [synthetic chemicals] are everywhere in our lives—often where we least expect them.

DR. PHILIP LANDRIGAN, CHAIRMAN, PREVENTIVE MEDICINE, MT. SINAI SCHOOL OF MEDICINE: We are conducting a vast toxicological experiment, and we are using our children as the experimental animals.

NARRATION: Not a single child today is born free of synthetic chemicals.

AL MEYERHOFF, FORMER ATTORNEY FOR THE NATURAL RESOURCES DEFENSE COUNCIL: With chemicals, it's shoot first and ask questions later.

NARRATION: We think we are protected but, in fact, chemicals are presumed safe—innocent—until proven guilty.

SANDY BUCHANAN, EXECUTIVE DIRECTOR, OHIO CITIZEN ACTION: Years of [getting] documents [from the chemical industry] have shown that they [the owners of chemical factories] knew they were hurting people, much like the tobacco industry...

DAVID ROSNER, COLUMBIA UNIVERSITY: You kind of avoid as a historian the idea that there are conspiracies or that there are people planning the world in a certain way. You just try to avoid that because it's—it seems too—too unreal and too frightening in its implications. Yet, when you look at these [chemical industry] documents, you say yes, there are people who understood what was going on, people who thought about the crisis that was engulfing them or about to engulf them and tried in every which way to get out of that crisis and actually to, in some sense, to suppress an issue.

BILL MOYERS: Do you think all of this added up to, to use your word, a conspiracy?

ROSNER: In a moral sense, I think it was a conspiracy...

NARRATION: Instead of changing its behavior, the petrochemical industry turned to the courts to stop the regulation [on benzene]. The companies argued that reducing exposure to benzene would be too costly.

October 11, 1977

"We assert that there is no evidence that leukemia has resulted from exposure to benzene at the current concentration limits. The new and lower limitation on exposure would represent an intolerable misallocation of economic resources."

NARRATION: The Fifth Circuit Court of Appeals in New Orleans—in America's petrochemical heartland—ruled that the government had not proved the danger to humans to be great enough to justify the cost to industry. The victory propelled an offensive directed by the now re-named Chemical Manufacturers Association.

September, 1979 A Summary of Progress.
Presented to the Board of Directors.

"Gentlemen, this is a campaign that has the dimension and detail of a war. This is war—not a battle. The dollars expended on offense are token compared to future costs. The rewards are the court decisions we have won, the regulations that have been modified, made more cost effective or just dropped. The future holds more of the same...

WITNESS IN HEARING: The industry's gotten away with murder. That's why they don't move forward. Because it's cost them some money and some effort, and if they're not pushed, they won't move.

Despite this unseemly, nay criminal, behavior of the chemical industry, American society in general, and scientists in particular, fail to challenge companies whose products are using all of the world's children like experimental animals. Americans still consume those products. The chemical-by-chemical-regulation scientists represent a cancer model of science which, while convenient and highly profitable to its practitioners, is not asking questions to reveal those responsible for the destruction of our world. We should not forget we are also part of nature. We belong to those very ecosystems under stress. Therefore, we need an ecopolitical or nature-human model of science with ecosystem integrity and protection, and prevention of human disease its most important values. Nature and an abiding respect and veneration for life must be guiding our policies.

In "Trade Secrets," the physician Philip Landrigan made the following utopian recommendation. "What's needed," he said, "is an unpolluted political structure that is empowered to set regulations that protect the public health." Theo Colborn, co-author of *Our Stolen Future*, a great book on the impact of the hormone poisons on women, was more straightforward than Landrigan. She became exasperated with the games of the scientists, the shenanigans and lies of the chemical industry owners, and the timidity of the government's regulatory crew. She put it like this:

> We've fooled around for years with a cancer model. We've never been very successful with our cancer model, there are still many assumptions and questions. We're moving into the realm of a developmental model, where there are trans-generational effects, two and three generations down the line—far more questions. We are dealing with how many vital life systems now? We'll never be able to come up with a risk model to protect us from these chemicals. The problem is too complex. So what is the answer? Don't release any more.[37]

Peter Montague agrees. He says we need to regulate chemicals not one at a time but by whole classes. "And the dangerous classes need to be phased out and banned. Zero discharge. Pollution prevention. These are the keys to sustainability and survival."[38]

Unfortunately, Colborn's and Montague's message, like the powerful proposal of Rachel Carson decades earlier, remain challenging ideas that may never be translated into policy. Yet the cancer system in place is like the cancer alley of Louisiana.

I visited the cancer alley of Louisiana several times during 1991-92 while on a visiting professorship at the University of New Orleans. But I want to preface my reaction to the cancer alley with my memories from a journey I took to the University of Colorado. Students are connected to the cancer alley. I went to the University of Colorado at Boulder for a conference sponsored by the Student Environmental Action Coalition or SEAC.

Twelve students from the University of New Orleans and Tulane University and I left New Orleans for Boulder at 7:30 pm on Thursday the third of October 1991. We drove for 25 hours straight. We passed through Louisiana, Mississippi, Arkansas, Oklahoma, Kansas and Colorado in our trek from New Orleans to Boulder, some 1,200 miles apart. Near the border between Kansas and Colorado, the horizon was extraterrestrial: immense, flat, a fantastic synthesis of a blue sky with huge hanging white clouds and a dry earth of the same manufactured consistency of small grass for cow grazing and grain cultivation. Largely empty of people, this part of the Great Plains has a beauty and solitude unmatched anywhere. It's a gods' and native Americans' country going through its cyclical destructiveness of dust bowls every 20 years or so. Without its precious prairie grasses, the nearly naked and violated land blows away in the arms of fierce winds. But its mad conquerors have not given up yet. They continue to extract the land's last wealth. Entire kingdoms of flat territories belong to banks and agribusiness.

The other surprise of our travel to Boulder was the chemical corridor and, no doubt, cancer alley of Denver. We passed this major city around 7:30 in the evening on the second day of our trip. The toxic chemistry of the factories floated in the air next to our fast-moving van. Fumes, clouds of pollutants rose lazily from the chimneys of Denver's Coketown. Hundreds of lights and the poisons floating in dense formation over the metallic skeleton of the oil refineries and chemical plants gave the entire conglomeration a strange barbarian architecture and appearance. I could not help but feel pity and contempt for the foolish and irresponsible people who built such a potential Bhopal in the midst of their city.

American college students expect to hear the ecological crisis is an ephemeral aberration of capitalism. Yet some of them hear that capitalism is the ecological crisis; that progress hides a baggage of illusions and destructive practices; that science mostly follows power rather than truth; that the so-called primitive people understand nature better than the so-called civilized people of Europe and North America; that their education fails to prepare them to manage and, much less, do away with the ceaseless poisoning of the earth.

Those of the students who grasp what is at stake with the environmental crisis are unhappy with the hypocrisy of their parents and teachers. They fear the future. They fear that forces beyond their control will force them to become like the models they resent. This explains why so many students are apathetic and apolitical, offering their heads like empty vessels to be filled with capitalism's formulas and rigid dogmas, something that their corrupt professors do immediately. They rush to pour their technical religion down those innocent young people's throats.

My engineering colleagues at the University of New Orleans, for example, polite and indifferent on the outside, were like police cops guarding their students from me. With the exception of Abdel-Alim Hannoura, a professor who sided with me, most of the engineering faculty refused to list my spring 1992 classes for credit to engineering students. They said my emphasis on policy and international environmental issues was not appropriate for engineers. They also became concerned when they discovered I planned to take my students on a field trip to Louisiana's cancer alley in their own backyard. The dean of the engineering college said this would compromise the objectivity of the university. He did not allow me to use university vans for the trip.

The narrow-minded professors had good reasons to feel unease with the reality of their cancer alley. I visited that stretch of 70 miles of factories, north of New Orleans on River Road next to the great but poisoned and captive Mississippi River, for the third time on October 12, 1991. Seeing up close the large factories of the cancer alley between New Orleans and Baton Rouge is overwhelming but instructive. It puts meat to theory. Students ask questions. Who benefits from these giant conglomerations? What happens to the effluents? What about the Mississippi River that drains the poisons oozing from the factory pipes? Where do these poisons end up? After all, we drink the water of the river and eat its fish. And why are most of these factories located in black communities?

These factories of fertilizers, petrochemicals, pharmaceuticals and plastics are strange technological structures of tubes and vessels, their smoke and poison rising in the sky. A human being next to such hot and boiling vats and coils of steel barrels feels insignificant, humiliated, frightened. Flames burn from the stacks, small in the day but huge at night, illuminating the darkness with blasts of leaping fire, hissing sounds and bad smells.

For the largely black neighbors of these factories, it has been an experience of a perpetual inferno of fires, stinking air, tremors, cancer, and other deadly illnesses—even losing their homes. I remember meeting Wilfred M. Greene, a 70-year-old black man in Wallace, a small town in the St. Johns Parish right next to the Mississippi River where Formosa Plastics wanted to build a large wood pulp and rayon plant right in a black neighborhood. The Chinese multinational corporation, Formosa Plastics, had no trouble with the local white politicians. The only resistance the company faced came from some environmentalists and Wilfred Greene who defended his besieged community with eloquence and passion. He was a retired teacher and principal. He said most of the black people in his town were illiterate, jobless and victims of white racism. His grandfather purchased his land in the 1870s and, he assured me on October 13, 1991, he was not about to let it be taken from him by Formosa Plastics. His determination defeated Formosa Plastics. The Chinese giant company abandoned its Wallace site and built a factory for petrochemicals and plastic resins in Baton Rouge instead.

However, the cancer alley in Louisiana, and other sacrificial zones in the country, are evidence that the owners of chemical factories can go on manufacturing and dumping with impunity. Even less than the tobacco companies, they face no public scrutiny or resistance to what they do. On the contrary, their products—plastics, drugs, and petrochemicals— are the fuels of industrialized societies. Yet the owners of cancer alleys know they hurt the people in their neighborhoods badly. That's why they surround themselves with secrecy, security, and barbed wire.

Things Fall Apart

One of the major differences between cancer alleys and industrialized food plantations is that the chemical factories are concentrated power and occupy small space usually out of public view. Large farms are everywhere, yet they are not easy to see. The effects on nature and society, however, are not that far dissimilar.

Rural America is becoming an immense cancer alley—and it is falling apart: In the place of flourishing rural communities, one sees poor people and decaying social organizations, rural ghettos with farmers on public assistance, main streets of dealers, brokers, agents. The farmers raise not so much food as they *produce* commodities for a handful of agribusiness corporations with enormous power. But even among the farmers themselves, there are great inequalities that shift land, food, wealth and power to a tiny agribusiness class. By the late 1970s, 3.6 million farms of less than 50 acres represented 57 percent of all farms but only 6 percent of all farmland. However, 1.6 percent of farms larger than 1,000 acres owned 34 percent of the farmland. And those farms larger than 5,000 acres, a mere 0.2 percent of America's farms, had control of 14 percent of the farmland. Five percent of the landlords owned slightly more than half of the farmland. The largest 5 percent of the landlords owned 70 percent of the farmland in the Pacific States and 66 percent of the land in the Mountain States.[39] In the late 1980s, about 1.4 percent of the large agribusiness persons produced more than 30 percent of our food. And it is these large "growers" who benefit the most from billions a year of federal agricultural subsidies. By the late 1980s, the beneficiaries of federal and state government favors and subsidies (giant agricultural companies and very large farmers) forced 70 percent of 2 million farmers into obscurity verging on extinction. These are America's "family farmers" producing less than 10 percent of our food in their "hobby farms."[40]

By the dawn of the twenty-first century—the year 2000—the subsidies to giant agriculture were high enough to hurt the already moribund family farmers even more. Direct government payments to America's farmers in the 1990s were in this order and magnitude: 1991 ($8.2 billion), 1992 ($9.2 billion), 1993 ($13.4 billion), 1994 ($7.9 billion), 1995 ($7.3 billion), 1996 ($7.3 billion), 1997 ($7.5 billion), 1998 ($12.2 billion), 1999 ($20.6 billion), and 2000 ($23.3 billion).[41]

This national policy, says the Center for Rural Affairs, a civil society farm organization from Nebraska, of paying giant agricultural companies billions so they drive "family farms out of business…represents a failure of democracy."[42]

This unjust policy is no small "failure" of democracy, an accident that can be fixed quickly. The willful destruction of family farming represents the corruption and crippling of democracy in the United States. And yet the dream and the living of democracy through family farming was, to some degree, alive in the United States in the late 1970s—at the very moment the entire legacy of family agriculture was at its unstoppable decline. Louis Harris and Associates reported in 1979 to the US Department of

Agriculture that "the public's preference is for a country which has a relatively large number of small farms.... Significantly, there is a broad-based consensus on this issue, with strong support for the small family farm in evidence in every region of the country and in every significant demographic subgroup of the population."[43] A family farmer from Oak City, North Carolina, William C. Beach, explained why this was so to the US Department of Agriculture. He said:

> The family farm is democracy and free enterprise at its best, a family running and working a business together, working together to produce food and fiber.... The family farm is not the agribusinessman in town, the lawyer at the courthouse, the doctor at the hospital, the professional man in his office. He is not people looking for a farm to buy as a hedge against inflation, nor the person looking for ways to reduce his income tax while making a safe investment. This group also includes the multinational corporations, food processing industries and vertical integrators.[44]

The US Department of Agriculture, however, ignored the public's preference for small family farms, and many of them all over the country, and continued with its pro-agribusiness policies, and their inevitable push of democracy out of rural America and the rest of the United States. The annual public gift of billions of dollars to private giant agriculture is the arrogant showing off of a tyrannical plutocracy doing favors to its clients. Democracy is written all over everything this plutocracy does, but it is just a cosmetic decoration, this constant and forced reference to democracy, that has nothing to do with democracy. Giant agriculture, if not the sole participant in the demise of democracy in America, is, without doubt, a chief perpetrator of that political crime. That is why debt, federal farm policies, and agribusiness power go on so freely in forcing many farmers out of agriculture all together.

In addition, America's agricultural schools or land grant universities, just like the US Department of Agriculture, side with agribusiness, so they produce agricultural industrialization, science and machines for large farmers, not organic farming or sustainable agriculture for small family farmers. Don Paarlberg, a senior official of the US Department of Agriculture in the administration of president Jimmy Carter, admitted in 1980 that land grant universities were largely responsible for driving the family farmer off the land:

> "The land-grant college system," he said, "whatever its intent,

whether real or professed or both, has served to speed the trend toward an industrialized agriculture. It simply has not been possible to make such great advances in efficiency as have occurred without having profound effect on the structure of agriculture.... The Extension Service, with its advice that a farmer should have a business 'big enough to be efficient,' undoubtedly speeded up the process of farm consolidation and reduced the number of farms. In the classroom, emphasis on modern management helped put the traditional family farm into a state of total eclipse."[45]

The land grant college system came into being in the 1860s and 1890s as a practical means of helping the small family farmer prosper and stay on the land. The federal government donated land to the states for agricultural schools. The agricultural universities had also a political purpose of keeping rural America democratic. Solving the technical problems of all family farmers by the translation and application of knowledge to skills, tools and power was the contribution of the state to nourishing a prosperous and just rural society. The South, however, had plantations with slaves, a political fact that undermined American democracy. In 1863, Isaac Newton, US Commissioner of Agriculture, informed president Abraham Lincoln that plantations were responsible for the fall of Rome. So with the plantations of the South in mind, the Commissioner warned America not to follow the example of Rome.[46]

The United States fought a civil war over slavery and plantations and the plantations won. The twentieth century confirmed the plantations to the pinnacle of power undreamt in the time of Abraham Lincoln. The family farmers who survive the traumas of the agribusiness economy of America are overwhelmingly white and old. In Nebraska, for instance, in the period of 1978 to 1987, the number of farmers declined by 12 percent. Those of 45 to 54 years old declined by 38 percent and farmers of 25 years or younger left agriculture at the rate of 43 percent. However, farmers older than 65 years increased in numbers by 16 percent and increased their land by 43 percent, farming Nebraska's nearly one-fifth of the land.[47]

The rapid loss of young people from agriculture, the loss of experienced farmers, particularly those of black and other ethnic minorities, and the rising age of all farmers provide hard testimony of how bad the social and political situation in rural America has become. However, rural America is part of a developing agribusiness world. Those who take over the land of failing family farmers in Iowa and California are the same plantations that grab the peasant's land in Brazil. The concentration of land among aging farmers and agribusinesses, and the near monopoly power of a few multinational companies in agricultural production in the United States and the rest of the world augur a new dark age for rural people and democracy and food. The spread of this land-grab, and deceptively, science-based agricultural model or, more accurately, corporate-based under the veil of science, throughout the globe, is unsettling the culture and ecology of the earth. In fact industrial agriculture is responsible for the greatest discontinuity in both planetary ecosystems and the social, political, and cultural traditions of the world's people.

The Western industrial agricultural paradigm reached the Americas, Africa and Asia in 1492 as an intricate part of the Western invasion and colonization of the tropics. Five centuries of that violent Encounter sufficed to institutionalize Western farm practices all over the world with the result of massive social and ecological upheavals in Africa, Latin America, and Asia. As previously noted, the "green revolution" of the last 50 years is the latest attempt by Europe and North America to finish off traditional peasant farming in the Third World.[48]

North America's Third World neighbor, Mexico, has been a green revolution guinea pig since the 1940s. The results have been—predictably—disturbing. Angus Wright, professor of environmental studies at California State University at Sacramento, spent 10 years documenting the social and environmental effects of Mexico's agricultural "modernization." "The evidence strongly indicates," he says, "that the [green revolution] policies [in Mexico] favored large farmers over small, monoculture over diversity, and chemical farming over traditional methods. In addition, they changed the food patterns of the nation, with wheat favored over corn, the North American researchers going a long way to accomplish what the wheat-loving Spanish had attempted to enforce on Mexican farmers for three hundred years." [49]

Sultan Ahmed Shah, a Bangladeshi engineer, studied the ecological dilemma of growing rice in his country under the strict regime of the green revolution. His 1994 report on the "Environmental Impact of Irrigation Agriculture" is telling of the "profound environmentally damaging effects" of the green revolution technologies in the world's most densely populated country of 110 million people. Shah says that pesticides are having a "visible and profound ecological damage to numerous aquatic and terrestrial wildlife species." He also argues that overuse of synthetic fertilizers for several years is having deleterious effects on the land itself. He concluded that "Bangladesh soils are hungry, sick and almost lifeless."

Up to mid-1980s, Indonesia faced Bangladesh's problems in its green revolution rice production. The insect, brown planthopper, destroyed so much of Indonesia's rice that, eventually, those who made policy in Indonesia understood that insecticides and brown planthoppers don't mix. An American entomologist working for the Food and Agriculture Organization (FAO) of the United Nations, Peter Kenmore, said in 1991 that "Trying to control such a population outbreak [of brown planthoppers] with insecticides is like pouring kerosene on a house fire."

Kenmore made that statement in "Indonesia's Integrated Pest Management—A Model for Asia," a report published by FAO in September 1991. That report gives the history of Indonesia's transformation from a green revolution paradigm—with severe environmental costs—to an alternative agroecological system of rice growing supported by ecological principles and good farming methods.

The so-called "green revolution" is a failure because of its half-baked and crude science—its insistence on treating tropical ecosystems like temperate factory farms—and because of its social agenda of tipping power on the side of the landlords. The paradigm of the green revolution—of doing farm work with machines, chemicals, and seeds fixed to match water and chemicals—has spread throughout the world. Yet the dissemination of this industrialized farming model, particularly that of wheat and rice in Asia, parallels the growth of hunger and ecological destruction throughout the Third World. Starvation is rampant in Africa and social and ecological crises are pronounced in Asia and Latin America. The extraordinary crop genetic diversity and richness of the tropics are rapidly becoming a thing of the past. India, for instance, relies for its wheat and rice on seeds that must have plenty of water, fertilizers and pesticides. These seeds respond well to fertilizers and irrigation water but their crops don't leave much in the land for either animals or the land itself. These seeds give rise to crops that are much more vulnerable to insects and diseases than the old peasant varieties. In fact, without a good dosage of irrigation water and fertilizer these science crops yield less than the traditional food crop varieties of wheat and rice. And because of the need of these scientifically engineered seeds for expensive chemicals, machinery, and water, they have fallen primarily in the hands of affluent farmers, hardening considerably the social crisis in the countryside of the Third World.

The Bhopal pesticide catastrophe in India in 1984 raised further doubts about the fate of industrial agriculture. Could agricultural factories producing poison gases be controlled? Was it even appropriate that cancer-giving, monster-forming, deleterious chemicals to all life be used in the raising of food for people? And is it possible to prevent poisoned food from moving from one country to another?

In the United States in 1989 the National Academy of Sciences issued its report, *Alternative Agriculture*, in which it said the ecological effects of industrialized agriculture in America were becoming serious enough that the country ought to look at working with non-toxic alternatives to grow its food.

Thus the evidence from both the Third World and the United States seems to indicate that the very fate of industrial agriculture is open to question. This is the case even if a strict global regime could guarantee a fair assessment of the risks of the hazardous chemicals used in industrial agriculture. It is the ecological factor, even more so than the political danger giant agriculture poses to democratic institutions, that makes industrialized farming incompatible with life on earth.

Industrialized agriculture is poisoning a considerable amount of the world's drinking water. This happens to a considerable degree because of irrigation—the plumbing engineers construct to bring fresh water to the farmers' fields. By the year 2000, some 17 percent of the world's agricultural land used irrigation water for the crops grown on that land. Irrigated land increased 72 percent from 1966 to 1996. Agricultural irrigation accounts for 70 percent of all water withdrawn from rivers, aquifers, and lakes. Now, this fresh water that engineers take from rivers, lakes, and deep in the ground, could be drinking water for humans. Of this huge amount of freshwater going to agriculture, about 30 to 60 percent returns to rivers, aquifers, and lakes as water loaded with agrotoxins and fertilizers and other wastes. Industrialized agriculture is the world's largest user of the earth's fresh water. It is also the world's largest polluter. More that 30 percent of the river basins in the Americas, North

Africa, Southeast Asia, and Australia are under intensive agricultural production. The situation is worse in Europe and South Asia where more than 50 percent of the river valleys are the plantations of agricultural systems hooked on chemicals and machines for their survival.[50] It is this toxic, irrigated, and mechanical factory in the world's countrysides that is impoverishing and killing the very biological diversity that keep the earth's ecosystems alive.

Chapter 4

Organic Farming and Genetic Engineering in the United States

Look to the Land

Even organic farming, a tiny, almost invisible, and imperfect form of developing biological agriculture that abstains from agrotoxins, gets very little support in the United States precisely because of the power of giant agriculture. The US Department of Agriculture is a perfect administrator and mirror of this immoral policy. This mammoth bureaucracy in the heart of federal government lavishes a lot of gold yearly in pushing the cause of agribusiness. In 1995, for instance, it spent $1.8 billion for agribusiness research and education, and $1.5 million for a few projects that had some relevance to organic farming.[1] Organic farming is the most visible expression, if only a modest application, of the idea of bringing agriculture back to the family farmer in the United States. Both the Europeans and the Americans adopted the name "organic farming" or "biological agriculture" as a protest, and alternative farm system, to the rising agribusiness colossus in Europe and North America.

This happened in the early twentieth century when the British landlords' 400-year war against the peasants, politely known as the "enclosures," had come to its violent and bloody end. England had no longer a peasant class. The British government had sided with the landlords and either killed the peasants, drafted them into its factory system, or sent them as indentured servants or slaves to North America, New Zealand and Australia. Agricultural industrialization was simply an extension of the triumph of the British landlords. It blazed throughout England, other Western European countries and North America, leaving behind it abandoned villages, and devastated countrysides, dust bowls, synthetic fertilizers and pesticides, while slowly building the infrastructure of the giant one-crop plantation and animal farm.

Agricultural thinkers were overwhelmed by the spread of this brave new mechanical farming in the rural world and nature. The British farmer and scholar, Lord Northbourne, writing in the late 1930s, tried to resurrect the dying wholeness of nature and agriculture. The farm, he said:

> must be a living entity, it must be a unit which has within itself a balanced organic life. Every branch of the work is interlocked with all others. The cycle of conversion of vegetable products through the animal into manure and back to vegetable is of great complexity, and highly sensitive, especially over long periods, to any disturbance of its proper balance. The penalty for failure to maintain this balance is, in the long run, a progressive impoverishment of the soil. Real fertility can only be built up gradually under a system appropriate to the conditions of each particular farm, and by adherence to the essentials of the system, whatever they may be in each case, over long periods. Such building up of a coherent living unity is utterly incompatible with frequent changes of system and with specialization. Yet the modern farmer is continually up against the temptation to make changes in order to secure a quick return where it appears there may be a chance of a profit for a few years in some particular line and to specialize in that line. In doing so he is tempted to use up accumulated fertility and trust to luck for the future. It is chiefly for these reasons that mixed farming is right, for it is only on the principle of constant exchange of living material, which is the basis of such farming, that real farming (as against forced, artificial, or imported productivity) can be built up. Mixed farming is real farming. Unduly specialized 'farming' is something else; it must depend on imported fertility, it cannot be self-sufficient nor an organic whole.[2]

It is possible that both the name "organic" and Lord Northbourne's ideals of mixed (organic) farming influenced organic farming in the United States. Yet the fortunes and politics of organic agriculture in the United States mirror the peculiar American phenomenon of draining theory from social life, pretending to live democracy on the face of overwhelming raw power. Going to an ecological conference in California opened my eyes to the sophistication of this national deception.

I wanted to go to California for the twenty-first annual Ecological Farming Conference for more than my deep affection for those raising food as a way of life. My interest was in seeing some evidence that traditional family agriculture was slowly coming back to life in the United States under the wonderful but deceptive names of "organic," "ecological," and "community-supported" farming.

The expectation, not yet tested, is that ecological, organic and community-supported agriculture will usher in "sustainable"—meaning non-deleterious and free of oppression—farming and rural societies.

In theory, of course, that is possible. But in the more than twenty-five years I have been monitoring agricultural and rural development in the United States, theory rarely guides government policy or what farmers do. In fact it's the lack of theory based on agrarian and ecological and political values that explains the devouring of the family farm in the United States by agribusiness. In addition, I was never under any illusion of a utopian yeoman hiding under the family farmer of North America. I knew that even in the best of circumstances, the small family farmer has nearly always been trying to become like his big brother next door, the agribusinessman. But with all its problems, and they are many, family farming appeals to me as a reasonable institution to raise food and democracy. Just as importantly, I consider family farming the only hope we have to bring to an end factory agriculture devastating rural America and the countrysides of the world.

The agricultural meeting in California was planned for the end of January 2001. California was my Ithaca in America. The image of the redwoods and the Trinity River remained burning in my mind. I spent 1988-1989 in Humboldt County in northern California. That brief experience had given me a taste for the magnificent and violent that is California. In Humboldt County, in the heart of California's redwood forest, I came face to face with the beautiful in nature and the criminal in corporate capitalism. The two realities—one permanent, the other ephemeral—played out their dance and, often, deadly embrace. I was a bystander to that drama, and I wanted to take sides, and I did take sides. I was a visiting professor at Humboldt State University. My teaching made me a book easy to read. I stood for the integrity of nature and the inviolability of the redwood forest in particular. I knew some of those ancient trees were growing up while my ancestors were building the Parthenon some 2,500 years ago. I fell in love with them instantly. There was no way I could justify their "harvest" by barbarians in corporate armor.

My students and I explored the world of the red giants in Humboldt County. But the moment we came across a grove that had been "clearcut," my mind raced to war—the violent and immoral war timber corporations have been fighting in northern California for decades. In the place of the ancient trees, only stumps remained and, in many instances, even those stumps had been blown apart. But along with these memories, were the pleasant memories of weekly evening seminar in the large and beautiful house of a librarian friend, Gloria Fulton. Over bowls of hot homemade soup, homemade bread and good wine, I would guide a passionate discussion about nature and culture. My students would bring their friends and the seminar would become a symposium. I also remember the pleasures of walking in the silence and majesty of the redwood forest. I remember the metamorphosis of nature after the exquisitely beautiful but gloomy land would soak the thin rain and then absorb the bright light of the sun, pushing aside to temporary oblivion the heavy dark clouds. All nature looked like a gorgeous bride—shining and laughing.

So on January 2001 I went to California's Monterey coast for the conference of organic farmers—and others. And despite my endless questioning of everything agricultural in the United States, I was interested to see what would happen bringing together about 1,400 people, some of whom would be organic farmers, some would be curious students like myself, and others would be there as part of a legal effort to destroy organic farming.

Wednesday, January 24, was the first day of the Ecological Farming Conference. About 300 people met in Watsonville to take a bus tour through four farms in the prosperous Pajaro Valley. Wednesday was another rainy day for which I was ill prepared. Yet I was kind of fortunate that at the motel office I met a woman with a car also attending the conference. She graciously gave me a ride to another part of town from where we took the busses for the farm tour. She was a retired computer management consultant who wanted to expand her garden in a small organic farm so she could sell vegetables at the local farmers market in Albuquerque, New Mexico. She spoke with so much passion about growing vegetables I was extremely happy there were people like her. In the bus I sat next to a former employee of a global seed company. He was an organic farmer who made a modest living growing tomatoes on two acres near Santa Cruz. He said he quit the agribusiness firm because he disagreed with its immoral behavior. "What you hear of Monsanto," he said, "is nor practiced by Monsanto alone. Agribusiness companies are not trying to feed the world. Their game is power, monopolies, and profits."

Monsanto, of course, is the American giant multinational seed and drug company pushing genetic engineering to its limits, particularly in the manipulation of crops. Some of the seeds Monsanto is selling to farmers are designed to bring traditional farming to an end. The Monsanto farmers, if they decide to do agriculture according to the Monsanto gospel, must buy their seeds from Monsanto every growing season. This is what my organic farmer had in mind with his warning about Monsanto. And he was right.

The US Department of Agriculture worked together with Delta and Pine Land, the world's largest cotton-seed company that almost became a subsidiary of Monsanto, and developed a seed-sterilizing technology designed to prevent farmers and peasants from saving seed from their harvest for their next growing season. USDA used public money to create a high-tech biological weapon with no possibility of public benefits, in this case benefits to family farmers, but with huge possibilities to enslave them even more to agribusiness like the seed, biotechnology, and agrochemical giant Monsanto.

The US Department of Agriculture will probably give Monsanto or another biotech corporation the exclusive license it needs to commercialize a technology that is biological and social warfare itself. The very idea of engineering food seeds for only one harvest is so antithetical to agriculture and agrarian life that it becomes equal to ending farming as we have known it for millennia.[3] Not even the gods have the right to act in such arbitrary and violent way. And the loss of farmers' rights—to be able to use the seeds from their harvest for the next agricultural season—will punish and humiliate the small American family yeoman even more. For the peasant, however, such violation will probably become civil wars, hunger, destitution, and starvation—even death.

Monsanto is also behind biotech crops like the New Leaf Superior, a potato, which is both a potato and an insecticide at the same time—the bioengineered spuds are toxic enough to kill their persistent enemies, the Colorado potato beetle. As I already said, biotech foods, like so much else in agricultural bioengineering, create a chasm between people and food, crops that coevolved with human beings for millennia are forced to become extinct or end up in some refrigerated collection. Biotech foods, and biotechnology in general, give the illusion we can beat nature by making nature do our bidding.[4] Agribusiness giants like Monsanto use their fancy scientific, engineering, and political skills to extract political power in return for their myths of endless production. Monsanto's New Leaf Superior is impoverishing both nature and the American family farmer. But Monsanto's bioengineered potato is also playing God.[5]

In addition, Monsanto manufactures the Recombinant Bovine Somatotropin (rBST), a growth hormone that forces dairy cattle to produce more milk. The US Food and Drug Administration approved the drug for cows in the United States in 1993 despite the fact the United States already produces too much milk, and despite the fact this hormone makes cows sick from swollen and ulcerated udders, skin rushes, and hoof disorders, medical problems that are mostly treated with antibiotics that find their way into both the cow's milk and meat.

Because of the ethical, economic, and potentially dangerous health effects of rBST in the milk of cows, Canada has had second thoughts about allowing Monsanto to sell their hormone to its dairy farmers. In fact, Canadian regulatory scientists complained of intense pressure from both Monsanto and their own supervisors to approve rBST. One of those scientists, with thirty years of experience with Health Canada, Shiv Chopra, testified on October 20, 1998 before the Canadian Standing Senate Committee on Agriculture and Forestry that he and his colleagues were "pressured and coerced to pass drugs of questionable safety, including rBST." Another scientist, Margaret Haydon, also testified that Monsanto tried to bribe Health Canada with a sum of one to two million dollars in an effort to boost their chances of selling the dangerous hormone.[6]

Finally, a small British printing company, Penwell, shredded 14,000 copies of the September / October 1998 issue of *The Ecologist*, England's leading environmental magazine, because that issue of the periodical was devoted entirely to the history of Monsanto—its links to biological warfare, the cow drug rBST, herbicides, bioengineering, genetically engineered foods, sterile agricultural seeds. Penwell had printed *The Ecologist* for the last twenty-six years.[7]

In an open letter to Robert Shapiro, chief executive officer of Monsanto, the editors of *The Ecologist*, said this:

> You tell us in your advertisements that you want to help preserve the environment, yet Monsanto has caused environmental pollution on a massive scale—not least through the production of enough PCBs [polychlorinated biphenyls] to kill all mammal life in the world's oceans. You tell us that your aim is to feed the hungry of the world, yet Monsanto has been directly responsible for undermining one of the key practices of sustainable, subsistence agriculture—that of saving and improving locally-adapted

seeds from year to year. And you tell us that you see genetic engineering as a means of *reducing* the need for pesticides, yet Monsanto is the producer of Roundup, one of the biggest-selling pesticides in the world.[8]

We don't know if Shapiro bothered to respond to these charges—an impossible task of refuting the truth from some 100 years of poisoning the United States and the rest of world. For about 40 years in the twentieth century, for example, Monsanto drenched Anniston, Alabama with its extremely toxic and lasting industrial coolants known as PCBs.[9] We also don't know why Penwell pulped the Monsanto issue of *The Ecologist*, or why the largest retailers of England refused to carry the reprinted Monsanto issue on newsstands. Probably they worried that Monsanto would use the libel laws against them. But the problem goes much deeper than libel. During the cow drug hearings in Canada, October 22, 1998, Senator Eugene Whelan, deputy chairman of the Canadian Senate Committee on Agriculture and Forestry, spoke angrily about Monsanto's $600,000 donation to Agriculture Canada "to find a wheat that is immune to Roundup," Monsanto's billion-dollar herbicide. Senator Whelan tried to find out who is pulling the strings behind the academic research supporting the work of agrochemical giants like Monsanto. He discovered that those agricultural researchers and professors serving agribusiness are "scared to death." So he turned to the courageous Canadian bureaucrats testifying before his committee, Shiv Chopra and Margaret Haydon and a few others, and said to them how proud he was they were "not scared to death."[10] However, these honest scientists paid a price for blowing the whistle on corruption and wrongdoing within the government. Health Canada fired them in July 2004.[11]

With this background in mind, I was startled by the forthrightness of this former company man who had also been a professor of plant breeding at North Carolina State University, and a consultant to the United Nations Food and Agriculture Organization. He had traveled widely and had respect for traditional agricultural knowledge. Yet this intelligent man felt that government should stay out of agriculture. He had little trust that any government would or could benefit him and other small farmers. He feared anything the federal government did with the "organic regulations" or other policies would add to his costs of raising tomatoes—and, maybe, put him out of business. He did not say it, but probably his close observations of how governments served the interests of giant global companies made him skeptical that the organic rule of the federal government was in fact designed to protect the organic farmers. This organic rule, defining the practices of organic farming and the quality of organic food, became final on April 21, 2001, and assumed the power of federal law on October 2002. The former company man probably thought that the US Department of Agriculture's organic rule was another scheme setting up a sector of the agricultural economy whose "certified" farmers would be secure in earning a better price for their produce. Yet his comments about Monsanto sounded chillingly familiar right in our first stop in the fabulous Pajaro Valley.

Farmers Renting Their Crops

Amigo Cantisano, an organic farming advisor and the shaker and mover behind the Ecological Farming Conference, was our friendly farm tour guide. This is a man who loves Watsonville and the Pajaro Valley. He also knows the history and politics of both the agribusiness and organic farm communities of California. He was wearing shorts and a huge hat. He spoke to us with a megaphone tied to a long wooden pole he held like a flag. He felt perfectly comfortable addressing several hundred people and leading them through greenhouses, answering technical questions about the land and crops and seasons. He repeatedly emphasized how rich and expensive was the land of the Pajaro Valley.

Amigo's first choice for us was the Sandpiper Farms. What struck me immediately in this large operation—I hesitate to call it a farm—was the several trucks, tractors, sprayers, and other machinery all over the place. This is the armament of giant agriculture, not of family or organic farming. In addition, there were two huge greenhouses. A manager named Dan Schmida spoke to us about the strawberry, raspberry, and blackberry varieties he and his staff develop for his company's clients. He said his was not a research station but a "land for designer berries for rent." Yes, he said his company "rented" varieties of strawberries, raspberries, and blackberries and other plants to "farmers" who grew these crops for his company. At that moment I remembered Monsanto and I shivered. Not one of the 300 or so organic farmers and others listening to him asked how it was possible for a farmer to be a farmer and "rent" his crops or seeds. In fact we were witnessing the present version of feudalism in

America; the so-called farmer was a contract worker doing in the twenty-first century what the landless tenants and sharecroppers did in the early twentieth century. I was stunned. I realized, then, I was in the brave new rural world of California, always first in agribusiness. Dan Schmida also spoke of his "organic" strawberries and the beneficial insects his company reared for selling to farmers. The two large greenhouses served that purpose. I took some pictures of the machinery and the exquisite land around the Sandpiper Farms. I asked Schmida if he did genetic engineering and he said no. I climbed the bus for the second farm thinking of "farmers renting their crops." And if farmers rent their livelihoods and receive orders on what to produce and how to produce it, how different are these farmers from tenant farmers and factory workers? Farmers, who once nourished their customers, do so less and less and their control over what they do is shifting into the hands of corporate farmers. I did not forget I was in California, but I did not expect to come so close to raw power so soon—at an ecological farming conference.

Our next stop was at the Lakeside Organic Gardens of Dick and Bill Peixoto, two brothers farming hundreds of acres in the Pajaro Valley and Hollister. The farm we visited was on the grounds of a school near the Pacific Ocean. The Peixoto brothers explained they grew vegetables with and without agrotoxins. They pointed to fields of "organic" celery (grown without pesticides) and "conventional" beans and cabbage (sprayed with pesticides) very close to each other. But like the Sandpiper Farms, this operation was loaded with heavy machinery. Indeed, from the number of men dressed in boots and blue jeans and carrying cell phones watching us and waiting for orders, I knew we were in the midst of a highly mechanized factory of agricultural production with subsidiaries in the United States and abroad. We could see trucks leaving the property full of the harvested vegetables sold under the owners' brands. The "organic" part of this business was tiny, perhaps five percent, and it served the interests of creating a good reputation—hence the provocative and tempting name, Lakeside Organic Gardens—besides earning a higher price for its boutique organic vegetables. Organic farming, of course, is a tiny sector of agriculture growing rapidly. And while it improves some farm practices, it has been implemented with hardly a change in the dynamics of power.

Organic Lunch

We drove to a park overlooking the Pacific Ocean for lunch. There, in a wet and slightly rainy weather making nature brown and slightly dark and gloomy but periodically interrupted by short-lived shafts of light transforming everything to color and happiness, and in the midst of tall ponderosa pine trees, we enjoyed a wonderful organic lunch provided by the Lakeside Organic Gardens. We then continued our tour to two organic farms, which had the appearance of being both family farms and farms raising their food probably agrotoxins. The first we visited, the Thomas Farm, is on the hilly edge of a wonderful small valley on the Central Coast of California near Santa Cruz. The owner of this nine-acre family farm, Jerry Thomas, explained he has been making a living on this farm since 1971 growing cut flowers, fruits, and vegetables, which he sells at farmers markets in Santa Cruz and the affluent towns of the Monterey Peninsula. The gravest threat to Jerry Thomas, and other small family farmers, is the high-tech industry wealth of the region that has raised the price of land to extraordinary heights (computer and software executives pay millions to convert tiny farms into vacation mansions). I took pictures of the lush and exceptionally beautiful valley where Jerry Thomas earns a living. During the busiest season he employs nine workers. At our last stop, I took pictures of a couple of roosters in their colorful plum. Surrounded by three hens, they paid no attention to the heavy handed "crowd of people" that invaded their territory. In this farm, which was very small, two men raised organic strawberries. Meanwhile, the sun was out and setting, the entire valley, sliced by a country road, looked vast and green and flat. Our farm tour had come to an end.

The aspiring Albuquerque gardener gave me a ride to the conference site, Asilomar, some 45 minutes by car from Watsonville. I woke up early next day, Thursday, 25 January, and attended a sumptuous breakfast of pancakes, hot cereal, and coffee. The dining room was spacious. Each round table was covered with linen, and had complete sets of silverware and dishes for eight people. I introduced myself to those having breakfast with me, and noticed that they, like the vast majority of the 1,400 conference participants, were white men and women in their late forties, early fifties and older. There were no more than two black men, one from the United States and the other from Ethiopia. Those who served our food, however, were primarily from the Philippines.

I spent the rest of Thursday and Friday going to a series of discussions and plenary sessions that covered all one needed to know about the terrible mess the country found itself thanks to its plutocratic ruling class and illiterate faith in high-tech, agrotoxins, and biotechnology. The corporate owners of those technologies have been given license to test their products on the people and the natural environment of the United States. They never paid a price for the sporadic silent springs of their agrotoxins or the genetic pollution of nature that, if left unchecked, promises to overshadow even the half-century of ecological devastation of industrialized agriculture. America's faith in high tech has been good enough for the priests of that new religion. Their corporations built their empires from the wealth and exploitation of rural America, which they have designed to their specifications.

Genetic Engineers at Work

Of course, not all the news at the Asilomar ecological conference was bad. There were encouraging reports of resistance at the local level and, unexpectedly, resistance at the international level with the European Union and Japan refusing to buy American food originating from animals and plants whose genetic make up had been altered. The genetically modified organisms(GMOs)—the symbols of genetic engineering— were becoming an embarrassment and a liability in Europe. Professor Anne Clark from the University of Guelph, Canada, said the problems biotechnology has created are so insurmountable that, for all intents and purposes, the technology is dead. But is it? Hundreds of millions of dollars from giant "life science" corporations and foundations "purchase" entire science departments at the country's greatest universities. That big bundle of money directs the talent and vision of university scientists to the solution of problems at the molecular level designed to make life itself a commodity and a colony. Genetic engineers are remaking cotton, corn, soybeans, tomatoes, strawberries, milk, and farm animals—or, at least, that's what they think they're doing. The owners of the biotech companies are so powerful, however, they have convinced governments to license their "live products" on the basis of hardly any credible scientific studies—declaring their products no different than those whose genetic make up is still intact.

America's worship of technology has given the boost to this terrible idea that engineers—imperfect little human beings—are better than perfect and immortal nature. In fact, bioengineers tried to make their "Brave New World" schemes look innocent enough with their proposal to include genetic engineering, sewage sludge, and irradiation of food in what is allowed in the legal definition of organic food and farming. more than a quarter of a million Americans sent comments to the USDA about that agribusiness proposal. The overwhelming majority of those comments refused to buy the giant agribusiness' deception, and the feared genetic manipulation of organic food, including the proposal for sewage sludge and irradiation of food in organic farming, died at their inception.[12]

Genetic engineers scramble the genes of organisms that could never breed with each other, like flounder and tomato, creating terata, monsters with no possibility for life of their own. But these engineers work for the likes of Novartis (Syngenta), DuPont (Pioneer Hi-Bred), Monsanto (Pharmacia), and Aventis—giant global companies trying to take over the drugs, food, and agriculture of the world. Weed killers or herbicides are an essential part of maintaining the plantations producing most of the food of the industrialized North—Europe and North America. To protect and extend the life of the extremely profitable weed killers, selling in the world market in 2000 for about $20 billion, the largest global agribusiness and drug corporations (which fancy themselves as life-science organizations) have used genetic engineering to make the world's major crops resistant to their own toxins. They manipulate the molecular world of those important crops so that their brand of weed killer will not kill them. Then they turn to the gullible farmers and sell them their toxic combination of herbicide and seed, the two working together, the seed having being made immune to its companion herbicide. Monsanto, for example, has redesigned canola, corn, and soybeans to withstand its toxic and powerful roundup weed killer. In 1998 and 1999 more than 70 percent of the bioengineered crops were products of that narrow vision. They could be sprayed with a herbicide, which would kill everything else but them.

Genetic engineers have also added genes from a soil bacterium, Bacillus thuringiensis (Bt), into the genetic code of corn. Bt kills the European corn borer belonging in the same insect family with the beautiful Monarch butterflies and moths. Out in the land, Bt does have the opportunity to kill the European corn borer and butterflies. But that opportunity is rare because of the countervailing forces of nature. First of all, the Bt toxin kills certain insects only when it is in the gut of those insects. Something in the digestive system of the insect activates the Bt molecules, making them lethal to the European corn borer or butterflies. No such complexity (and protection for the insects) exists in the bioengineered Bt corn. The entire corn plant and its pollen become killers to the Monarch butterflies and the European corn borers. The activated lethal Bt toxin is in every cell of corn. And considering that the toxic pollen of the Bt corn moves with the wind, and that cornfields are huge and include billions of corn plants very close to each other, then the danger for the Monarch butterflies and other related Lepidopteran insects is overwhelming. In addition, pollen from the Bt corn contaminates other cornfields and nature. There are 18 Lepidopteran insects (related to the Monarch butterflies), which are endangered or threatened under the provisions of the Endangered Species Act. These insects would be doomed if their diet were to include lethal pollen from the spliced Bt corn, a prospect that is simply unacceptable.[13]

Bt corn and other genetically modified food can cause allergic reactions in some people. Putting Brazil nut genes into soybeans, for instance, caused allergic problems to those who had nut allergies. And some of the nut allergies are serious and sometimes fatal. The Bt toxin in the soil is safe to humans. But eating a lot of Bt corn (in many foods) and for a long time could not, in theory, be without any adverse effect, however minute or mild that effect might be for humans or animals. In fact genetically modified food may not be as safe as Monsanto and the government assert. Jeffrey M. Smith, an American researcher on agricultural genetic engineering, says genetically modified food is not safe to eat. He documented the bad science and politics that prop the genetic engineering of crops and the selling of the genetically modified food.[14]

In addition, the taco shell scandal in the winter of 2000 and early spring of 2001 in the United States illustrates that the gene is out of the bottle and, quite possibly, beyond social control. Aventis, a French agrotoxins, drugs, and biotechnology giant, put the Bt insecticidal gene into corn and called that corn StarLink. In 1998 the government licensed Aventis to feed its StarLink corn to cattle but not to people. Government scientists were concerned that Aventis' Bt corn, which produces a protein, Cry9C, might be a human food allergen. So they told Aventis to use their StarLink corn for animal feed only. Yet StarLink was used in the production of hundreds of corn products for human consumption. The only reason we discovered the insecticidal corn in dozens of taco chips and taco shells was the foresight of a civil society organization, Friends of the Earth, which tested taco shells and found the StarLink corn in them. In the winter of 2000 and spring of 2001 Aventis spent nearly a billion dollars recalling those illegal and potentially hazardous foods, and in compensating farmers ruined by its toxic corn. And yet, StarLink was also found in the seed corn farmers were buying for planting in the spring of 2001.

In October 2000, Aventis asked the government to cancel its registration of the StarLink corn. However, the StarLink political grab for power (its contamination of so much of the corn-based food in the United States) was no fluke or accident. Rather it was a deliberate challenge of society norms and authority by Aventis and the agribusiness industry. Aventis says there's nothing anybody can do to stop the deliberate and accidental mixing of the processed non-engineered crops with the genetic engineered crops. The same farmers grow both and use the same machinery to harvest them. The arrangements farmers make with companies like Aventis to keep GMOs separate from non-GMOs are meaningless, paper exercises designed for use as a defense in court. The grain elevators that store crops are barely any more reliable places than farmers trying to satisfy both the organic and the conventional food markets. Their allegiance is with no one but their pocketbooks. In addition, both the agricultural system growing crops and the food system processing those crops support Aventis.

Between the Scylla of Biotechnology and the Charybdis of Regulators

The farmers growing organic food find themselves between the monster Scylla of the Aventis-like giant companies and the whirlpool of Charybdis of government agencies saying no substantial difference exists between genetically modified and natural food. Organic farmer David Vetter of Nebraska says he is facing probable extinction from the genetic contamination of his corn. He created a buffer of trees between his organic farm and the neighbors producing genetically engineered (GE) crops, but nothing worked. "It's now clear that we won't be able to have both genetically engineered and non-GE crops," Vetter says. "As an organic grower, I can no longer guarantee that my crops are GE-free. The only resolution I can see is a ban on biotech crops."[15] Yet some food processors are using a label that says their food is "GMO-free." The StarLink political scandal, and the movement of GMO pollen by air, however, cloud nearly all efforts to keep organic farming and the processing of organic food organic.

Such a dreadful dilemma illustrates the awesome power of agribusiness. It is like the entire tribe of American "farmers" takes orders from one supreme boss (the foreign company, Aventis, in this case). The giant corporations, Aventis, Monsanto, and Novartis, or a handful of other "life-science" firms, tell the farmers they are selling x genetically engineered seed which promises to get the farmer y more bushels of z crop per acre. And the farmers, like illiterate robots or dependent servants of the giant companies, rush to plant that unknown seed, risking everything in the process, their property, income, even liberty. How else is it possible to explain that the novel, and largely untested genetic engineering versions of fundamental crops like corn, spread like wildfire in the United States?

For example, by 1998 Bt corn varieties were planted to about one fourth of the land growing corn, something like 20 million acres. The discovery that the pollen of the Bt corn was lethal to Monarch butterflies did not exactly lead to the rethinking of either the government's policy or the mad rush into the hazards and immorality of playing god in the farm and nature. The bioengineers created a rumor that John E. Losey, assistant professor of entomology, Cornell University, who did the first study showing the toxic effects of the Bt corn pollen on Monarch butterflies was incompetent and corrupt. They also made fun of another professor from Iowa State University, John Obrycki, who found that Bt corn pollen was deleterious to Monarch butterflies. They said he was biased because he was associated with the Maharishi University.

The bioengineers also keep saying their Bt corn is designed to kill the European corn borer, saving nature from chemical contamination and saving the farmer money from not spraying insecticides. Yet many farmers do not use insecticides to control the corn borer, an insect that harms corn only sporadically. And when insecticides are used against the corn borer, the planting of Bt corn has had practically zero effect in diminishing the lethal sprays. If anything, Bt corn and sprays go hand in hand in increasing the amount of insecticides used against the European corn borer.

The manipulated plants also don't accept the violence against their integrity without resistance. Sometimes the inserted genes force the plant to direct its poison making to the fruit rather than the leaves. At other times plants kill the foreign genes introduced by the engineers. And between the determined engineers remaking the plants and the plants rejecting their crude products, the process of genetic engineering has been converted into a violent battleground. The genetic engineers shoot the desired genes (wrapped with other genes of viruses and bacteria, including antibiotic resistance marker genes) into the organism whose genetic make up they are trying to alter decisively. The blasted genes end up somewhere in the genetic code of the targeted species, inevitably injuring its genetic structure and threatening its survival. The viral and bacterial genes accompanying the engineers' design genes are weapons intended to destroy the target species' defenses. The antibiotic resistance genes, part of the armor of the design genes, may also become part of the bacteria in human and animal digestive tracks. Such eventuality bodes ill for the rising antibiotic resistance in the disease-causing bacteria for life-threatening diseases like pneumonia, tuberculosis, and salmonella. The antibiotic resistant genes, as I said, are used like props for the desired genes in the plant. But once in the gut of humans or animals, they will make a bad situation, the rising ineffectiveness of antibacterial drugs, worse. This is because agribusinessmen feed confined animals antibacterial drugs on a regular basis. They do that to keep their animals alive in a very unhealthy environment.

Genetic Engineering at the Farm Will Never Feed the World

Genetic engineering is bad and immoral science. It turned DNA, deoxyribonucleic acid, a long molecule wrapped tightly within the nucleus of every living cell, into the king of molecular biology, the oracle whose message might even lead bioengineers to make men. Genetic engineering said DNA alone is the key to inheritance, with each DNA segment, gene, developing a protein for a specific trait. Yet one gene may produce hundreds and thousands of different proteins. The Human Genome Project discovered that humans have around 30,000 genes but 100,000 proteins. Also, it's not DNA alone but DNA genes and protein-based processes working together that pass on traits of inheritance. However, starting from the "central dogma" of genetic science, which says more precisely that a DNA gene controls no more than a unique inheritance trait, genetic engineers moved aggressively to test their wrong theory at the farm by altering food crops. They assumed, for example, that the DNA bacterial gene, Bt, which they inserted into corn, would produce nothing but a poison for the insects feeding on corn. However, moving the Bt gene into the alien environment of corn, in addition to the insect-killing protein, the Bt gene could give birth, and often does give birth, to dozens of other proteins with unpredictable behavior and possibly toxic effects on human health and nature. We suspect that is what is happening not from studies, which don't exist, but from the failures of experiments. Many clones are not doing well. Kidney and brain malformations often kill the cloned animal. Bioengineered pigs suffer from arthritis, hearts larger than usual, renal disease and dermatitis. All this spoils the bioengineers' idea that each DNA gene, like each biotech boss, orders things to be done alone without interference from anybody or anything. But in real life, like in the instances of millions of plants having an alien molecule replicating independently within themselves billions of times in their cells, often, and, almost inevitably, with countless number of transgenic crop plants, errors crop up, causing chaos in an otherwise elegant plan or experiment. Without careful studies of those plants, we are headed for big trouble. In addition, genetic engineers show perfect contempt for nature, their hubris knows no bounds. They willfully ignore that, in nature, genetic material moves freely only within a single species. Butterflies don't mate with fish, and neither humans make love to hogs.

Barry Commoner, a distinguished biologist and philosopher of science at Queens College in New York, was right to warn us in 2002 about the premature licensing of agricultural genetic engineering in the United States. We don't know anything about the presumed safety of the genetically modified (GM) food. "The genetically engineered crops now being grown," he says, "represent a massive uncontrolled experiment whose outcome is inherently unpredictable. The results could be catastrophic."[16]

Commoner is not exaggerating. The hazardous nature and global spread of agricultural biotechnology constitute another attack against the fragile food security of the world and the integrity of traditional food systems feeding about three billion human beings at the dawn of the twenty-first century. In late July 2002, for example, Zimbabwe, on the brink of famine, said no to thousands of tons of free gene-altered corn from the United States.[17] Zimbabwe rejected the humanitarian food from the United States probably because of the near certainty that such GM corn, if planted, would contaminate its own corn with undesirable traits with long-term dangerous consequences for food security. The British science journal, *Nature*, explained that the policy of some nations in southern Africa, hungry for food and on the verge of famine, to reject international donations of GM food was not as bizarre and irresponsible as one might think. Rather, their decision to go hungry or buy non-GM food goes to the heart of "a chasm of misunderstanding [between them and countries like the United States trying to have them eat GM corn]." Such misunderstanding "is only exacerbated by exaggerated claims for the benefits of the [GM] technology."[18] Yet despite the threat behind the inoculation of food crops with alien DNA genes, five genetic engineering companies (Pharmacia/Monsanto, DuPont, Bayer, Syngenta and Dow) and four countries (the United States, Argentina, Canada and China) are moving the genetically modified or "transgenic" crops all over the world—fast.

From 1996 to 2001 the global amount of land growing GM crops increased more than 30-fold, from 1.7 million hectares in 1996 to 52.6 million hectares in 2001. About 91 percent of the 52.6 million hectares of GM crops in 2001 came from the GM seeds of Monsanto. More than a fourth of that GM land in 2001, about 13.5 million hectares, was in the Third World growing transgenic crops. Soybean was in 2001 the global king of GM crops, taking up 33.3 million hectares or 63 percent of the land. In addition, the transgenic soybean of 2001 was giving a stiff competition to the "regular," non-manipulated soybean. It represented 46 percent of the 72 million hectares of soybeans planted in the world. In 2001, GM corn grew in 9.8 million hectares (19 percent), cotton in 6.8 million hectares (13 percent), and canola in 2.7 million hectares or 5 percent of the total GM land in 2001.

In 2001 the herbicide trait in soybeans, cotton, and corn was present in 77 percent or 40.6 million hectares of the GM crops. This trait made the seeds and mature plants immune to designer weed killers. The Bt gene was used in 7.8 million hectares or 15 percent of the GM crops. The Bt gene made the seeds and plants toxic to insects. About 8 percent of the planted area included crops that had both the herbicide and the Bt traits.[19]

These GM crops have had two commercial purposes. One, selling farmers seeds of soybeans, cotton and corn which, growing to full plants, would be unaffected by weed killers. The farmer would purchase his herbicide from the same company that engineered his seeds. Second, the farmer would buy more expensive seed corn and cotton inoculated with the Bt gene that makes corn and cotton resistant and lethal to insects. Thus, in both cases, herbicide-resistant seeds and Bt seeds resistant to insects, are matters of convenience to the farmers. The traits of the seeds have nothing to do with feeding the world or making agriculture less toxic.

In fact, genetic engineering at the farm is becoming an almost transparent "science fiction" experiment—with straightforward political effects in concentrating all power in a handful of corporations. Biotech companies are getting so bold, shameless, dangerous and unethical that they are shuffling genes between unrelated species to manufacture drugs and infant formula, right within the milk of cows, goats, and sheep. They are also using the cells of corn, tobacco, soybeans and rice for the production of drugs. After all, who would suspect that essential food crops may be growing in the field for purposes eons removed from their real being, which is no more no less than giving us food? Can we suspect corn living a double life? Or, is it human to even imagine in our most frightened dreams that food crops would be secret factories for vaccines, contraceptives, growth hormones and other designer drugs? Yet field trials for the production of drugs through food are going on in farms of Nebraska, Texas, Illinois, Puerto Rico, Maryland, Kentucky, Indiana, California, and Florida.[20] And as with Bt corn, pollen from corn, tobacco, rice and soybeans pregnant with the genetic stuff of drugs is bound to fly in the wind, contaminating food crops and nature. The US National Academy of Sciences warned of the hazards of this experiment in nature and society.[21]

Yet to criticize this immoral policy is to be branded an enemy by those selling genetic engineering in the United States. One such propagandist, Hembree Brandon, uses the rhetoric born of terror in the United States when on September 11, 2001 Islamic enemies of America killed thousands in New York and at the Pentagon in Washington, DC. He denounced the "anti-biotech radicals" like they are the enemy of the state. These "anti-biotech radicals," he says, "are a lot like Osama bin Laden and his al-Qaida loonies: They want to take the world back to the Stone Age. Regardless of the consequences to humanity as a whole, they want to dictate the pace of scientific progress according to their own messianic insight into what is right for the world."[22]

Of course, this is utter nonsense. I am a critic of genetic engineering and of the kind of technology that brought us the nuclear bomb, but I don't have problems with technologies that are serving human needs without polluting or destroying our natural world. Machines have a role in farming, for example. Yet such machinery ought not to become a weapon for the illusionary domination of nature. Small-scale tractors are useful to work the land. It is not the biotech critics who are taking the world to the Stone Age, but those who misuse science for personal gain. Rachel Carson spoke about the "Stone Age of science" in order to help us understand the harm to science done by the developers and proponents of pesticides who do everything—so they keep saying—on the name of science. These people kill insects so that they control nature. They arm themselves with weapons, which are self-defeating, because each time they point them against the insects, they point them against the earth.[23]

Chemical weapons like herbicides are not mirrors of scientific progress but instruments of war. Science, in its original Greek meaning of *episteme*, knowledge for defending the integrity of the person and truth, is the antithesis of violence and war. We need vigorous critics and good scientists with public purposes in mind to study biotech and give us honest answers about its effects on nature and humans. It is the immoral policies of biotech companies, which corrupt science and violate the integrity of nature, man, and civilization. If such unethical practices continue, reflecting too much power in too few hands, it is possible that humanity may plunge into the "Brave New World" of Aldous Huxley, a high tech version of Dark Age—and barbarism. In other words, our dilemma is not so much about ethics as it is about political power. When it becomes concentrated in the hands of a few wealthy companies, they run over regulations (or gut them by buying politicians) to further their own venal interests, the interests of investors demanding increased profits from one quarter to the next. Restraint is not a matter of teaching ethics to corporations but of making sure their power and ability to do damage is limited by a balancing power of democracy that insures other interests have control.

So the surreptitious use of genetic engineering to produce pharmaceutical proteins and chemicals in farmers' fields, dubbed "biopharming," has no place in a civilized society. It is no longer agriculture or drug manufacturing. It is, instead, a political movement adding biological weapons to the mechanical and chemical armory of the plantation, broadly defined to include pharmaceutical conglomerates. It is agribusiness' new "green revolution" (assisted by genetic engineering companies) manufactured to bury the peasant and the family farmer. This is particularly true in the genetic engineers' production of sterile seeds, which, should they ever reach the market, would be forcing both the farmers and peasants to buy new seeds every growing season. This immoral technology is married to chemicals. The sown seeds will express one or more traits only with the assistance of sprays. What this means is that the farmer's seeds will thrive or die on the presence of a chemical, which will trigger or abort their fertility. In this way genetic engineering comes out in its true colors—the best friend of giant corporations and large farmers, the worst enemy of family farmers and peasants, and pure poison for nature.

This green giant of high tech (genetic engineering) will very likely stumble and fall primarily because it is an immoral intervention in agriculture, without doubt the most sacred of all life-giving human actions and traditions. The corporate owners of genetic engineering, however, are not disturbed by philosophical issues. Their strategy is the cigarette strategy: Make false claims true into received truths by constant advertisement. It worked for the tobacco and pesticide companies, so why would it not succeed for their similar message? They purchase a dominant position within the public mind with a constant barrage of misinformation in the media. For instance, the Council for Biotechnology Information, a mouthpiece of the corporate owners of genetic engineering, says that biotechnology is "helping provide ways for developing countries to better feed a growing population."[24]

Tewolde Berhan Gebre Egziabher, director of Ethiopia's Environmental Protection Agency, disagrees:

> Even if genetic engineering managed to double, triple, or quadruple food production, it would still remain an irrelevance.... Without local control, local availability of food can never be certain...the threat [of genetic engineering] is not only to the South; it is to life as a whole. The major threat is that we are combining genes that have not previously been combined. We are creating new traits and we simply don't know what could happen.... I think genetic engineering is really going wild because it is not controlled by society but by selfish individual [corporate] interests.... When I am in negotiations with the United States, Canada, and Australia... corporate control [of government and genetic engineering] is clear.[25]

The corporate control of genetic engineering makes it difficult to defeat. Its rejection in Europe and Japan is not complete, but it assures delays in its global reach. The resistance against genetic engineering is not feeble, but insufficient to bring the technology to an end. Companies soldier on in the knowledge that they can outlast the resistance or subvert it. The Japanese's fear of American farm biotech is the fear of becoming guinea pigs once again. Hiroshima and Nagasaki are images of horror not likely to diminish in the Japanese mind and soul any day soon. Europeans understand that American bioengineered food means the destruction of their own agriculture—with possible deleterious consequences on their political freedom. They even resent the strong-arm tactics the United States is using on hungry Africa to eat and grow GM crops. David King, chief scientific advisor to Tony Blair, British prime minister, denounced the United States during the World Summit on Sustainable Development in Johannesburg, South Africa, August 26 to September 4, 2002. Professor King questioned the morality of America trying to spread GM crops in a continent whose people are facing starvation. He saw such efforts as "a massive human experiment."[26] The same thing is happening in Latin America.[27]

Aside from the danger of agricultural genetic engineering, it's not that, suddenly, Europe and Japan are abandoning their legacy of mechanization of nature and society. After all, Germany, and the other major states of Europe, North America and Japan, which fought the world's bloodiest and most horrific war ever in the 1930s and 1940s, were armed with biological weapons poised against each other. Germany's holocaust against the Jews and, to some degree, the Gypsies, was the product of crusading hatred and social genetic engineering based on racism. The Germans, like most Christians for more than 1,000 years, believed that Jews were inferior human beings. The Japanese experimented on their American and European prisoners. North Americans and Western Europeans used biological weapons against the indigenous people of the Americas, Africa, and Asia.

Mad Cow Disease or Illness of Civilization?

Moreover, England gave birth to both the industrial revolution and to the mad-cow disease, twin children of the same mechanical monster. Rather, Europe acknowledged that mad-cow disease, bovine spongiform encephalopathy (BSE), is in Europe and, particularly, in England.[28] The British government appointed a commission to study the history of BSE in England. The commissioners' 16-volume report is thorough and, at times, blunt. Among their "key conclusions" we find these:

> BSE has caused a harrowing fatal disease for humans. As we sign this Report [in 2000] the number of people dead and thought to be dying stands at over 80 [in England], most of them young. They and their families have suffered terribly. Families all over the UK [United Kingdom] have been left wondering whether the same fate awaits them. A vital industry has been dealt a body blow, inflicting misery on tens of thousands for whom livestock farming is their way of life. They have seen over 170,000 of their animals dying or having to be destroyed, and the precautionary slaughter and destruction within the United Kingdom of very many more. BSE developed into an epidemic as a consequence of an intensive farming practice—the recycling of animal protein in ruminant feed. This practice, unchallenged over decades, proved a recipe for disaster.[29]

BSE is a fatal illness dissolving both the brains of infected animals and the brains of humans eating the diseased meat of those infected animals. It is the result of Europe's and North America's abominable animal factory system peppering the feed of cows and other farm animals with animals—a standard practice in all countries with industrialized agriculture. This factory system took root in 1962 when the European Union started importing about 50 million tons of feedstuff per year from the United States. These American animal meals in Europe fostered intensive milk production and frantic measures to cut costs in the industrialization of agriculture. In addition, the huge American feedstuff imports led Europe to producing surpluses in milk, beef, pork, poultry, eggs, and cereals. This situation translated into low prices to farmers and the violent exodus from agriculture of the small family farmers and the emergence of giant agricultural producers—exactly like in the United States. It was in such a life-and-death competitive environment that the mad-cow disease was born.

Those who own animal factories cut ethical and biological corners by feeding dead cattle to cattle,[30] or, to use the polite expression of the British commissioners, they recycle animal protein in ruminant feed. At the same time, scientists urged farmers to feed their cows animal protein to boost milk production and to accelerate their rate of growth. An entire industry came into being *rendering* animals into meals for other animals. So that American dairy farmers, for example, have been given their cows not merely hormones and drugs to speed their growth but feeding them rendered supplements of animal by-products—meat, bone meal, fat, and blood for more than fifty years.

The horrible death from mad-cow disease of several children and adult European men and women sombered Western Europe. The slaughter of thousands of diseased cattle in England (and in smaller scale in France and Germany) scared the Europeans to the degree they are beginning to see another mad-cow-like disease coming out of eating food born or grown from spliced animals and plants. So they want nothing to do with such food. In addition, the burning of dozens of thousands of farm animals struck by the foot-and-mouth epidemic in the spring of 2001 intensified the food anxieties of Europeans. They don't want to eat food that has been irradiated and pumped with hormones and agrotoxins. But, above all, many Europeans detest food made up by engineers from the genes of different organisms.

The mad-cow crisis and scandal in Europe, the holocaust of farm animals because of the foot-and-mouth disease, and the public fear (in Europe and Japan) of genetic engineering mean more sales for food "labeled" organic—since organic farming is legally prohibited from indulging in dangerous animal meals and genetic or agrotoxic fixes. The German government promised in 2001 to push organic farming to cover ten percent of its land during the next five years. Austria, in 2001, was already using ten percent of its land for organic food. Germany, and possibly other Western European countries, intend to subsidize the transition of their farmers to sustainable agriculture.

The US Department of Agriculture blamed Canada for two cattle it detected in 2004 and 2005 with mad cow disease. So the US closed the US-Canadian border to Canadian cattle, a move that pleased the US producers of beef. But mad cow disease in the United States, no less than in other countries with animal factories and regimes of feeding cattle animal protein, is part and parcel of the food system. Only organic farming forbids the recycling of animal protein to cattle and other farm animals. So, in the United States, unless one eats organically grown meat, any amount of beef is potentially a career of the mad cow disease. We only hear about mad cow disease when the code of silence between cattle producers, slaughterhouses, and government inspectors breaks down.

The Glassy-Winged Sharp Shooter

So organic farming serves its purpose. In 2002, there were 11,998 certified organic farms in the United States.[31] However, organic farmers are confused. They bask in the huge global demand for their food. Most of them earn good money; and some of them make money hand over fist. In California, organic farming is quickly and dangerously following in the footsteps of giant agriculture.[32] It is growing too fast, entangling itself with its agribusiness parent, sponsor, partner, and model. Since 1998, more than 2,200 California organic farmers doubled the amount of land they converted to organic production. In 2001, this was over 170,000 acres. In 2000 alone, organic farmers earned more than $250 million.[33] In 2003, some 1,765 organic farmers, cultivating 173,821 acres, made $330 million.[34]

California organic farmers are cannibalizing each other, arming themselves to the teeth with machinery, and treating migrant farm workers like slaves they rent. In addition, they keep these issues under wrap. They forcefully and, sometimes, deceptively project innocence and health. They say nothing about their warfare with the spray "growers" who are jealous of them and would love to subvert them or put them out of business. Yet organic farmers are saying even less about pesticides— that they are not using them for reasons other than their legal prohibition. They also remain silent that the food they grow without agrotoxins is better for people and nature. They just want to keep making money in the dark shadow of the agribusiness giants. It is possible, of course, that, in the future, they will overshadow their conventional rivals. By producing more and more, and bringing the price down, they are challenging the chemical-dependent farmers.

Yet organic farmers in the United States and, in particular, California are in danger. They could be wiped out tomorrow. In California, an insect, the glassy-winged sharp shooter, is already determining the fate of some organic farmers. This tiny insect has most of California's farmers worried. The insect, on its own, is almost harmless. But the trouble it causes to California's grapevines is its habit to transmit a bacterium, Xylella fastidiosa, to the xylem tissue of the grapevine. The bacterium then cuts off the water of the infected plant and the result is usually death. The infection the glassy-winged sharp shooter spreads to the vines is known as Pierce Disease—first detected in California more than a century ago. Both the State of California and the US Department of Agriculture are spending lots of money for immediate "eradication" of the glassy-winged sharp shooter—spraying land and orchards with the agrotoxins carbaryl, imadicloprid, and chlorpyriphos. They are also working on long-term solutions by discovering other insects to eat the glassy-winged sharp shooter. Meanwhile, organic farmers, unfortunate enough to raise food in counties of California where the glassy-winged sharp shooter has been discovered, are facing possible extinction. If the county agricultural commissioner determines that sharp shooters are in the fields of organic farmers, he has the legal authority to spray their land, thus effectively putting them out of agriculture, destroying their dreams and organic farming at the same time. The wine agribusiness made certain that the legislature of California declared the glassy-winged sharp shooter "a clear and present danger to the grape industry."

On the face of this precarious situation for the organic farmers of

California, I was startled by the silence of the participants in a workshop dealing with the "ecological pest management for the glassy-winged sharp shooter." Bruce Kirkpatrick, professor of plant pathology at the University of California-Davis, and Charlie Pickett, a scientist with the Department of Food and Agriculture of California, explained, in relatively neutral and technical language, the basics about the sharp shooter. They also described the efforts in the entire State of California to "eradicate" the glassy-winged sharp shooter. "Eradication," a concept from the cold war of agricultural development in the United States in the 1950s, and one of utter contempt for nature, means massive spraying of farms and orchards with deleterious agrotoxins. Yet no one present at the workshop of some 200 people challenged it as a bad idea and disastrous state policy. Only a woman said she suspected the enemies of organic farmers had brought the glassy-winged sharp shooter to northern California in order to kill organic farming. The workshop speakers dismissed that claim and they resumed their instruction. They came to Asilomar to educate us with the facts, not to indulge in useless speculation. They left no room for debate, discussion. I sensed a lot of frustration, fear, and apathy in the huge silent crowd. The organic farmers were there—in force. But they said nothing.

At another workshop, the silent organic farmers heard the booming voice of Bill Liebhardt, professor of biology at the Davis campus of the University of California, saying that science at the land grant universities, including his own school, was not objective. In the simplest terms possible, Liebhardt was telling the organic farmers two things. First, they should not be intimidated or frightened by the pronouncements of scientists corrupted by the idea of eradication; and, second, the science of the land grant universities was against them because of the tainted money behind that science. In other words, the agrotoxins industry was funding the agricultural research of the University of California-Davis, and that university, like all other land grant colleges, was producing research results in support of agrotoxins and the agenda of the giant agribusiness corporations. It was that immoral. It was that insidious.

I congratulated my good friend, professor Bill Liebhardt. For ten years or so, he directed the University of California's small but pioneering effort to fund research for farmers wishing farming to be less dependent on agrotoxins and power, otherwise known as sustainable agriculture. Now this scientist, marginalized at his university, is retiring. Another powerful voice of reason and family agriculture was about to be eclipsed from rural California and the country.

Farming Bioengineered Grapes of Wrath

I had come to this California of Asilomar primarily because of my memories of Humboldt County. Listening to the polite speeches and, occasionally, bursts of passion, did not convince me things had gotten any better since my visiting professor days in the redwoods forest in the late 1980s. To cool my rising anger, I left the silent workshops and walked to the edge of the Asilomar grounds where giant foamy waves of the Pacific crushed on the coast. I walked to the Asilomar beach as often as I could. I kept looking at the massive waves slowly and perpetually rising from the invisible depths of the vast green ocean. The water would surge and withdraw quickly as if its movements were regulated by an underground machine. I was fascinated by the rapid change of color, the huge size of the waves, the sounds, and the light and beauty of the coast—still wild but tamed.

There is a highway very close to the water. This highway becomes "sunset drive" in front of Asilomar, and, then, in the direction of Pebble Beach and Carmel, the highway becomes the "seventeen mile drive," and, again further down, "scenic drive," etc. In addition, an endless number of homes, hotels, and golf courses have been built within short distances from the raging Pacific. In fact the Asilomar retreat is part of the Monterey Bay National Marine Sanctuary. Yet the entire Monterey Peninsula has been made into a shopping mall and playground for the rich. Here's where world-class golf, wine tasting, boating, dining, and boutique buying and selling take place every day.

On January 27, 2001 the twenty-first Ecological Farming Conference came to an end. I took a taxi to Pacific Grove, a small beautiful town close to Asilomar. I had come to Pacific Grove in order to take a van to the San Jose airport. The one-hour or so drive was not unusual except going through Salinas. The land of agribusiness was flat and shining with light and plastic to perfection. One could not see anything stirring. Salinas was the agribusiness empire that forced John Steinbeck (1902-

1968) to write *The Grapes of Wrath* in 1939. The van driver directed my attention to a tall building in Salinas where the papers of Steinbeck are kept. I thought of Steinbeck and of the tragic fact Salinas and California and the United States are still farming grapes of wrath—some of which are now products of genetic engineering.

Genetic engineering, of course, is much more than the child of giant agriculture. It is the daughter of early twentieth century experiments with political eugenics and racism. Two British writers, George Orwell (1903-1950), and Aldous Huxley (1894-1963), codified the barbarism of the genetic engineers in their nearly prophetic books, *Nineteen Eighty-Four* (1949) and *Brave New World* (1932). Unless genetic engineering is universally condemned and brought to an end as an immoral act, crop and farm animal manipulation will spill over into more troubles for the family farmer and the rest of us.

Organic farming, with all its deficiencies, is just a hope away from that nightmare. It is trying to add agrarian values to a brutal system of factory production on the land. We ought to join organic farmers, however, and help them become our family farmers raising our food. This is particularly urgent now—in the dawn of the twenty-first century. The US government is implementing the corporate agenda of giant agriculture under the guidance of President George W. Bush. In fact, the temporary takeover of the US Department of Agriculture by a representative of agribusiness, a woman from California named Ann Veneman, all but wrecked the US National Organic Program (NOP). The federal regulation of organic farming became the law of the land on October 2002, but USDA, for all intents and purposes, killed it by the well-tested bureaucratic method of indifference and subterfuge. It could not happen otherwise. The year 2002 was especially full of corporate plutocratic schemes, malfeasance, and corruption. Corporate executives stole their way to fabulous riches through the hard-earned money of countless investors. Such kleptocratic politics not merely impoverished millions of Americans, but reinforced the bias of the government against the small, the indigenous, the sustainable, the society of non-corporate culture. Organic farming, always a fringe movement, became invisible within USDA. The first blow in this hidden war was that USDA stopped its communication and contacts with organic farmers and their representatives. Even the word "organic" did not exist in Secretary

Veneman's political lexicon.

Mark Keating, a young USDA employee whose commitment to organic farming caused him endless troubles with his supervisors, which eventually led him to leave USDA in 2004, denounced the policy of USDA towards organic farming. On May 20, 2002 he charged that USDA was:

> stumbling badly in meeting its responsibility to implement a productive NOP [National Organic Program] through active partnership with the organic community. At a time when the positive truths about organic agriculture are ever more conclusive in the eyes of producers, researchers and consumers, the USDA has re-inserted its head in the sand.... [T]he current Administration has not expressed any measurable interest, support, or even much cognizance of organic agriculture. The absence of leadership has a paralytic effect on the regulatory process.... The USDA has long had difficulty accepting responsibility to support or advance organic management due to its commitment to an agricultural production system that is often incompatible if not antithetical with organic principles. The schizophrenia of being responsible for these conflicting paradigms has created a paralysis at USDA that affects only the organic parts of the body. The [US] Department [of Agriculture] is moving forward with its program of agricultural biotechnology, concentration of production and dependence on WTO [World Trade Organization] markets while the organic [farming] program is relegated to leper status.

On the face of this harsh reality at home, Europe's tilt towards organic farming merits close attention. To grasp the significance of this we must take a look at the historical evolution of American agriculture. The next chapter moves into history because the American debate—silence would be a better term—on organic farming is part of a superficial global assessment of conventional agriculture.

Chapter 5

A Republic Cannot Have Large Farms

The Danger of Plantations

We say the United States is the world's foremost breadbasket but we neglect to point out that giant farm plantations mine the soil, and water, and life of rural America in order to produce the bountiful harvests of corn and wheat and all the dazzling varieties of the agribusiness supermarket. And the destruction of nature, and the human costs of expropriating land and lives from the rural underprivileged find no place in the power-hungry calculations for policy.

For four centuries African slaves were the pillars of the southern American economy. A black tenant farmer from East-central Alabama, whose father was a slave said, in 1971, that "the nigger was handicapped to death."[1] This was true in cotton plantations for black people and, to some degree, for white tenants as well. Every one knows that the cotton plantations were slave camps.

James Agee, a magazine reporter, wrote with passion and love about white tenants in Alabama in the 1930s. He described them as undefended and appallingly wounded human beings working and living under savage and crippling conditions in the American South. Agee denounced the plantation. He said:

> [T]his awful field where cotton is made, infinitesimal, the antlike glistering of the sweated labors of nine million....a tenant can feel, toward that crop, toward each plant in it, toward all that work, what he and all grown women too appear to feel, a particular automatism, a quiet, apathetic, and inarticulate yet deeply vindictive hatred, and at the same time utter hopelessness, and the deepest of their anxieties and of their hopes: as if the plant stood enormous in the unsteady sky fastened above them in all they do like the eyes of an overseer.[2]

Perhaps the most threatening aspect of American agriculture is the metamorphosis it has undergone in the last century. It has moved from a system based primarily on family farming and plantations to a system based on industrialized agriculture. This change has transformed a way of life for raising food and sustaining democratic society to making money for giant agriculture. One can visualize this giant agriculture as a massive factory that has taken roots in the land, industrializing both farming and food and farmers, making rural America a colony for the extraction of profit. The tragedy of this metamorphosis is that it has been taking place for decades, leaving behind millions of broken family farms, contaminated water and land, and a wounded rural America opened to conquest by urban culture and power.

In the 1880s the fear was that "there will be too few farms and these too large. A republic cannot long survive when the lands are concentrated in the hands of a few men. Any man will fight for his home, but it takes a very brave man to fight for the privilege of working for half wages."[3] Sadly, this premonition has come to fruition.

F. H. Newell was the first director of the US Reclamation Service, implementing the 1902 Reclamation Act to water the desert in the American West for the purposes of creating family farms. Newell said in 1905:

> The object of the Reclamation Act is not so much to irrigate the land as it is to make homes. President Theodore Roosevelt...has emphasized again and again that the primary objective of the law was to make homes. It is not to irrigate the lands which now belong to large corporations or to small ones; it is not to make these men wealthy; but it is to bring about a condition whereby that land shall be put into the hands of the small owner, whereby the man with a family can get enough land to support that family, to become a good citizen, and to have all the comforts and necessities which rightly belong to an American citizen.[4]

The provisions of the Reclamation Act held that the federal government would deliver water to farms *no* larger than 160 acres. Landowners with farms larger than 160 acres would have to sell their excess land to the federal government under the law. Unfortunately, these democratic political ideas and noble sentiments were never translated into policy.

Large landowners and agribusinesses in the West have been corrupting the county, state, and federal governments throughout the twentieth century. They siphon off billions of dollars of public subsidies while they cannibalize the family farmers and wreck the communities and ecology of rural America. In the Westlands of California, for example, 10 farmers own about 260,000 acres of irrigated land. It costs the federal government $2,200 a year to deliver enough water to irrigate an acre in the

Westlands. Every year each Westlands farmer with 960 acres of irrigated land receives subsidized federal water worth more than $2 million. David Lavender, a student of California history and politics, encapsulated the situation: "Mom-and-pop farms? Oh, sure, run by computers from a boardroom high in some San Francisco financial tower."[5]

Paul S. Taylor, professor of economics at the University of California at Berkeley and expert on the Reclamation Law (designed to deliver water to farmers with farms 160 acres or less) testified in Congress on July 29, 1966 that the federal government would better serve the public interest if it limited its water subsidy to *one-acre* farms for areas located near cities. Furthermore, he added, that the government should purchase all excess land in order "to help 'save' the future of the West... [and] to hand down to our children's children our heritage of natural beauty and many of the values of a Great Society associated with it. The federal government, spending billions of dollars to bring water, does not end its proper responsibility upon the arrival of that water."[6] The federal government, however, stayed out of corporate farms. It just delivered water to them.

John Steinbeck wrote *The Grapes of Wrath* in 1939 to protest the destruction of rural America by the emerging mechanical monster of anonymous and impersonal corporate power. He warned the American people of the undemocratic agribusiness in the countryside, invisible banks farming on paper the expropriated land of the Okies, tractors— "great crawlers moving like insects, having the incredible strength of insects"[7]—devastating the nature and culture of rural people. Steinbeck condemned the coming into being of huge farms, mechanical operations that pushed one-crop farming over thousands of acres of land, building animal factories and treating animals no different than pieces of machinery. Steinbeck's Okies were a metaphor for the catastrophic cultural effects of giant agriculture on rural people. These effects include the loss of their homes, churches, schools and culture. In other words, agribusiness was responsible for America's internal refugees, drastically reducing the number of family farmers, expanding the size of the surviving farms, reducing the social and biological diversity of rural America for a one-dimensional view of the world. This has been a model of "development" and agricultural "production" that has been dangerous and destructive from the very beginning.

On April 16, 1968 the Governor of North Dakota, William L. Guy, wrote a letter to Senator Gaylord Nelson in which he explained why he detested agribusiness. He said:

> It should not take a very sophisticated study to show that large corporation farming eliminates the need for small farm units living on the land. When small farm units are eliminated and the families who farmed them are moved to the cities, some very grave economic and social problems arise in the rural areas. Personal property tax income diminishes; and the financial support and, for that matter, the need for such things as schools, churches, recreation and health facilities in rural communities diminish.... North Dakota has barred corporation farming since the middle 1930's. During those depression years, land foreclosures placed so many farms in the hands of the corporate lender, that there was grave danger of the majority of our state's farm land being in the hands of corporations.... I grew up in the shadow of the corporation farm in North Dakota.... This corporation owned its own grain marketing facilities in several adjacent towns. It bought its machinery direct from the Minneapolis-Moline farm equipment manufacturing company. It formed a cooperative gasoline and oil company which granted credit and gave service to the farm tenants of the corporation. The retail gasoline dealer was forced out of business. At one time, this corporation owned every building in the corporation town. Businesses were run on a concession basis. It might be argued that this could never come to pass again, but I believe that it could.... I am strongly opposed to corporations taking over the farming industry.[8]

Few American politicians understood the danger of agribusiness as Governor Guy did. Senator Nelson from Wisconsin spent the 1960s and 1970s holding hearings about corporate power. He, like Governor Guy, opposed the take over of rural America by factory farms. Yet his legacy was that his hearings forced the country (and particularly the leadership of the country) to listen to voices—many, eloquent, and passionately defending family farming—it did not wish to hear.

Antidemocratic Consequences of Agribusiness

Those voices kept saying family farms and small rural towns in the United States were falling apart because agribusiness had been sucking the life out of them.

Consider, for example, Arvin, a small rural town in southeastern Kern County in the fertile Central Valley of California. In 1940, factory-like farms surrounded Arvin. Arvin, however, did not share in the prosperity of those factory-like farms. The average farm size of Arvin was 500 acres. Only thirty-five percent of Arvin farmers owned their land. Only four percent of the people of Arvin were native Californians. Sixty-three percent were Dust Bowl migrants with less than five years of residence in the town. They earned little and did not have much interest in their community. Even the managers of the large farms were absentees. If any businessmen lived in Arvin, they went to Bakersfield and Los Angeles for recreation. Arvin's schoolteachers found the town so distressing that most of them lived in Bakersfield, commuting 22 miles daily. The elementary schools, churches, and the economy of Arvin were impoverished. Arvin had no high school. The town had no elected political leadership of its own. It was unincorporated. Its large farms converted it into a slum and a colony.

We know these things about Arvin because of Walter Goldschmidt, an anthropologist with the US Department of Agriculture in the early 1940s. Goldschmidt studied Arvin and compared his findings with what he discovered in another rural town that was dominated by small farms. This was Dinuba in northern Tulare County in California's Central Valley.

In 1940 the average farm in Dinuba was 57 acres. More than three-fourths of the farmers of Dinuba owned their land. Dinuba's economy and culture were vigorous and democratic. Its elementary and high schools were good. The teachers lived in town and made outstanding contributions to the culture of the community. Dinuba's residents were middle class persons with good income and strong interest in their town. Nineteen percent of the people of Dinuba were native Californians and 22 percent Dust Bowl migrants. The median length of residence at Dinuba was between 15 and 20 years. Dinuba's prosperity was the prosperity of its small farms.

Yet Dinuba and Arvin were similar rural towns. They enjoyed the same climate and fertile land. They were equidistant from small and large cities and had access to highways and railroads. They had the same industrialized farming, relying on laborers to do the hard and dangerous work. They specialized in single crops, which they produced exclusively for cash sales. Dinuba raised fruits, especially raisin grapes, some cotton and vegetables. Arvin produced largely cotton, potatoes, fruits and vegetables, grapes, and grain.

The sole factor that made Arvin and Dinuba different was the size of the farms—Arvin had large farms and Dinuba had small farms. Ninety-one percent of Arvin's land was in farms larger than 160 acres but only 25 percent of Dinuba's land was in farms of over 160 acres.

The economic, social and democratic consequences of farm size in Dinuba and Arvin were dramatic: Dinuba's small-farm economy supported 62 businesses, Arvin's large-farm economy 35. The volume of retail trade in Dinuba for a year was $4,383,000 and for Arvin $2,535,000. The small-farm community spent over three times more money for household supplies and building equipment than the large-farm community. More than one-half of the breadwinners of Dinuba, but less than one-fifth of the breadwinners of Arvin, were independent businessmen, white-collar workers or farmers. Less than one-third of the breadwinners of the small-farm community were agricultural workers while nearly two-thirds of those gainfully employed in the large-farm community were agricultural workers. Dinuba had three parks and two newspapers. The town had paved streets, sewage, and streetlights. Arvin had but a single playground loaned by a corporation and one newspaper. Arvin had practically no paving, streetlights, or sidewalks. It had inadequate water and sewage facilities. For these reasons, Goldschmidt said, Arvin was "less a community than an agglomeration of houses."

Goldschmidt was right. Arvin was not merely a disintegrating rural community in California's Central Valley but the nightmare of rural America. Agribusiness was killing family farming and industrializing the countryside. Even the government, USDA, was becoming a subsidiary of agribusiness.

This was bad enough, and not merely because of the concentration of land and power at the hands of a few men. Goldschmidt accused agribusiness of destroying the "American character" which, he said, "was forged in its rural hinterland: the frontiersman melding into the freeholding farmer created a pattern consisting of egalitarianism, personal independence, the demand for hard work and ingenuity, self-discipline, with the ultimate reward in a personal success."

Despite the national importance of the freeholding farmers, however, the United States abandoned them to agribusiness, which either kicks them off the land or, Goldschmidt says, remakes them into "organization men in overalls." Both Governor Guy and Senator Nelson were aware of

Goldschmidt's 1944 study on the adverse effects of huge farms on small communities in California's Central Valley, probably the richest land in the United States. They also knew of Goldschmidt's troubles with his superiors at USDA who were very unhappy with him. Goldschmidt had stirred a hornet's nest with his study and the large landlords of California wanted his blood. He wisely gave his report to Senator James E. Murray who was Chairman of the Senate Special Committee to Study Problems of American Small Business. Senator Murray appreciated the importance of Goldschmidt's investigation so he published that study as a committee report on December 23, 1946.[9]

In the introduction to his study, Goldschmidt described the family farm as "the classic example of the American small business enterprise... the spread of the family farm over the land has laid the economic base for the liberties and the democratic institutions which this Nation counts as its greatest asset." He then explained why Dinuba was part of the American tradition of agrarianism and why Arvin was a rising threat to that tradition. Even the businessmen of Arvin frequently expressed "their own feelings of impermanence; and their financial investment in the community, kept usually at a minimum, reflects the same view. Attitudes such as these are not conducive to stability and the rich kind of rural community life which is properly associated with the traditional family farm."[10]

Goldschmidt's fear was an ancient fear. He discovered, in the fertile land of California, "too few farms and those too large." He knew that large farms were inimical to the health of democracy—there's simply no way to misread history at this crucial political evolution of societies. Political observers in California were right to say (in the 1884 *Transactions of California State Agricultural Society*) that "A Republic cannot long survive when the lands are concentrated in the hands of a few men."

Greek peasants (very small family farmers) put together the foundations of the polis (the state) and the political institutions of law and liberty that blossomed into the religion, art, philosophy, science, literature and social life that made Greek civilization so powerful and lasting—at least until down to the Roman conquest in 146 BCE when the small peasant farmer was undermined by the emerging large farms that, in substantive political issues, became the icons of the new imperial state in both Greece and the Roman Empire. Victor Davis Hanson, a family farmer and professor of Greek at California State University, Fresno, studied the political significance of Greek farming and he is right to argue that agrarianism made Greek political culture. "Only a settled countryside of numerous small farmers," he says, "could provide the prerequisite mass for constitutional government and egalitarian solidarity." [11]

The lesson of Greece and Rome suggest that the takeover of farming by large interests is not entirely a function of the industrial revolution. I tell the story below in greater detail, especially documenting the idea that large farms are problematic independent of their industrialization.

Both Hanson and Goldschmidt—steeped in the theory and practice of the democratic harvest of family farming and the authoritarian and other deleterious consequences of large-scale corporate agriculture— are bitter about the ceaseless conquest of the countryside of America by the very form of factory farming they despise. Hanson denounced giant agriculture in a personal account of his own efforts to survive as a family farmer. Indeed he talks as if he is writing a "postmortem" to the millennium "agrarian Armageddon" responsible for the obliteration of family farming in the United States. [12]

I don't think Armageddon—agrarian or otherwise—has a place in the fate of agriculture. But I understand the fury of anger that has consumed so many family farmers[13] and others who believe passionately not merely in the ability and, clear necessity, of eating our food from the family farmer's field, but, just as importantly, hold true that several million family farmers throughout the land in America are a must for the preservation of freedom and a democratic form of government. The collapse of that democratic and agrarian dream is causing a nightmare to those who like Hanson and Goldschmidt are certain of the deleterious alternatives to family farming.

Goldschmidt testified before Senator Gaylord Nelson on March 1, 1972—twenty-six years after another Senator, James E. Murray, made it possible that his path-breaking study of the destructive effects of large farms on family farming and human communities saw the light of the day. Goldschmidt said Congress ought to know more about "the increased encroachment of agribusiness on American rural life" primarily because he was convinced that "corporate farming creates an urbanized and impoverished rural community." He also accused agribusiness of decimating the number of family farmers and the federal government for making all that possible—particularly with its policies of agricultural support and farm labor [14]

I met Goldschmidt in 1987 in Florida at an academic conference. I asked him if the country had a chance to break up agribusiness and distribute its lands to small family farmers, in other words, do to America's large farmers what the American general, Douglas MacArthur, did to the large farmers of defeated Japan. He said my proposal was not feasible without a willing dictator-president. I was stunned and rejected his argument. But, deep inside, I knew he probably was right.

I was in Washington, DC, in the mid-1970s when the Small Business Committee of the Senate held extensive hearings on the fate of the family farmer. Senator Gaylord Nelson of Wisconsin was one of the very few voices behind Congress' belated interest on family agriculture. Witness after witness would describe the crimes of agribusiness against family farmers and rural America. Yet, listening to the testimony of the defenders of family agriculture, I felt like I was at a funeral. It made no difference how passionate the testimony was. The victim was already dead. And no one was there to listen. Congress and the USDA pretended the tragedy of family farming did not exist.

That tragedy, however, affected me profoundly. I spent the best years of my life studying agrarian issues. Moreover, I paid a heavy price for defending the idea of family farming in my work with the federal government, especially with the US Environmental Protection Agency, 1979-2004. It was not merely USDA, which sided with giant agriculture throughout the twentieth century. The agribusiness disease afflicted the entire government of the United States. I could diagnose the symptoms of that disease and feel the transformation because I see the world with Greek eyes. The meaning of this translates into my tremendous respect for nature, which I believe is full of gods. Remembering the ferocity and violence of the Christians against my Greek ancestors, is another reason I feel so uneasy and frightened by the industrialized (Christian) societies' war against nature. The Christians annihilated the Greeks because of hatred. They called them pagans, heathens, idolaters, etc. They smashed the beautiful Greek temples, schools, libraries, and culture. They murdered countless Greeks. The result of such a paroxysm of barbarity was the Dark Ages. Now, I wonder, what is to follow their new paroxysm of barbarity against nature? Another Dark Age worse than the original model?

I consider human fortunes ephemeral under the best of circumstances. Sophokles, a tragic Greek poet of the fifth century BCE, was certain of the precarious nature of human fortunes. Everything about men, he said, is full of danger and fear. Even good fortune and prosperity may suddenly turn to evil and impoverishment.[15] For those who remember the nuclear bombs and the twentieth century, ought to take Sophokles' warning seriously. In addition, didn't the Dust Bowls of the 1930s, 1950s and 1970s leave any memory behind? I try to live with courage, moderation, and justice. I strive for arête, which for the Greeks was a life guided by moderation, courage and virtue.

A Fly in the Undemocratic Ointment of EPA

My greatest challenge, however, was how to make a living. I earned a doctorate in history, but could find no teaching history job anywhere. I went back to school. This time I went to Harvard for postdoctoral studies. With that experience and my first book on global agriculture, *Fear in the Countryside*, I did find a promising opportunity on Capitol Hill. Yet in my positions with the Congressional Office of Technology Assessment, Congressman Clarence Long (Democrat of Maryland), and the US Environmental Protection Agency I could not and did not become a typical employee because I took my education, knowledge, and the public interest seriously.

That's what I meant by saying I looked at the world with Greek eyes. I had to defend that world because I love that world. I attended meetings at EPA where toxicologists and ecologists recounted their findings on the poisonous effects of certain pesticides, which they were considering for some kind of regulatory action. They would conclude that some of those toxins would "fill EPA's risk cup," by which they meant such chemicals out in the environment would have killing effects on wildlife and, possibly, deleterious effects on people eating food, particularly children. Several times I suggested that we should sign a letter to the director of the Office of Pesticide Programs saying, in effect, that prudent caution demanded we ought to withdraw those toxins from the market. My colleagues smiled at that proposal, some of them laughing that anyone would dare think of abolishing the bread and butter of the pesticide industry. But, in any event, they ignored my suggestions completely, never following up with a vigorous rejection of the demands of the industry for expanded use of the toxins, which, in their own vocabulary, were problematic, pushing to overflow the risk in the magic cup of EPA. I could not do what my colleagues did. I would never even dream of harming nature and human beings. In addition, I always felt I worked for the people of this country, not the "regulated industry," pesticide companies, agribusiness, the World Bank, or other corporations. I kept asking questions and initiated research projects that thoroughly embarrassed and angered my supervisors.

Another example from my EPA work will suffice to illustrate the price I paid for trying to do the moral thing, using my knowledge for defending nature and public health: On October 10, 1989 the *Chicago Tribune* published an op-ed essay I wrote about climate change. I argued that lowering the earth-threatening heat would more likely be the consequence of protest and action by peasants and city people, not state intellectuals and corporations. About six months later, on April 20, 1990, the *Wall Street Journal* reprinted two paragraphs of my article under its "Notable and Quotable" section. Those paragraphs included my critique of corporate behavior. I said, in a sense, corporations created the global crisis of a warmer earth. It would be foolish to assume that the same companies would sacrifice their profits for a less threatened world. I also did not have anything nice to say about the technocrats of industrialized development. I accused them of tilting science to cover up corporate crimes against nature at home, and for using their influence with Third World governments in doing two additional evil things: Forcing the peasants off the land, and bringing about more mechanical cash crop plantations.

The troubling thing of the *Wall Street Journal's* innocent-looking reprint was what happened at the place of my work, the US Environmental Protection Agency. The day the *Wall Street Journal* made me "famous," April 20, 1990, was EPA's Earth Day and the day I found an official "letter of reprimand" on my desk threatening me with "removal." It's not important to mention the name of the author of the letter of reprimand or to list his allegations against me. What is important is that this branch chief (and almost certainly other senior EPA managers) tried to have me fired because of my political views.

In addition, some one brought Congress into this trifling but mean-spirited fight. On September 4, 1990 Senator Conrad Burns (Republican from Montana) wrote to William Reilly, administrator of EPA, asking him whether or not my views were private or represented those of EPA. The Senator, nevertheless, found my ideas disturbing. At the end of September, Linda Fisher, a Republican political appointee at EPA for the position of the assistant administrator for Prevention, Pesticides, and Toxics, assured Senator Burns that I wrote as a private citizen and not as an employee of EPA. Even before Senator Burns' inquiry on my political beliefs, on July 9, 1990, another senior EPA official, Lewis Crampton, associate administrator from the Office of Communications and Public Affairs, wrote a letter to the editor of the *Wall Street Journal* in which he explained my article was my personal opinion, not official EPA policy. Crampton dismissed my article, nevertheless, because it was a "fanatical diatribe against capitalism as an earth-heating, destructive, suicidal system."

My survival at EPA was not easy. I use "survival" with caution, of course. Yet with the exception of brief normal periods of time, most of my service with EPA was service under stress, sometimes too uncomfortable for any enjoyment or clear thinking. This was because I looked at environmental protection differently than many officials of the Agency did. I thought we should have been enforcing the country's environmental laws, they did not. I thought we should have been supporting organic farming as a serious alternative to agribusiness, they did not think so. Nevertheless, I had to support my family, so I had to have a job. And despite the indignities I endured from time to time, I stayed at EPA without compromising my principles. I was also fortunate I had a couple of friends who, when it was necessary, intervened with EPA on my behalf. The first was Congressman George E. Brown, Jr. (Democrat from California). This was a wise politician who did not like the narrow-mindedness of bureaucracies and, more important than that, he liked my contributions to the debate about agriculture. The other friend was James Aidala who worked at EPA and Congressional Research Service for several years before he came back to EPA in 1993 as a political appointee of the Clinton administration. Aidala, an ambitious insider, had his own agenda. He worked with the chemical industry, and after the victory of George W. Bush in 2000, he left the government to exploit his connections with the multinational corporations making and licensing agrotoxins. He knew where I stood on issues of pesticides and industrialized agriculture, so he kept his distance from me, but, in an ingenious manner, he spread the message that bureaucrats ought to leave me alone. From time to time, we had lunch together, a symbolic event that sufficed to buy peace for me in the late 1990s.

Nevertheless, America's agricultural tragedy, which led me to the writing of this book, left its permanent mark on me. Throughout my life in this country I felt the pain of witnessing the undoing of America's rural culture. That pain brought me in touch with my own Greek upbringing— entirely agrarian and almost ancient.

Most Things in Agriculture are Death Systems

Thomas Jefferson respected the ancient Greeks. His affection for Greek culture found expression in the agrarian model of democracy he designed for the United States. Jefferson's yeoman farmer was the Greek farmer. Yet, by the twentieth century, the United States dismissed the Greek agrarian example and followed the imperial Roman model. Its agriculture became one of its most violent impulses.

America's agriculture was loaded with corporate-oriented science. The farmer sowed the turned prairie sod with hybrid corn and the consequences were just as dramatic as those of the plow, ax, and livestock. First of all, the yield of this science corn increased spectacularly so that between 1930 and 1965 the United States produced an additional 2.3 billion bushels of corn on a corn acreage that had been reduced by more than 30 million acres. In fact hybrid corn replaced the open-pollinated corn very fast. In 1933, one percent of the Corn Belt was sown with hybrids. In a little more than 10 years, in 1944, eighty-eight percent of the Corn Belt was growing hybrid corn. And because farmers cannot replace hybrid corn without considerable yield loss, a new hybrid seed corn industry came into being. In 1934 that industry made about $70 million in sales. By 1981, the hybrid seed corn companies earned about $2 billion.

The choice of hybrid corn over open-pollinated varieties also meant that the farmer could mechanize because the essentially identical hybrid corn plants were ideal for machine harvesters. Iowa corn farmers, for example, went to mechanization as rapidly as they could. In 1935 fifteen percent of them had mechanical pickers. By 1945, seventy percent were using harvesting machines. In addition, hybrid corn farmers planted their hybrids closer to each other and fertilized them more heavily. In the years 1950 to 1980 the amount of hybrid corn used as seed for each acre nearly doubled. Despite the fact that the total area of land growing corn increased by only 2 percent in those same 30 years, the volume of hybrid seed corn sales increased by 60 percent and the tonnage of nitrogen fertilizer went up by a factor of 17. Of course, growing corn plants very close to each other with abundant fertilizer contributed not merely to larger harvests of corn, but also to significantly larger harvests of weeds, insects, and disease. This, inevitably, made corn dependent on pesticides, particularly, weed killers.

All these changes were taking place in the early 1940s—a period of war that had a powerful impact on the growth of the chemical industry and industrialized agriculture. World War I made fertilizers available to agriculture. The great devastation of that global conflict left Europe with huge supplies of munitions from fertilizers but not a bright prospect for immediate sales for those explosives. So the fertilizer / munitions industry taught the farmers to feed fertilizers to their crops. The farmers with the ambitions of conquerors learned to apply synthetic chemical food to their land, slowly abandoning the agrarian methods of their fathers. In the same manner, the second global conflict wounded more of the traditional heart of agriculture. The Germans discovered the nerve gases, chemical weapons lethal to people. After World War II, the nerve gas weapons moved to the armory of large farms all over the world. Nerve gases kill men and insects in the same manner—by suffocation. They were recycled in the form of an insidious insect and man killer, parathion, belonging to a class of nerve poisons known as organophosphates. Just like fertilizers, parathion, and dozens of other nerve gas agricultural sprays, reveal the often-intimate relationship between war and industrialized agriculture. The first is the conquest of one society by another through the killing of many men; the second is the conquest of nature through the extermination of insects, unwanted plants (deceptively called weeds), birds, and other forms of wildlife farmers find troublesome.

It was DDT, however, that was the granddaddy of the farmers' agrotoxins and agrarian war. It came into being in 1939 when Paul Herman Mueller, a chemist working for the Swiss company, J. R. Geigy, discovered DDT's killing power against insects. The military did not use nerve gases during World War II, but it used DDT to control a typhus epidemic in Italy in 1943 and 1944. Soon thereafter, DDT became the Western man's golden bullet for the control of nature. Industrialized farmers and malaria workers made DDT a global spray with nearly miraculous effects. So much was DDT at the center of the exhausted life in the West that it was praised to heavens. In 1948 Mueller received the Nobel Prize in Physiology and Medicine for his research on DDT. But, in fact, it was not Mueller who received the honors of the Nobel committee. The Nobel Prize went to DDT.

Yet the Nobel committee learnt nothing from this embarrassing episode. In 1970 it awarded its prestigious peace prize to an American, Norman Borlaug, an agronomist of the Rockefeller Foundation who sparked Mexico's destructive conversion to the agribusiness farming of the United States. When Borlaug delivered his Nobel lecture on 11 December 1970 in Oslo, Norway, he was right to defend food as a moral right. He saw himself as one of millions of farmers, most of whom were small and humble. Yet he also defended agribusiness to the hilt, saying that without the "green revolution," or the industrialization of Third World peasant farming, and continuous and increasing food production, there would be famine and hunger. Borlaug's "green revolution" was a "miracle" producing bread for the "underprivileged billions in the forgotten world." To keep that "miracle" going, Borlaug prayed for the replacement of the peasants' "stagnant traditional agriculture" with a farming fuelled by the Mexican dwarf wheat, the "powerful catalyst" of the green revolution. He praised the rapid "transplantation" of the high-yielding varieties of wheat, along with chemical fertilizers, which powered the forward thrust of industrializing the Third World countrysides. His big dream was emptying Third World villages of bullocks and filling them up with tractors and threshing machines.[16]

A few months later, in 8 November 1971, he delivered the 1971 McDougall Memorial Lecture at the UN Food and Agriculture Organization (FAO) in Rome. At this time, Borlaug addressed like-minded agronomists, technicians from all over the world who also dreamed of seeing the globalization of the Iowa cornfield, Africa and Asia and Latin America full of pesticides, fertilizers, tractors and threshing machines. Proud of his accomplishments, he hit the nail on the head straightaway:

He sided with the cold war policies of the United States, seeing agriculture but a mere tool in the broader goal of defeating communism. The United States was then, in 1971, fighting the un-winnable but brutal war in rural Vietnam against the communist regime of North Vietnam, which was fighting the joint armies of America and South Vietnam. The strategy of the United States was to avoid dominoes in southeastern Asia: If North Vietnam won, Cambodia, Thailand and Laos would become communist. That, the United States said, was the reason it was fighting communist North Vietnam. This was also the strategy of Norman Borlaug in Mexico. The Rockefeller Foundation sent him to Mexico so that the hungry peasants would not launch a revolution on America's doorsteps. His "green revolution" was counterrevolutionary: It won ground by shredding peasant culture, plowing through the peasants' land, fields of knowledge, seeds, festivals, gods, and traditions. In fact, in time, Borlaug's American farming in the tropics emptied the countryside of bullocks, filling the villages with tractors and threshing machines.

So, Borlaug, among friends in Rome, expanded the polite speech of his Nobel Lecture, his litany of what made his wheat improvement program possible, offering a hymn to DDT, which, at that time the US Environmental Protection Agency threatened with extinction. He praised the "green revolution" (agribusiness) to the heavens, a gift of the Judeo-Christian civilization. He then denounced the enemies of industrialized agriculture, the "hysterical environmentalists—who are provoking fear by predicting doom for the world through chemical poisoning." Borlaug had in mind the environmentalists of the United States whom he described as the "new aristocratic environmentalists." These city folk employed "impulsive emotional myopic tactics" against agriculture and pesticides in particular. Borlaug lashed at the audacity of non-experts criticizing agricultural chemicals, especially Rachel Carson who exposed, in 1962, the ecological dangers of the farmers' sprays in her eloquent book, *Silent Spring*. Borlaug denounced the public critique of agrotoxins as a "vicious, hysterical propaganda against the use of agricultural chemicals, being promoted today [in 1971] by fear provoking, irresponsible environmentalists." He traced the origins of the anger of the environmentalists to Rachel Carson, slandering her book as "half-science-half-fiction novel," "a diabolic, vitriolic bitter one-sided attack on the use of pesticides, especially insecticides and weed killers. DDT was the main villain." His wrath was sweeping: He used the vocabulary of fundamentalist Christians, quoting the Bible, using terms like cult, conversion, and crusade. He attacked the "fickleness of nature" and the idea of the "balance of nature," replacing it with his own mantra of "evolve or perish." He insulted ecologists, environmentalists, organic gardeners, organic farmers, calling them irresponsible doomsayers, privileged folk who preached fads, being followers of cults. Borlaug, finally, said that without the "improved technology and higher yields" of agribusiness much more land would have to come under the plow. So he blamed the environmentalists for shortsightedness, being responsible for the hesitation of the "privileged world" in converting the "forgotten world" to its agricultural cornucopia.[17]

Norman Borlaug was a missionary for the Rockefellers. The Rockefellers sent him to Mexico and he stood by them. He, and the missionary movement to spread the technologies and political message of the mechanized plantation throughout the world, became one of the defining characteristics of the cold war era. Now, on the dawn of the twenty-first century, genetic engineering, an adjunct of agribusiness, is becoming the "new green revolution" and, once again, a missionary movement is retracing the steps of Norman Borlaug. Food is an incomparable asset. Without it, people die. So whoever controls the food and agriculture of the world, would be its master. The US government and corporations know that truism well. Industrializing agriculture became the means for the control of all the contested areas in the cold war between the United States and the former Soviet Union. So Borlaug became the global icon of doing good, his tenacity in spreading American seeds and the know-how of manipulating those seeds, including pesticides, fertilizers, tractors and threshers, increased food production in Mexico and Mexico did not have another revolution. He collected dozens of honorary degrees, and a tremendous variety of international distinctions and honors—all for becoming one of the agents of undoing the peasants' world. But the 1950s to 1980s was a terrible age darkened by the cold war. Few sensitive scientists like Rachel Carson and Robert van den Bosch saw through the fog of war, and denounced the horror of the industrialized farmers trying to crush nature. But agriculture was on a war footing, and Norman Borlaug was a steady agricultural soldier who never gave up. Toxic sprays served him well. They are weapons, capturing the hatred and bullets of war. They offer simple, violent solutions to complicated biological and social problems.

The appearance of the DDT-like weed killers, 2,4-D and 2,4,5-T, which the Americans were ready to spray over Japan in order to starve the Japanese just before they dropped the atomic bomb on them, increased public confidence, especially the confidence of farmers, that pests would not have a chance against the new weapons of chemistry. Such confidence, of course, was misplaced. Agricultural pests adjusted to the farmers' toxic barrage and evolved into super bugs. Insects, microorganisms causing plant disease, weeds and rodents are becoming resistant to the agrotoxins used against them. From 1900 to 1980, 428 insects, ticks and mites became resistant to one or more pesticides. But the incidence of resistance picked up considerably in the decade of the 1970s. The number of insects, ticks and mites alone, which developed resistance to chemicals between 1970 and 1980 nearly doubled from 224 to 428. By the mid-1990s, there were more than 500 species of insects and mites, 270 species of weeds, and over 150 plant pathogens and about 6 species of rats resistant to pesticides. There are also pests like the Colorado potato beetle, spider mites, houseflies, some mosquitoes, cotton bollworms and cattle ticks, which can put up with nearly all poisons thrown at them. By 1980, 51 of the 60 anopheles mosquitoes capable of transmitting malaria to people had become immune to the most widely used poisons against them. Such hardy mosquitoes exist in more than 84 countries. Pests eat a lot of the farmers' crops, and some of them are becoming nearly indestructible. Despite the billions of pounds of poisons they spray yearly on their crops, despite the genetic engineers making the crops themselves deleterious to insects, American farmers lose a third or more of what they produce to insects and other pests. In the Third World farmers hooked on pesticides lose to pests as much as half of the food they produce. In 2004, American farmers lost approximately 29 percent of citrus, 18 percent of vegetables, and 12 percent of apples.[18] In general, however, American farmers have been losing about 35 percent of their crops to insects, weeds, and diseases.[19] The cost of this loss on the dawn of the twenty-first century is between \$20 billion to \$33 billion per year.[20]

The effects of sprays add to the damage of pests, which, adapting to the sprays, become ever more destructive. But these costs, social and ecological, however, don't seem to matter to agribusiness. Tony T. DeChant, president of the National Farmers Union, testified in Congress on May 20, 1968 that corporate farm "represents power without conscience." [21] Ben H. Radcliffe, president of the South Dakota Farmers Union, also testified on May 20, 1968 before Congress. He told the Senators that social and economic decay follows large farms all over the country. "You can drive almost anywhere in the rural areas," he said, "and see the results of our failure to weigh social consequences in determining our economic objectives: the weathered, abandoned farmhouse, a curtain flapping through a broken window; the soaped-up plate glass of the store front with the 'closed' sign taped to the door; the weeds standing tall around the vacant service station, and the growing ratio of older people on our main streets in areas like South Dakota." [22]

Migrant farm workers, even more than the threatened family farmer, have become the classic icons of the social, economic, and political decay that comes with giant agriculture. John Steinbeck's *Grapes of Wrath* have simply become *Corporate Grapes of Wrath*—a technical model of agrarian oppression that is more sophisticated and mean than the crude violence of the earlier era of economic depression and dust bowls.

America's migrant farm workers follow in the footsteps of poverty, unemployment, underemployment, and malnutrition and hunger of the harvesting gangs of *The Grapes of Wrath*. The "Okie" lives dangerously. He moves 3,000 to 4,000 miles from one crop covered with pesticides to another farm with crops treated with more poisons. He lives with the terrible knowledge that he is beyond the protective reach of the law. He does not know that his wife and child are likely to die at a rate two and one-half times the national average. And he does not know that his life, should he survive death from poisoning, may well be cut short twenty years sooner than the life of other people.[23]

The Tolan Committee of the House of Representatives concluded on January 2, 1941 that the hardships and poverty of the agricultural migrant worker "bring ills not only of the body but of the spirit."[24] On October 19, 1942 Senator Robert LaFollette took the Senate Floor to talk about those "millions of forgotten and disadvantaged farm workers and their families."[25] Eighteen years later, in 1960, the CBS documentary, "Harvest of Shame" explained that the migrant farm workers were "the forgotten people, the under-protected, the under-educated, the underclothed, the underfed."[26] In 1968 the National Educational Television studied the harvesting gang of a farm labor camp in Cutchogue, Long Island, and reported that the migrant's "living conditions too often do not respect his sanctity as a man."[27] An NBC White Paper revealed in 1970 that 2.5 million migrants harvest America's food for very few if any benefits to themselves. In Florida, "the Sunshine State," some 200,000 farm workers try "to put down roots" but they soon discover they enjoy none of the rights of the rest of us—"the migrants live in poverty and despair."[28]

The Senate Commerce Committee probably had this migrant destitution in mind in 1972 when it recommended that the health of farm workers should become "a vital criterion" in all the regulatory actions the US Environmental Protection Agency would take under the pesticide law.[29] In 1978 the President's Commission on Mental Health used language on the farm workers of America, which would have been perfectly understood decades earlier. "There are farm workers in virtually every state of the Union;" the Commission said, "yet domestic farm workers are systematically underremunerated, underpaid, underprotected by the law, and underserved by even those programs categorically designed to assist them. A labor system which fosters an oversupply of workers, encourages geographic migration, and permits the continuation of virtual peonage under the present crewleader system impedes the farm worker's own efforts to substantially improve his harsh existence."[30] Finally, in 1997, the US Department of Agriculture, silently recognizing the peonage of those who harvest America's food, noting that "Hired farmworkers were more likely than all US wage and salary workers to be male, Hispanic, younger, less educated, never married, and non-US citizens."[31]

This abstract declaration of the US Department of Agriculture about farm workers, many of whom are immigrants yet essential to the harvesting of the food we eat in the United States, mirrors the Manichean side of giant agriculture: Its successful strategy has been to use the state and science to grind down the family farmer, enslave the domestic and foreign farm worker, and emptying the countryside of people—first the Indians and then the family farmers. Now, on the dawn of the twenty-first century, giant agriculture nearly owns all that vast territory of farms, pasture, and forest. The "hobby" family farmers that survive have been made largely irrelevant in terms of food production.

This American farming system (which is the icon of the world's industrial agriculture) has become a giant mechanical factory that, for about a century, has been mining and cannibalizing its way through rural America—leaving behind desolate land, communities falling apart, and fearful people.

In the midst of the depression and dust bowl—a massive ecological and social disaster that destroyed the land and lives of millions of Americans primarily because of very aggressive and violent farming practices—the Secretary of Agriculture, Henry A. Wallace, spoke the truth. He said that while the Indian "did little to change the virgin character of the land," the white man "came with ax and plow and livestock. Advancing rapidly, farmers, lumbermen, and stockmen pushed the frontier farther and farther westward, cleared the land of forests, turned the prairie sod, and overstocked the range.

"They bared millions of acres to the wash and sweep of rain and wind, and soils which had been thoroughly protected for thousands of years began to erode."[32]

I discuss the plight of the black farmers below. Suffice it to say that black family farmers, who are descendants of slaves exported from Africa to man the Europeans' cash crop plantations in America, have suffered the erosion of the land, the wash and sweep of rain and wind, even the erosion of their very survival. The violent racism that followed their emancipation washed and swept them from the land. America's giant agriculture worked them nearly to death for 400 years, inevitably, bringing their entire black experience in farming, their exquisite knowledge of rice cultivation,[33] fragile ownership of land, and rural culture on the borders of extinction. Gary Grant, President of the Black Farmers and Agriculturalists Association, described what happened to black farmers this way in 1998:

> African Americans have been losing land at extraordinary rates, averaging 9,000 acres per week. Discrimination within and by the USDA [United States Department of Agriculture] is at the root of the Black farmers' struggle to save his land, his livelihood, his health and his family. In 1920, 1 in 7 farmers in America was Black, but by 1982 only 1 in 67 farmers was Black. The most recent figures show that since 1982 alone, the number of Black operated farms in the U.S. has decreased over 43 %.... Black farmers do not suffer from some temporary aberration for justice and fairness. Instead we and our families are subjected to a persistent and

degrading suppression of our living standards, our mental and physical health, and of our dignity and humanity.[34]

Gary Grant is right. The combination of racism and the plantation technologies of power of giant agriculture make for a determined adversary.

Bill Mollison, the Australian who founded *permaculture* (permanent agriculture and culture) in the late 1970s, a means of raising food based on Third World traditional peasant farming knowledge and wisdom, described this new rural adversary with precision in 1992, the year of the Earth Summit in Rio, Brazil. He said:

> Most things in agriculture today are really death systems...Agriculture today grows nonsensical crops for nonsensical reasons. It grows practically all of its soybean to feed animals; fish are caught to be turned into powder and fed to pigs...Beef agriculture has destroyed the world's drylands...And the world's largest agriculture is the European and American grass lawn... Agriculture lost its way in the 1940s. Once it was there to produce food for people; now it's there to produce money for large interests. With present day agriculture, the Third World is made to feed the First World, the reverse of aid in its true sense.[35]

In the United States farmers don't even like to be called farmers. They are right. They are not farmers. "The modern farmer," says Jose Lutzenberger, one of Brazil's greatest environmentalists, "is only a tractor driver or a poison sprayer. He is only a tiny cog in an enormous and highly complicated techno-bureaucratic structure that begins in the oilfields, goes through the whole chemical industry and the huge agribusiness industry—I'd rather call it the food-manipulating, denaturing and contaminating industry—and ends up in the supermarkets."[36]

For these reasons, so well-captured by Lutzenberger, American farmers, who are the models of modern farmers, describe themselves as growers, ranchers, or agribusinessmen. This is especially true of the tiny minority of businessmen that have the largest stake in the perpetual financial prosperity of the giant agricultural system. These growers *produce* "plant or animal products" under rigid chemical and one-crop, monocultural regimes. They probably never heard of permaculture or Bill Mollison or sustainable agriculture or that black farmers in the United States are disappearing. They would be shocked to hear they work for something made up mostly of "death systems."

Yet Bill Mollison characterized the situation correctly. Almost nothing in large farms is part of traditional agricultural practices. The logic of profit and the mechanical routine of the factory taking over agriculture make up Bill Mollison's death systems. Such industrialization is corrupting agriculture through and through. Now, on the dawn of the twenty-first century, even synthetic fertilizers are used as another mechanism for the disposal of a great deal of the hazardous wastes of the chemical and manufacturing industries. Farms growing food "are being transformed into toxic waste dumps, one season at a time."[37]

There's practically nothing in the conventional agriculture of America that is in accord with human needs, democratic institutions, social justice, respect and love of nature, and respect for science. Giant agriculture is using and misusing science to justify the huge public subsidies it extracts from a corrupt political culture—including a corrupt and cowardly academic class of "scientists" who keep silent on the face of daily ecocide and social disintegration and fear in the countryside.

Why not say, for example, that pushing black farmers out of farming is bad for America? Or that what passes for "modern" and "advanced" and "high-tech" in agriculture (like sowing entire plantations with only one crop) is against human culture and nature? That, in fact, such a practice is nothing but the expression of the violence and greed of colonialism and cash cropping?

The social effects of giant agriculture have been equally catastrophic to the welfare and political and cultural life of most farm communities— and farmers. Wherever big agriculture settles in rural America, it is almost certain it will rapidly destroy the democratic, cultural, and economic institutions of the community and convert everything around it to a plantation. In 1992 we hear that "Abandoned farmsteads and closed businesses haunt rural Kansas."[38] Marty Strange, an agricultural policy analyst for at least 20 years with Nebraska's Center for Rural Affairs, says that a fundamental demographic shift is taking place in the farm communities of America: Farmers are getting few and old, fast. Strange sees nothing good from this unsettling of the land. He says that while "wholesales of fertilizer" increased during the 1970s and 1980s, "sales of groceries, shoes, haircuts and everything else that has to do with people fell. This has left rural Main Street with little more than dealers, brokers, franchisers and agents—businesses designed to siphon money of the community."[39]

Giant agriculture is an industrial system that has very little to do with traditional farming. It relies on "producing" one crop at a time in expanses of the land, plantations, huge spreads, feeding that one crop with synthetic fertilizers, and protecting it from insects and diseases with powerful toxins. Giant agriculture is also concentrated livestock operations, and food processing and marketing of food. Moreover, industrialized agriculture mines the land. Nearly half of the world's wrecked agricultural soil, some of it moderately eroded, some of it severely degraded, is in Africa.[40] Yet economic analysis obscures the degradation and, sometimes, destruction of the natural resources in the absence of which no agriculture is possible.

Yet the persistent policies of conventional agriculture of using only a handful of crops to *produce* most of the world's food—in largely huge farms displacing the tiny but immensely rich in biological and cultural diversity peasant farms—are responsible for the tragic loss of a considerable amount of genetic resources for food and agriculture. In 1903 there were 13 known varieties of asparagus. Only one variety of asparagus existed in 1983. Nearly 98 percent of asparagus varieties became extinct between 1903 and 1983. There were similar losses for carrots, radish, and lettuce. In 1903 there were 287 varieties of carrots, more than 460 varieties of radish, and about 500 varieties of lettuce. By 1983 there were 21 varieties of carrots, 27 varieties of radish, and 36 varieties of lettuce. Clearly the twentieth century was a killer century. Nearly nothing survived the cash croppers and scientists who set to reinventing nature. *During the twentieth century about 75 percent of the varieties of food crops disappeared.* In the tropics, says Hugh Iltis, the world-renown botanist at the University of Wisconsin, cash crop agriculture causes biological genocide and utter devastation.[41] And with a collapse of agrarian culture brought about by cash cropping and the spread and globalization of Western culture and farming, there's a dramatic decline and killing of cultural diversity, particularly the disappearance of spoken languages among indigenous people and small ethnic groups. The United Nations Environment Programme estimates that *the globalization of Western culture is likely to kill about 90 percent of the world's 5,000 to 7,000 languages in the next 100 years.*[42] The situation is so bad in the impoverishment of both cultural and biological diversity that determine what people have been worshipping, growing, and eating for millennia that one can describe the loss of agricultural biodiversity and the erosion of cultural diversity as a biological and cultural meltdown.[43]

Huge and Rapid Seizure of Power by Mammoth Farms Run by Hirelings

The incredible paradox in the United States transcends the genetic diversity meltdown. It's about another deadly metamorphosis—of the self-reliant and democratic family farm into an undemocratic and aggressive agribusiness. Only a relatively few persons, and the surviving family farmers themselves, are conscious that things are falling apart in rural America.

Giant agriculture and its purchased professors have been inundating the brains of urban people with "news" about the "modernity," "progress," and "high tech" efficiency of things giant, including larger and larger farms, that the advertising lie has become the accepted value, the normal in American culture. However, this paradox does nothing to dispel the ugly truth. What about the future? What about a possible disaster, a catastrophe, when a disease, for instance, wipes out the monocultures of corn and wheat? What then? Can we even dream that the 50,000 or so "farmers" who "produce" most of our food disappear into thin air? Or that the next few years may be dreadfully quiet which is a melancholy prospect because our entire land and food economy will pass into the private domain of a huge hacienda? What then? Who is going to continue with our civilization?

We cannot be neutral to rural culture, the growing of food, the industrialization of agriculture, and the disintegration of human and ecological communities resulting from the transformation of what used to be a way of life to a factory in the field. Replacing biology with mining / production is profitable to the owners of agribusiness capital but deleterious to society and nature. Whether the so-called modern people like it or not they have to eat. And what they eat has a lot to do with who they are. Besides, the fate of agriculture determines the fate of about three billion people raising food throughout the world. Thus, for reasons personal and ethical, I consider agriculture the most fundamental issue in human affairs.

My personal reasons have to do with my birth and upbringing in Greek peasant culture. The moral paradigm of my courageous and decent father. The tasty and uncontaminated food. The white *robola* wine of god Dionysos. The human scale of the peasant enterprise: Families working together by the season with their hands and a few simple technologies. Nothing would be wasted. Traditional knowledge at the hands of the peasants / very small family farmers makes these people of the land masters of agroecological practices but without the envy of industrialized farmers or academic experts. Small family farmers are significantly more efficient than conventional "growers." They don't willfully pollute the environment, and they protect biodiversity. Family farmers learn to work with and respect nature primarily from nature.

Yet small-scale farming communities do exist precariously and, often, in conditions resembling insurrection, within larger state and global systems of agricultural production and power. Who owns land is a key ingredient in the local, national, and international struggles for power. You need land to raise food. But you need land even more to have power.

And power, no doubt, is central to the fate of family farmers, the culture they represent, and to the evolution of the industrial agricultural systems. The only reason the idea of sustainability has been dragged into the debate on global agriculture is as a last ditch effort to legitimize the biocidal system of conventional agriculture and, therefore, perpetuate the power of the landowning class.

Agriculture has almost always been sustainable—if by sustainability we mean the perpetuation in the countryside of an agroecological and socially just system of food cultivation and human culture. Land makes agriculture possible. Land is agriculture. You cannot raise food if you don't have land or if your methods, technologies of food production, degrade and destroy the land. In this later case, which is largely the case of giant agriculture, you are putting yourself out of the business of producing food. In other words, giant agriculture is destroying land / agriculture, and, therefore, it is an unsustainable system of ecological and social exploitation. That such a system exists in hegemonic relations to the rest of us in the United States and the rest of the world, says more about political power rather than farming.

Giant agriculture in the United States leaves no doubt that homogenization has gone far enough. We wonder: Can this process be reversed? Will further research prove that corporate factory farming is a bad idea?

Research, like traditional agriculture, has a legitimate place in the generation of new knowledge and the formation of public policy. But "research" can also become an excuse for avoiding responsibility or a sophisticated strategy to support the corporate position. In the case of agriculture, is it realistic to expect that "research" can affect policy when power is overwhelmingly on the side of agribusiness? It is research, after all, that has made giant agriculture what it is. Public funding of the land grant universities slowly tilted farm technology in favor of industrialized agriculture.

Stewart Smith, an economist at the University of Maine, predicts that farming in the United States will end sometimes in the early part of the twenty-first century. Biotechnology will deal a fatal blow to what is left of farming because the technology holds "the promise of non-soil based agriculture." Smith explains: "Biotechnology being developed today with the support of the LGUs [land grant universities] will lead to a more industrialized system, with most farming activity conducted by part-time farmers and nonfarm firms performing much of the production activity away from the soil. Full time, family-owned and managed farming, as we have known it, will cease to exist."[44]

What a dreadful prospect! No more farming in the United States beyond the year 2020. And yet only in 1853 a physician, Daniel Lee, proudly reported to Congress that "Agriculture gives employment to more capital and labor in the United States than all other pursuits combined; and its progress marks, in a peculiar manner, the advancement of the republic in wealth, civilization, and power. The natural fruitfulness of the American soil, its vast area, and wide range of climates, between the gulf and the great lakes, the Atlantic and the Pacific oceans, present for consideration resources and capabilities almost unlimited in extent and quite inestimable in value."[45] However, by 1992, professor Stewart Smith could project the disappearance of that vast bucolic dream in the United States. When I spoke with him he said the eclipse of family farming is a nightmare. He is right. If we continue to avoid challenging the power of giant agriculture and place our hopes on the salvation of research, Smith's nightmare will become a political reality probably as dangerous as nuclear power plants and even nuclear weapons. As the United States starts growing its food in laboratories, sustainable agriculture in the Third World will be threatened even more than it has ever been by conventional "green revolution" schemes. The camouflaged ecocide and the taking of the land away from the family farmer of the last several decades will become open state policy. Rural America will cease to exist—with the incalculable social consequences of a society falling apart. Consider the power behind this calamity:

In 1987 some 85.7 percent of the net cash farm income and 61 percent of direct government subsidies went to no more than 317,000 "farmers." These "growers," "farm operators," own plantation-like farms, the average size of which is 1,873 acres. These plantations represent no more than 14 percent of all American farms.[46] In 1992 only 2 percent of all farms sold about 50 percent of all food produced in the United States. On average, each of these large farms earned more than $500,000 per year.[47] The 1996 farm bill confirmed and strengthened these huge inequities between the small hemorrhaging family farmers and the powerful large growers. Giant agriculture got another license to continue with its profitable harvesting of the political system—and its deadly mining of most of rural America. Marty Strange, who has been struggling for about twenty years to bring public purpose in farm policy from the Center for Rural Affairs in Nebraska, spoke with not a little bitterness about the perpetuation of injustice in the 1996 farm legislation.

> "The 1996 farm bill," he says, "in many ways represented the final collapse of public purpose in farm programs. It is difficult to justify legislation that transfers guaranteed sums of money to people notwithstanding either their individual need or the general condition of the economic sector in which they operate. The larger the farm, the larger the guaranteed payment. Big farms get big help to bid land away from moderate-size farms. And for next to nothing in return."[48]

Victor Davis Hanson traces the insidious roots of agribusiness right into the consumer culture of the United States, "the desire of the American consumer to have instant, attractive food, cheap and in surfeit, at any time of the year from anywhere, regardless of the environmental or cultural consequences. In that sense, agribusiness, which is godless, does a far better job, with its vast array of vertically integrated shipping, processing, and distributing branches, of fulfilling this constant need of the consumer. It is almost as if we didn't have agribusiness, we'd have to invent it, given the tastes and values of our citizenry. Out here [in California] we are more efficient in growing fruit than agribusiness, and I'd like to think better for the local community, but what we can't do is on our own get cheap plums to New York—only large conglomerates can do that—and they are getting larger every day. And people forget that out here in California, family farming is essentially gone, if by that term we mean a family deriving its livelihood from the land. Most of the few that are left are like me, commuting to town to pay for losses on the farm. Almost all my neighbors are renting to agribusiness or selling out. That has been a real untold story, the vast and accelerated disappearance of viable family farms in the 1990s—witness the latest reincarnation of the Farm Bill, which once more gives to those who already have plenty."[49]

Meanwhile, the top seven leaders of giant agriculture—Cargill, RJR Nabisco, Safeway, Continental Grain, Mars, Southland, Supermarkets General—had an income in 1989 of $106.4 billion. Cargill alone in 1989 had revenues of $43 billion.[50] Three companies—Cargill, ConAgra, and Iowa Beef Processors—control the vast meat packing (slaughter) industry with sales in 1987 of approximately $47 billion. This concentration of power is hazardous to farmers, ranchers, packinghouse workers and rural communities. Close to a third of the United States has been set aside for the grazing of cattle. About one-half of all farms raise livestock feed, and cattle drink as much as half of all potable water in the country. To get a pound of feedlot-finished beefsteak, it is necessary to start with five pounds of grain, about 2,500 gallons of water, close to 35 pounds of eroded topsoil, and the energy equivalent of a gallon of gasoline.[51]

Giant agriculture also uses violence to "produce" meat. Its animal factories cram millions of animals into small spaces, causing diseases, pain, and suffering of cruel proportions. "Milk-fed" veal comes from baby calves spending their short lives in the dark chained to a wooden box so small the animal can't even turn around. The calf is made anemic in order to give its meat a special color. And to keep calves and all the other factory animals alive, they drug them as much as they feed them.

In December 1997, US Senator Tom Harkin (from Iowa) released a report documenting the staggering amounts of waste coming out of those animal factories of livestock and poultry production in the United States. In 1997 the total animal waste was 1.37 billion tons of solid manure—1,229,190,000 tons from cattle; 116,652,300 tons from hogs; 14,394,000 tons from chickens; and 5,425,000 tons from turkeys. This is as if every man, woman, and child in the country produced 5 tons of waste in 1997. The animals of giant agriculture—in 1997—generated

130 times more manure than the human waste of all the people of the United States. What to do with such a mountain of manure when, for instance, outside of Washington, DC, in the Delmarva Peninsula, 600 million chickens produce 3.2 billion pounds of raw waste every year— releasing as much nitrogen in the environment as a city of nearly 500,000 people. A 50,000-acre swine factory in southwest Utah is designed to "produce" 2.5 million hogs every year—and its potential waste per year could be larger than that of the city of Los Angeles, California. It's hardly surprising that staggering amounts of manure, concentrated usually not where they could be used as fertilizer, cause pollution of rivers, ground water, and other severe environmental problems. The Mississippi River, for example, drains a huge swath of the country bringing animal waste, and "nutrients" from farm runoff to the Gulf of Mexico with the result that almost 7,000 square miles of the Gulf water is dead.[52]

In August 2000, the Water Keeper Alliance, a civil society organization from New York and several North Carolina environmental groups, filed a legal complaint at Wake County, North Carolina, against Smithfield Foods and its subsidiaries—Carroll's Foods, Brown's of Carolina, and Murphy Farms. The complaint said that Smithfield Foods (and its dependent hog companies) have been poisoning the Neuse, Cape Fear, and New River of North Carolina, the basins of those rivers, and the land adjacent to the hog factories and slaughterhouse of the Smithfield Packing Company. Smithfield Foods, the suit charges, has been maintaining open hog cesspools full of untreated hog feces and urine and other wastes from pigs. This waste is contaminating surface and ground water and aquifers, and poisons the air with ammonia from the nitrogen in the hog cesspools. The owners of the hog factories willfully kept the hog cesspools overflowing with pig waste and did nothing to prevent the poisoning of the environment from their business. These hog factory owners also knew of the detrimental effects their hog farms are having on the people near their pigs. During September / October 1999, Smithfield Food's hog lagoons overflowed into the rivers of North Carolina causing massive contamination of the surface and ground water. Smithfield Foods illegally sprayed untreated pig waste onto land that was not fit and large enough to absorb the waste. The company also sprayed huge amounts of untreated hog waste into the creeks and rivers of North Carolina. Among other deleterious substances, like copper and zinc, all this pig waste was equivalent to dumping more than 29,000 metric tons of phosphorous every year into the rivers and creeks of North Carolina. Smithfield buried thousands of dead and drowned hogs in its own sprayed fields. The result has been massive contamination of water, land, and air. The worst poisoning of the water is in the river systems of the Neuse, Cape Fear, and New River. Seeing it in a different light, Smithfield's hog waste reaching the rivers of North Carolina is larger than the human waste of the entire population of North Carolina and New York State. In addition, pig waste is loaded with poisons, including heavy metals, which poisoned the water of North Carolina. Smithfield has had devastating environmental damage to the rivers, creeks and natural environment of North Carolina. Smithfield has been poisoning the water, land, and air of North Carolina in a manner that is negligent, wanton, callous, and reckless. It operates with a disregard of the rights and safety of the public. Its business practices are abusive. And its conduct is "deceptive, immoral, unethical, oppressive, unscrupulous, and substantially injurious."[53]

The social consequences of the animal factories that produce America's meat are also ominous—and not just in North Carolina. In 1995-1996 animal farms were inhabited by 103 million pigs, 58 million non-dairy cattle, 7.6 billion chickens, and 300 million turkeys. From 1969 to 1992 the number of chicken factories declined by 35 percent, yet the number of chickens *produced* almost tripled. A mere 2 percent of the non-dairy cattle factories sell more than 40 percent of the cattle for slaughter. And since 1982 a drastic concentration of power has been taking place in the pig factories—their overall numbers were reduced from 600,000 in 1982 to 157,000 in 1997.[54] Chuck Hassebrook, director of the Center for Rural Affairs in Nebraska, said in November 2001 that since 1996 giant hog owners have driven half of the family hog farmers out of business. That way corporate agriculture replaces "genuine middle class self-employment opportunities in family farming with low-wage jobs that most rural people won't take…Mega livestock production will not offer lasting growth. Big hog production is already shifting to Mexico and Brazil…The animal science departments of land grant colleges, with some exceptions, have not stepped up to help us chart a better course. Too often, they have acted as cheerleaders for industrial livestock production rather than public institutions with a responsibility to empower rural people to create a future that reflects their values."[55]

John Helmuth, an economist who teaches at Iowa State University, saw the rotten core of animal factories quite early. He said in 1990: "The meatpacking industry has rapidly become an industry where literally every day fewer and fewer individuals are making more and more of the economic decisions about what America eats...this consolidation of economic power in the meatpacking industry has resulted in (and is resulting into a greater degree every day): lower prices paid to farmers and livestock producers, lower wages and deplorable working conditions for meat industry workers, serious questions about the quality and nutritional safety of meat, and higher prices paid by consumers. When an industry drives its best small and medium companies into bankruptcy, when cattle producers and farmers are driven into bankruptcy by lower and lower prices, when workers are treated like animals and injured and maimed for life, and consumers are charged higher and higher prices for minimum quality, often unsafe meat, something is wrong."[56]

Of course something is wrong. Helmuth illustrates the nature of that wrong by highlighting the "breathtakingly rapid" consolidation and concentration of economic power in the slaughter or meatpacking industry, particularly in the 1980s. "Never in any American industry in any other time period," he says, "has there been such a huge and rapid seizure of economic power."[57]

For example: In 1998, four companies—Iowa Beef Processors, ConAgra Beef Companies, Excel Corporation (Cargill) and Farmland National Beef Pkg. Company—controlled 79 percent of beef slaughter in the United States; Smithfield, Iowa Beef Processors, ConAgra (swift), and Cargill (Excel) slaughtered 44 percent of all pigs in 1992; Tyson Foods, Gold Kist, Perdue Farms and Pilgrim's Pride slaughtered 49 percent of all chicken in 1998; Cargill, ADM, Continental Grain, and Bunge control America's grain trade: their elevators hold 24 percent of the country's grain, and own or control 39 percent of the grain facilities and 59 percent of the port facilities for grain trade. Finally, ADM Milling Company, ConAgra, Cargill Food Flour Milling and Cereal Food Processors controlled 61 percent of flour milling business in 1990.[58]

Redistribution of land to the landless tenants and farm workers, and other people willing and able to become farmers, and support for family farming could go very far in the United States in light of the power of these companies. The government must break up these giant corporations into thousands of very small businesses—not merely in the United States but throughout the industrialized world. Giant agriculture is diminishing the democratic institutions and human rights in this country. And the concentration of power in the global food system is threatening democracy everywhere.

In fact, the hegemony of the fast food corporations in America's agribusiness-food industrial complex accelerated the industrialization of cattle-raising and slaughter of farm animals, a change that is wrecking rural America. Slaughterhouses in Nebraska, Colorado, Kansas, and Texas cripple immigrants by the thousands. In the 1980s and 1990s these slaughterhouses used illiterate migrant workers to destroy organized labor. Jobs in the slaughterhouses as a result are some of the most dangerous and lowest paying in America. Moreover, the paradigm of how the slaughterhouses crushed labor unions is quite unsettling for the rest of the workers of the United States. The fallout of fast food in the United States is also bolstering an ugly and killing homogenization of every aspect of American culture. In addition, fast food companies have a tremendous power over America's food and agricultural economy. These corporations are responsible for the assembly line slaughter of farm animals. Their carcass-dismembering system is something out of a nightmare. They produce food for people in a hurry with limited taste, usually children and impoverished adults in the United States and the rest of the world.[59] This comes from Eric Schlosser's *Fast Food Nation*, a comprehensive 2001 report on the business of fast food. His data are compelling.

Fast food is not a fad. It is everywhere in the United States—restaurants, zoos, cruise ships, trains, elementary schools, universities, high schools, gas stations, hospitals, government cafeterias, and shopping malls.

In 1970, Americans spent some $6 billion buying hot dogs, hamburgers, cheeseburgers, pizzas, chicken, French fries, and milk shakes. By 2000, they spent $110 billion. McDonald's, the corporation that blazed America's path into fast food, owned about 1,000 restaurants in 1968. By 2000, there were 28,000 McDonald's fast food restaurants all over the world. About one of eight American workers has probably worked, temporarily in most cases, for McDonald's. This giant buys the largest amount of beef, pork, and potatoes in the United States every year. It is the largest owner of retail property in the world, earning more from renting its land to its franchisees than selling food, and spending huge amounts of money for advertising, eclipsing Coca-Cola. McDonald's operates the most playgrounds in the United States and it is one of the largest distributors of toys. About 96 percent of American schoolchildren identify with the mythical Ronald McDonald; and the Golden Arches of McDonald's are more widely recognized than the cross of Christianity.

Fast food came into being at exactly the time that the industrialization of agriculture and the cold war were at their zenith—in the early 1950s. This was a time that life itself looked precarious, what with the clouds of the global slaughter that had just come to an end with the explosion of two atomic bombs over Japan. This was an era of hatred in international relations, a revived crusade between West and East, American-led capitalism and Russia-led communism—Christians fighting their ancient battles under new names. However, both sides glorified technology. Praises for nuclear bombs, scientific socialism, sleek machinery, cars, electronics, and automation went hand in hand with slogans like "Better Living through Chemistry" and "Our Friend the Atom."

In 1948, the McDonald brothers built a restaurant in San Bernardino in south California on the model of factory specialization—selling only hamburgers and cheeseburgers. Short-order cooks, skilled on food preparation and cooking were no longer necessary. The new order of fast food had one person grilling the hamburger, another "dressing" and wrapping it; another making the milk shake, and still another preparing the French fries. McDonald's Speedee Service System replaced restaurant workers (carhops, waitresses, dishwashers and bus boys) with the customers who were asked to serve themselves the fast food they purchased.

Ray Kroc bought out the McDonald brothers, and founded McDonald's on the principles of QSC and V—Quality, Service, Cleanliness and Value. He was born in Illinois in 1902. He served in the ambulance corps of WWI next to Walt Disney, the founder of America's children entertainment industry. Both men ended up in southern California. And both men were obsessed with cleanliness and control. They believed in the survival of the fittest and run their corporations like boot camps. Kroc, exactly like Disney, targeted children. He wanted to make them his customers. So he used huge sums of money for toys, playgrounds, and TV and radio advertisements to capture their appetite and imagination. His strategy worked. Every month, something like 90 percent of American children, ages three to nine, visit a McDonald's fast food restaurant with their parents. McDonald's food culture has become the popular culture of American children.

Fast food comes out of a kitchen that is like a small factory: The food is pre-cooked and frozen. Adding hot water to the frozen food is all it takes to get it ready for "cooking." Strict and elaborate rules govern both cooking and serving fast food. Such regimentation goes hand in hand with the assembly line technology and philosophy behind fast food—a process of work that de-skills the worker, making him easy to replace and cheap to hire. That is one reason why teenagers make up the bulk of its workforce. Fast food companies design technologies that would require zero training for their workers. And, yet, the same companies get grants from the government to "train" workers. Fast food chains pay their teenage workers minimum wages without any medical or other benefits. They are also firm in discouraging their young workers from joining unions. No union represents any of the workers in 15,000 McDonald's restaurants in North America. Bad working conditions, monotonous labor, high turn over, and low wages may be partly responsible for the violence afflicting fast food restaurants in the United States. It's not too unusual for fast food workers to rob the very restaurants that employ them or, in some instances, to murder the managers of those restaurants.

What McDonald's did for hamburgers—assembly line making of food and de-skilling of the workers—IBP (Iowa Beef Packers), a slaughterhouse founded on the McDonald model in Denison, Iowa, did to the slaughtering of cattle. The owners of IBP consider business (the slaughter of cattle and sales of beef) like war. This means resurrecting the worst legacy of the beef trust and slaughterhouses of the early twentieth century. Eric Schlosser documents how IBP broke worker unions, paid workers low wages, and even collaborated with gangsters in order to introduce its boxed beef to the people of New York City. IBP's low-cost beef forced the Chicago slaughterhouses to shut down and move west and become like IBP. New meatpacking factories (slaughterhouses) were built in Iowa, Kansas, Texas, Nebraska, and Colorado—all following the ruthless tactics of IBP. In fact, these slaughterhouses now hire almost exclusively migrant workers from Mexico and Central America.

Eric Schlosser is right to lament those jobs in slaughterhouses "that had once provided a middle-class American life now offered little more than poverty wages." In fact desperately poor people from Mexico and Central America rush to slaughter cattle for the IBP-like meatpacking factories (slaughterhouses). These immigrant laborers do hard and dangerous work, wounding and crippling and killing themselves on the job. Among them, the sanitation workers, cleaning the killing beds of the slaughterhouses every night, suffer the most accidents and most deaths. Says Eric Schlosser: They are often "ground up and reduced to nothing."

The fast food-slaughterhouse complex is responsible for a number of hazardous consequences. Pathogens like the killer of children, E. coli 0157:H7, find ideal conditions to grow and spread in the feedlots where manure gets re-circulated. That way E. coli 0157:H7 multiplies in the food of the cattle and survives in the manure for close to three months. Feedlots are also places for other ghastly practices. In addition to grain, cattle are fed animals and the wastes of animals. Some 75 percent of American cattle have been fed, for several decades, the "rendered" products of dead sheep, cattle, cats, dogs, hogs, and poultry. With the outbreak of the mad cow disease, bovine spongiform encephalitis, in England because of these "scientific" feeding regimes of forcing grass animals to eat their own, the US government forbade animal farmers from feeding cattle to their cattle. However, animal farmers are allowed to feed their cattle pigs, horses, poultry, and cattle blood. And one can still feed cattle to poultry. All this frenzied feeding domestic animals to other domestic animals goes with an additional ingredient—animal wastes. Chicken manure, sawdust, and newspapers used as litter, become meals for cattle.

If one adds to these practices—admittedly cruel, dangerous and barbarous—what happens in the slaughterhouses, then meat comes under suspicion. The killing workers and the killing machines of the slaughterhouse slaughter so fast that they become the cause of contaminated and, in many cases, diseased meat, which ends up with hair, insects, manure, urine and other wastes.

Giant slaughterhouses are the antithesis of hygiene and sanitation. They are mechanized factories of slaughter. They are not an improvement over the filthy slaughterhouses of the early twentieth century. Upton Sinclair's 1906 book, *The Jungle*, captured precisely that bloody and dirty past in America's animal farm. The slaughterhouses, Sinclair said,

> were simply honeycombed with rottenness...the bosses grafted off the men, and they grafted off each other...every man lived in terror of losing his job. So from top to bottom the place was simply a seething cauldron of jealousies and hatreds; there was no loyalty or decency anywhere about it, there was no place in it where a man counted for anything against a dollar....[I]n the room where the men prepared the beef for canning, and the beef had lain in vats full of chemicals, and men with great forks speared it out and dumped it into trucks, to be taken to the cooking room. When they had speared out all they could reach, they emptied the vat on the floor, and then with shovels scraped up the balance and dumped it into the truck. This floor was filthy, yet they set [the worker] Antanas with his mop slopping the 'pickle' into a hole that connected with a sink, where it was caught and used over again forever; and if that were not enough, there was a trap in the pipe, where all the scraps of meat and odds and ends of refuse were caught, and every few days it was the old man's task to clean these out, and shovel their contents into one of the trucks with the rest of the meat!"[60]

A century later, "the jungle" is reinventing itself, reigning supreme. The new trusts, giant conglomerates of power—fast food chains, supermarkets, slaughterhouses, livestock companies and animal farms—restrict even the government' authority to end the contamination of meat. They blithely ignore that it is their cattle-raising methods, the cannibalistic feed they give to the animals, and the fast, relentless assembly-line slaughter of those animals, which are responsible for the suspect quality of their meat. Instead, they embrace another magic bullet technology, irradiating their meat with gamma rays and x-rays, in order to convince themselves and consumers that the meat they sell is safe to eat.

This is bad enough for the health and well being of the United States. However, fast food—with all its undemocratic and ecologically destructive values—has become global. In 1990, McDonald's had 3,000 restaurants outside the United States. By 2000, McDonald's had 15,000 restaurants in 117 foreign countries. Fast food chains, says Eric Schlosser, have become "imperial fiefdoms," exercising power far and wide. They don't import American beef and potatoes but buy food from the farmers of the countries where they have their fast food restaurants. Yet they bring with them the assembly line thinking and practice of raising and preparing food. Thus McDonald's goes abroad, bringing along the entire

American system of industrialized agriculture and the slaughtering and processing of animals and other food. Giant American agribusiness firms follow McDonald's, gaining considerable shares or buying outright the beef, poultry or grain industry of foreign countries. Then, once the American fast food chains get a foothold abroad, they target their host country's children with deceptive advertisements so that they can do to them what they did to America's children—hook them and their parents to hamburgers, fries, chicken nuggets, and, indirectly, to American culture. No wonder the children of Beijing love "uncle McDonald."

American fast food is conquering and making the rest of the world like America so fast that, like imperial Rome, it puts its defeated enemies on display for all to see. In March 1999, fast food companies put Mikhail Gorbachev on display in Las Vegas, paying him to extol the virtues of fast food. Gorbachev was the Soviet Union's / Russia's last communist boss and the man who, single-handedly, ended the worst aspects of the cold war. No small fry, Mikhail Gorbachev. In 1989, he was one of the two most powerful men in the world.

America is also paying for being a fast food nation. Fast food, from restaurants and in supermarkets, is responsible for an "obesity epidemic," second only to smoking in the number of Americans it kills. Neal Barnard, president of the Physicians Committee for Responsible Medicine, accuses the food industry for contributing to "the obesity crisis and its related epidemics of heart disease and diabetes." Big food, he says, has been very successful "in manipulating the public, the government, and even the scientific community." Fast food companies employ "myriad techniques" in making us believe that their products are good for us. They are pushing "Cheeseburger" bills in state legislatures and the US Congress, granting the fast food industry sweeping immunity for bringing about the obesity crisis in the United States. Such selfish legislation would kill reform and also prevent tobacco-like lawsuits to effect social and political change.[61] That obesity epidemic is spreading to the rest of the countries that now have McDonald's. Britain, Germany and Japan are only second to the United States in obesity from indulging in the Happy Meals of McDonald's.

Inevitably, however, foreigners were bound to see behind the slogans and bad food of American fast food corporations. For instance, I, who have lived most of my life in the United States, resent seeing a

McDonald's at the center of Athens, Greece. The Greeks have had an ancient and distinguished tradition of raising and eating food that is good for their health. So why did they allow the mechanical food factory of McDonald's to stand up like an alien intruder at downtown Athens? Clearly not for the hamburgers and frozen, reconstituted fries. Could then it be that the Greeks opened to McDonald's to be in the good graces of the United States? But both the Greeks and other people elsewhere in the world look at McDonald's as an icon of American political and cultural power, the obsessive effort of the United States to globalize its way of life, even create a world after its own image. Probably, that explains why McDonald's restaurants have been burned, bombed or trashed in Denmark, Holland, France, Germany, Japan, England, China, India, Greece and other countries.

Could consumer pressure make a difference in the behavior of one or all of the fast food chains? For instance, "forcing" one of these chains, McDonald's, not to use bioengineered potatoes or to increase the pay of its workers are good policies, but they do not alter the history and nature of fast food. Even if McDonald's started cooking the best of food, McDonald's would still be a bad idea for nature, society, and culture. You simply can't use a factory model to replace family cooking and family farming in the raising of food.

Eric Schlosser says the bosses of McDonald's, Burger King, Kentucky Fried Chicken, Wendy's, Subway, Pizza Hut, Taco Bell, Jack in the Box and other fast food corporations, "are not bad men." I disagree. His study says something different to me. It is a carefully crafted document that, reveals the dark side of both agriculture and the all-American meal. The data in this book show that these fast food executives, often indistinguishable from other agribusiness leaders, with a possible exception or two, are not good men. They are scheming abhorrent policies in support of an assembly-line food system, giving the consumer often tainted food and meat full of toxins and fat, creating a train of ecological disaster and rural ghettos in order to sustain their lucrative food profits. The fast food chains have so much power that they have accelerated the industrialization of agriculture and rural America. They have become a model for the obliteration of diversity and the emergence of sameness everywhere. Both of these new trends are bad for nature and society.

Of course, fast food executives are businessmen. And, yes, they could serve "free-range, organic, grass-fed hamburgers." But why don't they? After all, consumers have been demanding healthy food free of agrotoxins for several decades. The entire environmental movement came into being because of the "silent spring" of the deleterious sprays of large farmers supplying fast food executives with food.

The dilemma with fast food is not a result of consumer apathy. The story is different. Fast food executives represent economic and political interests, which are the antithesis of organic food and family agriculture and society. Indeed, fast food executives are enemies of ecology and democracy: They buy food from companies, and have tremendous stakes in companies, which are devastating rural America and the rest of the world by poisoning nature and by marginalizing and destroying family farmers and peasants. Fast food executives are also the missionaries of American power: They see the world as their conquered province. Consumer pressure is good, but democracy and global resistance would be better to putting giant fast food chains, and their agribusiness suppliers, out of business.

Concentration of power in agriculture in the United States, allowing the growth of "mammoth farms run by hirelings,"[62] expanding the borders of silent spring with ever more potent sprays, is having deleterious effects on both wild nature and human nature. The farms of giant American agriculture are not that much different from the state farms of the former Soviet Union-present Russia: The same mania for mechanization; the same madness for the control of nature; the same contempt for venerable agrarian traditions and peasants / family farmers; the same fatal attraction to animal factories.

One has to visit an animal factory to be convinced that giant agriculture does not care about nature, culture, or our society's long-term interests. The smell and stink of death hang around animal factories like a plague. These killing operations are made to print money for corporations through the administration of enormous inhumanity, cruelty, suffering, and outright violence against hundreds and thousands of caged animals spending their short lives under conditions of mechanical barbarism. No civilization here. Pure slaughterhouse.

In chapters two to four I discussed the deleterious nature and effects of agrotoxins. At this point I need to close the circle with a brief examination of the political nature of the farmers' sprays.

In 1987, at the height of the anti-environment Ronald Reagan administration, probably one of the worst governments the United States has ever had, both the US Department of Agriculture and the National Academy of Sciences concluded that chemical pesticides "are responsible for a wide array of unacceptable negative effects on the environment."[63] They are right—but few people listened in 1987 or any time since 1987: America's fertile land is being poisoned entirely for political purposes. Pesticides have replaced the slaves at the plantation. And the owners of the plantation are addicted to their farm toxins.

One of the many nasty consequences of the addiction farmers have for pesticides is that they are paying a terrible price. They are giving birth to more and more terata, yes, human monsters, babies with severe birth defects, are born to farmers and to those who live near farmers. Researchers from the University of Minnesota and the US Environmental Protection Agency report that the deleterious human effects of agribusiness are pronounced in the spring wheat, potato, and sugar beet regions of western Minnesota whose farmers use extensive amounts of chlorophenoxy defoliant herbicides like 2,4-D and MCPA and fungicides. These scientists documented life-threatening birth defects in rural Minnesota among children born in the spring to pesticide applicators, farmers, and others who reside next to farmers.[64] The National Academy of Sciences also concluded in 1989 that conventional farming in many states is "the leading nonpoint [unregulated] source of water pollution."[65]

"Part of the trouble with talking about something like DDT," says the American poet Gary Snyder, "is that the use of it is not just a practical device, it's almost an establishment religion. There is something in Western culture that wants to totally wipe out creepy-crawlies, and feels repugnance for toadstools and snakes. This is fear of one's own deepest natural inner-self wilderness areas, and the answer is, relax. Relax around bugs, snakes, and your own hairy dreams."[66]

I agree with Gary Snyder. I also agree with professor Warren Porter of the University of Wisconsin who says "The world cannot afford to raise a generation of children with high proportions of altered aggression levels and reduced learning abilities." Porter complains that there is very little money for research to find out what pesticides do to people and nature. "There are more than 77,000 pesticides registered in this country," he says. "Almost none have been tested for neurological, endocrine, AND immune effects combined. Researchers who choose to pursue this work are often confronted with threats to job security and threats to the financial security of their immediate family."[67]

Despite this ugly and dangerous situation in the United States, there are plenty of scientists, bureaucrats, and businessmen who would swear of the safety of pesticides used in the farm. They say these biocides, which the chemical industry has dubbed them "crop protection chemicals," are a must for food production, providing "benefits" to society. Americans have cheap food because of pesticides. I don't wish to enter into any theological discussion over the public "benefits" of pesticides, which, in reality, are abstractions plucked out of thin air. In fact, a handful of global corporations manufacture these poisons and don't wish to have several scientists like Porter documenting the deleterious effects of their products. I already cited Bill Moyers' documentary, "Trade Secrets," which demonstrated that it is these corporations—not scientists or governments representing the interests of society—that define everything of importance, including science, around pesticides and other chemicals.[68]

All arguments on favoring "safe exposure" of humans to these poisons are ideological. And they mirror the views of corporations making money from them. Similarly, it is misleading to talk about a "threshold" determining the 'limit' of the deleterious or innocuous impact on life of any one of the toxins released into the environment. Say Barry Castleman and Grace Ziem, experts on occupational and environmental health, "the very concept of 'safe' exposures to any chemical is inherently unscientific. Indeed, the term 'threshold limit' embodies this unproven and probably unprovable concept that there is some known level of exposure which does not adversely affect the organism. Discarding the term 'threshold limit' is a necessary first step in correcting this false ideology of the past. Rather, the numerical values for exposure limits selected as 'acceptable' by one social group (scientists) for another social group (workers) is very much a political as well as a scientific process."[69]

Clearly there's a compelling story worth telling about the American society's deadly political dependence on agrotoxins, but this is not the place for that story. Suffice it to say, the defoliant herbicides, and some of the neurotoxin insecticides, were born in the heat and hatred of war. And herbicides were used as a weapon during the Vietnam War.[70] Herbicides also transformed agriculture, and because of that role of changing agriculture, primarily making it possible for farmers and agribusiness to own and cultivate huge expanses of land, herbicides became an important glue that keep giant agriculture together: Now it's easy for haciendas to remain haciendas. And for that reason, J.D. Fryer, a British scientist and director of the Weed Research Organization in Oxford, England, says weed killers "are considered to be among the greatest scientific advances" of the twentieth century.[71] The world's haciendas spent $20 billion in the year 2000 for herbicides. Finally, the global trade in pesticides in 1996 measured $30.5 billion. Ten agrochemical companies controlled 82 percent of that global market in agricultural poisons.[72]

The Dark and Shady Deals of Corporations Masquerading as Farmers

The idea of family agriculture in the United States is a paradox. Despite the fact there have always been farmers who have raised food in non-destructive ways, the dominant paradigm (of giant haciendas loaded with agrotoxins) has never allowed America's struggling small family farmers to operate at the center stage of agricultural research, public policy, government subsidies or public attention.

By the mid-1970s—when I used to attend those wrenching Congressional hearings on whether or not the family farm had a future in America—the family farm was dying. In 1975 Angus McDonald of the National Farmers Union spoke on the survival of family farming in testimony to a Senate subcommittee. He defended the wisdom of a 1902 acre-limitation law that forbade the federal government from subsidizing water to farmers with more than 160 acres of land. He spoke of the "dark and shady deals" of agribusiness giants in the Westlands Water District of California's Central Valley. McDonald said:

> My conclusion is that the purposes of the limitation law have been largely ignored. It appears that every subterfuge imaginable has been used in the Westlands District to sabotage honest and sincere enforcement. The disclosure of apparently fraudulent sales to individuals and to corporations masquerading as farmers calls to mind the Land Office scandals of the 19th century. Congress has ignored its oversight responsibility, and the Department of Interior seems to have become a creature of speculators and great landowners.[73]

Donald Worster, one of America's most eloquent environmental historians, argues that in the American West the alliance of agribusiness, water technicians, and the state bypassed democracy to exploit the water of the Colorado River for agribusiness crops. Worster's thesis, confirming the evidence from Greek and Roman history, is that you cannot mix wealth and empire with democracy and freedom. Agribusiness made the American West a "hydraulic society" fueled by a "coercive, monolithic and hierarchical system" of close relations.[74] Another brilliant analyst, A.V. Krebs, speaks for the fate of democracy and agribusiness in the entire country. He makes a powerful case that corporate agribusiness is killing America's family farm and its democratic institutions:

> [I]t is the very structure of our current [agribusiness] food production and delivery system and the self-serving policies that it generates that cause starvation throughout the world and hunger in our own country, while at the same time methodically eroding many of our most cherished moral values and democratic ideals...corporate agribusiness...[is] clearing millions and millions of human beings off productive land and relocating them where they might better serve the interests of an economic and politically powerful elite.[75]

The jacket of Krebs' book pictures a family farm next to a cemetery—the symbolism could not be more potent.

Thus it is all the more remarkable that, in the midst of forced evacuations from the land, there is an elementary experiment and discussion occurring in the United States on "sustainable" agriculture, meaning family farming. It is not surprising that the public experiment with alternative farming methods, funded since 1988 at about $12 million per year, has barely scratched the surface. Public and academic confusion persists as to what "sustainable" agriculture is all about. Most of my former colleagues in the Department of Natural Resource Sciences at the University of Maryland censor themselves when it comes to issues of family farming or sustainable agriculture. They keep studying and teaching the program of giant agriculture, always finding technical answers to the minute details of how you dominate nature, making the farmer an efficient grower. With the rare exception of professor Ray Weil, who teaches soil sciences, they refuse to admit there's such a thing as sustainable agriculture. In addition, there are few studies that point the way to radical change in public policy. Sustainable agriculture has barely taken a foothold in the United States. The power of the agribusiness system scares politicians, farmers, and researchers from even asking the proper questions. And when they do, they find little if any money for research. But they do face overwhelming disapproval.

Inimical to the Natural Order

This makes the Third World connection—how other people raise food—vital to America's civil society. Indigenous people, even more so than peasants, are close to perfecting sustainable methods of food and agriculture and development. Guillermo Delgado of the University of California-Santa Cruz says that "indigenous communities actively retrieve ancient sustainable agricultural practices to oppose environmental collapse and share their knowledge to promote self-sufficient methods."[76] Both rich and poor countries need to protect traditional agriculture. "This invaluable inheritance is nothing less than our ability to preserve the mutually symbiotic and always changing relationship between human society and nature. It takes concrete shape in the diversity of human culture and its most essential artifact, the ability to produce food under varying and unpredictable circumstances."[77]

H. David Thurston, professor of international agriculture and plant pathology at Cornell University, has a great deal of respect for traditional farming. Like other American scientists sent to the tropics with little if any appreciation for the complexity and science of peasant agriculture, he learned to respect the wisdom of peasant farming after several costly mistakes. He realized that the Andean peasants of Colombia have a superior mastery of growing potatoes—they are better farmers than those trained in the agricultural schools of the North. Thurston does not claim that traditional agriculture is scientific. He monopolizes science for modern, Western farming. Yet he recognizes sustainability in what the peasant does, particularly in the tropics where indigenous farming systems are a picture of natural ecosystems with their diversity, resilience, stability and efficiency. He says if only we could breed the 10,000 years of the peasant and indigenous farming experience and wisdom with "modern agricultural science" then we would be much closer to sustainability.[78] If only we could!

This is all well and good. Preserving traditional agriculture in the global political system of corporate hegemony is like installing in an anthropology museum beautiful Indian artifacts while the Indians themselves are slaughtered and then pushed to extinction. Traditional agriculture is of no more use to industrialized people than high-tech microwave ovens are of any practical significance to peasants. Traditional agriculture is sustainable because it is a live tradition of people unwilling to dominate nature or each other. Traditional agriculture is a fantastic science and legacy of living human cultures, which, unfortunately, has been threatened with perpetual mutilation, poisoning, and total destruction for millennia.

In a papyrus document in the British Museum dated 3,200 years ago, we get a glimpse of the landlords' violence against the peasant raising Egypt's grain. In this case, the scribes enforce the crippling taxes and the wretched conditions in the countryside. The ancient Egyptian observer asks:

> Do you remember the condition of the peasant-farmer confronted by the registration of the crop-tax when the snake has carried off one half [of the grain] and the hippopotamus the remainder? Mice infest the fields; locusts descend; cattle consume; sparrows impoverish the peasant-farmer. The residue which is on the threshing floor is lost: it is for robbers. The investment in hired cattle (?) is forfeited; the ox-team is dead through threshing and ploughing. The scribe has landed at the riverbank to register the crop, the agents carrying staves, the Nubian attendants palm ribs. They say: "Give grain", but there is none. They beat him violently; he is tied up and thrown into a well.[79]

Leo Tolstoy, writing nearly 100 years ago, explains why the violence against rural people continues. The peasants, he says, starve because they don't have enough land. Yet they toil that land even when they are on the verge of starvation. But the landlords sell the peasants' grain abroad to enrich themselves.[80]

Despite the vicious policies of the landlords and the state towards them, the peasants never waiver from their purpose, which is to raise food and culture in accord with the seasons and the gods. "Peasants," says Jose Lutzenberger, the agronomist and engineer who was the Minister for the Environment of Brazil from 1989 to 1992, "want to grow food and make a good life. Peasant culture leads to a diversified landscape, even though the original landscape may disappear. There will be a variety of production—tomatoes, fruit, vegetables, goats, sheep, handicrafts.

Where there is healthy peasant culture, there is social justice. When landlords own all the land, they don't care about food production—they can import it from anywhere. They care only about making money. And that means monocultures—whatever will grow under local natural and market conditions—coffee, sugar, cattle, coconuts. They ensure that the population remains as poor as possible, because of the need for cheap labor in the plantations."[81]

Lutzenberger is absolutely right. Peasants and landlords represent the ancient and the modern, the South and the North, traditional farming and agribusiness, the gentle and the plundering of the natural world, the polytheistic and multicultural with the monotheistic and monocultural (one-crop farming) in civilizations. The peasant / landlord schism is the greatest divide splitting the globe into perpetual wars of annihilation and crusades.

It is the landlords and their corporate creatures in the North and South that sponsor the "green revolution" project. Matthias Uzo Igbozurike, an American-educated Nigerian biologist, damned industrialized one-crop (monoculture) farming as a catastrophe—"inimical to the natural order, deleterious to ecospheric safety, and lethal to man's long-term interests."[82]

Uzo Igbozurike's warning in 1971 has done little to stop the voracious colonialism of one-crop industrial farming. Some of the choicest real estate in the Third World is used for the production of cash crops for export. The cruel paradox of hungry regions of the South exporting food to the already well-fed North makes up the bulk of international food trade.

The highly prized cocoa-chocolate bean, for instance, brings pleasure to consumers in the North but poverty, exploitation, and ecological impoverishment to the people of the South.[83] Africa's cocoa bean does become sweet chocolate for millions of people every day of the year. The road of this sweet bean from the fields of Ivory Coast to the candy store of North America and Europe, however, is paved with the toxins of the cash croppers and the tears of stolen children. The cultivation of cocoa is hard farming. It must follow all the nature-killing practices of plantations— growing one crop alone in vast quantities, poisoning everything else on the land, feeding that crop synthetic food. In addition, cash cropping demands monotonous, back-breaking labor, work that is increasingly done by child slaves from Benin, Mali and other impoverished African countries. These children are sold to slavers who then sell them directly to large cash crop farmers and cocoa plantations in Ivory Coast, Gabon, Cameroon and elsewhere. Chocolate comes to North Americans and Europeans often wrapped in much more than sweetness and flavor. Children's blood may just be one of the chocolate's ingredients.[84]

The outbreak of the Chiapas peasant rebellion in Mexico on January 1, 1994, the day that the North American Free Trade Agreement (NAFTA) took effect, was meant to awaken the whole world to the simmering discontent of peasants not just in Chiapas, Mexico, but elsewhere in the Third World as well. The Zapatista National Liberation Army that launched the Chiapas insurrection saw NAFTA as an effort to destroy the *ejido*, the communal land system, and steal indigenous farmland for industrial production. The rebels' seizure of private ranches sent out an unambiguous message that, just like the 1910 Zapata revolution, their fight was also for land.

Humbling the Global Power of Corporations

Concentration of power in land and agriculture on a global scale is pretty much the equivalent of a state of planetary siege. Militarization of the world food economy is incompatible with democratic institutions, food security, and sustainable human development. Breaking up agribusiness monopolies would have the virtue of releasing enormous wealth and creativity for the reconstruction of both rural societies and ecosystems. All the people of the earth live in the same commons. We can no longer import tropical fruit while indigenous people and peasants die of hunger.

Joan Dye Gussow, professor of nutrition at Columbia University, said in August 1994 that the rich people of the North better realize they are not alone in the world. They:

> share the biosphere with the poor. If the World Bank, the International Monetary Fund [IMF] and other representatives of our unjust economic system continue to starve them, their struggle to survive will change the planet for all of us. We cannot save ourselves without saving everyone. So we need to begin the urgent task of educating people about food—where it comes from, who produces it, at what cost to the environment—before it is too late.[85]

I agree with Joan Gussow: Food is nutrition, politics, ecology, and culture, all rolled into one. I would expand her food education to include a national and global political campaign to capture the ideas, enthusiasm, talent, dedication and commitment of countless civil society groups, non-governmental organizations (NGOs) struggling in defense of ecosystems and indigenous systems of knowledge and social relations.

In the United States reinventing agriculture would have the support of women, particularly those women who, through suffering, have realized they pay a disproportionate cost in disease and death from toxins in the environment. In February 1994, representatives from two NGOs, Greenpeace and WEDO (Women's Environment and Development Organization) met in Austin, Texas to initiate a campaign against toxic poisoning. They drafted a consensus statement, which says:

> We are Rachel's Children, named in honor of Rachel Carson, who was the first to sound the alarm on the link between pesticides and cancer. We are women from the United States, Canada, and Mexico, dedicated to ending the silence about the deterioration of women's health and its connection to the misuse of the environment.
>
> We are initiating a worldwide campaign to take action to prevent cancer—particularly breast cancer—as well as other diseases caused or triggered by preventable environmental factors. We do not accept the fact that one out of three people will get cancer, and one in every four will eventually die from it.
>
> Man-made toxins—such as organochlorines and nuclear pollutants—are being produced without regard to our lives, the lives of our families, future generations or the planet. These poisons are being disproportionately produced and dumped in neighborhoods of the poor, the disenfranchised and people of color. The United States, Japan and Germany, and many other countries export toxins to developing countries. In some areas, whole communities are being poisoned and destroyed.
>
> We demand accountability from corporate polluters who are sacrificing the health of millions for billions in profit. As a beginning, we seek the phase-out of the entire class of chlorinated organic chemicals and an end to the production and use of all nuclear power and weapons. With careful transitional planning, the use of hazardous materials and toxins can and must be replaced with clean production, renewable energy and healthy work.
>
> Women's lives and health have been compromised by the cancer establishment. We hold these agencies and institutions responsible for their inaction and failure to PREVENT cancer. We demand immediate action with a priority on prevention in all programs, policy and research areas.

We hold accountable our governments that are supposed to be protecting us. We challenge them to confront the polluters that are poisoning us and to stop them before millions more die. For too long, women have been excluded from decisions that profoundly affect our lives and our families. We demand our right to participate in all stages of decision-making about health and environmental matters.

We have the right to live in communities where the air we breathe, the water we drink, the food we eat and the places we work are clean and poison-free.

We invite all women to join us in our campaign to achieve these most basic of human rights. Together, with effort, we can create the political will and awareness necessary to address these urgent issues.[86]

What is remarkable about Rachel's Children is not merely their denunciation of the nexus of government, the cancer establishment, and the polluting and hazardous industries for giving them disease and death, but their recognition of the corporate source of their troubles. Breaking the American national silence about corporate power and control is probably the beginning of a new politics of ecological and social resistance.

In September 1994, some 173 citizens from around the country sent a letter to the nation's 15 leading environmental organizations telling them that their work would be peripheral if they failed to educate their members on the corporate cause of the country's environmental crisis. The environmental groups complained in July 1994 that not even "during the Reagan/Watt/ Gorsuch years" did they face polluters as determined as the corporations of the 1990s, companies determined to weaken federal environmental laws.

Taking corporations off our backs is no less ambitious than legislating agrarian reform in the land of agribusiness. Agrarian reform can only take place when American citizens take control of their destiny—when they understand the origins, fate, and importance of the food they eat; when they value agriculture as a way of life; when they appreciate the ecological unity and fragility of the planet. They must be ready to get the corporations not merely off their backs but off the backs of the people of Latin America, Asia, and Africa.

Education for the twenty-first century must emphasize that we are in this—the excruciatingly difficult task of building a gentle and sustainable global economy—together. No longer can we plunder the Third World while we say we mean well in our plunder. A South American researcher saw through the West's uncivilized mission. He said:

> How long will the West continue to believe itself involved in an act of charity towards the Third World? First, it was to 'civilize' it and the Third World was despoiled of its precious metals and sovereignty, then it was to 'develop' it and the Third World was dispossessed of its raw materials, then to 'modernize' it and the Third World was drained of its financial reserves whilst the North got rid of its industrial surplus and got back three dollars for every dollar it lent, and now it is to 'feed' it. What price will have to be paid this time for Western charity? Those in the majority in the Third World, the peasants, are already suffering the consequences. Enough of the hypocrisy! The countries of the South ask only for their freedom and respect for their sovereignty. The process of decolonization is not yet complete. Under such conditions, how can the North speak of co-operation, of aid?
>
> The peasants of the South are not asking for help or financial charity, any more than they asked for aid in foodstuffs. They ask only that their environment cease to be destroyed, that they cease to be deprived of natural means of production (land, water) and that they be paid a fair price for their products. In short, they want to be allowed to get on with their work.[87]

The family farmers of America, especially those with modest acreage, also want "to be allowed to get on with their work." Most of them are scared to death. When corporations move against them, they don't fight back. They are not organized to resist the agribusinessmen. Slowly, steadily, one by one, small farmers face the wasting machinery of banks, government policies, land grant universities, the merchants of technologies and poisons, the power and control of corporate agribusiness.

For example, Don Deichman is a failed Missouri farmer who tries to farm the volatile political and agricultural cropland of the Washington, DC metropolitan region. On our way to an academic conference, Deichman, his four-year-old daughter Hilary, and I spent the evening (June 4, 1994) with Deichman's mother-in-law, Joan Hershberger.

Joan is a former farmer in the exquisite Morrisson Cove of the bucolic Bedford County, Pennsylvania. She used to own a successful 300-acre dairy farm but after an accidental fire in the barn in 1981, she never made it back to farming. She sold her 90 milk cows and most of her land in 1988. Joan now looks after her granddaughter and prepares food for a catering service while her husband, Max, sells lemonade at a nearby shopping mall.

Joan Hershberger is unhappy about her condition, which reflects the much larger deteriorating state of thousands of farmers like her throughout the country. She talks about her personal tragedy in stoic terms but also wonders what would have been left for Hilary.

Deichman and I left her hospitable home early in the morning. She lives in a modest house, which is falling apart, with the ruins of a silo, abandoned agricultural machinery and chemicals telling the story of an engulfing social and ecological crisis in rural America. As we drove from Joan's abandoned dairy farm in New Enterprise to State College where Penn State University was hosting the conference, we passed through several communities with boarded barns and decaying farms. The countryside of Pennsylvania and the United States is increasingly becoming an immense rural factory sliced by main streets of bankers, insurance agents, merchants of fertilizers, pesticides and machines.

It was in the midst of this disintegrating rural society that the esoteric discussion of nearly 200 academic people about "environment, culture, and food equity" sounded so incongruous. Inside the academy, experts with steady jobs debating issues of life and death for absent rural people.

Of course, not all of the academic discourse at Penn State was marred by jargon and a depoliticized vocabulary. Bill Liebhardt, professor of biology and then director of the sustainable agriculture program at the University of California-Davis told the conference delegates that California barely has any more "wiggle room" left as a result of the toxic agricultural practices and policies of the last 50 years. And Gustavo Estava, a Mexican grassroots activist, described the "green revolution," the Western policy of funding the industrialization of Third World agriculture, as a monstrous experiment. "Technically speaking," he said, "what seemed to be the culmination of millennia of agricultural knowledge and experience happens to be just an extremely ephemeral, unsustainable productive regime, transmogrifying agri-culture into agro-business and destroying both nature and culture."

The Penn State conference gave a glimpse of the huge struggle ahead. The land grant universities and federal and state governments are locked to a considerable degree into the toxic practices and politics of agribusiness corporations. The only bright light in this bleak landscape is the emerging global grassroots resistance movement to industrial farming.

You Are for the Landlord or You Are for the Peasants

Peasants and landlords are fighting for land all over the globe. Supreme Court Justice William O. Douglas was right when he said, "You are either for the landlord or you are for the peasants."[88] Douglas appealed to the Americans' pride in their revolutionary political traditions—their Declaration of Independence, Constitution, and Bill of Rights. He urged them to come to their senses and, instead of trying to stop the peasant revolutions sweeping the world, they should join the peasants and make the revolutions.

Douglas's courageous stand took place at the peak of America's cold war, in 1952. The situation was so explosive that Douglas was convinced one needed to stay in a Third World village no more than a week to witness the unfolding cosmic drama for survival and hegemony.

Thirty-six years later, the Guatemalan bishops stated that the peasant's struggle for land was the singular characteristic of the tortured life of their country. And like Justice Douglas, the bishops sided with the peasants. In their Joint Pastoral Letter of February 29, 1988, the bishops said that:

> The cry for land is undoubtedly the strongest, most dramatic and most desperate cry heard in Guatemala. It bursts forth from millions of Guatemalan hearts yearning not only to possess the land, but to be possessed by it. It is a cry from the People of the Corn who, on the one hand identify with furrows, sowing and harvest, and who, on the other hand find themselves expelled from the land by an unjust and punitive system. They are like strangers in the land which belonged to them for thousands of years; they are considered second-class citizens in the nation forged by their extraordinary ancestors.
>
> Perhaps there is no subject which awakens more fierce passion and gives rise to more radical and irreconcilable positions than does the subject of land ownership...
>
> It is a fact that the majority of arable land is in the hands of a privileged few, while the majority of campesinos own no plot of land on which to sow their crops. This situation, far from pointing toward a solution, becomes day by day more harsh and painful. Certainly the critical problem of land ownership is at the very heart of the propagation of injustice...
>
> Campesinos have extreme difficulty in trying to move beyond their marginalization because of scant opportunities, lack of preparation, and due to the very structure of Guatemalan society which is organized for the benefit of a minority and with no regard for the vast majority of Guatemalans. It has come to seem natural for us to see the campesino or Indian dressed in rags,

sick, dirty, despised. We call the damp, unlivable and unsanitary shacks "folklore" and tourist attractions. We are not shocked to see tiny children trudging off with their machete or hoe early in the morning beside the men, to carry out a hard and poorly-paid day's work. We fail to react before the shameful spectacle of thousands of Indian peasants transported to the coastal plantations in trucks without security or even minimal comfort.[89]

One can substitute Third World for Guatemala, and the desperate reality is the same. The Zapatistas of Mexico and peasants all over Latin America, Asia and Africa are fighting for land and the integrity of the ecosystems they have been nurturing. A global coalition of NGOs, North and South, is chipping away at the monolith of industrialized societies—their orgiastic excesses and waste; their proselytizing, monotheistic, anthropocentric, messianic ideologies; their culture of violence and colonialism.

Elting E. Morrison says that in his country, the United States, there is:

> A developing mismatch between our extending knowledge of what we can do with the materials and forces in the world and our older, but less certain, understanding of what we have to do to be ourselves. And in this mismatching—such is the power in our machinery and such is the confusion about our real needs—we are likely to come away losers—ground down, blown up, twisted out of shape, crammed into computer-designed compartments, bored to death.[90]

Jose Lutzenberger of Brazil is convinced that "we are in a situation where people can no longer distinguish between the gallows and the plough; they cannot tell the difference between an instrument of domination and one of liberation."[91]

It is the peasants and the non-governmental organizations (NGOs), the entire civil society, which is providing the antidote to the gallows. United Nations conferences in the 1990s—including the Earth Summit, the United Nations Conference on Environment and Development (UNCED), in Brazil in 1992, the nutrition conference in Rome in 1992, the population meeting in Cairo in 1994, the 1995 summits in Copenhagen for social development and in Beijing for women, and the World Food Summit in Rome in 1996—have been a huge magnet for NGOs and private individuals to support the struggles for social justice and the protection of nature. Their networks—the connections between civil society organizations—spread their subversive message of liberation throughout the globe.

If grassroots organizations in the United States can join in solidarity with the groups in the Third World, together they can humble the hegemony of corporations. This would open the door for democratic and ecological ideas, technologies, and politics. Above all, we must put agrarian reform on the international agenda and re-legitimize the biological significance and wisdom of traditional systems of farming.

The farming practices of indigenous people are mirrors of nature: they preserve biological diversity, variability, natural selection and evolution. Rather than destroy, we must recognize the genius with which these cultures have cultivated food.

Hugh H. Iltis, professor of botany at the University of Wisconsin, recognized the crucial importance of what he called "primitive" or traditional farming systems. He knew that the green revolution, America's industrial agriculture exported to Latin America, Asia, and Africa since the 1940s, threatens the survival of the genetically rich ancestors of our most important crops. The wild, weedy, ancestors of corn, potatoes, wheat, and rice need absolute protection in their cradle regions by forbidding American agricultural scientists from interfering with the evolution of crop diversity in those regions of the world where the diversity of corn, rice, wheat, potatoes and other food crops is pronounced. He felt so strongly about the preservation of food crop diversity that he appealed to the world community and to his colleagues around the planet to *freeze* selected areas of the global agricultural genetic landscape to protect the treasures of primitive or traditional farming. Writing in 1974 he said that:

> 'Progress'-oriented agriculture and massive technology, often blindly conspiring with greed, hunger, population pressures and ignorance, deliberately replace this low-yielding primitive diversity [of traditional agriculture] with high-yielding advanced uniformity...the only way we can hope to save a crop's dynamic evolutionary potential is to literally protect the diverse 'ancestral' genotypes in their cradle region from modern agricultural interference, in effect, by 'freezing' the genetic landscape, even to the extent of subsidizing primitive agricultural systems. In the case of truly wild 'ancestral' species we need to preserve them outright...
>
> Only by the deliberate and permanent preservation of selected specific local genetic landscapes, scientifically justified, politically negotiated, and perhaps internationally subsidized, and by the deliberate exclusion of agriculture "improvements" as represented by the Green Revolution and

modern agricultural technology is there any hope for long-range success in
continuing the evolution of our crops.[92]

So, for example, we could protect the Andean potato stocks because
they are the original source for our commercial potatoes; the survival
of these genetically rich but poor-yielding potatoes guarantees that
our potatoes will not become extinct. Second, Peruvian potatoes are
genetically diverse and rich in proteins—assets of great value. It would
make sense to make a potato preserve of Lake Titicaca basin, the home
of the Peruvian and Bolivian potatoes. Western potato experts would be
prohibited from pushing their potato schemes in this potato preserve.
This kind of protection would also be necessary for maize or corn in
Mexico and Peru.[93]

Feeling at Home in America

Iltis is right. Negotiating the "green revolution" out of much of the
Third World would be a boon both to the social and biological systems
sustaining life on earth. Agrarian reform of a planetary scale and scope
may even help us understand the significance of indigenous or native
agriculture.

In the United States, we must recognize the wisdom of our rapidly
disappearing Native American culture. We have a great deal to learn from
our own indigenous peoples. Explains ethnobotanist Gary Paul Nabhan:

> To feel at home here, to learn from our predecessors on this continent,
> each of us must kneel on the ground, put an ear to the earth, and listen...
> the Native American agricultural legacy is more than a few hard, tasty
> cultigens waiting to be "cleaned up" genetically for consumers, and then
> commercialized as novelty foods. Our goal must be something beyond
> blue corn chips, tepary bean party dips, amaranth candy, sunflower seed
> snacks, and ornamental chiles. These nutritious crops deserve to be revived
> as mainstays of human diets, and not treated as passing curiosities. These
> cultivated foods are rich in taste and nutrition, yes, but they are also well
> adapted to the peculiarities of our land.[94]

Nabhan is right, but we must also water our imaginations and
crops with political action. The solution to environmentally destructive
agribusiness is not mysterious: It demands the courage of an entire
generation. A generation of environmentalists, small family farmers,
organic, sustainable farmers, farm workers, factory workers, politicized

women such as Rachel's Children, and students. We must form alliances with our partners in the Third World to resist toxic exploitation and the loss of our democratic institutions.

Family farmers, peasants, and indigenous people must have their share of the land. Agrarian reform is the mechanism by which land and power can be redistributed for sustainable human development. In the United States, a rural class of small-scale family farmers, Native Americans, and black farmers must take back the land that has been taken away from them by large agribusiness corporations.

Congress granted homesteads of 160 acres in the 1860s to those willing to take up farming as a way of life, but the effort did not last very long. Corporations, breaking the social contract of the homestead law, and land grant universities, stole the land with false promises and loans; they also corrupted the government, and pushed American agriculture toward perpetual crisis. During the New Deal programs of the 1930s, the federal government assisted families of sharecroppers and helped over 10,000 families become landowners. The federal government purchased and then divided 1,865,000 acres of land. Previous tenant farmers were empowered by owning their own land, and inequitable relationships in the rural South were rectified forever.[95]

Approximately 2,267 families among the New Deal land-reform beneficiaries were black, a revolutionary program in the midst of the racism and rigid caste system of the rural south. Creating a black land-owning class in a white plantation economy was both disruptive and de-colonizing. It politicized the recipients: Landless tenants who received land in Mississippi created the Mississippi Freedom Democratic Party. They elected the first black to the Mississippi legislature since Reconstruction and galvanized political support for the Civil Rights Movement.

In 1943 Congressional racism and hostility killed America's only land-reform experiment in the twentieth century. At the same time, preparations for World War II, the building of military bases and war factories, struck another blow against black farming. The federal government disproportionately dispossessed rural black communities in Southeast. Many blacks did not have clear titles to their lands. So the US military confiscated some of those lands. Black communities lost land in Alabama, Georgia, Florida, South Carolina, North Carolina and

Tennessee.[96] Nevertheless, despite such racist policies against the black rural society, more than 50 percent of the black beneficiaries of the New Deal agrarian project survived the military's taking of black land during WWII, maintaining ownership of their land for 30 years.[97]

Agrarian reform begins with simple arithmetic: Divide America's 420 million acres of cropland by 40, for instance, and you create 10.5 million 40-acre-farms: Enough to provide a comfortable living to probably 10.5 million farmers and their families. Of course, it would be madness to hope that agrarian reform could have been successful in the 1990s, and on the dawn of the twenty-first century, given the hegemony of the Republican Congress, a legislature usually crafting laws to legitimize the outright theft of our country's resources by corporations, particularly land under federal jurisdiction. Yet there is logic and morality to the dream of agrarian reform: If we do nothing, catastrophe is certain, and rural America and family farming will disappear within 20 years.

The murderous Oklahoma bombing of a federal government building full of civil servants in April 1995 was a very violent episode in the social disintegration of rural society in America. Hysterical anti-government rhetoric regarding property rights provides the ideological justification for predatory policies on behalf of corporations. Yet the hate talk also divides the family farmers: Fertilizers can feed crops, but they can also become lethal weapons.

The struggling and disappearing family farmers are witnessing their own demise by no fault of their own. And like in so many other disasters, the twentieth century was the killer time for agriculture in the United States: In the 1920s, about 600,000 farmers per year were forced to abandon farming. The extremely violent rural exodus became a stampede from 1940 to 1960 when more than 1,000,000 farmers per year had to say goodbye to rural America and their dream of a good life from raising food. America's farm population in 1940 was 30.5 million people. In the early 1970s, the number of farmers in rural America had dropped to less than a third of what it was merely 30 years earlier. In other words, there were less than 10 million farmers and their families in the United States in the early 1970s. In the next chapter I explain why black farmers rushed to get out of agriculture as if their lives depended on that desperate act. From 926,000 black farmers in the 1920s, there were some 46,000 left in 1974. The loss of 95 percent of black farmers in 54 years was a calamity for the black people of the United States. The former slaves lost nearly everything they gained after centuries of servitude.

In 1979, the farm population had sunk to about 6 million.[98] The 1980s dealt another violent blow against rural America. Rapid and unprecedented disintegration struck hundreds of farm town and communities throughout the contiguous Farm Belt States. So many farm people were kicked off their farms and communities that society and social services and institutions nearly collapsed in a huge swath of the countryside of the United States. And on the dawn of the twenty-first century, rural America has been cleansed of family farmers, with most of the food (more than 75 percent) being produced by a few thousand very large farmers and corporations.

On the dawn of the twenty-first century, the majority of the surviving family farmers live and work below the poverty level, and most incomes are earned outside of farming all together. Giant agriculture is responsible for this national disaster. For example, it is causing the horrendous persistent poverty crippling rural life and family farming in the countryside of the Great Plains (Iowa, Kansas, Minnesota, Nebraska, North Dakota, and South Dakota).[99] Dozens of thousands of family farmers are forced out of agriculture every year. In the 1980s about 200,000 family farmers per year abandoned agriculture. In the 1990s the cruel departure from agriculture claimed some 100,000 family farmers per year.[100] Does anyone pay attention to these signs of social collapse?

Meanwhile, the top one-half percent of American families, the ruling class, *increased* its wealth between 1983 and 1989 alone by $1.45 trillion[101]—taxable money that the government could use to finance a significant portion of an agrarian reform project.

Perhaps the argument for agrarian reform is best summarized with this anecdote. In 1992, John Pitney, a United Methodist minister, led a tour of religious leaders through California's San Joaquin Valley, an irrigated desert controlled by agribusiness. The desert now produces fruit, nuts, and vegetables in great abundance. John Pitney and his friends were astonished to discover these high-tech haciendas, "farmers" such as Tenneco, Castle and Cook, Gallo, J.G. Bosworth and H.J. Heinz. Says Pitney:

> We left [eastern San Joaquin Valley], a country full of small orchards, communities and visible activity, where we had driven along winding

roads following the contours of the land. We entered [western San Joaquin Valley], a country where, for miles and miles on straight roads through straight-rowed vineyards, we drove and saw no people, no homesteads, no community. The bus began to stir with hushed conversations at the woe of an economy that *'joins house to house and adds field to field'* until a great loneliness is made in the middle of the land.[102]

Chapter 6

What Happens to a Dream Deferred?

In the Heart of Darkness

The legacy of the plantation is loneliness and fear, which is why I decided to go to North Carolina during the third week of February 1998 to attend a conference on the loss of land by black farmers in the United States. I thought I was well prepared for what promised to be a forum for academic discussion and grassroots solidarity for the remaining black farmers and their few supporters.

I was scheduled to deliver one of the "academic" papers—and I chose to talk about the loss of land by African peasants as a result of the violence of European colonizers of Africa who forced Africans to grow cash crops for them and the European market. Cash cropping, I was going to argue, became the royal road to making African agriculture the antithesis of African culture. With cash cropping, and the plantation model of development that such a policy implied, the Europeans sowed seeds of hunger and colonialism in Africa.

I borrowed the title of my paper, "All of Africa's Gods Are Weeping," from Chinua Achebe, the Nigerian author of *Things Fall Apart*, the powerful 1959 indictment of European colonialism in Africa. I connected slavery and cash cropping in Africa with the African slave trade that Europeans engaged in when they sent Africans to American plantations to develop cash crops in the new world. The descendants of those African American slaves are the disappearing black farmers of the United States in the 1990s and 2000s.

Despite my thinking quite comprehensively about the legacy of colonialism in both Africa and America, I felt unease that it was possible—as it happened to me at numerous other conferences—that for at least three days I was probably going to be trapped in useless and seemingly endless discussions.

In 1982, I told a group of professors (at an academic conference about food and agriculture) that America needed agrarian reform to increase the number of family farmers from thousands to millions. By agrarian reform I meant that the government should break up the huge agribusiness plantations and give the land to deserving family farmers. However, a philosophy professor from the University of Florida characterized my proposal as "un-American"—an insidious, illiterate, and mean perspective that was probably shared by many of the conference participants because no one found it objectionable to denounce it.

I also knew from living in America since 1961 that black people were still crippled, nearly handicapped to death, from the powerlessness and poisons of four hundred years of slavery. Yes, black Americans are "free," but what kind of freedom do they enjoy? Those among them who are farmers are becoming almost extinct. What kind of freedom is that? According to the US Bureau of the Census in 1900 there were 740,670 "Negro and other" (black) farmers in the United States. In 1920 black farmers increased to their highest number ever: 922,914. There has been a downward trend since 1920. In 1969 there were 90,141 black farmers left in the United States, and by 1992 the number had been reduced to 18,816. In other words, black farmers declined by about 98 percent between 1920 and 1992.

And in North Carolina where I was going to the Second National Black Land Loss Summit, the situation is equally tragic: In just fourteen years, between 1978 and 1992, black farmers declined by 68 percent, the number going from 5,820 to 1,866.

Pearlie Reed said at a government hearing on the fate of small farmers, September 11, 1997, that black farmers were convinced that the US Department of Agriculture—for which he served as its chief black spokesperson in the position of the acting assistant secretary for administration—was discriminating against them, cheating them of their dignity—and loans that could keep them farming. This senior government official dared suggest that the agency that paid his salary, the US Department of Agriculture, was probably conspiring to take the land of black farmers. I was so impressed by his honesty that I sent him a memorandum on September 17, 1997 asking him if he would agree I could do a study of that awful policy.

I never heard from him but, instead, I met with his soft-spoken yet determined white chief-of-staff, Catherine Gugulis, who shared Reed's suspicion of the likely monstrous behavior of the US Department of Agriculture. Finally, I knew that some of the aggrieved black farmers had taken USDA to court charging all the things that Reed implied USDA was responsible for several decades against black farmers—harassment, delayed loans, no loans, misinformation, paternalism, outright racism— and foreclosures, the taking of their land.

With all these things in my mind, I was certain my early misgivings were misplaced. This could not be a typical "academic" meeting—with so much useless talk by people with so little courage and practically no political and social consciousness or responsibility. The stakes were too high. It was bound to be a very interesting, even provocative, political event staged as it was in the midst of Halifax County, North Carolina's largest slave-owning plantation economy for centuries.

On Wednesday, February 18, 1998, I drove the four-hour 200-mile trip to the conference site, Franklinton Center at Bricks, Enfeld, North Carolina. The Franklinton Center at Bricks, where I was to spend four days and nights, was not just another southern plantation with a cruel history of oppression and slavery. It was also the plantation society's police, "a massive farm property where slaves were afflicted." It provided training on how to make slaves of men and to "subdue" and "break in" unruly slaves. Right outside of the Guest House where I slept there was once a "whipping post" for "breaking the uncivilized nigger."

We get an idea of that "breaking process" for the destruction of the slaves as human beings—the kind of work done at the Franklinton Center at Bricks—from a letter disseminated during the land loss summit. This letter was written in 1712 by William Lynch, a plantation owner from West Indies, and was addressed to plantation owners in Virginia. The slaveholders of the colony of Virginia invited William Lynch to teach them more effective methods of slave control.

Lynch said to the "gentlemen" of Virginia on the bank of the James River:

> Take the meanest and the most restless nigger and strip him of his clothes in front of the remaining male niggers, the female, and the nigger infant, tar and feather him, tie each leg to a different horse faced in opposite directions, set him afire and set both horses to pull him apart in front of the remaining niggers. The next step is to take a bull whip and beat the remaining nigger male to the point of death in front of the female and the infant. Don't kill him, but put the fear of God in him, for he can be useful for future breeding. Then take the female, run a series of tests on her to see if she will submit to your desires willingly. Test her in every way because she is the most important factor for good economics. If she shows any sign

of resistance in submitting completely to your will, do not hesitate to use the bull whip on her to extract that last bit of bitch out of her. Take care not to kill her, for, in doing so, you spoil good economics. When in complete submission, she will train her offspring in the early years to submit to labor when they become of age.... We reversed nature by burning and pulling one civilized nigger apart and bull whipping the other to the point of death—all in her presence. By her being left alone, unprotected, with the male image destroyed, the ordeal caused her to move from her psychological dependent state to a <u>frozen independent state</u>. In this frozen psychological state of independence she will raise her male and female offspring in reversed roles. For fear of the <u>young male's life</u> she will psychologically train him to be <u>mentally weak and dependent but physically strong</u>. Because she has become psychologically independent, she will train her female offspring to be psychologically independent. What have you got? You've got the nigger woman out front and the nigger man behind and scared. This is a perfect situation for sound sleep and economics.

It was this monstrous making of an American holocaust—on top of the genocide of native Americans—that supported the plantation political economy of the United States and North Carolina in general and Franklinton Center and Tillery in particular.

One of the most politically relevant, intriguing research findings came from the technical work of Bob Edwards from East Carolina University and Anthony Ladd from Loyola University of New Orleans, Louisiana. These two sociology professors study pigs in North Carolina. They said that "pork production" has gone through quite a dramatic transformation since the early 1980s when some 11,400 hog farmers raised about 2.5 million pigs. By 1998 the hogs of North Carolina soared to almost 11 million while the hog farmers dropped to around 3,000. But one of their main conclusions is that "where the pigs are, is where black people live in North Carolina." This harsh reality mirrors the brave new emerging plantation in the United States—the breaking process at work.

In this rural world, things are not what they appear to be. A system of giant corporations and government agencies is making most of the decisions of what millions of people will eat, if they eat at all. A handful of corporate executives have the final say of what gets sown, produced, harvested, processed and marketed. This is a system, furthermore, that treats animals like cogs of a machine, and land as a mere commodity. In contrast to the original plantation with its slaves and its usual one cash crop—for instance: cotton, sugar, peanuts, tobacco, corn—the new plantation (going under such names as conventional farm or agribusiness) is still the production of one or a few cash crops, but it is a much more violent place than the slave farm it replaced. Now this giant food and agriculture organization considers the entire world as a potential hacienda. It no longer "breaks" unruly slaves to a Christian god-fearing work ethic. Instead, it puts out of business any family farmer who refuses to become its voluntary slave.

Thus, the foreclosures, the taking of the land of black farmers by the US Department of Agriculture, is probably part and parcel of an agribusiness scheme to empty rural America of unruly people, particularly people who are descendants of unruly plantation slaves. It is not surprising, then, that mechanical pig farmers are invading black rural communities in eastern North Carolina. The stink, filth, ecocide, and human-life threatening pollution of the hog factories bring the deleterious urban industrial development model into the countryside and make a factory out of rural society. And because the black people of rural North Carolina are so few and largely powerless, they become the targets of large hog operations and other plantation farmers.

When my turn came to address the conference, I summarized my paper. I said the gods of Africa are weeping over the hunger and destitution of more than 200 million human beings in sub-Saharan Africa. I traced that calamity to cash cropping, the original plantation model of food and agriculture devised by the European slavers of Africa to "break" Africans into slaves. I explained that the slavers moved their plantation model to the Americas with the result they slaughtered millions of Native Americans who refused to become slaves, and imported millions of African slaves to man their cash cropping plantations. And, finally, I made the connection between that plantation agriculture practiced in the United States and the destruction of the black farmers.

I don't know what impact, if any, my modest contribution, and that of the sociology professors revealing the insidious corporate pig invasion of rural black communities, had on the audience. Certainly the "academic" discussion that followed the presentations was too cursory to reveal the changing mood of the participants. In addition, during Thursday afternoon there were practically no black farmers in the conference room.

The Theft of Black Land

All that changed during the next day, Friday, 20 February 1998: Black farmers had come in relatively large numbers in an audience of some 200 people. At about nine in the morning Gary Grant, the black man who organized the conference, opened the day's program with a denunciation of the US Department of Agriculture that spearheaded the theft of land from black farmers all over the United States. He spoke with great passion and immense sorrow about his father, Matthew, who did not survive the twenty-two year foreclosure proceedings, the "breaking process" against him by the US Department of Agriculture. Gary said that some of the people who marched in the civil rights struggle of the 1960s and 1970s are the farmers who are losing their land. Besides, those farmers opened their homes to those who marched for civil rights. Marcus Tillery, a young black professor at the black North Carolina Agricultural & Technical State University at Greensboro, North Carolina, continued Gary Grant's message: The black people of Mississippi, he said, are well represented in Congress, but they are getting nothing back in return. Black leaders are failing black people throughout the United States, including Halifax County, North Carolina, where black farmers are losing a lot of land. "We negotiated," he said, "this far in the hole. We need to get back swinging. Be ready to take the land back taken away from you. We must target people who have their feet on our throat. This must become part of our agenda."

Marcus Tillery got a standing ovation. The passion for land was evident—not merely stopping foreclosures, but, just as fundamentally, getting back all the land that was stolen from the black people through the plantation "breaking" process. Now I began to understand why Gary Grant entitled the 1712 letter of the slave owner, William Lynch, "And the Message is Still True." He obviously meant that the plantation had mutated, but had survived. Its brutal "tar and feather" method of teaching the slaves a lesson by tearing them apart was no longer feasible as it would be a criminal offense. But its psychological warfare and soul-killing "breaking process" was very much alive in foreclosure, a technical legal term designed to hide the cruelty and violence of taking a person's land.

Foreclosure is also related to the British tradition of enclosures whereby the English landlords used the parliament in passing laws for taking the land from the English peasants and their tenants, converting the English Isles and Ireland into their private haciendas. It took the British landed ruling class several bloody centuries to destroy the English peasants and enslave Ireland. Foreclosure captures all that violence in what appears to be a nonviolent process of lenders auctioning property to be repaid. The violence is in the destruction of the moral economy and soul of the foreclosed farmer; the legal process becoming the breaking of his being, separating him from the land he loves, crushing his dreams. Foreclosure also ends with the farmer's utter humiliation, finding himself in the street with nothing, becoming a victim of the technology of power developed in the plantation. Its "breaking process" (now foreclosure) slowly wears down a person's defenses—psychological, economic, social, political, and cultural. And, indeed, foreclosure does "break" a person.

Pearlie Reed talked to all the people at the conference at lunchtime about his own understanding of foreclosure. Pearlie Reed, one of eighteen brothers and sisters in a black family living several miles away from the closest rural road in eastern Arkansas, was the US Department of Agriculture's assistant secretary for administration in 1998. "The only reason my parents saved their farm from foreclosure," he said, "is that they had the good sense not to deal with the US Department of Agriculture. I am 49 years old and I have been [an employee] of the US Department of Agriculture for 28 years. Don't believe that USDA has no money to resolve the financial problems of black farmers. USDA does have money to fund its projects. With the possible exception of five or six people in the entire bureaucracy of the US Department of Agriculture and the US Justice Department, there's no one who wants to give one red cent to black farmers. Nobody in power is taking black farmers seriously. Some listen to them, but they don't follow up. The system of the US Department of Agriculture in the countryside, the county committee system, does not give a damn about what the Secretary of Agriculture thinks. This committee system is accountable to state and local powers, which, in turn, reflect the interests of old plantation owners. It's a patronage system. The President himself can do nothing to change what these farm county committees do. It's in the law. Black farmers need good lawyers—that's the way for any recourse. Don't bother with

USDA officials. Finally, the lawyers of the US Department of Justice who represent USDA in its dispute with black farmers don't give a rat's ass what I think."

Pearlie Reed had tragedy etched on his face. He spoke the truth. He probably knew he was doomed. He probably knew he was used by the very US Department of Agriculture that had put him temporarily in such a senior post. His presence, his blunt talk, his spontaneous siding with the powerless and discriminated black farmers probably encouraged them to hope the hopeless dream of making it in the plantation. But he tried to dispel that dream. He warned black farmers to stay out of USDA reach—exactly like his dirt poor father did. He too cut short his high visibility position as assistant secretary—abandoning any pretense of helping black farmers—and on March 2, 1998 he went back to his technical assignment in USDA's natural resources conservation service. He probably said enough of keeping up appearances. But another farmer, Eddie Slaughter, had something different to say about the vanishing Pearlie Reed.

The Skin Game

Eddie Slaughter is one of the black farmers who joined several other black farmers in 1997 suing USDA for "willful and continuous racial discrimination." His experience includes nineteen years of putting up with the humiliations of the bureaucracy of USDA both at home, the white patronage farm committee system of Buena Vista, Georgia, and in Washington, DC. He is playful and even philosophical at the pain and suffering he has endured, a process he describes as the "skin game."

"Did you see Pearlie Reed," he said to me as we stood outside the Guest House after Pearlie Reed's keynote address. "He is stressed to the breaking point. He won't last much longer, I guarantee you. All the time his fingers are pressing his forehead—as if they are trying to take the pain away. He looks so much older than his age. He is 49 and I am 47. The skin game is doing him in."

"What do you mean by the skin game," I asked.

"Here's what I mean," he said. "Long time ago, a couple of black freemen were pretending to sell each other. But the joke turned deadly when they accepted money from a white plantation owner who immediately treated them as slaves. And when one of the black men explained to the planter he had it all wrong, this was a skin game they were playing, the planter had him bull whipped and enslaved. The difference between then and now is this: The skin game has become extremely sophisticated. Now black people are not selling each other for money, but they are sold nevertheless. They are used as a level of protection for those whites holding power. The white leadership of USDA, for example, put Pearlie Reed to face the wrath of black farmers while they stay aloof from the despicable consequences of the racist policies of their agency. It's like Pearlie Reed said. No one with power (and that means white people) takes us (black farmers) seriously. The skin game covers up the racism of America. White agribusiness corporations and farmers and USDA are taking our land by design. No secret in that."

Eddie Slaughter is probably right. He can almost smell racism. He has a keen sense of detecting feelings of hostility between white and black people—however much that antagonism is being camouflaged and adapted to the convenience of the moment. His "skin game" is another form of the plantation owner's "breaking" of the unruly slaves. The system continues, but in a different structure, organization, and agenda.

Consider this: In February 1997 USDA's Office of the Inspector General and Pearlie Reed's Civil Rights Action Team released information denouncing the state of civil rights within America's federal agricultural bureaucracy from 1983 to 1997. We need to remember that the Reagan administration dismantled USDA's own legal mechanisms for civil rights in 1983. This certainly gave a signal to the 2,750 white patronage farm county committees in the countryside to ignore the needs of black farmers—and probably sparked works of outright racism against them. But Reagan's policies, bad as they were, do not explain the disorder, indeed, moral collapse, of USDA on everything that has to do with being fair to *all* farmers, protecting them from discrimination, intolerance, racism. USDA could not even keep count of how many black farmers filed complaints for abuses they suffered in trying to get a loan to farm or to enter agriculture.

The incidents that black farmers describe in their dealings with agriculture officials—harassment, misinformation, arbitrary reductions of their loans, getting loans not at the growing season, not getting loans at all, forcing them into foreclosure and taking their land, and visiting on them other acts of frustration, anxiety, humiliation, and mental distress—are mind boggling. In addition, one would be overly charitable to characterize USDA's own lawyers in the Office of the General Counsel as merely hostile to civil rights. Pearlie Reed's February 1997 report, "Civil Rights at the United States Department of Agriculture," page 55, says that the legal positions of these lawyers on civil rights "are perceived as insensitive at the least, and racist at worst."

And, finally, despite the fact Pearlie Reed—as the assistant secretary for administration—was USDA's senior official on civil rights, he had neither the authority nor the resources to do what he had to do to enforce the civil rights laws of the United States—and the regulations of his own agency—see to it that qualified black farmers who needed loans got them, and bring to an end all past discrimination. Thus between 1983 and 1997 black farmers filed 874 complaints because (1) they were denied equal protection under the law (which is a violation of Title VI of the Civil Rights Act of 1964); and (2) they were also deprived of due process in the handling of their complaints (a violation of the Fifth Amendment to the US Constitution). Neither of these injuries to the human rights of so many black farmers is a minor infraction of domestic or international law.

The US Department of Agriculture did the awful things it did in the 1980s and 1990s because it is following a long-standing tradition coming out of the "breaking" of human beings, using persistently extreme violence to crush any spirit of freedom in the slaves of the plantation economy of the American South. With this theory—which Eddie Slaughter captures so perceptibly with his "skin game" metaphor—I am explaining what, otherwise, might be interpreted as bizarre behavior, a fluke in the daily work of a law-abiding federal farm service bureaucracy.

Resistance

Eddie Slaughter's troubles started in 1978 when he tried to borrow some money from the US Department of Agriculture—always the last resort for farmers in need—to purchase a farm from a relative. The farm county committee turned him down and, as revenge, funded a couple of white farmers to buy that piece of land. Eddie Slaughter blew the whistle. He complained about his troubles with USDA over National

Public Radio. But nothing made a difference. And now, nearly 20 years later, in front of the Guest House of what was the bloody ground of a slave plantation at Franklinton Center at Bricks, Halifax County, North Carolina, he was telling me his story, trying to help me understand the skin game while his two teenage sons, his most important crop, dressed in huge colorful fluffy outfits, milled around us saying nothing but listening intensely. I too listened to Eddie Slaughter intensely while he spoke fast with that distinctive southern accent—what Richard Wright describes as "hurried speech, in honeyed drawls"—speaking and moving and dancing in place, grinning the smile of a man, angry, but in full control, and even charitable towards his enemies.

Another black man, Samuel Taylor, the executive director of the Black Farmers and Agriculturists Association—and a friend of Eddie Slaughter—added a crucial detail that made the insidious and explosive paradox of the skin game more tenable as a theory.

Taylor, son of a farmer from Alabama, is one of the lawyers representing the black farmers in their class action suit against the US Department of Agriculture. I met with him at ten-thirty in the morning on Tuesday, January 27, 1998 in his Washington, DC, Georgetown office on Thomas Jefferson Street. Taylor is an ambitious political man, but he was also born in the plantation system of the South, in the "hateful web of cotton culture." He speaks softly, slowly, deliberately and with precision. He handed me *The Movable School Goes to the Negro Farmer*, a 1936 book written by Thomas Monroe Campbell, a student of Booker T. Washington and one of the first black farm extension agents in the country. This remarkable autobiography of this daring man was published by the Tuskegee Institute in Alabama, a school devoted to the uplifting of the black people from the shackles of the plantation. Campbell concluded that the black farmer, whom he tried to help, "is constantly in debt, hungry, sick and cold, and without civil protection."

Thomas Campbell did not exaggerate. A white employee of the US Department of Agriculture, Frank D. Alexander, reached similar conclusions in 1944 about the black people living under the brutal hegemony of the cotton plantations in Coahoma County, Mississippi. Alexander studied the cotton plantation society of Coahoma very carefully from its inception in 1833. He found that when blacks moved to the white plantations in the rich flat lands of Coahoma County in the 1840s from the nearby hill counties, they lost the little food self-sufficiency they had. In the cotton plantation of Coahoma the tenant and, especially, the sharecropper, had nothing but daily hard work. He was forbidden to have a garden. He had to buy his food from his landlord. He was forbidden to talk or have any relations with anybody in the neighborhood or from the outside world without the explicit approval of the owner of the plantation. In fact all agencies or services of the state and the federal government were meaningless unless they went through the good offices of the plantation. The planter class had absolute control over their tenants and sharecroppers. For all practical purposes, the sharecroppers and, to somewhat lesser extent, the tenants of Coahoma County, Mississippi, were slaves of the cotton plantation when Alexander put together, in 1944, his extraordinary report, "Cultural Reconnaissance Survey of Coahoma County, Mississippi." The only civilizing influence in the barbaric culture of Coahoma came from the Methodist women at Clarksdale, the county seat. These women tried, sporadically and quite unsuccessfully, to bring to an end their husbands' habit of lynching their black slaves. Alexander is right to say that Coahoma County "never experienced an invasion of a new political, social, or religious movement." Even the Grange, a national political club advancing the interests of family farmers, did not last long in Coahoma. It opened a local chapter at Clarksdale in 1875, and abandoned Coahoma in 1887. Alexander said:

> The great mass of farmers in the county are Negro sharecroppers who, as one of them pointed out, do not have 'the privilege' of being a good farmer which according to him would be to 'raise some of everything he can'. It is interesting that several Negro sharecroppers who were interviewed conceived of a good farmer as one who carried on a diverse operation. One Negro cropper said a good farmer is 'a man who keeps his crops jam up, including his house—a worker who don't need nobody to stay on him.'…The Negro group is defined by all whites of whatever status as an inferior group which must be kept in its low caste position. Care is taken to maintain segregation and prevent the Negro group from assuming any position which might be called 'social equality'. Negro people are almost universally thought of as farm laborers and domestic servants. It is difficult for most whites to conceive of them as capable or desirous of occupying any other role. Because Negroes are conceived of as inferior and work animals, the whites see little wrong with the poor educational facilities provided for Negroes or the denial to them of the ballot. A peculiar ambivalent attitude to the Negro exists among the whites. They will complain of the inefficiency

of Negro labor, condemn them violently for their shiftlessness, and even wish they had fewer of them; yet at the same time they constantly display their dependency on them, revealing beyond a shadow of doubt that they are unwilling to give up their Negroes without considerable protest."[1]

Samuel Taylor, speaking to me sixty-two years after Thomas Campbell, and fifty-four years after Frank Alexander, confirmed those men's harsh assessment of the plight of the black rural people in the United States. Taylor painted a picture of oppression that sets the "skin game" in the sweat and terror of the young black men down to nearly yesterday. He said:

> What happened to the black farmers since the Civil War is nearly a holocaust of racism and violence. The US Department of Agriculture is the only government agency that delivers paychecks to farmers. But that kind of money goes through the state and, particularly, the county committee system. White Catholics may dislike white Protestants, and Protestants may despise Catholics, but all white farmers hate black people. Also, up to very recently, many black farmers were not educated as to how USDA does business. The combination of white racism at the county committees and the illiteracy of black farmers conspired to run them out of agriculture. Moreover, those of the blacks who were tenants to plantation owners were slaves under all circumstances, hence the rapid exodus of black people from rural America to cities in the North. My father owned his farm. The practical consequence of that was that I rarely worked for white farmers. But most young black men finishing high school down to the late 1960s were entrapped to become captured laborers for the planters. The sheriff would simply arrest any of those kids who did not have a document identifying them with a plantation. The white farmer would then pay the prison fine and the young black man would work for him—most times, forever. We literally helped some of those young fellows escape for one or other city in the North.

It's this fear of the black people for the dreadful plantations and their white owners—Richard Wright's *Lords of the Land*—that paralyzes everything about the black farmers, their history, their relations with the US Department of Agriculture, the plantation's umbilical cord of power with the state. The continuing theft of the little land black farmers still own is devoured in this awesome fear. Yes, Samuel Taylor is right. It helps to be literate about how USDA goes about in its business. But what about the lasting hostility, hatred, the pain, the suspicion, the terrible memories of the landlords always lynching some of them at harvest time and the sheriff chaining the young men into slavery? "Fear is with us always," says Richard Wright in his 1941 *12 Million Black Voices*. "Even when the sprawling fields are drenched in peaceful sunshine, it is war. When we grub at the clay with our hoes, it is war. When we sleep, it is war. When we are awake, it is war. When one of us is born, he enters one of the warring regiments of the South."

The incredible thing is that, with such a constant war, there are any black farmers left so close to the land of their torture, the land of their love and power, and, above all, that those who survive the plantation mean to fight to retain their land—and more. Langston Hughes put it best in 1938: "We must take back our land again, America!"

I was fortunate to come across men like Eddie Slaughter and Gary Grant—keeping the agrarian spirit of resistance alive, not in the least accommodating themselves to the encroaching new plantation, and unwilling to abandon their culture for some soul-crushing urban ghetto. In fact Gary Grant's conference was defiance in itself. He said repeatedly that in the conference crowd—of about 200 black farmers and their black and white supporters—one could find the leaders of an emerging movement to preserve farming for African Americans and take back the land black farmers have lost.

And that explains, in part, why the conference was a combination of learning exercises, listening to experts and farmers, numerous opportunities over coffee breaks, breakfast, lunch, and supper for people to get to know each other, and cultural events that connected black farmers with the decolonizing experience of their African ancestors: Gary Grant led a Kwanzaa celebration that became a stirring passion play for the suffering black farmers of America.

In the end, after our last breakfast together on Sunday morning February 22, 1998, we gathered in the front of the cafeteria for a prayer, a worship service inspired by Reverend C.F. McCollum, Sr. This black preacher recapitulated the history of black people in the United States: The plantation with its African slaves, the debasing consequences of that slave economy and society, the endless struggle of black Americans for human rights, dignity, jobs, acceptance by the white people; the failing of that vision in the white society's stubborn indignities for black people, the perpetuation of a mechanized version of the old plantation system continuing with its theft of the land of black farmers. But, he said, there was no reason to doubt that, in good time, the righteousness of the cause of black farmers would triumph.

I liked this preacher because, like Eddie Slaughter and Gary Grant, he did not try to confuse the issue with trivia—in his case, with the Christian legitimization of oppressive forms of power and social relations. Instead, he made the struggle of the black farmers a struggle for himself and his congregation. And, for me, that's good preaching—an emergency signal to the whole country of what has to happen to safeguard not merely the black farmers who are already too few and powerless, but to protect and increase the numbers of small family farmers (both white and black) from thousands to millions at the expense of the plantations out to break the rest of us into obedient servants / consumers. We need to break the plantations instead. And to do that, most Americans must make the struggle of the black / white threatened farmers their struggle.

The crisis of the black rural Americans trying to protect their land and continue with farming as a way of life is a welcome opportunity for national mobilization, the creation of a mass movement to infuse society with democratic principles and institutions. Start this renewal with the dismantling of the plantation's patronage system, the national farm county committees delivering treasury checks to their faithful members, primarily white farmers and businessmen, mostly owning giant farms or animal factories in the countryside. It is these men who get the lion share of government subsidies to remake rural America and agriculture to fit their monstrous science and business vision. The 11 million pigs of North Carolina in 1998, for example, translated into a series of deleterious effects for both nature and human beings. It is as if these hogs brought an additional 30 million people in the state of North Carolina but without any additional waste treatment facilities. The US Department of Agriculture, and to a significant degree both white and black land grant universities, have become wholly owned subsidiaries to hog factory owners and other plantation men. We can undo this undemocratic process by demanding and funding only their service of the small family farmer, black and white.

The issue is starkly simple and clear: The forces taking the land of the black farmer are also eyeing the white small family farmer. When the black farmers become extinct, it will only be a matter of time before the small white family farmers also become landless and disappear. What then? Of the thousands of black farmers who sued the US Department of

Agriculture in the late 1990s for denying them loans, only one in ten found restitution. By 2004, the US Department of Agriculture paid out $814 million to 13,445 black farmers, disregarding and rejecting the claims of 80,555 black farmers. The *Philadelphia Inquirer* concluded bluntly that such a dismal record "has sown more injustice."[2] Yet the struggle of the black farmers is about much more than land. It should not be allowed to fail. Black farmers are a huge symbol of the ceaseless crucifixion of black people, the crushing of their hopes and dreams. Langston Hughes speaks about dreams that are endlessly postponed:

> What happens to a dream deferred?
> Does it dry up
> like a raisin in the sun?
> Or fester like a sore-
> And then run?
> Does it stink like rotten meat?
> Or crust and sugar over-
> like a syrupy sweet?
>
> Maybe it just sags
> like a heavy load.
>
> *Or does it explode?*

Chapter 7

The Land Howls

Africa's Cash Cropping Road to Development

The agricultural and social situation in Africa is not as bad as that of black rural America. Yet with about a third of its population hungry—more than 200 million people in the dawn of the twenty-first century—sub-Saharan Africa is probably the most impoverished region of the world. Poverty, wars, foreign powers' cold war food politics in the continent, droughts, the plundering of the land for trees, petroleum, diamonds, and gold, environmental degradation, rapid population growth, foreign debt, AIDS, and inappropriate industrial development policies are partly responsible for Africa's massive hunger, but they don't explain it.

The idea of progress and Western development theory are twin sisters that emerged out of the fateful 1492 encounter between Europe and the rest of the world. Progress and development came to describe primarily the class position in the international political system of Africa, Asia, and Latin America. Of course, Europe, and Europe's successor states in North America, won the confrontation with the non-white societies of the Americas, Asia, and Africa, which they colonized as a means of appropriating their tropical wealth.

However, since Europe abandoned the slave trade, slavery, and the colonies themselves, but was determined to maintain its hegemony over its former imperial territories, England and other European powers wanted uninterrupted access to African resources. As a result, they educated Africa to maintain its colonial institutions for achieving "progress" and "development."

This gave birth, among other things, to an entire stream of literature on economic development intended to legitimize the perpetuation of colonialism in Africa under the guise of development. Even the 1960s post-colonial Western-style farming exported to the former colonies of Europe and North America—now conveniently known as "the Third

World"—indicates that this form of industrial agriculture, also dubbed the "green revolution," is cash cropping, the old-style colonial cash cropping dressed in the technical panoply and impressive discourse of modern science.

Thierry Brun, a French scientist with the Agronomy Mediterranean Institute in Montpellier, France, argues that it is not possible to separate cash cropping from colonialism: "One was the justification of the other."[1] This is true because cash cropping, appropriating the peasants' best land, is about the growing of luxury crops (coffee, tobacco, tea, cotton, sugar, cocoa) for export. In addition, forced African labor built the infrastructure of cash cropping in Senegal, Gambia, Guinea, Ivory Coast, Ghana, and Mali—with immense destructive cultural, social, and ecological consequences, including the establishment of one-crop farming (centuries before the green revolution) and the denigration of indigenous agricultural systems.

Because in West Africa it is Africans who own, for the most part, cash cropping, the prices they received for their commodities were kept low enough that the profits nearly always went to the Europeans who processed and traded the tropical crops for export to Europe. But even the small amounts of European money African peasants earned from selling their export crops did not last long or bring substantive benefits to them. European grocery stores all over West Africa, usually managed by Lebanese, imported into Africa Europe's manufactured goods. The very slave traders of the eighteenth century funded these grocery outposts in West Africa in the nineteenth century (from Liverpool, Amsterdam, Nantes and Bordeaux). Colonial administrators used forced labor to support these grocery stores, which eventually evolved into corporations. In fact the entire economic system of West Africa (banking, railways, agricultural research stations, roads) was designed to support and serve cash cropping.[2] Development for Africa became cash cropping.

Export cash cropping in sub-Saharan Africa is the strongest legacy of European colonialism. The Europeans made the Africans pay taxes by forcing them to produce a few tropical crops out of which the Europeans made desserts and beverages. By forcing cash cropping on Africa, Europe did more than assure herself of exotic desserts, drinks, and valuable tropical commodities like rubber, cotton and timber. Cash cropping remade Africa in the image of Europe.

The production of crops for export—cash cropping—became the royal, hegemonic part of African agriculture and political life. Cash cropping brought benefits to men who owned small farms and plantations, city merchants who sold the crops, and state bureaucracies that approved the transactions of trade. So cash cropping made African agriculture pro-male, pro-city, pro-state, and pro-plantation—the very antithesis of pre-colonial agriculture that was almost a model after nature, growing food for rural people in societies in which women did most of the farming and decided the price of food.[3]

Sub-Saharan Africa is paying a terrible price for her cash-cropping road to development. Cash crops condemn Africa to impoverishment and hunger—even periodic starvation. The very essence and culture of Africa, subsistence peasant agriculture, with its extraordinary variety of indigenous food crops, is ignored for cash cropping. Maxwell Owusu, an African scholar, says that "the terms of Africa's incorporation into the global capitalist market since the colonial days have up till now [in 1993] condemned Africa to the production of agricultural export commodities of little or no immediate use in Africa, which promotes African underdevelopment, and which by its very nature also promotes hunger and starvation as subsistence output is neglected in favor of export production."[4]

Clearly, Africa's cash cropping for export equals to hunger for tens of millions of Africans. About 25 percent of the population of West Africa, counting some 50 million people in 1998, and probably more than 60 million in 2005, are perpetually hungry. And nearly 17 to 48 percent of the children under five years old never grow up because of chronic malnutrition. They are stunted for life. But cash cropping is also responsible for the growing exodus of peasants to the cities. Between 1970 and 1995 the urban population of West Africa grew by 388 percent while the number of peasants increased by 160 percent.[5] This imbalance between city and country is ominous, creating huge cities with all the characteristics of slums.

It's almost tempting to suggest—though it's not true—that Africa was better off under colonialism. Better, that is, than the season of hunger and war of post-colonial days. Certainly, during the centuries of colonialism, when cash cropping was taking roots in the continent, Africa was a net food exporter, but, since the 1960s, Africa has been importing food.[6] The United Nations Food and Agriculture Organization (FAO) says that sub-Saharan Africa produced less food in 1998 than it did in 1968.[7]

FAO classifies 86 nations around the globe as "low-income food-deficit countries" (meaning these countries don't grow enough food for themselves). In fact the vast majority of the world's 800 million "chronically undernourished people" live in these countries. Forty-three of these hungry nations, with 200 million hungry human beings, are in Africa. They include: Angola, Benin, Burkina Faso, Burundi, Cameroon, Cape Verde, Central African Republic, Chad, Comoros, Congo, the Democratic Republic of Congo, Cote d' Ivoire, Djibouti, Egypt, Equatorial Guinea, Eritrea, Ethiopia, Gambia, Ghana, Guinea, Guinea-Bissau, Kenya, Lesotho, Liberia, Madagascar, Malawi, Mali, Mauritania, Morocco, Mozambique, Niger, Nigeria, Rwanda, Sao Tome and Principe, Senegal, Sierra Leone, Somalia, Sudan, Swaziland, Tanzania, Togo, Zambia, and Zimbabwe.[8]

The United Nations Food and Agriculture Organization also reports that agriculture uses more than two-thirds of the world's drinking water. And just like there are countries that cannot feed themselves—the so-called food-deficient countries—there are 26 countries that FAO describes as "water deficient." Eleven of these water-poor nations are in Africa. FAO predicted correctly that by the year 2000 "six out of seven East African countries and all five North African countries bordering the Mediterranean would face acute water shortages. All the countries in North Africa, except Morocco, already import half or more of their grain."[9]

Africa imports much more than grain. The entire panoply of industrialized agriculture has been seeping into the continent for centuries—and that includes pesticides as well. Yet synthetic agricultural poisons, like the massive mechanical beast of machines and factory infrastructure of industrialized farming, have very limited scope in Africa. In West Africa, for instance, 95 percent of all pesticides used in agricultural production go to the growing of cotton.[10] This is because cash cropping is Africa's primary trade route to earning foreign money. Uganda's entire exports trade (from 93 to 99 percent) comes from cash crops—coffee, tea, cotton, tobacco, maize and beans.[11] This is bad because the good land of Uganda, which could be sowed to food crops for local consumption, is feeding Europeans who have already plenty of food.

Because Africans spend no more than $250 million to $500 million per year for pesticides—which equals to one to two percent of the world's annual budget for agrotoxins that in 1992 was about $25 billion—the global pesticide companies don't go out of their way to push their latest products on Africans. Instead, they dump on them toxins no one else will use. The pesticides industry, says the US Agency for International Development, "regards Africa as a residual market, where pesticides whose patent protection has expired can still be sold in small amounts for a profit...[and] considerable stocks of pesticides that are banned in developed countries, especially older organochlorines, are traded and used in Africa."[12]

We don't really know whether or not this global poison dumping on Africa, including the use of DDT, is causing an environmental crisis on the continent—a huge part of the earth. But considering that hardly an African country has even the rudiments of law and bureaucracy and money and commitment to defend nature and human beings from the injury of industrial poisons and dangerous development, it would not be much of an exaggeration to describe the African ecological situation as verging on anarchy and violence and death for wildlife and nature. The coastal region of West Africa, for example, fabulously endowed with biological diversity and fish, is under a regime of careless exploitation and destruction. To complicate matters, all foreign "donors" to Africa (primarily Japanese, Western European, and North American governments) have different guidelines regarding encouragement for the use of pesticides or the use of ecological alternatives to pesticides in the projects they fund and in their overall development policy towards Africa. Japan, for example, donates pesticides to African governments. Since the foreign donors in Africa have no common agenda or approach to assisting African agriculture (and, therefore, deal with the issue of agrotoxins or less hazardous pest management alternatives), the resulting consequences, says the US Agency for International Development, are "deleterious" for both African food security, Africa, and her North American, Japanese, and European donors.[13]

For several centuries, Africa's relations with Western Europe (particularly England, France, Portugal, and Belgium) and other ambitious colonizers—the United States and Japan in the twentieth century—have been deleterious, with the poison hitting Africa exclusively. Humiliated, angry, and desperate people, the Africans are still handicapped to death from the long winter of colonialism. They are all messed up, broken into the alien religions of Christianity and Islam, forced to adopt and adapt to political organizations and geographical divisions not in their own tradition and history, even made to embody and live in the culture of their slavers. Africans are even forced to discard their heavenly food for the impoverished and hunger staples of foreigners.

Such is the conflict of values in African culture and the desperate effort of Africans to find some familiar part of themselves, that the struggle often becomes schizophrenic and suicidal. In Rwanda, one of the most Christianized of all African countries, the colonial legacy exploded into desperate violence, senseless slaughter, barbaric genocide, and raw cannibalism.

Rwandan Hutus murdered 800,000 Rwandan Tutsis in about three months in 1994 while the rest of prostrate Africa and the immoral international community looked on. And the model of the Rwandan genocide, the ultimate in the madness of remaking human beings with fear and loathing of themselves, trap them in shame for what they used to be, is becoming a weapon of war in the vast Democratic Republic of Congo. Central Africa is engulfing the continent with foul murder as loud as the howling of the land from cash cropping.

I will never forget going through, in the spring of 1998, the villages of the lush and rich Rivers State of Nigeria—the petroleum bank of the former kleptocratic and violent military rulers of West Africa's largest country. There was that intense heat, the bright sun sucking my hunger and energy in the green land of sweet yams, with only water uppermost in my mind.

Everywhere I looked I could see the smoldering skeleton ruins of deformed peasant culture, destroyed roads, buildings left unfinished, hovels decorated with the deep green vines of the engulfing forest, piles of garbage rotting, half naked black people dazed and mad with anger with the tragedy and injustice of military siege, the outright theft of their resources and the poisoning of their sacred land.

But in the air-conditioned coolness and comfort of the luxury hotels in Port Harcourt, the capital of the Rivers State, Lagos, the southern metropolis, and Abuja, Nigeria's new federal capital, I saw another Nigeria—the Mercedes Benz ruling class, men and women feeding on the Rivers State's oil, moving comfortably in their silk flowing robes, eating European food, talking to each other and the visiting foreigners in English, thinking non-African words and worlds. The Hilton Hotel in Abuja, in particular, is a cement icon of this other Nigeria. It is a fortress designed to withstand any attack from the bleeding and screaming red land or the conquered peasants slowly seeping in its neighborhood at the center of the military city, which is also at the very center of Nigeria. Both the Hilton Hotel and Abuja were built with zero respect for African architecture and traditions. From my ninth-floor hotel window, I could see in Abuja an immense replication of a "modern" asphalt city—and a huge mosque.

I walked to the mosque to admire its elaborate Arabic design and observe, up close, its beautiful art. I talked to a young woman on my way back to the hotel and I heard from her what I heard, with great difficulty and some risk, in the countryside of the Rivers State. Nigeria's military tyrants killed Ken Saro-Wiwa on November 10, 1995 because he and the civil society organization he created, the Movement for the Survival of the Ogoni People, had the courage to expose the corrupt relations between Shell, the giant Dutch petroleum company, the generals running the country, and the destruction of his homeland, right in the Niger Delta, the oil-rich region of the Rivers State in southeastern Nigeria where the Ogoni people live.

In his closing statement to the Tribunal that condemned him to death, Ken Saro-Wiwa appealed to history: "Appalled by the denigrating poverty of my people who live on a richly endowed land," he says, "distressed by their political marginalization and economic strangulation, angered by the devastation of their land, their ultimate heritage, anxious to preserve their right to life and to a decent living, and determined to usher to this country as a whole a fair and just democratic system which protects everyone and every ethnic group and gives us all a valid claim to human civilization, I have devoted my intellectual and material resources, my very life, to a cause in which I have total belief and from which I cannot be blackmailed or intimidated...[the] Shell [oil company] is here on trial...the ecological war that the Company has waged in the [Niger] Delta will be called to question sooner than later and the crimes of that war be duly punished. The crime of the Company's dirty wars against the Ogoni people will also be punished.... The military do not act alone. They are supported by a gaggle of politicians, lawyers, judges, academics and businessmen, all of them hiding under the claim that they are only doing their duty, men and women too afraid to wash their pants of urine."[14]

Even the illiterate young peasant woman, working in Abuja as a waitress to send money home to her parents in a village in the southern part of the country, had heard of Ken Saro-Wiwa. The man touched the soul of both the Ogoni people and the Nigerian population in general. His denunciation of the experts in corruption, the managers of the foreign oil corporation, Shell, and the kleptocratic and colonial oligarchy of military men and men of business, politics, law, and the academy, was full of passion, anger, madness, heroism. There was no way Ken Saro-Wiwa would survive his campaign to lead the Ogonis to defend their land from the cannibalism of Shell and the Nigerian army generals.

Just like international connections did not help an authentic Brazilian peasant hero, Chico Mendes, in the Brazilian Amazon in 1988 from the murderous attack of landowners, no one with power in the United States or Western Europe intervened with either Shell or Nigeria's dictator, General Sani Abacha, to stop the state killing of Ken Saro-Wiwa in 1995. The lesson is clear: Contest corporate profits at your own risk.

The young woman also spoke with anxiety of corruption, extreme poverty, the oppression of the Ogoni people, the murder of Ken Saro-Wiwa—the heart-breaking picture of impoverishment I saw in the villages of the poisoned and crucified Ogoni land very much alive in my mind. I almost felt embarrassed to admit to her, and other Nigerians who asked me to explain the purpose of my visit to their country, I was an observer from the United States to what turned out a fake Congressional and gubernatorial elections cooked up by general Sani Abacha to give the illusion to Europe and America that Nigeria was about to switch to civilian democratic rule. Yet, however disturbing my misgivings were about my mission to that vast West African country, I consider myself fortunate to have taken that leap of faith and danger in a society in so much pain, a society, nevertheless, with so much potential to lead Africa in the not too distant future.

Nigeria and West Africa, however, are becoming suicidal Rwandas and nobody cares. Ken Saro-Wiwa was right. The army said no to my request to visit any of the Shell oil installations in the Ogoni region. Indeed, some members of the African American delegation visiting Nigeria as election observers tried to block my journey to the Rivers State all together. They discovered early on that I had a sympathetic view of Ken Saro-Wiwa. But a Nigerian colonel took me and some other election observers, including the black Americans hostile to Ken Saro-Wiwa, to see a destroyed oil transfer station, which, he said, was torched by the followers of Ken Saro-Wiwa. I listened in silence to the terse monologue of the young colonel speaking of "terrorists" and petroleum in a land that had suffered both the poisoning of petroleum and the dissolution of gentle human communities that revered it. I said to the colonel that Shell ought to clean up the oil pollution we could see all around us and he agreed. I sensed that this soldier—despite his programmed outburst against the Ogoni—was a bright man eager to learn. So I raised the issue of the warming of the earth as a result, among other things, of the huge amounts of petroleum burned in industrialized countries. The role of giant companies like Shell, I said, was crucial in the destruction of the global environment. The colonel listened politely and smiled. The black Americans kept snapping pictures of each other and the tense soldiers who kept at a distance, stony-faced in the tropical heat and bright sun.

I was armed with a camera and a bottle of water but our escort, the military officer, and his soldiers were armed with machine guns and jeeps. I was afraid I might be caught in the cross fire of hatred and oppression. My sympathies were obvious. Being in the Ogoni land was exhilarating and sad. The land and the Ogonis are devastated. Everything is a skeleton—people, buildings, entire villages. The passion of Ken Saro-Wiwa was secret but diffused. Nigeria depends on Ken's vision.

But in the midst of tragedy, there was so much green life everywhere we drove and walked. In addition, the intense temperature, the Potempkin election stations, the young soldiers hugging their weapons and keeping us in constant view, the diplomatic and not so diplomatic efforts I made to talk to peasants, pressed on me the violence of daily life and the virtual state of war in the Rivers State.

The tyrant Sani Abacha died from a heart attack in June 1998. He came from Nigeria's Moslem north that siphons the country's $10 billion per year petroleum wealth from the Christian south. The death of Abacha brought to power another general from the Muslim north, Abdulsalami Abubakar. This man promised that Nigeria would return to democracy by May 1999. He kept his promise. He even searched for Abacha's stolen Nigerian treasures. And he did not order the army to crush the rebels in the Niger Delta. Does this mean Abubakar was better than Abacha? Highly unlikely. Abubakar's policies were simply better tuned to the outside world's revulsion with brutal power. Yet the gaggle of local and foreign politicians and experts push for more oil and more cash crops which fuel rebellions and ecological wars in the Niger Delta, all over the coast of West Africa, and against traditional people trying to live from the land. The cash croppers are so busy appropriating oil revenues, the secret value of nature, harvesting money, less and less from more and more land, that they are deaf to the coming earthquake.

Simeon T. Numbem, a Cameroon scholar, said, in 1998, that whenever peasants lose their earnings from "crops like cocoa" they push the "slash and burn agricultural frontier into pristine forest. The rate of poaching for bushmeat [wild animals killed for food, which, according to the *National Geographic* of September 2005, is a multibillion dollar business, and which, in 1998, was on the menu of the Abuja Hilton], and encroachment on protected areas and forest reserves is increasing as rural population seek to increase rural income by all means possible." And, of course, governments follow the example of the peasants. "Cash strapped" governments in the Congo basin, says Numbem, go after logging "as a means of fetching foreign exchange"[15] so that they can privatize and deregulate their economies to satisfy their debt masters—to whom they owed in 1994 about $313 billion, a sum of money equivalent to 234 percent of all of Africa's income from exports.[16] Africa's debt represents another form of colonialism. The continent is a slave to its debtors. Africa borrowed about $540 billion between 1970 and 2002. It paid back some $550 billion, but, by 2002, it still had a debt of $295 billion. The debt peonage is worse for sub-Saharan Africa where most poor people live miserable lives, suffering hunger, civil wars, and plunder of everything that is valuable like trees, petroleum, and diamonds. Sub-Saharan Africa borrowed $294 billion, paid back $268 billion in debt service, and, in 2004, had a debt of $210 billion—a classic example where the poorest of the poor support the richest of the rich.[17]

Time for Africa is Running Out

With such debt hanging over Africa, nothing gets done, especially in agriculture. Cash crops assume almost a divine status. The neglect of subsistence farming for plantation cash cropping, however, is having ecocidal effects on huge swaths of the African continent. R.D. Mann, an English agricultural researcher with 30 years of experience in Africa, warned in 1990 that "Africa's arid regions are edging towards catastrophe. An area of 635,000 square kilometers has already been over-run by desert in the past 50 years, and the semi-arid belt 300 to 1,100 kilometers wide stretching across the continent is becoming sterile. Time for Africa is running out fast; as soil is eroded and the micro-climate continues to disintegrate across the whole continent, field-crop and livestock-production is decreasing yet further, and widespread hunger is increasing in frequency."[18]

Mann argues that "unsustainable modern agricultural practices" are clearly a significant factor in the ecological destruction of Africa. This is particularly true of cash cropping. "In the Sahel and sub-Sahel," he says, "the connection between the expansion of the area devoted to the cultivation of annual export crops and the desertification process is obvious. Whole rural communities have been [and] are still advised to clear woodland at the expense of ecological stability, leaving behind a trail of exhausted land."[19]

Despite the trails of exhausted land and devastated rural communities all over Africa, international agencies like the United Nations Food and Agriculture Organization (FAO) lament the failure of the colonial model of plantation agriculture in Africa which, in reality, has mutated into American-style industrial farming, but, for political reasons, goes under the name of the "green revolution."

FAO would like to see more of Africa's land come under irrigation, more intensified chemical and mechanical farming replacing the gentle practices of the peasant. FAO does not give rainfed agriculture much of a chance to feed Africa, thus "neglect of irrigation may seem to be unthinkable."[20] Besides, FAO says that unsustainable farming follows rainfed agriculture. One wonders what African peasants did before the white invaders of their land hooked up their cash crop plantations with water from rivers or pulled water from the depths of the ground. FAO blames "soil mining" and "destruction of biodiversity" on those farming without irrigated water. This is a preposterous claim. And one may reasonably say that centuries of colonialism left nothing unchanged—not even the peasant. But the blame for ecocide is primarily on the side of the plantation producing cash crops for export rather than peasant subsistence farming.

Decolonizing Plantation Africa

Growing luxury crops like tea, cocoa, coffee and sugar for export in sub-Saharan Africa is a legacy of European colonialism that, in early twenty-first century, translates into hunger for more than 200 million people and biological and cultural meltdown for the entire region.

The Europeans forced the Africans to pay taxes by forcing them to produce a few crops out of which the Europeans made desserts and beverages. In fact this process of extracting desirable commodities from the tropics was so massive and violent that, for 300 years, millions of Africans were sent to the Americas as slaves to work sugarcane, cotton, and coffee in huge plantations. J.H. Bernardin de Saint Pierre, a French royal officer, said in 1769, he was not so sure that coffee and sugar were "really essential to the comfort of Europe," but he was certain that these two crops "have brought wretchedness and misery upon America and Africa. The former is depopulated, that Europeans may have a land to plant them in, and the latter is stripped of its inhabitants, for hands to cultivate them."[21]

Africa is still unhappy from her European encounter—a largely muted displeasure, bitterness, coloring all relations of most Africans with each other and their former colonial masters. After all, Africans are producing, more or less, the cash crops they used to produce under French, British, Portuguese, Belgian, Italian and German colonialism—cocoa, coffee, sugar, peanuts, cotton, rubber, tea, palm oil, timber, and tobacco. The violence of the old system has not diminished or vanished. It has, instead, gone underground, reappearing in the hunger, destruction of nature, and other forms of invisible yet deleterious manifestations of ecological and social disintegration. The signs are all over Africa—and beyond:

(1) Cash crops for export take more and more of the best land from local food production, forcing peasants to bring additional marginal

land under cultivation. The social and environmental results of such policies are devastating.[22]

(2) Women are crucial for food production in Africa. But when men out-migrate for jobs, the entire burden of subsistence farming falls on women who frequently have no land tenure rights. Female labor is also important for the production of men's cash crops. These social arrangements often result in hungry and malnourished women, food insecurity, bad gender relations, and bad development policies. Women are also responsible for growing and processing of cassava, the most important subsistence food in sub-Saharan Africa.[23]

(3) Paul Richards, the British geography professor with extensive agricultural research and teaching experience in Africa, argues convincingly that the dramatic modernization option of industrializing agriculture in Africa has been such a failure that time has come for something fundamentally different—like designing a support system for peasant farming which he credits with strong innovations in food production. He calls his pro-peasant strategy "the people's science option." He says: "a peasant-focused, decentralized approach to research and development in West African agriculture is an option worth serious consideration because it is appropriate to the region's environmental circumstances. People's science is worth pursuing in West Africa not out of spontaneous admiration for the peasantry (though on my part I am quite ready to admit such admiration) but on the grounds that it is good science."[24]

Another British scientist, Laurence Roche, believes, like Paul Richards, that time is of the essence in siding with the African peasant: The social and ecological emergency of Africa demands that selfish schemes be abandoned. Roche spent fifteen years of work and travel in Africa and became furious with the waste and destruction of the imported economic growth model of development fueling the ambitions of African leaders. But he said the needs and culture of the peasant ought to be the sole priority of those who care about Africa, discarding, at the same time, the fixation of the elites with capital-intensive projects that usually benefit a few Africans living in the city and industrialists in Europe and North America.[25]

Has the people's science option, the evidence from scientific research that the peasant in fact mirrors Africa, that traditional farming is the most credible and appropriate method of raising food in Africa, any better chance in the dawn of the twenty-first century? An American researcher, Bill Rau, confirmed in 1993 the admiration of Paul Richards, Laurence Roche, and other students of Africa for African peasants. He reported: "African agricultural knowledge offers the strongest hope for igniting and promoting sustained development throughout the continent."[26] Incidentally, I have advanced the same thesis for Third World peasants in general in both of my books, *Fear in the Countryside* (1976) and *Harvest of Devastation* (1994): Peasants and their traditional knowledge do matter.

Yet, in Africa, colonialism is even threatening not merely how much people eat but what they eat. The United Nations Food and Agriculture Organization reports that, increasingly, Africans eat mostly imported wheat, corn, and rice. About half of the African people eat roots, tubers and plantains for something like 40 percent of their diet.[27]

Why Africans eat less and less of their own food goes to the very heart of their hunger and dependency on others. Colonialism forced them to produce export cash crops and to eat imported grains. The Europeans heaped scorn on the fantastic variety of Africa's indigenous cereals. And Western scientists classified the African grains as cattle feed. That is why—and not so much because of urbanization, perishability of food or labor requirements—many of the 2,000 varieties of indigenous grains, roots, fruits and other food plants have been "lost," at least from the daily diet of most Africans.

But these foods still exist in Africa and they are the answer to the tremendous food insecurity of so many millions of human beings in both Africa and elsewhere in the world. In a 1996 study, *Lost Crops of Africa*, the US National Academy of Sciences says that Africa's native cereals like rice, finger millet, fonio, pearl millet, sorghum, tef, guinea millet, and dozens of wild cereals, present a "local legacy of genetic wealth upon which a sound food future might be built."[28]

Resurrecting Africa's own food plants—in other words, getting back to peasant agriculture by putting sustainable human development to practice in Africa—would heal the ecological wounds of the Sahel. Africa's cereals are tolerant of heat, cold, drought, waterlogging, and infertile land. And they are also nutritious and tasty. The National Academy of Sciences study says that Africa's "lost" plants may benefit more than Africa because "they represent an exceptional cluster of cereal biodiversity with particular promise for solving some of the food production problems that will arise in the twenty-first century."[29] In fact, those problems already exist, threatening industrialized agriculture, which has a very narrow biological diversity. That handicap could be corrected with borrowing from the rich genetic diversity of African crops.

The "lost crops" of Africa present Africa, the rest of the world, and the international development community with a great opportunity to give substance to some of the theory one hears at United Nations fora on "sustainable human development"—and join the African peasants, who still use many of these indigenous food plants, in building Africa's food security around Africa's own food, people, and culture.

This means, above all, the dismantling of the colonial cash cropping culture—and the distribution of that cash crop land to the peasants. Clearly, coffee and sugar made Africa very unhappy. The French observer of the mature but beastly colonial system, Bernardin de Saint Pierre, was right in 1769: Europe, and the Europeans in America, tore Africa to pieces for their pleasure. In the Congo, for instance, Belgian and French soldiers and agents of cash cropping companies carried "fire and sword from one end of the country to the other" in order to force the Africans to work rubber.[30] And an African observer of the evolving but still evil colonial system, Chinua Achebe, captured in 1959 the anguish of Africa when he said "all our gods are weeping" with the imposition on Africans by the white colonizers of a "lunatic religion"—Christianity—that disrupted the peasants' sacred farming with cash cropping and forced them to abandon their ancestral gods.[31]

Certainly it would not be easy for Africa to return to her pre-colonial (pre-Islamic, pre-Christian) culture. The entire international system, including Islam and Christianity, would oppose that kind of metamorphosis for Africa primarily because both the international system and the foreign religions benefit from Africa's impoverishment and political weakness.

The global state political arrangements in the start of the twenty-first century—that confront the massive hunger of Africa with icy indifference—may center around the moral idea of the United Nations but, nevertheless, they are a sophisticated if mutant high-tech version of slave-days state balance of power without formal slavery. They are long-winded on issues which, on their own right, are terribly important, but which become abstractions at the hands of their public relations men and women. Issues like sustainable development, peasant farming and democracy, gender, indigenous knowledge, human rights, biological and cultural diversity, and nature are drained of meaning and political significance. It's as if they are saying to the world "We are not about to do anything to end hunger, poverty, biological and cultural meltdown, environmental destruction, racism, inequality, but we are doing a lot to define those problems." No bread, no clean water, no biodiversity, but plenty of words.

That downpour of coded vocabulary is sprinkled with plenty of acronyms, and, from time to time, the flash and excitement of international conferences. Such deceptions, however, suffice to keep, for the most part, the civil society's "best and brightest" busy fighting for the good cause. Yet they are often frozen in place by the global political system. In all this protracted world dramatic theatrical exercise, the protagonists are very careful with anything that touches the interests of those few who hold power. These include the multinational corporations and the 358 billionaires who, in 1996, owned more money and wealth than 2.5 billion human beings or 45 percent of the world population.[32] In 2005, there were 691 billionaires worth about $2.2 trillion, a fantastic amount of money. More than half of these billionaires live in the United States.[33]

In the presence of these barbarian realities in the global organization of power, even scrapping sub-Saharan Africa's plantation agriculture alone would cause alarm (and even violence) in Europe, North America, and Africa (and probably panic in the international system's powerful agencies like the World Bank and the World Trade Organization). Yet cash cropping for the benefit of a few Africans and foreigners ought to find no more room in Africa. Only then the gods of Africa would cease weeping. The lengthy process of reconstruction might then have a chance to heal the enormous wounds of foreign domination and ruthless colonialism.

Besides, self-sufficiency in all matters of importance, and food self-sufficiency and food sovereignty in particular, is a good idea. Aristoteles called that *autarkeia*, autarchy, self-rule, and thought it should be both the end and the best of state policy.[34] And Xenophon, an Athenian writer and a friend of Sokrates, considered agriculture the mother and nurse of the arts and sciences and the pillar of political independence and freedom.[35] The French philosopher, Jean Jacques Rousseau, some 2,200 years after Xenophon and Aristoteles, in the eighteenth-century, also appreciated self-sufficiency, especially in food and agriculture because, he believed, only enough food raised at home could guarantee the independence of a state. "Commerce," he said, "produces wealth, but agriculture ensures freedom."[36]

In Africa, agriculture will nurture freedom when all land from the cash crop plantations passes on to the peasants who are certain to grow both food and democracy, the two most fundamental ingredients for both self-reliance and happiness, and the resurrection of that ancient continent. In addition, giving land to the African peasants is certain to inspire their distant relatives in the United States, the threatened and endangered black family farmers, to keep fighting for their land and freedom.

Chapter 8

The Development Syndrome
is Becoming Pandemic

Whose Common Future?

In the fourth chapter I touched on "organic" farming in the United States as the economic and political expression of what, for reasons of philosophy, convenience, or desperation, goes under the name of "sustainable" agriculture, a subsidiary of "sustainable" development. The argument has been that "sustainable development" is the rediscovery of a paradise lost.

I also used the epithet "sustainable" to describe a desired moral agricultural system primarily because, in one sense, sustainable for the civil society implies something good that lasts. This is true in some cases. However, the ideologues of the World Bank, multinational corporations, and not a few environmental organizations, argue that sustainable development is something necessary, nearly an ideal in the principles guiding the political and economic life of societies and their institutions, including the United Nations. The story of how the concept of "sustainable development" came to be a hotly contested issue, however, is both complex and relatively new.

The 1987 United Nations report, *Our Common Future*, set the tone and the economic arguments for the life of this often confusing, deceptive, and colonizing idea—sustainable development. The confusion over "capitalist sustainable development" is deliberate. For industrial societies, development is the mining of nature and human communities for the production of commodities that bring wealth and power to the ruling class. Development, therefore, is synonymous with power—usually corporate power, the power over nature and culture—and violence—the violence of ecocide, the destruction of social organizations, including genocide. Capitalist sustainable development means the perpetuation of this violent system.

Gro Harlem Brundtland is the woman associated with the political concept of sustainable development. She was the prime minister of

Norway and the head of the World Commission on Environment and Development, which published *Our Common Future*. The deceptive message of this book is this: As long as we leave enough resources for future generations, while we take care of the needs of the current population, we are practitioners of sustainable development. Brundtland said economic growth was the linchpin of her model of sustainable development. That means, in a sense, she left out of the debate corporations and the plutocracies of North America and Europe and the Third World, which, in any case, are the same. She also avoided any accounting for the crisis of development, a gigantic violence colonizing and ripping apart societies all over the world.[1]

Gro Brundtland was never serious about the protection of nature. As prime minister of Norway she undermined international law by her insistence her country had the right to continue to violate the ban against the hunting and slaughter of whales. She argued, unconvincingly, that Norwegians had to kill whales for scientific research. Japan is using the same dishonest language to justify its violation of international law, which would otherwise protect the whales from further slaughter.

Gro Brundtland then became the secretary general of the UN World Health Organization, an assignment that lasted from 1998 to 2002. She belongs to an international class that rules the planet. This global ruling class, which is defending its predatory policies under the seductive cover of sustainable development, is made up of a select number of multinational corporate executives, directors of foundations, government representatives, and a few wealthy persons. This class is still invisible because of its sophistication and immense power. The nation state is also a fantastic mirror that shields the covert governance of this global plutocracy.

It was the multinational corporation which put together the ideological and economic foundations for what is often known as the new world order—meaning a system of international relations conductible and protective of capitalist business flowing unhindered from state to state. As long as communist Russia kept Eastern Europe communist and in its empire, capitalist corporations found it difficult to sell their ideas and products behind hostile borders. But with the collapse of the Berlin Wall in 1990-1991, the entire Russian system of control throughout Eastern Europe and Asia disintegrated. It was like communism Russian-style never existed. The subject states and Russia, having gone through a convulsive but relatively peaceful transition in abandoning their bureaucratic socialism, rushed headlong into the embrace of capitalism, and, therefore, into the guidance and eventual control by multinational corporations.

Only China, Vietnam, North Korea, and Cuba still pretend they are not capitalist states. Yet their economies are becoming, gradually, capitalistic. Millions of Chinese workers receive nearly slave salaries for manufacturing goods for United States corporations and business of other capitalist societies. China uses its countless workers to accumulate both dollars and technologies, and Western corporations make huge profits from their exploitation of the workers of China. Vietnam says the Yankies are welcomed back. North Korea, prostrate from hunger, but potent with missiles and possibly nuclear weapons, is causing trouble for crumbs of capitalist aid. Even Cuba, which the American ruling class detests because of its hatred of Fidel Castro, is sliding into non-mechanized agriculture and tourist capitalism.

The significance of this restructuring of the Russian empire (and the remaining bureaucratic socialist world) is this: Never before was the entire planet left with only one supreme state power and ideology as it is now on the dawn of the twenty-first century. The surviving global power, of course, is the United States. Which is to say the globalization of America follows exactly the globalization of Christianity in the fourth and fifth centuries: More and more of the world will be forced to come down to the same denominator—worshipping the same god and the same emperor. Mechanical and largely meaningless American culture——movies, TV, fast food, destructive giant factory farming, corporate monopolies, selfish plutocratic policies and politics—is having a field day all over the world.

The rise of the United States to the top of the world is not good for the global environment: Planetary ecological threats and the toxic contamination and poisoning of the world environment are not theoretical issues for some more acrimonious debate. The poisons of industrial and industrializing societies are both changing the global climate and, as a result, raising the world's temperature. They are also destroying the ozone layer around the planet, which protects life from the sun's harmful ultraviolet radiation. The consequences of slowly undermining and, in time, crippling the balance that the earth and the sun reached after billions of years of coexistence in the cosmos are necessarily very bad, global—and lasting.

For instance, Alaska's permafrost is disintegrating. The falling and melting of snow in the Antarctic are changing with the result penguins in the West Antarctic peninsula are losing their summer breeding habitat. In addition, and more ominously, glaciers are retreating and gigantic floating ice sheets are collapsing. Meanwhile, increasing ultraviolet radiation, because of the ozone depletion over the Antarctic, is causing morphological abnormalities, genetic damage, impairment of metabolic processes, decreases in growth, and death to a variety of life forms—all deleterious effects on the water animals of the continent.

Donald Brown, an American legal expert on climate change, is accusing the United States of wrecking the international efforts to deal with the climate crisis. At a Harvard seminar, December 13, 2000, he said "a stream of disturbing facts"—oceans rising, ice caps and glaciers melting, disease infected mosquitoes moving to higher grounds, animals changing their migrations, more intense storms killing people and destroying communities all over the world—leave no doubt that humans are heating the world.[2]

Of course, Brown is right. On February 22, 2001, he addressed some of the climate issues in a civil society discussion at the Stewart Mott Center in Washington, DC. What struck me the most about Brown, a dear friend and former colleague at the US Environmental Protection Agency, was his passion and anger about lost opportunities for the United States to face responsibly the grave global climate disaster.

The world's other governments have, like the United States, known of the ugly climate facts for several years. In fact, the United Nations Intergovernmental Panel on Climate Change (IPCC), an international organization representing over two thousand climate experts from more than 100 countries assessing global warming since 1988, was set up to inform the world's governments about the weather. Was the globe getting really warmer? And if it did, what could the world community do? The UN Intergovernmental Panel on Climate Change issued another draft report, February 19, 2001, which lays out bare the consequences of warming the earth with the gases of industrialization, particularly the poisons from the burning of oil, gas, and coal. The effects of global warming would be the most severe on the poor countries of Africa, Asia, and Latin America. One would expect to see more flooding, less food from reductions in crop yields, less fresh water, more stress from higher temperature, and more diseases.[3]

These are real threats and real world dangers. And by the gravity and global scope of what they portend, they—along with a multitude of other global ecological risks—erase national borders: They are the most deadly cosmic warning yet to humanity responsible for interfering with forces in nature billions of years old. The "national state," a creature of an older, ecologically-illiterate era—since at least the emergence of the monotheistic religions of Christianity and Islam, some 1,600 and 1,300 years ago respectively, when humans spent most of their talents and power in predatory schemes and genocides—is deeply problematic.

Only through the remaking of the national state into a polis, a state designed to be as close as possible to the original Hellenic democratic model, we have a good chance of crippling the vain imperial schemes of some huge national conglomerations striving for planetary hegemony. We also need the ethical and ecological values and mechanisms of international law to be vigorously applied and enforced throughout the world. This will be especially relevant if we allow the world's global organization, the United Nations, to absorb at least the environmental protection powers of the national states. Such authority ceded to the United Nations must, in all cases, be higher than that of the national state. In other words, we need a World Environment Organization whose decisions will have priority and be of higher standing than those of the World Trade Organization. In no case should a commercial project be allowed to proceed, if it can be shown it will have ecocidal effects. If we do that, we have a fighting chance to put a break to an otherwise slow-moving and often invisible destruction of the entire planet.

That is why each one of us has the moral responsibility to do our part in diminishing the effects of this global crisis. I wrote this book, and my other two agrarian books, for this reason. All together, they are as much a prayer to the gods as they are useful theory and suggestions to bring to an end the agribusiness threat and return us to the time-tested moral economy, democracy and food of family farming. This book brings to a conclusion the argument I started in 1976.

Power

In the discourse of the managers of international political power, sustainable agriculture—like sustainable development—is conventional agriculture and development plus power, their power to sustain a deleterious system for a very long time. That power says that you only have to change your vocabulary, and with enough money, you purchase the understanding of what others think of you. Thus the international political system orchestrated a sophisticated campaign in the 1980s to neutralize the emerging subversive movement of global green ecological concerns about the fate of the Earth. *Our Common Future*, the 1987 UN report on the global environment, baptized industrialized or conventional agriculture with the worthy name of sustainability. And then the real power politics began. Many international institutions like the World Bank announced programs of sustainable development. Even the US Congress funded, in 1990, Low Input Sustainable Agriculture for the United States. And in 1992 the Rio UN Conference on Environment and Development, the Earth Summit, put the touchstone of international respectability on the politically loaded concept of sustainability for nearly all branches of capitalist economy.

The 1992 World Summit gave birth to SARD or Sustainable Agriculture and Rural Development. No one could possibly be against such a noble idea. On superficial examination, there is nothing wrong with wishing for the advancement of the purposes of those advocating the permanent well being (sustainability) of farmers and rural people. In fact the Earth Summit documents spoke eloquently about the horrors of soil erosion, misuse of agrochemicals, the destruction of forests by invading hungry peasants, the benefits of using less pesticides.

But underneath the soft green rhetoric of the UN SARD creators, there is a real agenda of the global agribusiness brokers: Yes, conventional agriculture causes pollution but it also feeds the world. The population of the planet continues to increase, so, while we tinker with the machinery of the industrial agricultural system—with technical schemes like herbicide-resistant crops and a more discriminating use of pesticides often described as Integrated Pest Management—we must bring the peasants' unproductive holdings into that system.

Robert Paarlberg, professor of political science at Wellesley

College, elaborates the camouflaged international agribusiness agenda of the Earth Summit in *Countrysides at Risk: The Political Geography of Sustainable Agriculture*, a pamphlet he wrote in 1994 for the Washington, DC think-tank, Overseas Development Council. Paarlberg makes the industrialization of Third World agriculture, euphemistically dubbed "the green revolution," to be environment-friendly, an increasing food-production mechanism for closing the huge global food gap between North and South. In translating an ecocidal and upper class-driven system, industrialized agriculture, into a savior of the environment and food stocks, Paarlberg transforms the peasants' traditional farming, making it responsible for most environmental degradation in the world's countrysides.

Yet attacking the peasants has little to do with sustainable agriculture but everything to do with a rigorous defense of selling pesticides, fertilizers, machinery and agricultural research. This is the program of the World Bank's sixteen international agricultural institutes, which manufacture agribusiness methods of farming and distribute industrialized agriculture throughout the Third World.

Three of these research institutes are in Europe and the United States and thirteen are all over Latin America, Africa, and Asia. They cover the world from these locations: (1) Cali, Colombia: Centro Internacional de Agricultura Tropical; (2) Lima, Peru: Centro Internacional de la Papa (Potato); (3) Mexico City, Mexico: Centro Internacional de Mejoramiento de Maiz y Trigo (Corn and Wheat); (4) Washington, DC: International Food Policy Research Institute; (5) The Hague, Netherlands: International Service for National Agricultural Research; (6) Rome, Italy: International Plant Genetic Resources Institute; (7) Bouake, Cote d' Ivoire: West Africa Rice Development Association; (8) Ibadan, Nigeria: International Institute of Tropical Agriculture; (9) Nairobi, Kenya: International Livestock Research Institute; (10) Aleppo, Syria: International Center for Agricultural Research in the Dry Areas; (11) Nairobi, Kenya: International Centre for Research in Agroforestry; (12) Patancheru, India: International Crops Research Institute for the Semi-Arid Tropics; (13) Colombo, Sri Lanka: International Irrigation Management Institute; (14) Manila, Philippines: International Center for Living Aquatic Resources Management; (15) Los Banos, Philippines: International Rice Research Institute; and (16) Bogor, Indonesia: Center for International Forestry Research.

The World Bank manages this global farm educational empire through the Consultative Group on International Agricultural Research (CGIAR). Maurice Strong, the Canadian businessman who in 1992 presided over the Earth Summit in Rio, also chaired a panel of experts in 1998 and found that without the leadership and participation of CGIAR nothing can be done in the Third World to "eradicate" poverty, end hunger or ensure "sustainable food security."[4]

Despite such global standing befitting a World Bank subsidiary enterprise, which, however, is entirely a fiction designed to buttress the World Bank's elaborate illusions of self-importance, both the CGIAR and its planetary network of research centers are invisible. With more than $330 million per year, 1,800 scientists, and 10,000 technicians, these institutes are in the forefront of the Western world's secret but ceaseless campaign to abolish the peasants. They are producing and selling non-tropical agriculture in the tropics with crops such as wheat, corn, soybeans, and rice. Much more than food, these Western organizations are manufacturing culture—their own culture. They are the monasteries of the religion of Western science and capitalism, high tech mechanisms for the perpetuation of Western colonialism in the tropics. Their sole purpose is to undermine the world's millennia agrarian culture. They are afraid of the peasants.

Says Octavio Paz, Mexico's Nobel-prized writer: "The peasant— remote, conservative, somewhat archaic in his ways of dressing and speaking, fond of expressing himself in traditional modes and formulas— has always had a certain fascination for the urban man. In every country he represents the most ancient and secret element of society. For everyone but himself he embodies the occult, the hidden, that which surrenders itself only with great difficulty: a buried treasure, a seed that sprouts in the bowels of the earth, an ancient wisdom hiding among the folds of the land."[5]

But the World Bank scientists don't see the peasants that way at all. These mostly European and American men, and their Third World pupils, are full of apocalyptic visions of Africa and Latin America and Asia exploding with another two billion peasants in the next twenty-five years. Knowing that their artificial science could not possibly come up with more tricks to increase by, at least, 50 percent the yield of their exhausted crops by the year 2025, they are turning all their anxieties to biotechnology or genetic engineering. They are working for some kind of a miracle. Their engineering of the food crops at the molecular level of life is the perfect secret mechanism of biological warfare they are directing against the peasants and those peasants' seeds of food and culture.

The thousands of projects of these missionary outposts of American and European agribusiness subvert very ancient agrarian traditions of raising food, steal indigenous agricultural knowledge, and sow the ground with explosive seeds of hunger. They have managed to replace 70 percent of the Third World's fantastic wheat and rice varieties, and 10 percent of the peasants' indigenous maize, potatoes, and sorghum with the hunger seeds of the European and American scientists. The scientists' seeds of wheat, rice, maize, potatoes, and sorghum produce more per acre than the nature seeds of wheat, rice, maize, potatoes, and sorghum of peasant societies. Yet the fatal flow in the factory / science seeds is that they have hunger bioengineered into them. They are useless without pesticides, fertilizers and water. They are also defenseless against most pests and diseases.

Paarlberg leaves these matters out of his discussion. All things political become matters of production. He pretty much writes off Africa, lamenting in particular that the industrial agricultural model developed by five of the World Bank's research institutes in Africa did not yet set strong roots in the black continent which has the unfortunate distinction of leading the South in rapid population growth and poverty.

Paarlberg, however, is very sophisticated in his biased assessment of traditional farming. He condemns Third World mega dam projects and state policies destroying village commons and forests. He says that greater gender equity is necessary in Africa, and land reform would be good for Latin America. He is also critical of the "second generation" problems of industrial agriculture—overuse of pesticides, fertilizers, increasing resistance of pests to poisons. Running through his superficial critique of high-tech agricultural practices, however, there are repeated allegations, indeed a systematic denunciation of peasants for causing the "first generation" problems of development. Paarlberg says that peasants destroyed the rural environment, cutting down forests, mining the land of its nutrients, and, in general, they degraded nature. This is a preposterous accusation against peasants, practically the only people on earth who in fact are practitioners of a socially just and sustainable way of life and culture.

Clearly Paarlberg's brief was designed to drum up support for the morally bankrupt World Bank international agricultural research institutions by creating the dangerous image that those missionary icons of American agribusiness power in the Third World are paragons of environmental protection and food security. Yet Paarlberg's faith is not his alone. The same idea, expressed differently, came out of the Rio Earth Summit in 1992, and the same proposals dominate the discussion on "sustainable agriculture" at the highest levels of governments, universities, and international organizations.

For instance, since the 1996 World Food Summit, the UN Food and Agriculture Organization keeps talking of the urgent need to promote the "sustainable intensification of agriculture." And during the "International Centers Week" in the last days of October every year in Washington, DC, scientists and administrators of the World Bank's international research institutes get together and fill the place with similar slogans. Their public reports become sponges that take up the entire vocabulary of the civil society, using powerful words like capacity building, pro-poor, pro-environment, bottom-up development strategies, two-way learning, and sustainable development. That way, they conceal their real purpose of pirating the tropical world's fantastic agrarian culture in the peasants' seeds and knowledge.

On the one hand, almost surreptitiously, these missionaries admit their agribusiness experiment (the Orwellian "green revolution") failed. It failed to accomplish what their public relations men said it would do, help peasants. In fact, this green revolution hurt the peasants because the Western missionaries' agribusiness methods strengthened the cash croppers, the large farmers, and, furthermore, exacerbated rural impoverishment and grinding poverty.

On the other hand, the funders of the "green revolution" rush to their conventional wisdom of preparing themselves for a "second green revolution" by bringing together "biotechnology" and "information technology" to "give a new opportunity to mankind" "to disappear the hunger menace from the world."[6] Translated into English this is an ominous message: The men, who leveled peasant farming in Western

Europe and North America, are now arming Third World agricultural scientist and agribusinessmen with ingenious biotechnological processes, chemicals, seeds, and information. They do that to extend the life of their "green revolution" to buy or steal the genetic food crop wealth of the Third World for the benefit of the North and its corporate elite.

Professor Robert Paarlberg preached a similar catechism with his crisp reminder that, in places like Africa, agriculture faces a "modernization and intensification imperative."

It is both laughable and tragic to still think of the intensification (industrialization) of peasant agriculture as a high tech bullet supposedly able to close the world's food gap. First of all, the intensification of agriculture, including the genetic engineering of crops and farm animals, in the societies of Europe and North America over the last hundred years and, since the 1960s, in selected regions of Latin America, Asia, and Africa, has left a dreadful global legacy of broken democratic institutions and ecological and social and political violence. Rachel Carson, an American biologist, documented merely the ecocidal dimensions of that violence in the United States in her 1962 book, *Silent Spring*. And an Ethiopian agricultural scientist, Melaku Worede, accuses the intensification of farming practices in Ethiopia and Africa for Ethiopia's and Africa's famine and irreversible losses of crop diversity.[7]

There is also a structural reason why biotechnology won't end hunger: It isn't designed to. What it is designed to do, as all products are, is create more profit for those who create the product. The well being of the customer is usually important at least to some minimal degree, of course, since without it sales will dry up. But the customer in this instance isn't the peasant farmer but the consumer of the crop—those living in the countries importing it. Agribusiness can make absolutely no money out of enhancing the well being of the peasant, and thus biotech is not designed with that in mind. BUT the propaganda that it is designed to end hunger really is worth something as a fig leaf behind which to hide the further destruction.

Third World countries like Mexico, the Philippines and India, which are the leading guinea pigs of the North's agribusiness management, produce much more poverty and hunger than food. Indeed there is nearly a mathematical relationship between violence and agribusiness management in both North and South. The indigenous people of Mexico's

Chiapas state launched their insurrection on January 1994 because of the misery and starvation the hegemonic hacienda / agribusiness system has been producing for them for generations. Agrarian discontent has been at the heart of the ferocious civil wars in Guatemala, El Salvador, and Nicaragua; the Brazilian army occupation of Brazil from 1964 to 1990, and the tyranny of the military assassin governments of Chile from 1973 to 1990 and Argentina from 1976 to 1983.[8]

Colombia has spent the entire twentieth century in violence, much of which has agrarian roots. Colonial relationships in the countryside are outward manifestations of a secret war of assassinations, fear, internal refugees and violence. One of those refugees, Alvaro Arcila Bedoya, was visiting Washington, DC, in 7 March 1995, with a woman from Peru, Isabel Susanabar Huarocc, also a victim of the bitter war between the Maoist Shining Path guerrillas and the Peruvian state. Both spoke eloquently and with passion on the plight of the hundreds of thousands of "internally displaced" Colombians and Peruvians. Alvaro Bedoya said that most of the violence in Colombia results from the aggression of large landowners and corporations producing food for export. The more wealthy a region in natural resources, land in particular, the more widespread the violence against the campesinos and indigenous people. Land grabbing in Peru, Isabel Huarocc argued, is not the chief source of internal upheaval as it is in Colombia. But land struggles are also critical in the violence and transformation of Peru as well. Both Alvaro Bedoya and Isabel Huarocc are indigenous people, Native Americans. Isabel Huarocc burst into tears when she described the assassination of her grandfather by the guerrillas and the assassination of her father by the state. Indigenous people and peasants pay the price of development.

The global political system condoning and tolerating such aggressive state violence in Colombia and Peru is the same system of North American and European countries that inherited the racism and colonialism of more than 500 years of imperialism of European and North American power over Latin America, Asia, and Africa. Indigenous people are still fighting for their political independence. Anamaria Guacho, Quechua peasant and General Secretary of the Movimiento Indigena del Chimborazo of Ecuador, says: "So many state offices, so many development agencies are well meaning but destroy us nonetheless. They have taught us to beg but we want liberation by our own means. Our Inca ancestors were our pioneers. Their gold drove the white man mad and cruel, they themselves only used it to make jewelry. Theirs was the right attitude. Wealth is not our goal. What is important is the spiritual element, and economic, cultural and political independence."[9]

The corporate agents of hegemonic power, and their Third World elite collaborators, however, don't listen to powerless people. They continue to impoverish the Third World of its natural resources. Peru exported its guano fertilizer and fish to feed the industrial agriculture of affluent Europe and North America, just like Mexico exports petroleum to the over saturated chemical machinery of agribusiness in the United States. Peru earned nothing from mining its nature for the benefit of foreigners. But the unequal relationship between Peru and the hegemonic foreigners did prepare the ground for the misery, poverty and violence that assassinated both the father and grandfather of Isabel Susanabar Huarocc.

Oil development was killing the Ecuadorian Amazon in the 1990s for the equivalent of 13 days of US petroleum needs. For the last thirty years or so, "American oil development in the Orient—as the Ecuadorian Amazon is known—has proceeded virtually without regulation. Everyday, the petroleum industry dumps millions of gallons of untreated toxic pollutants into a watershed extending over fifty thousand square miles of rain forest, and it has opened vast stretches of the region to colonization and deforestation. The impact has been so devastating that at least one tribe, the Cofan, has all but disappeared."[10]

Development is cannibalizing more than Ecuador's rain forest and indigenous people. For example, the country has been in a frenzy of producing bananas and shrimp for export. But the very modern agrochemical "medicine" sprayed on the bananas to cure them from the spreading and persistent black leaf wilt disease, *sigatoka negra,* may also be the poison that prevents the shrimp from molting to form new exoskeleton. This insidious teratogenic ecological disaster is hitting the shrimp farms in the North of the Taura River in the Gulf of Guayaquil. And the poison that kills 60 to 80 percent of Ecuador's shrimp moves down the Gulf of Guayaquil through the drainage basin of the Taura River, a vast area contaminated with mercury and cyanide of gold mining, untreated sewage from the metropolitan city of Guayaquil, and other dangerous industrial wastes.

The destruction of mangroves and wetlands near the shrimp farms completes the development ecocide that speeds up the disintegration of nature and culture in Ecuador. Nearly half of this Andean country's population of some ten-and-a-half million people may be suffering impoverishment from the collapsing ecosystems of the banana and shrimp economies. These people, and their plundered environment, are the shadow, in its latest version in the 1990s, and the beginning of the twenty-first century, of an evolving development catastrophe.

The symptoms of the banana-shrimp ecocide in Ecuador are also evident in Honduras, Peru, Colombia and Southeast Asia. The development syndrome is becoming pandemic: Intensive prawn agriculture in Asia is leaving "death and destruction in its wake."[11] Malaysian and Japanese timber companies and "a stampede of foreign loggers" are plundering "the last rain forest" of Papua New Guinea,[12] clearcutting the island nation's nature and culture.

I already explained why sub-Saharan Africa is falling apart. Yet Wangari Maathai, a Kenyan professor who inspired the Green Belt Movement, an indigenous environmental protection organization, accuses the international community and Africa's military oligarchy for the diachronic disintegration of Africa. She says:

> There is little willingness on the part of the international community to support genuine, mutually-supporting and cooperative solidarity with the African region, despite all the public statements to the contrary. It is not as if the causes and the symptoms of under-development and deprivations are unknown. They are discussed in a myriad of words in books, magazines, evaluation reports and development plans, many of which are written by experts from the same international community. So why do national and international development agencies, nevertheless, prefer to spend huge resources in curative social welfare programs (famine relief, food aid, refugee camps, peace-keeping forces and humanitarian missions) rather than use the same resources in preventive and sustainable human development programs? Why is the rich and developed world unwilling to adopt levels of production and consumption which would ensure that all peoples of the world can have a development model which is environmentally sustainable and morally just?
>
> African leaders have tended to take advantage of their people's state of disempowerment and debilitating poverty to rule them with an iron fist...
>
> It is suspected that huge sums of money given to the African people for development and which is partly responsible for their huge international

debts have been corruptly taken from the national treasuries and elsewhere and are stashed away in secret bank accounts within the same nations which control the Bretton Woods institutions [World Bank and International Monetary Fund]. Such sums of money are then available for use by the very same nations which demand that they be paid by masses of Africans who never got the money to begin with. Top secrecy surrounds such financial transactions. It is said that if all the sums of money which African leaders have in secret vaults outside Africa were returned to the rightful owners and made available for development, Africa would no more be in need of loans and foreign aid and there would be no more 'donor fatigue.'

Since it is known that these funds are stolen wealth why can't the international community accept that it is a crime to have stolen it and a crime to hide it for those who stole it? If it is a crime to kill half a million people in Rwanda why isn't it a crime to steal millions from national treasuries and indirectly cause the death of millions?[13]

In October 2004, Wangari Maathai received the Nobel Prize for Peace. But the tragedy she denounced continues. I am sure that no African "leader" or development professional would dare answer her questions. Furthermore, why this ceaseless poisoning of life, the destruction of the forests, the dangerous simplification of complex plant and animal communities, the homogenization of the immense diversity of human cultures and the diversity of life not merely in the Ecuadorian Amazon, Papua New Guinea, and in the entire continent of Africa but all over the Earth? Probably because the hegemonic industrialized culture of East and West, its scientists, bankers, and development experts believe, erroneously, that man can and should dominate nature. These men of progress are also under the treacherous illusion that their magic bullet technologies will get them out of the ecocidal trap they have been building around the globe. Peter Raven, director of the Missouri Botanical Garden, broke rank with his class during the XVI International Botanical Congress on August 1-7, 1999. He denounced the world of the twentieth century for hounding so much precious life to extinction.[14]

The victims of this violence have no illusions about the darkness of Western progress and development. Jorge Terena, a Brazilian Terena Indian representing the Alliance of Forest People, called Westerners spiritually blind. He said in 1992:

Indians, tappers and river-dwellers have ancient ties with the environment. Spirits dwell in forests and rivers, and when these are destroyed, it is a destruction of the sacred. The equivalent would be if we were to come and lay waste the Vatican and St. Peter's in Rome. We'd be jailed and calumniated. But that is what has happened to us, and no one in the West recognizes it. Our sanctuaries have been trampled. One old shaman said to me he could no longer dream, and could therefore no longer guide his people, because the animals had fled and the spirits departed from the damaged landscape...

Development for Indians is death. In order to protect the Western system, human sacrifices are made. Which is the more irrational, superstitious? How can such spiritual blindness be called civilized? Once you destroy the spirit of the environment, people go wandering in search of that spirit; the psyche is messed up, the spiritual part of human beings ruined. People then start to question their own self-worth. The West believes only in body and soul, they don't understand the importance of cherishing the spirit. In the village where I grew up, there was no prison, no child-care provision, no home for the elderly. When I first went to Sao Paulo, I was looking at lost people, kids on the streets, beggars, the desperation for money. You could see what these people had lost, and it was frightening, because they didn't know what it was. Victims of development. That is why the relearning of the traditional ways is a matter of survival, not only for the people themselves, but also so that the rich and powerful may become wise and recognize the errors they have made.[15]

Mexico loses dignity and wealth in its relations with the colossus of the North, the United States. In fact Mexico's very survival has been a matter of American foreign policy since the United States dismembered Mexico in the 1840s. California, Nevada, Utah, New Mexico, Arizona and Texas—a huge region of the United States—came from the American colonial war against Mexico. Thus Mexico's export of petroleum to the United States is a colonial tribute. Petroleum is not made in nature with the speed of corn. Eventually petroleum will disappear from Mexico. Meanwhile, the United States sells Mexico cheap corn produced with Mexico's own cheap oil. But inexpensive American corn in Mexico is an additional pressure against the oppressed Mexican campesinos who raise corn, the indigenous people's sacred food.

The United States forced the Mexican state to abandon its price support of Mexican corn and to scrap the constitutional protection of the ejido or communal land system for the peasant. These policy changes were part of NAFTA, the 1993 North American Free Trade Agreement that tie Canada, the United States and Mexico into a common market. The Zapatistas of Mexico's Chiapas started their rebellion against the Mexican state on January 1994, the first anniversary of the signing of

NAFTA. The Zapatistas are right to see NAFTA as another powerful tool of colonial oppression, which will accelerate conventional development—mining, extraction, production, and export—of their indigenous resources. Under these colonial conditions in both Chiapas and the rest of Mexico, there is hardly a place for development that is sustainable. Which is to say development that protects the environment and promotes the interests of the Mexican people rather than the profits of the foreign and domestic elites. The poor, especially the landless among the impoverished rural Mexicans, are desperately trying to grab any land that is not already owned by the rich. Such ruthless struggle for survival often wrecks forests and nature. In that sense, the agenda of the Zapatistas for self-reliance, food security and food sovereignty, an end to the colonial exploitation of Chiapas, and dignity for the indigenous people of Chiapas, is a sustainable development agenda.

The Zapatistas' struggle, no less than the struggles for green or ecopolitical human development throughout the world, have a long way to go. Both movements face state power and the hegemony of the northern colossus, the United States.[16] The plutocracy of America funded the creation of the concept and illusion of capitalist sustainable development. While its corporations plunder the environment and human communities at home and abroad, its massive academic and government bureaucracies are managing the global debate on military and food security, poverty, and conventional development—underneath the stylish slogan of sustainable development.

Imperialism

The prevailing thesis is this: The United States is the end of history. American power defeated Russia's evil empire, therefore, America is the only global superpower. Its policies are planetary, nearly unchallenged, but enforceable at great cost: The emergence of India and, especially, China in Asia challenge America's global hegemony. Nevertheless, if the United States says that economic growth is necessary for sustainable development, it is. If the United States says all peasant land holdings must come under the management of an agribusiness hacienda, the liquidation of traditional farming is a foregone conclusion. Academic experts, glued to imperial schemes, grab these rumors and make them elaborate policy studies with options for all contingencies, including the possibility of the spread of the Zapatistas' movement beyond Chiapas and the political radicalization of the civil society. After all, the civil society of Eastern Europe and Russia used the innocence and subversiveness of ecology to bring down mighty bureaucratic socialist states. The lesson is clear. Non-governmental organizations (NGOs)—the heart and brains of civil society—are growing everywhere. Gods forbid that the civil society in the United States would subvert and replace the corporate state. Human liberation might also reach the North American plantation.

The United States remains an imperial state bent on the uninterrupted exploitation of the world's resources. America's invasion and conquest of Iraq in 2003 is an illustration of that imperial policy. America is using its power and science to confuse, frighten, and convince the civil society at home and opinion and policy makers abroad that managing nature is a responsible policy, that American corporations are good stewards of resources, that "free" markets and trade fuel sustainable development. And since the Third World is Third World because it is "under-developed," what a better chance to reduce and, perhaps, eliminate poverty in those huge regions of the world by more development, more intense sustainable development. Of course, not everyone buys this deceptive message.

Gabriel Garcia Marquez, a Nobel Prize-winning Colombian writer, said that the trouble in Latin America started over tropical fruit. He says: "Look at the mess we've got ourselves into just because we invited a gringo to eat some bananas." The gringo settled in the tropics—and the tropics have never been the same again: "When the banana company arrived...the local functionaries were replaced by dictatorial foreigners... brought to live in the electrified chicken yard so they could enjoy...the dignity that their status warranted and so that they would not suffer from the heat and the mosquitoes and the countless discomforts and privations of the town. The old policemen were replaced by hired assassins with machetes."[17]

From these modest banana origins, gringo scientists, corporations, religious missionaries and officials continue to be in charge of the industrial world's strategy to destroy the diversity and power of indigenous peasant culture. They lead a crusade to rebuild the world in their own image. They have so convinced or frightened the ruling classes of Asia, Latin America, and Africa that the Western way is the *only* way that, together, they force the natives to work bananas, rubber, oil, aluminum, asphalt highways, airports, computers, plastics, fertilizers, genetic engineering and pesticides.

The managers of the gringo colonial system consider the Third World like a huge jungle from which they import designer foods, cheap raw materials, a select number of skilled / wealthy persons, temporary farm workers, and products from factories belonging to their corporations. The idea of free trade with Mexico, of course, was to institutionalize even further the ability of American companies to jump borders and produce their commodities the cheapest way possible. With practically no enforceable worker health and environmental protection standards, Mexico gives American corporations a Dickensian world of big profits and power they use against their workers at home. In fact, American corporations tried but failed to globalize their colonial relations with Mexico through the Multilateral Agreement on Investment (MAI), a proposed international trade pact that would transform all global commercial relations on the model of the North American Free Trade Agreement—NAFTA. But, in a real sense, MAI—should it ever become a binding international agreement among the nations of the world—would become a license for corporations to loot the earth and its people.[18] The United States also sees the Third World as a dumping ground for its surplus wheat, corn, chemicals, drugs, machinery, fertilizers, weapons, aid, geopolitical / strategic experiments—and wastes.

The World Bank is the gringo's premier international development agency. It lends Third World governments tens of billions of dollars a year for projects designed to strengthen the colonial relationships between North and South. Which is to say, World Bank money goes to the clearcutting of forests for timber, damming of rivers for hydroelectric power plants, the building of chemical, fertilizer, mining factories, urbanization schemes, and the industrialization of traditional agriculture, particularly the duplication of cash crop enclaves for the export of food.[19]

Mechanizing the Third World, accelerating the often kleptocratic and piratical processes of extraction, production, and export of its material, biological, and, particularly, genetic wealth, is impoverishing the entire planet. For instance, the nuna bean is a nutritious food that is a treasure to the Andean people. They roast rather than boil the beans, thus saving their scarce firewood. The nuna beans are popping beans as well. They have been grown and bred for centuries in Peru, Bolivia, Ecuador and Colombia. Yet, in the year 2000, an American company, Appropriate Engineering and Manufacturing, was granted a US patent over this vital food crop and cultural tradition of the indigenous people of the Andes. The patent is, without doubt, morally offensive and unacceptable to civilized people. Julie Delahanty, an analyst for Rural Advancement Foundation International, a North American civil society organization, said the patent "usurps the genius of Andean farmers for the commercial gain of a US company."[20] This is happening because the international legal system cares very little about indigenous people, and even less, about agricultural genetic diversity. Says Darrell Addison Posey, a British scholar on indigenous people: "International laws that guarantee protection of traditional knowledge and genetic resources are inadequate to non-existent, making most bioprospecting, food and agricultural development, trade and alternative product initiatives predatory on local communities, rather than supportive of them."[21] That is why the world is an alien place where sophisticated violence is the guiding principle of all international relations.

The Third World, nevertheless, is the home of the tropics, the Amazon, biological and cultural diversity. But the economists of the World Bank are trained in the brutalities of imperial piracy and power, not the wisdom of traditional cultures or the vital importance of biodiversity and ecosystems or the liberating influence of self-reliance and food sovereignty.

On June 30, 1997, I participated in a day-long "brainstorming workshop" of the World Bank concerned about the tendency of the state in Southern Africa—Malawi, Mozambique, Tanzania, Zambia, Zimbabwe and South Africa—to involve itself persistently in food markets, particularly to hold stocks of grain reserves, and even put restrictions in international trade in grain. The World Bank thinking in this academic exercise of "food market reforms in Southern Africa" is revealing not merely of the actual policies of the World Bank towards Africa but, just as importantly, throws light on the West's heart of darkness. Africa may no longer be a colony of Europe, but colonialism is still the currency of discourse guiding African development.

Economists from the International Food Policy Research Institute, a Washington think-tank closely tied to the World Bank, and economics professors from Michigan State University and Purdue University, spent a lot of time explaining their convoluted theories around the behavior of the state in Southern Africa. But despite the trite academic monologue or, perhaps, because of it, there was never a doubt about the World Bank's dislike of the role of the state in the food economies of Africa. The Bank said it simply wanted to see the region "move towards more developed grain markets and market based solutions to national food security objectives."

With rare exceptions, listening to economists describe their studies of a variety of food market reforms in Southern Africa, added nothing to real understanding of why, for instance, Zimbabwe, a country with rich and plentiful land, was on the verge of internal explosion from landless and marginal rural population. The obvious need to me and to Tobias Takavarasha, Zimbabwe's permanent secretary of agriculture, sitting next to me, was land redistribution from the 4,000 largest landowners to the landless. But the World Bank—and its professors—had no interest on the great potential of land or agrarian reform to make Zimbabwe a powerhouse in Southern Africa.

World Bank men and women see things differently. They see Latin America, Asia, and Africa as population factories, far away places for the raw data of "under-development," poor regions with close to a billion hungry people with huge unmet needs in clean water, sanitation, health, housing, roads, electricity, etc. Thus moving money at the World Bank towards developing countries is the reason for being,[22] demolishing the backwardness of non-white people, bringing them the gospel of development—even if that means pushing wastes to get to that desired goal.

In a December 12, 1991 internal memorandum, Lawrence H. Summers, then World Bank vice president and chief economist, said that "the economic logic behind dumping a load of toxic waste in the lowest wage country [of the Third World] is impeccable and we should face up to that." The Summers memorandum was leaked to environmentalists, including Jose Lutzenberger, Secretary of the Environment of Brazil. In early February 1992 Lutzenberger reacted with outrage at the Summers proposal. He said to him his reasoning for arguing in favor of dumping toxic wastes on the Third World was "perfectly logical but totally insane. It underlines...the absurdity of much of what goes for 'economic thinking' today...Your thoughts...[are] a concrete example of the unbelievable alienation, reductionist thinking, social ruthlessness and the arrogant ignorance of many conventional 'economists' concerning the nature of the world we live in. If it came from some insignificant teacher in a third grade school in the backwoods it might be laughable, but coming from a Harvard professor and a man in your position it is an insult to thinking people all over the world. If the World Bank keeps you as a vice president it will lose all credibility. To me it would confirm what I often said as an environmentalist, years ago, fighting ecologically devastating and socially disruptive World Bank 'development projects,' namely that the best thing that could happen would be for the Bank to disappear."

The World Bank has not disappeared, however. Jose Lutzenberger was fired as Minister of the Environment of Brazil in early 1992, and Lawrence Summers—who in 1999 became the US Secretary of the Treasury—was rewarded for his imperialism. In 1993 he became the Assistant Secretary of the US Treasury Department for International Affairs, the American official responsible for the behavior of the World Bank and other international financial institutions. In fact, Lawrence Summers was one of three candidates for becoming president of the World Bank. But in 2001 he achieved the pinnacle of power in the United States. He became the president of Harvard University—America's and, probably, the world's most prestigious school. However, in February 1995, he put together the multi-billion dollar package for bailing out Mexico that collapsed in less than two years after the North American Free Trade Agreement opened its borders and workers to Canadian and American corporations.

Lawrence Summers, finally, had his revenge on Jose Lutzenberger and the Amazon. He brokered Brazil's November 1998 structural adjustment agreement with the International Monetary Fund (IMF), the World Bank, and the US Treasury Department. Brazil borrowed more billions but, in the process, lost nearly all the funds the rich industrial countries gave her in the Rio Earth Summit in 1992 for slowing down the destruction of the Amazon. Begging Brazil in 1998 also promised to cut its domestic environmental spending by 66 percent. Says Steve Schwartzman, an anthropologist with Environmental Defense in Washington, DC, "The IMF, the World Bank, the US Treasury and the Government of Brazil have taken an insignificant step towards balancing Brazil's budget and a giant step toward the destruction of Brazil's ecological patrimony. This is more irresponsible than the harshest critics of the IMF and the Bank could have imagined."[23]

The American-dominated international political system is becoming more openly violent. World Bank technocrats manage a sophisticated yet crude machinery of colonial administration and oppression. Lending money and technology to Third World governments greases the global technocrats' levers of imperial control.[24] With no state power anywhere defending biodiversity, ecological patrimony, or the natural world, international agricultural research centers and financial institutions and corporations guide state bureaucracies and the media how best to protect capitalist investment and development.

The world, meanwhile, is reeling from the violence and piracy of corporate business: Hundreds of millions of people are consumed in hunger, poverty, war, landlessness, and exploitation. And nature and biodiversity—the indispensable foundations of life—are wasted as if there is no tomorrow. Hugh Iltis, the courageous botanist at the University of Wisconsin, has been waging a one-man war against indifferent scientists, cattle ranchers, greedy corporations, and the international financial institutions making a killing from the devastation of the natural world. In 1969 he explained why nature matters:

- First, because our species, *Homo sapiens*, evolved in nature, and was selected by nature, we need nature to survive.

- Secondly, because of our technological successes in conquering nature, we have been completely preoccupied with progress which to agriculture has meant ever-increasing production of goods and food to feed more and more people. This means ever-increasing destruction of the natural environment which made us. Our preoccupations have made us not only rich and civilized, but also arrogant and blind to inescapable biological realities. If we wish to continue our evolution, a radical shift from an exploitive to an ecological philosophy is a most urgent business.

- Lastly, only undisturbed ecosystems, such as virgin prairies or forests, can show us their vast ecological complexities. Such untamed lands are desperately needed for teaching and research, for a balanced stable environment and a beautiful and healthy world.[25]

However, by 1986, Iltis could see it did not matter what one said.

Industrial civilization was, almost by design, a big killer of life. All developers, he said, are

> recklessly destructive of nature and in an orgy of environmental brutality, clearcut the forests, burn the trees, and plow up the land to grow more food or graze more cattle, even before any scientist has had a chance to find out what lives there. In the name of growth, progress, and development, and with a colossal self-confidence, we humans are now messing up even the last wild lands and damming the last wild rivers, oblivious of the irreplaceable biological treasures that are being destroyed.[26]

In the midst of this global ecocide, state military bureaucracies spend a trillion dollars a year but fail to establish any security in and outside of their borders.

In March 1995 the Canadian Coast Guard seized a Spanish trawler fishing in the neighborhood of Canada's territorial waters east of Newfoundland, an area known as Grand Banks in which Canada forbids its own fishermen from catching fish simply because there are so few of them left alive.[27]

The collapse of one of Canada's most important fisheries, and the confrontation of Canada with Spain and the European Union over fish and North Atlantic fishing rights, are cracks in the international piratical and predatory management of the world's resources. Like conventional agriculture, marine fishing is *mining* the seas and oceans of fish and biodiversity. The industrialization of fishing has destroyed about 70 percent of once-rich fisheries all over the world. Because of wasteful overfishing, huge amounts of fish, ranging from 17.9 million tons to 39.5 million tons a year, are discarded at sea. And states spend more than $50 billion a year subsidizing their fishing fleets.

Sylvia Earle, former chief scientist of the US National Oceanic and Atmospheric Administration, says that the fishing practices of industrial countries are deadly. They are:

> destabilizing the nature of ancient ocean ecosystems through the relentless, pervasive removal of life from the sea.... Part of the reason for the swift decline of ocean wildlife concerns the absurdly destructive methods used for commercial fishing. If ducks and geese had been captured by dragging trawls through marshes or if songbirds were taken by bulldozing forests, or squirrels captured by dynamiting their trees or buffalo obtained by gathering them in nets along with rabbits, lizards, shrubs and clumps of prairie grass, the catch for market of these creatures would have ended much

sooner than it did. Even with the selective techniques used in the 1800's to obtain wild birds and mammals commercially, it was soon obvious that natural systems could not long sustain the high levels of new predation that we imposed. Nothing in millions of years of history of passenger pigeons, prairie hens, Carolina parakeets, turkeys, quail and other native gamebirds prepared them for sustained large-scale slaughter, coupled with the gradual reduction in the habitats required for them to reproduce and prosper. The same principle applies to cod, halibut, tuna, sharks, crabs, oysters and clams.[28]

The global violence and barbarism against fish and biological diversity in the world's waters mirrors similar violence and barbarism on land for other "resources." Peru and Ecuador, for example, have been fighting over petroleum in their Amazon forest. Herbert "Betinho" DeSouza, director of the Brazilian Institute for Social and Economic Analysis, says that "the world is more and more organized in terms of social apartheid. There is apartheid inside each country. If you go to Rio de Janeiro and you don't want to see poor people, that is possible because there is an area for the rich and one for the poor, a geographical apartheid...Brazil is a producer of hunger and misery for the majority, and wealth and goods for ten percent of the population."[29]

This is particularly true in Northeast Brazil, where I had the good fortune to visit in early 1992, with the result the first chapter of this book mirrors to some degree what I learned about the violence of the Brazilian and the global landowning class. Yet the situation in the Northeast hacienda is much worse than I thought. It is a nightmare.

In the United States, the Republicans in Congress, without knowing anything about the Brazilian Northeast, are pushing rural America in the direction of that murderous hacienda model. They display their hatred against family farmers, poor Americans and the environment. In the 1980s, under the administration of the Republican presidents Ronald Reagan and George Bush, class divisions reached a new height as the most affluent 2.5 million Americans made an after-tax income gain which equaled the entire income of the poorest 50 million people. It is not a secret that the anti-social and anti-ecological agenda of the Republican Senators and Congresspersons is the agenda of the American ruling class.

The corporate masters of the world's only superpower want more of the wealth of America and more of the wealth of the planet. Their Draconian legislation is designed to freeze blacks, Hispanics, indigenous Americans, other minorities, and poor whites in misery and powerlessness. The 1994 victory of the Republican members of Congress was a defiant step by that corporate ruling class to reverse even the possibility that civil society in the United States might mobilize against corporations. Republican policies aim to cripple public participation in decision-making, and gut any pretense that the government is anything more than a defender of corporate property and rights. Timber companies, for example, have been plundering America's nature and national forests with the supervision of the US Forest Service.[30] Such bad policies became the norm with the coming to power in 2001 of the Republican leader, George W. Bush. His administration confirmed the policies of plunder to permanence. And the attack of Moslem fanatics against the United States on the eleven of September 2001 gave George W. Bush the excuse he needed to push the country one step closer to police state management at home and warfare abroad. He invaded Iraq to grab that country's petroleum and enrich the corporations that funded his stealing of the 2000 election. "Security" and "terrorism," funded in the hundreds of billions of dollars, have replaced state social and environmental policies. So the corporate policies of the state, including legislation in Congress supported by politicians (nearly all of the Republicans and most of the Democrats) leave no doubt in the federal bureaucrats' mind whose servants they really are.

Industrialism is Giving Cancer to the World

The robber barons are here again, but, on the dawn of the twenty-first century, they operate with the powerful and colonizing assets of tobacco science, misinformation, a virulent anti-environmental rhetoric,[31] cost-benefit analysis, and the outright support of state and federal bureaucracies.[32] It's as if the country is moving back in time to the comfortable era of mining and cold war—the 1950s.

Wilhelm Hueper (1894-1978), a distinguished American scientist who understood the toxic effects of industrialization, and from 1948 to 1964 directed the Environmental Section of the National Cancer Institute, warned us against the prolific, money-making toxins of the industrial robber barons. He said this in 1976:

It is in the best interest of mankind that industry makes the proper

adaptations for eliminating and or reducing environmental and occupational
cancer hazards, since human beings lack the ability to make the appropriate
biologic adaptations for effectively combating the growing wave of toxic
and carcinogenic risks propagated by modern industry, which represent
biologic death bombs with a delayed time fuse and which may prove to be,
in the long run, as dangerous to the existence of mankind as the arsenal of
atom bombs prepared for future action.... A future potential cancer hazard
to rather young individuals may be connected with the consumption of
foodstuffs and drinking water contaminated with one or several of the
carcinogenic chlorinated hydrocarbon pesticides, despite the insistently
soothing assurances and indignant protestations of their manufacturers and
commercial users.[33]

The new American robber barons, and their domestic and foreign
subsidiaries, are a formidable phalanx protecting their property in a
world falling apart. The message of Hueper, like those of Rachel Carson
and Robert van den Bosch, were completely lost in a sea of slogans about
progress, the benefits of factories, and the nirvana of free markets and
free trade. Meanwhile, cancer has become the plague of the world—
killing about 550,000 people in the year 2000 in the United States alone.
Between 1950 and 1995 all cancers increased by 55 percent in the United
States. Lung cancer accounted for a quarter of this huge rise in cancer.
Non-smoking cancers—non-Hodgkin's lymphoma, multiple myeloma,
adult brain cancer and childhood cancer—also rose greatly. In fact
cancer in children rose by more than 20 percent.[34] Samuel S. Epstein,
professor of occupational and environmental medicine at the medical
school of the University of Illinois, explains the cancer epidemic in these
terms: "Cancer is now [in 1987] the only major killing disease in the
industrialized world whose rates are sharply rising.... Increasing cancer
rates are an expression of run-away modern industrial technologies
whose explosive growth has clearly outpaced the ability of society to
control them...industry has used various strategies to con the public
into complacency and divert attention from their own recklessness and
responsibility for the cancer epidemic."[35]

Yet the advertisements of the captains of industry did not mention
cancer but "sustainable development" because "sustainable development"
was part of their propaganda war against the emerging civil society, which
they threaten with another more sophisticated version of feudalism.

Industrialized countries have been setting the earth on fire for a very long time. Their agriculture, forestry, fishing, chemicals, and the industrial manufacture and production of countless technologies and products, are deleterious to civilization and to the continuation of life on earth. The most "advanced" of the industrialized countries have also chemical and biological arms, and atomic and nuclear bombs and the intercontinental ballistic missiles to deliver those ecocidal and genocidal weapons. All in all, industrialized countries are stressing the planet's social, political, cultural and natural systems often to a breakdown.

In 1984, Hugh Iltis, the fearless professor of botany at the University of Wisconsin, equated "economic development" to cancer feeding on "biotic destruction."[36] A few years later, in the early 1990s, Robert Ayres and Udo Simonis, scientists of the United Nations University, described the global spread of industrialization during the last two centuries as a cancer. "[I]ndustrialization, in its present form," they said, "is a process of uncontrolled, unsustainable 'growth' that eventually destroys its host—the biosphere."[37] In the late 1990s, British biologists warned that, since the 1960s, the industrialization of agriculture in Western Europe is having devastating effects on nature. One-fifth of Europe's birds are endangered and threatened. The overall decline of birds, insects, and plants in northern Europe was quite dramatic in the last thirty years of the twentieth century. This was a time when the homogenization of Europe's countryside was pursued with rigor and science. European farmers, earning huge subsidies, abandoned their centuries-old agrarian traditions and demolished their beautiful small-farm landscape for the icon of the plantation growing rarely more than one crop. This was crippling, disabling, and death to many birds and other wildlife. In England in the years 1968 to 1995, farm birds like the skylark and corn bunting declined by thirty percent.[38] The United Nations Environment Programme (UNEP) issued a similar dire alarm in 2001. "Human activities," UNEP says, "are destroying [the] Earth's biological wealth at an unprecedented rate. There is a strong consensus that the extinction spasm now being caused by human activities is greater than any [extinction] since the dinosaurs died out 65 million years ago. This damage is irreversible and—many believe—unethical. What's more, given humanity's dependence on food crops and other biological resources, it is also dangerous to our species."[39] The World Wildlife Fund (WWF), a global civil society organization, agrees. In its 2002 report, WWF confirms that humanity's onslaught against nature is taking an awesome toll. In the relatively short span of time between 1970 and 2000, the world's natural ecosystems declined by about 37 percent. This translates into a loss of 15 percent of the terrestrial species, the destruction of some 35 percent of all animals and plants living in seas and oceans, and the disappearance of about 54 percent of all species of animals and plants living in freshwater. With this extremely recent ecocidal history, the future does not look good. The killing of nature, which WWF politely describes as "the world's ecological footprint," will have more lethal consequences in the next 50 years or so. Such a bloody footprint is already exacting 20 percent above the earth's biological capacity when the human population is 6 billion. In the year 2050, when it is possible that there will be 9 billion humans on earth, the "ecological footprint" of these humans will reach a level of taking away from the earth more than 80 to 120 percent of what the earth can provide. This means the 9 billion humans in 2050 would need something like 1.8 and 2.2 earth-sized planets.[40] That, of course, is impossible.

The International Joint Commission, an international organization set up to prevent and resolve disputes between the United States and Canada under the 1909 Boundary Waters Treaty and to implement the Great Lakes Water Quality Agreement of 1978, has been documenting the poisoning and breakdown of nature between Canada and the United States. Its 1998 Ninth Biennial Report says this about the danger of the persistent poisons in the environment of the Great Lakes: "The evidence," says the Commission, "is overwhelming: certain persistent toxic substances impair human intellectual capacity, change behaviour, damage the immune system and compromise reproductive capacity. The people most at risk are children, pregnant women, women of childbearing age and people who rely on fish and wildlife as a major part of their diet. Particularly at risk are developing embryos and nursing infants."[41]

The struggle over what to do about these biocides—reduce the amounts reaching water, air, and land, release no more in the environment, clean up areas of contamination—as much as the fight over our understanding of the meaning and substance of "sustainable development" in general, is a metaphor of the anger, hatred, and passion unleashed by the global discontinuities of industrial production.

The international economic and political system that benefits from the prevailing processes of violent and piratical development is using propaganda and intimidation to confuse and purchase the potential power of honest scientists and civil society in general. Its representatives from multinational corporations, international organizations like the World Bank, and governments are pupils of Niccolo Machiavelli (1469-1527), the Florentine intellectual and bureaucrat who codified the cruelty and deception one has to follow in pursuit of power. Machiavelli offered his considered opinion to the aspiring princes of sixteenth-century Italy, but he could have also been an advisor to secretaries of state, corporate executives or World Bank presidents—the princes who decide the fate of the world in the dawn of the twenty-first century. He says it makes sense that the prince is in reality and also appears to be compassionate, truthful, kind, sincere, and religious. However, the prince ought to be ready, once it suits him, to do the exact opposite of truthfulness, kindness, sincerity and devoutness. In other words, Machiavelli advises caution with things humans do to get a reputation for virtue since to run a state a prince "is often forced to act in defiance of good faith, of charity, of kindness, of religion. And so he should have a flexible disposition, varying as fortune and circumstances dictate...he should not deviate from what is good, if that is possible, but he should know how to do evil, if that is necessary."[42]

Non-governmental or civil-society organizations, of course, are becoming politically mature. They have read Machiavelli. They know which princes are doing evil. They came into being to fight that evil. They were born precisely because the rulers of the world, the princes of industrialized societies, failed so utterly in safeguarding the public good. In its December 29, 1994 newsletter, "Environment and Health Weekly," an American NGO from Annapolis, Maryland, Environmental Research Foundation, identified civil society's chief adversary as "the corporate form." This corporate form "has poisoned much of our land and water, harmed our health, polluted our politics, hijacked our democracy, and diminished our common wealth."

The civil society knows, however, it cannot fight its corporate enemies in their Bastilles. Yet civil society organizations understand that sustainable development is much more their vision of the future than it is a slogan of the corporate elite.

Non-governmental or civil-society organizations and the millions of often powerless people who create them, are defending primarily themselves with their defense of ecology, peasant and small-scale family farming, democracy, and social justice—the absolute requirements of sustainable development. In about forty years they defeated the mighty empire of the industrialized states in Eastern Europe, the Soviet Union.

It will be more difficult for the civil society to undo, reinvent or destroy the Berlin Wall of capitalist business-as-usual, but there is no doubt about the outcome of the conflict in the long term. After all, the struggle for *real* rather than *fake* sustainable development, particularly the revitalization of family agriculture, is much more important than crusades over cold or hot wars or monotheistic religions. The fate of this struggle is no less important than the fate of the earth. At the core of that contest is land and agriculture, the seminal importance of traditional farming, the preservation of agricultural biological diversity, and the survival of enough peasants in the Third World and enough small family farmers in the United States and Europe for an alive rural world. That, of course, is the main ingredient for both food sovereignty and democracy. Agrarian reform is the key to such vision.

I now return to Robert Mugabe, president of Zimbabwe. He is a tyrant and certainly I don't share his ideas or policies or politics. Yet he said something profound about land and agrarian reform in 2002, which merits understanding. During the World Summit on Sustainable Development in Johannesburg, South Africa, on September 2, 2002 he said:

> The poor should be able to use their sovereignty to fight poverty and preserve their heritage in their corner of the earth. That is why we, in Zimbabwe, understand only too well that sustainable development is not possible without agrarian reforms that acknowledges, in our case, that land comes first before all else, and that all else grows from and off it. This is the one asset that not only defines the Zimbabwean personality and demarcates sovereignty but also that has a direct bearing on the fortunes of the poor and prospects for their immediate empowerment and sustainable development. Indeed, ours is an agrarian economy, an imperative that renders the issue of access to land paramount. Inequitable access to land is at the heart of poverty, food insecurity and lack of development in Zimbabwe. Consequently, the question of agrarian reforms has, in many developing countries, to be high on the agenda of sustainable development if we are to meet the targets that are before us for adoption at this Summit. In our situation in Zimbabwe, this fundamental question has pitted the black majority who are the right-holders,

and, therefore, primary stakeholders, to our land against an obdurate and internationally well-connected racial minority, largely of British descent and brought in and sustained by British colonialism. Economically, we are an occupied country, 22 years after our Independence. Accordingly, my Government has decided to do the only right and just thing by taking back land and giving it to its rightful indigenous, black owners who lost it in circumstances of colonial pillage.

Conclusion

Doing Away With the Persistent and Giant Wrongs of Giant Agriculture

As I said, one does not have to agree with the policies of Robert Mugabe in order to side with him, as I am, on his 2002 position on agrarian reform. Since 2002, however, he is using violence against the white farmers of Zimbabwe and more violence against his opposition. But he was right connecting agrarian reform to rural prosperity and food security because that is what this book is all about: I started my narrative with Brazil—and some reflections on agrarian reform, literally speaking, giving land to the land-poor peasants, indigenous people whose land was stolen from them, very small family farmers, and the landless who are willing and able to raise food and culture on the land. I argued that, in my scale of values, agrarian reform is of the greatest significance for bringing to an end the corporate war against America's family farmers and agrarian culture and the earth—by means of the pointed attacks of giant companies against peasants and family farmers. But for this land distribution project to go anywhere, it would be necessary to break up the giant agribusiness corporations that have almost brought slavery back into the world and particularly rural America—their plantation.

The dust bowl curse of the 1930s against the *God-dam'd Okies* is symbolic of the violence unleashed in rural America and the rest of the world by industrialized farming, mechanizing what used to be a way of life on the land into a factory for the extraction of profits. The wreckage and recklessness and aggressiveness and death of that inhuman system of food production are everywhere in rural America. That other United States is littered with animal factories, abandoned farmhouses, deserted land, impoverished farm towns, and the industrialization of the countryside into massive plantations. The consequences of such an upheaval have been there for all to see and feel—for several decades. Walter Goldschmidt, the honest USDA anthropologist, brought to light in the early 1940s the undoing of rural America by agribusiness. Yet despite the feeble attempts in the US Senate in the mid-1970s to put a break in the path of the agribusiness colossus, government policy never ceased lavishing America's large farmers with gold. In 1983, another researcher, Dean MacCannell, professor of rural sociology at the University of California-Davis, issued a severe warning that complemented the warning of Walter Goldschmidt: Size of farms matters in agriculture. Large farms destroy rural America. MacCannell said agribusiness policies "cut against the grain of traditional American values." His studies showed that giant farmers were becoming America's "neo-feudal" lords who, with government assistance, were converting rural America into a Third World of poverty, injustice, exploitation and oppression. When large farms are in or near small farm communities, he says, they ruin the rural communities, sucking all life out of them: "In the place of towns which could accurately be characterized as providing their residents with clean and healthy environment, a great deal of social equality and local autonomy," he explains, "we find agricultural pollution, labor practices that lead to increasing social inequality, restricted opportunity to obtain land and start new enterprise, and the suppression of the development of local middle class and the business and services demanded by such a class."[1]

The middle class has always been the heart of democracy. So the most lasting of the effects of the industrialization of farming include the decline of democracy, poisoned water and food, high rates of debilitating disease and death from poisoning, monstrous malformations of the newborn, higher rates of cancer in both farmers, other rural residents, and wildlife, the drastic decline of the small white family farmers and the near disappearance of the black family farmers.

In 1900, there were 746,717 black farmers in the United States. In the next ten years, by 1910, black farmers increased by 19.6 percent, becoming 893,377. The next decade, black farmers increased by 3.6 percent, reaching their highest number ever: 925,710. That was the year 1920. Then an unstoppable decline and fall took the form of self-destruction and strife. Black farmers rushed to abandon farming. Second, a pernicious turn of the white society, its government and large farmers, hit the landed black farmers with the force of a cataclysm. Their campaign waged an invisible war of cheating the former slaves of their promised forty acres and a mule. Large white farmers, agribusiness, and government agencies at the county, state, and federal level scared black farmers, giving them the wrong information, denying their loans, harassing them out of their land. And when black Americans started demanding civil rights in the 1950s, the wrath of the large white farmers boiled over. Black farmers ran away from the countryside to the northern cities as fast as they could. The legacy of slavery, the failure to distribute land to black Americans after the Civil War, and the racist working of the federal land grant university and extension service had had their terrible impact on black farmers as well.

Joel Schor, a historian with USDA, reminded USDA of its racism and destructive policies toward black farmers. He concluded that, by 1995, the vanishing black farmers were, at the most, one percent of the country's farmers. Agriculture for blacks was becoming "a cultural memory." It was no longer a way of life or a source of employment.[2] Their numbers told their tragic history: They declined by 51.3 percent in the 1950s, 50.8 percent in the 1960s, and 57.3 percent in the 1970s. By 1997, the brave new rural world of America had cleansed itself of black farmers. Less than 18,000 black farmers were still farming in the year 2000, their numbers hitting the catastrophic level of 98 percent decline in the twentieth century.

I remember walking with a few black farmers protesting the discriminatory and racist policies of the US Department of Agriculture. The silent protest took place in Washington, DC on September 28, 2004. We were walking from the headquarters of USDA to Capitol Hill where the Constitutional Subcommittee of the House Judiciary Committee was preparing to have a hearing about the legal problems of the black farmers suing USDA. What startled me was that there were so few people in the protest march, and those who marched, were overwhelmingly old and black. The Congressman who chaired the hearing, Steve Chabot, captured the tragedy of the black farmers, saying this: "When slavery was ended in the United States, our government made a promise—a restitution of sorts—to the former slaves that they would be given 40 acres and a mule…what is clear is that promise was intended to help freed slaves be independent economically and psychologically, as holders of private property rights. What also is clear is that the very government that made this promise, the "People's Agency" [US Department of Agriculture] established in 1862 under President Abraham Lincoln, has sabotaged it by creating conditions that make sovereign and economically-viable farm ownership extremely difficult."

That same USDA also wrecked the lives of the small white family farmers, never ceasing telling them to get big or get out. Its advice was wrong most of the times. Its science was not science at all but a technology of conquest, which it gold-plated with lavish subsidies, research, and policies disdainful of nature and human culture. Sowing pro-agribusiness seeds in rural America did bring forth the desired harvest—a few thousand giant companies and large farmers producing so much that, even with subsidies for the medium and small farmers, they sell their grains and food at prices that fail to match their costs of production. So, one by one, family farmers "go out of business," leaving behind them an empty and devastated rural America.

However, looking at the 2002 Census of Agriculture, another product of USDA, the picture of rural America is still pretty—not much has changed in the past quarter century: In 1974 the United States had 2,314,013 farms and in 2002 there were still more than two million farms in America, exactly: 2,128,892 farms. Also, the other spectacular finding of the USDA census was the nearly unchanged size of the average farm from 1974 to 2002. In 1974 the average size of the farm was 440 acres. That size zoomed to 491 acres in 1992 and then declined to 441 in 2002. But even the number of the largest farms did not change that much, according to the USDA data. In 1974 there were 62,225 farms of 2,000 acres or more and in 2002 those giant farms were 77,970. Yet a closer look at the USDA statistics gives out the secret of the political power and economic might behind the number-dense agricultural census: In 1974, for example, there were 11,412 farms, which earned $500,000 or more. In the mid-1980s, when the rural exodus became drastic, there were 27,000 farms earning half a million dollars or more. Those farms represented 1.2 percent of all farms, receiving 10.1 percent of direct government payments, and earning 38.5 percent of the net cash income. But, by 2002, the number of farms making $500,000 or more was 70,642. Meanwhile, thirty-five percent of America's farms in 2002 were completely impoverished, each earning less than $2,500, which represented one percent of sales and government payments. Three percent of the farms making $500,000 or more shared 62 percent of sales and government payments. Finally, there were 29,862 farms in 2002 worth one million dollars or more in sales and government subsidies. Each of these giant farms had an average net cash income of $698,345.

Numbers alone tell part of the story. But when a third of America is set aside for cattle and more than half of the country's cropland grows feed for that cattle and more than half of the country's drinking water goes to cattle, something fundamental is afoot. The meat trust has come back into being, anti-trust law or no law. Cargill, ConAgra and Iowa Beef Processors are the kings of meat. These, and other giant agribusiness companies, make and unmake agriculture in the United States. USDA's get big or get out is mirrors the policies of those giants, with the result rural America is drained of the democratic family farmers, their lands now under the dominion of corporations sowing the countryside with bad food and tyrannical economic arrangements. Meanwhile USDA is putting lipstick on the sod-busted prairies, the poisoned rivers, the sticking hog factories, the boarded main streets and poisoned land. It is proud that half of the American farmers have Internet access while 39 percent use a computer for their business. These farmers, however, are dying fast. The average farmer in 2002 was more than 55 years old. Only one percent of the farmers were younger than 25 years, while seventeen percent were seventy and more.

The only positive trend in American and global agriculture is the steady growth of organic or biological farmers blending traditional knowledge and ecological wisdom. The rest of the farmers either disappear or blend into the complex of agribusiness. Some of the surviving small family farmers make it as "hobby" farmers. Others have no option but becoming "contract" workers to a handful of agribusiness companies who pay them pitiful wages and incorporate them into their version of feudalism. Several of those companies are meat factories that produce bacon burgers and chicken nuggets while, Ken Silverstein says, they are "among the nation's largest polluters."[3]

If the United States does nothing to abolish its oppressive system of giant agriculture, the remaining white family farmers—who declined by about 66 percent in the twentieth century—will "get out" like their black family farmer brothers and sisters did before them. Rural America will increasingly become a plantation where the routine of the horror of animal factories will spread to include the routine of human suffering and everyday violence. Such a plantation, slowly becoming more and more like the death-without-weeping hacienda of Northeast Brazil, will not be a hospitable place for ecology, democracy, family farming or just economic development. Which is why I hope Americans will not allow this evil project (however flashy it looks in its science garb) to complete its orbit.

Evil project? Yes, indeed. Platon said that doing wrong is bad, nasty, evil. But doing wrong without making amends is the worst of all evils.[4] One would be hard pressed to find anything but persistent and calculated giant wrongs in the work of giant agriculture as it slices land and rural communities in its imperial conquest of nature and society.

Carl Buckingham Koford, an American ecologist decried, in 1958, the barbaric habit of ranchers, farmers, and government agencies of using sodium fluoroacetate, a chemical known largely by a number, 1080, to exterminate wildlife. "Aside from killing prairie dogs," Koford says, "continuous distribution of compound 1080 has had other effects on animal communities. The chemical is extremely toxic and kills other grain-eating mammals, such as cottontails. The poison is stable, even in animal tissue, so that carnivores which feed on poisoned rodents are often killed. Coyotes (*Canis latrans*) have nearly disappeared from the plains because of secondary poisoning. In addition, application of poison brings about a cataclysmic alteration in the relative populations of different mammals, followed by various coactions between species and changes in their effects on plants and soils."[5]

A cataclysm is a destructive upheaval, a blotting out of culture and life, an exact metaphor on what industrialized agriculture has been doing to nature and rural society alike. Koford was right. Spreading poison in dog towns was annihilation to more than the dogs that ate the poison. Just like rural towns fall apart when their family farmers go under, so does the community of wild animals around a prairie dog town go to pieces when prairie dogs get into trouble. Koford's affection for prairie dogs was the affection of a biologist who understood nature. Rodents, he said, were a beneficial species to man. They improved the soil and checked unwanted plants and shrubs. They were food to other animals, and enlivened the scenery. What more could we expect of any animal?

Douglas Tompkins, the enlightened American businessman who has been funding a number of worthwhile environmental projects in the United States and Latin America, is as angry in 2002 as Koford was in 1958 about the barbarism of industrial agriculture. He says the United States is wrecking rural America and culture because it converted its farming to industrial agriculture. He explains:

> Our conversion from agrarian, local, fully integrated food systems
> to industrialized, monocultural agricultural production has brought a
> staggering number of negative effects... [These effects include] soil
> erosion, poisoned ground waters, food-borne illnesses, loss of biodiversity,
> inequitable social consequences, toxic chemicals in foods and fiber, loss of
> beauty, loss of species and wildlife habitat, and myriad other environmental
> and social problems. To make the crisis even worse, we continue to export
> this destructive industrial system of food production around the world.[6]

In addition, is it not wrong and evil to destroy millions of small
family farmers in America and Europe, and take the land away from
countless millions of peasants in the Third World? And what about the
slaughter and extinction of wildlife following the massive machinery and
toxins of this mechanical agriculture? Moreover, plantations appropriate
most of the world's freshwaters. The international peasant and family
farmer civil society organization, Via Campesina, says that it is this
monstrous giant agriculture that is pushing family farmers and peasants
throughout the world to the brink of "irredeemable extinction."[7]

We need to do the right thing and globalize the peasants' hopes and
stop the war against them. Our conflict is with those landowners and
corporations who clear the forest and "produce" cash crops. They are
incapable or unwilling to understand that the roots of African hunger
lie deep in the structure of the most persistent of colonial institutions
in the continent—the export out of sub-Saharan Africa of plantation
agricultural cash crops to the markets of Europe and North America.

Such agricultural exports are bad for democracy and the land,
concentrating political power in a few hands and impoverishing Africa's
traditional food and agricultural economy. Scrapping that colonial model
of development—cash cropping—for a healthier and stronger peasant
economy is bound to invigorate both democracy and the raising of food
for local consumption. A peasant-driven development strategy is also
certain to heal the howling land and restore Africa to her values—give
the best land of Africa back to the peasant and bring into the field and
the village the fabulous biological and cultural diversity and wisdom of
traditional farming.

The fundamental difference between the plantations of Northeast
Brazil, Africa and the United States is not so much in the amount and

kind of violence they inflict on human beings and nature, but in their toleration of people around them. In contrast to African and Brazilian plantations surrounded by villages and towns, the American plantations have almost emptied rural America of people. They are doing to small family farmers what the first Europeans in North America did to the Native Americans. They are forcing them out of agriculture and rural America. In fact the United States, under the hatred of the cold war, did to its small family farmers what the Soviet Union / Russia did to its peasants. Both empires funded the development of plantations—agribusiness in the United States and state farms in the Soviet Union—as the expression of modernity, science, the factory system, agricultural productivity, and power.

And both America and the Soviet Union "domesticated" nature by breaking it apart, clearcutting its life, making it scream to death. The Soviet Union destroyed the Aral Sea in the 1950s for the production of irrigated cotton—in one of the most dramatic and violent ecological crimes of the twentieth century. The United States ploughed up its Great Plains for the industrial production of cattle, wheat, and corn. The result of sodbusting the fragile prairies was biological warfare against millions of buffaloes and genocide against the Native American people who relied on the buffalo for their survival and culture. Moreover, farming the semiarid Great Plains brought that vast region on the verge of a cataclysm, massive dust bowls in the 1930s, the 1950s and 1970s threatening to swallow farms, machinery, crops, and illiterate people.

Yet the United States failed to do more than cosmetic changes in the political economy of the prairies or the policies of the country in addressing the root cause of the dust storms and desertification in the Great Plains, namely industrial ranching and one-crop factory farming in particular. In addition, the plantations of America's Great Plains are using the ground water of the great Ogallala aquifer with abandon. The United Nations Environment Programme says that America's Great Plains are going through "another form of desertification—groundwater depletion."[8] The bountiful water of the Ogallala gives the illusion of permanence to both the desert-creating cash cropping plantation men and to the cattle-fattening factories producing beef no different than corn.

It's the same cruel plantation politics all over the vast southwestern region of the United States. The Colorado River—a water highway

1,400 miles long starting from the Colorado Mountains and ending in Mexico and the Sea of Cortez—is without doubt the lifeblood of the arid southwestern United States and northwestern Mexico. It brings water to about 30 million people and irrigates more than 3.7 million acres of agricultural land in both the United States and Mexico. Yet this life-giving river has to contend with an exceedingly brutal shackling of its nature and waters—no less than 29 dams capture its might and every drop of its water, which rarely reaches the Sea of Cortez.

The same people who drink the entire Colorado River, particularly the practitioners of giant agriculture in arid southwestern United States, convert forested wetlands and uplands to pine forests, cotton plantations, or other cash crop farms. Such conversion of nature from ecosystems to industrial systems wipes out biodiversity and kills wildlife on both land and water. New Mexico, Texas, Louisiana, Arkansas and Oklahoma, for example, destroy 30,000 acres of wetlands and uplands every year for pine plantations alone. Huge amounts of poisons are used for the maintenance of those plantations.

It's the globalization of this model of agricultural plantation of power, camouflaged under the flashy and imperial image of American science, which threatens the world's ecology and cultures. The sodbusters of the 1930s (*the God-dam'd Okies*) were the first victims of this emerging global food factory. They started as impoverished settlers of Oklahoma who applied to the prairies the knowledge of their betters—America's agribusiness men, agricultural university professors, and agents of the state and federal agricultural departments. However, neither the Okies nor the Okies' teachers had a clue about farming. Instead, they went into Oklahoma and the Great Plains with the determination and vengeance of the conqueror to subdue and to crush and to exploit. And they did all these things—both to the Native Americans and to the land. The deadly dust bowl was their first harvest. The dust storms are not safely tied in the sack of the Greek wind god Aiolos: They are merely waiting in the wing.

Millions of other "farmers" throughout the world are repeating the experience of the Okies with the result that countless millions of acres of good land have been made into desert. The more land goes to agribusiness production or cash cropping, the more acute pressures are exerted against poor people trying to survive. Landless peasants—like

those of Mexico, India or Africa—do cut down forests, and in other
desperate ways, degrade the land that gives them life.⁹

But unless the international community puts an end to the nature-
poisoning and society-destroying antidemocratic cash cropping and
factory farming—economic, political, and violent activities not of
peasants but of affluent farmers, landowners, corporations and states—
social disintegration and desertification are bound to overwhelm the many
societies and ecosystems. In addition, other related upheavals in nature
like the destruction of the life-protecting ozone layer around the world
by, among other industrial poisons, methyl bromide of cash cropping,
and global warming, are certain to put an end to ecosystems and human
societies already under tremendous stress.¹⁰

Industrialized agriculture destroys democracy and makes the land
howl—and not merely in the tropics. It is biological, social, cultural, and
political meltdown. It is the resurrection of the breaking of free human
beings and democratic communities into slaves and colonies. It is the
half-baked nightmare of a cold war America bent on global conquest. It
is a throwback to the dark age of lords and vassals, feudalism, political
absolutism, and empire. Industrialized agriculture, finally, is a global
plantation with both massive and intolerable impacts on both human
societies and nature. The stakes are much, much larger than the private
profits of corporations and the economic or strategic primacy of countries:
The earth and its people are at risk.

Globalizing the Hopes and Democratic Farming of Peasants and Small Family Farmers

I started this book by saying conventional or industrialized agriculture
must be stopped and abandoned and buried in the cemetery of the war
dead. Alternatives to this military farming exist both in the United States
and in every other society in the world. These alternatives—biodynamic
agriculture, organic farming, community-supported agriculture, biological
agriculture, peasant or ecological farming—are forms of applied biology
that have nature as their primary model. They are desired biological
pathways to family agriculture,¹¹ which has the potential to heal some of
the wounds of industrial agriculture.¹²

All these methods of raising food—and the indigenous people, peasants, and small family farmers who practice them—share a respect for the land and the people who eat what they raise on that land. This means they follow ancient traditions of agrarian knowledge and practice, and some even merge that heritage with the latest in agroecological thinking about agriculture.[13]

Indigenous people and peasants have detailed knowledge of nature. Their religion, just like the religion of ancient Greeks, is a spiritual form of farming—pleading to the gods to bring them a good harvest. Their celebrations, their fiestas, are prayers of enjoyment to their gods for their ancestors, animals, crops, harvest, the dead and the living. Indigenous people in the Philippines consider the land a gift of the gods. And land in the savannah grasslands of the Upper East region of Ghana is a sanctuary for the gods. The Dai people of southwest China protect and preserve sacred groves where they worship their gods—exactly like the ancient Greeks. The Dayak Pasir Adang people of East Borneo, Indonesia, practice sacred farming. If their reading of nature is auspicious, they use fire for clearing the land in order to plan their crops. They don't destroy or burn fruit-bearing trees or ground that has the graves of their ancestors. They sow seeds of spinach, bitter brassica, corn, and cucumber. But the most sacred of seeds and agrarian traditions of the Dayak Pasir Adang people are rice seeds and their cultivation. They place the first rice seeds in holes, each with a special name—father, mother, captain, and guardian. The community sows and harvests the rice. At harvest time, men, women, and children work together. They sing and pray to the gods. The unhusked rice grains that will become the seed for the next growing season are cleaned first, and, then, the rest of the rice grains are trampled and dried in the sun for two to three days. Finally, the rice is thrown in the air, its chaff and impurities blown away. In the same tradition of sacred farming, the Mende rice peasants of southern and eastern Sierra Leone use rice varieties best adapted to the ecological conditions of their land and region. And since rice is a self-pollinating crop, the Mende peasants do the shifting and choosing of rice seeds coming their way, in the rice fields, and next door in nature. They revere their ancestors for the rice bounty they left them. But they no more feel they own the rice varieties they developed than they own the breeze. Yet they are experts in combining and selecting seeds for their way of life, which is sacred agriculture. "Maybe," says Paul Richards, a British scholar on African traditional farming, "it makes more sense to concentrate on enriching the gene pool, leaving local talent to do the rest. Forget the Green Revolution. Treat local myths seriously. Charter a plane and scatter duplicates of the international rice gene bank collections to the four winds."[14]

Paul Richards is right. The Mende peasants are the real experts and best guardians of rice genetic diversity. The Dai's sacred groves or Holy Hills or Nong are rich in agricultural biodiversity. The Dai peasants, and peasants in the rest of the world, use a tremendous variety of plants for food, fiber, and medicine. The ethnobotanical knowledge of several indigenous people is remarkable. The Tzeltals and the Purepechas of Mexico recognize more than 1,200 and 900 plants respectively. It was from that careful study and understanding of the workings of nature that traditional farming came into being. Crop mixtures with animals, crops grown with trees near or within a forest, make up a traditional farming system. Mixing plants and animals is good farming because, together, they fertilize the land and keep pests under control. Crop mixtures attract insect predators and parasites that keep hostile insects and weeds in check. In addition, the traditional seeds of the peasant have a greater resistance to disease. Farm animals (hogs, chicken, cattle) give the peasant milk, meat, and draft power while they eat weeds and crop residues recycling them into protein and manure for the land.

The Chiapas peasants, who are fighting for survival, raise two tons of maize per hectare while the industrialized farmer next door produces six tons of maize per hectare. For this reason, the agricultural experts call the peasants backward and insist they leave the land or adopt the methods of the mechanical plantation. Yet the industrialized farmer gets nothing more from his land but the six tons of corn. The Chiapas peasant, however, grows not merely maize but, along with maize, he raises beans, squash and pumpkins, sweet potatoes, tomatoes and other vegetables and fruits and medicinal herbs. Some of his food the peasant sells for cash and the rest is for his family, chicken, and cattle. The Chiapas peasant "easily produces more than fifteen tons of food per hectare and all without commercial fertilizers or pesticides and no assistance from banks or governments or transnational corporations."[15]

The harvest of such a sowing of traditional knowledge and practice is predictably good for civil society organizations that work with peasant or small family farmer communities, sometimes reviving and protecting their culture. Civil society organizations also make it possible for some small farmers to move away from the one-crop chemical and mechanical model of raising food. They help them return to their own agrarian traditions of planting a variety of crops at the same time, rotating forage and food crops, forest and fruit trees, rebuilding their terraces, using cover crops to smother weeds and fertilize their hillside plots, planting trees.

Indigenous people and peasants in the Third World are defending the integrity of ecosystems, biodiversity, the priceless Amazon, wild rivers, earth-centered or gaiocentric sustainable development. These people know and practice what we must know and practice in order to put the brakes on the global ecocidal and anthropocidal (man-killing) policies of capitalist economic development. Their traditional beliefs, says Vandana Shiva, India's courageous ecological thinker, represent "the only cognitive resource we have to maintain the conditions of survival."[16] Shiva is right. Peasants and indigenous people do not separate the social from the ecological. Both are one. Sustainable development theories are theories to thinkers in industrial societies. But in the Third World these theories take flesh and blood. They are the stuff of life.

Peasants in the Andes, for instance, still have social institutions and knowledge to revive their pre-Hispanic ecological farming. Joan Martinez Alier, a Spanish scholar, says that agriculture in the Andes:

> gave to the global human patrimony a considerable number of domesticated vegetables whose benefits could hardly be evaluated monetarily.... On the coast [of Peru], where natural dryness necessitates irrigation, a hydraulic civilization arose unlike those of Egypt or Mesopotamia. It was not organized around the control of one or two rivers, but fifty rivers, creating systems of faultless fluvial connections like the Lambayeque complex which covers five valleys. Another example of original coastal agricultural technology is the hillside agriculture, capable of securing agricultural production using environmental moisture. In the Sierra, the struggle to expand the agricultural frontier was also a difficult challenge. Notable accomplishments include the large Andean systems of terracing and irrigation, the complex sectoral fallow systems controlled by communities, and the agricultural raised fields in the *altiplano.* Even more remarkable were the development and management of hundreds of varieties of potatoes adequate for diverse ecologies, as well as many varieties of other root crops and cereals.[17]

In addition, in Peru a pre-Columbian high-altitude farming method of raised fields (waru-waru) in the midst of water ditches is responsible for bumper crops of potatoes, quinoa, amaranth and oca (wood sorrel), better diet, better incomes, and healthier and more resilient land.[18] This waru-waru farming system of the Andes—with its canals for water, terraces, and raised fields—is very productive and sophisticated method of growing food in a harsh environment. The water in the canals slowly percolates to the raised fields. That way it moderates the temperature of the land and prevents the frost from hurting the growing crops. The peasants use the silt, sediment, and organic residues in the ditches to fertilize their vegetables or crops.

Raised-bed farming was a widespread agricultural practice not merely in Peru but throughout pre-Columbian Central and South America. In Mexico, raised-bed farming or chinapas had probably been invented by the Mayas and passed on to the Aztecs. When on November 8, 1519, Herman Cortes and his Spanish conquistadors entered Tenochtitlan (Mexico City), the metropolis of the Aztec empire with a population of 200,000 to 300,000 people, they discovered an advanced and rich indigenous culture that sustained itself from the food grown on the chinapas. One of Cortes' soldiers, Bernal Diaz del Castillo, left us an account of the Spaniards' destruction of the Mexican Aztec Empire of Montezuma. Despite his contempt for the Aztecs so he could justify their murder, Bernal Diaz was impressed by the Aztecs' cities, their running water, paved streets, temples, large markets, clothing, organization, gold, silver, abundant wealth. Diaz saw the chinapas lining the waterways of Tenochtitlan and he thought he was dreaming. He assigned those gardens to emperor Montezuma; they were so beautiful, what "with their many varieties of flowers and sweet-scented trees planted in order, and their ponds and tanks of fresh water into which a stream flowed at one end and out of which it flowed at the other, and the baths he had there, and the variety of small birds that nested in the branches, and the medicinal and useful herbs that grew there. His gardens were a wonderful sight, and required many gardeners to take care of them. Everything was built of stone and plastered; baths and walks and closets and rooms like summerhouses where they danced and sang. There was so much to see in these gardens, as everywhere else, that we could not tire of contemplating his great riches and the large number of skilled Indians employed in the many crafts they practiced."[19]

The chinapas, exactly like the waru-waru of Peru, were agricultural islands within lakes and marshes encircled by shallow water and dense vegetation. These raised beds produced maize, beans, chilies, tomatoes and fruits in abundance. They were very productive, allowing continuous cultivation. They were round year gardens. The chinapas also were an ideal environment for fish and wildfowl and forage for animals. But the Spanish vented their hatred, jealousy and Christianity and buried both the chinapas and Aztec Mexico. In one blow the Spanish conquistadors destroyed Mexico's prosperous and sacred agriculture (the chinapas and terrace cultivation) and Mexican culture.[20] On their ruins they built the hacienda or large farm and manned it with the slave labor of the surviving indigenous people. Industrialized agriculture was the harvest of hacienda.

When in November 1998 hurricane Mitch devastated Honduras and northern Nicaragua, the only region of Honduras that escaped the fury of nature was around the village of Guarita close to the El Salvador border primarily because the Lenca peasants of Guarita never changed their farming way of life. The massive rain and wind of the violent storm barely altered their land since that land is solidly anchored on the hills with the roots of ancient wisdom and traditional agricultural practices. The Lenca peasants don't slash-and-burn their hillside farms. And neither do they go for the cash cropping methods of farming taught at the colleges of Honduras in an effort to speed up the country's modernization. Instead, they plant their crops under trees, and build terraces to prevent erosion of the land. They also avoid plowing but use their traditional pointed stick for sowing.[21] In the same manner, in fighting against another deadly erosion, peasants have been waging struggles of resistance in defense of their culture, and struggles of liberation from all colonizers.[22] Thus it is almost part of their nature that they create and maintain crop genetic diversity. Their seeds are not the suicide seeds of genetic engineers. The seeds of peasants are their culture—ancient, rich in variety, resilient, tasty, aromatic, dependable for the next sowing and harvest of food. Says Jonathan King, professor of molecular biology at the Massachusetts Institute of Technology, "Peasant farmers [in Asia] are struggling to maintain control over the material basis of their livelihood, the agricultural crop plant on which they depend. They are also struggling to maintain control over their culture, as represented in the knowledge of producing and using rice."[23]

The seeds of peasants are also the backbone of plant breeding throughout the world. Some $200 to $350 million per year is needed to support gene banks for sharing, on a global basis, the peasants' seeds. In Tehran, Iran, in August 2000, representatives of major plant breeders and biotech companies agreed to pay a portion of the annual costs for the global peasant seed bank. But in the November 12-17, 2000 international meeting in Neuchatel, Switzerland, the United States objected to the "tithing" of industry and the global negotiations for the support of the peasant seed bank collapsed. Europeans and representatives of Africa, Asia, and Latin America accused the United States for wrecking the world's food security. "Most diplomats, most people," an Asian diplomat said, "don't understand how dependent the world's food supply is on the flow of plant genetic resources [from the seeds of peasants]. This is a tempest in our rice bowl—and that's important!"[24]

The seeds of the industrial farmer have their origins in the seeds of peasants. But because their genetic structure is perpetually redesigned to meet the needs of industrialized agriculture, they are poorly adapted to nature, thus they are genetically uniform, exotic species easily attacked by insects, weeds, and diseases. They require weapons for survival— synthetic poisons and fertilizers—not exactly a replacement for the eons-tested peasant seeds.

Moreover, non-industrialized family farmers and peasants (using appropriate machinery and tools) practice not merely good husbandry but, just as importantly, they and their agriculture are expressions of agricultural, ecological, and biodiversity principles, social justice, democracy, and very small-scale farming on the land. In contrast to the ruthless treatment of both land and rural communities by industrialized farmers, peasants and small family farmers raise food in ways that enrich the land and create strong rural society. Peasants in particular are inseparable from seeds—agricultural genetic diversity. There is simply no alternative to healthy peasant and small family farm communities for biological diversity. Seeds for food security survive and thrive only when peasants have been growing food for very long time.

In a March 22, 2001 letter to the Mexican Congress, Medha Patkar of India and Elias Dias Pena of Paraguay (and an additional 12 recipients of the Right Livelihood Award and the Goldman Prize), said that:

peasants and indigenous peoples of the world have been, through the centuries, the creators and conservers of biodiversity for survival, providing the whole humankind with the bases for the cultivated diversity for food, medicines and shelter. This has been an open and sustainable process, the heritage of humankind and intimately linked to cultural diversity and the fact that indigenous peoples could practice their traditional livelihoods and cultures, their political, economical and social ways of life, indissolubly linked to the access and sustainable and autonomous management of their lands, resources and territories.[25]

Organic farmers in the United States are not peasants, much less indigenous people, but, to some degree, they do things like peasants and indigenous people. For instance, to a large extent, they spray no synthetic pesticides in growing their crops. In 1994 they used 1,127,000 acres for raising vegetables, fruit, herbs, nuts, mushrooms, food crops, livestock feed, cotton, tobacco, nursery plants and flowers. By 1997 organic cropland and pasture included 1,350,000 acres in 49 states. The amount of land for organic crops doubled between 1992 and 1997. Dairy and eggs grew even faster in the 1990s. About two percent of top specialty crops like lettuce, carrots, grapes, and apples were grown under certified organic farming standards in 1997. Yet no more than 0.1 percent of corn and soybeans moved into organic production. In 1997 was a good year for organic vegetables and fruits. There were more than 49,000 acres of organic fruit in 1997 and 48,227 acres of organic vegetables in 43 states in 1997. A modest number of farmers growing organic vegetables did so on farms, which were five acres in size or smaller. There were 600 of those very small organic vegetable farmers in the United States in 1997. America's certified organic land is minuscule in comparison to the acres used for conventional food production—somewhat more than a tenth of a percent of the total agricultural land in the United States.[26] The same truth applies to organic food. Very small amount, but huge significance.[27] In 1998 organic agriculture made $4 billion while growing at 20 percent per year in the 1990s.[28] In the year 2000 sales from organic agriculture reached $7.8 billion. Those sales represented 1 to 2 percent of food sales in the United States and other countries with a commitment to organic farming—Japan, England, Sweden, Denmark, Netherlands, Switzerland and Germany.[29]

As I demonstrated in the fourth chapter of this book, the significance of organic farming is primarily moral and political: That organic farmers grow food without poisons (and earn a very good living in their working the land) neutralizes the lies of the plantation—that we would starve without pesticides. Organic farmers and non-industrialized farmers in general all over Europe and North America and, particularly, peasants in Latin America, Asia, and Africa represent a living counterrevolution to the factory food and power path of giant agriculture.

The problem of forgetting the "green revolution," moving away from the plantation—imperial, industrialized farming of the United States, and the most aggressive and colonizing impulse of Western culture—should that momentous decision ever be made—is not knowledge or productive capacity or talent. The problem is power. Political and economic. Huge amounts of money. Global monopolies.

Which is why all persons of good will, meaning all non-industrialized farmers and the civil society in general, have to organize to fight giant agriculture as if their lives depended on the success of that fight: "By destroying the genetically modified maize seeds on the 8th of January [1998] at the Novartis factory in Nerac, [France]," say members of the French peasant confederation, "we wanted to put this short-sighted logic into the spotlight.... Through the action which we undertook and for which we are being judged, we kicked-off a vast citizen's movement which refuses the use of GMOs [genetically modified organisms] in foodstuffs for animals and for humans. These actions will stop when this mad logic comes to a halt."[30]

In late November 1998, the peasants of India, particularly those from the states of Maharastra, Gujarat, and Madhya Pradesh, started a campaign to reduce to ashes all of the agricultural genetic engineering experiments in India of corporations like Monsanto, Novartis, and Pioneer. The wrath of the Indian peasants turned against Monsanto whose field trials of bioengineered cotton they burned down. The slogan of the angry peasants was to "cremate Monsanto." On October 2, 2000, more than 5,000 family farmers and peasants from 68 countries, meeting in Bangalore, India, under the auspices of their international civil society, Via Campesina, denounced the dangerous power of corporations in global agriculture. They promised to resist giant agriculture everywhere in the world. They also formulated plans to eliminate farm corporations and centralized systems of agricultural production.[31]

Ideally, the civil society of the United States and of other countries ought to emulate the courageous behavior of the French and Indian peasants, and the members of Via Campesina—if not to cremate corporations but to bring them down to size and power and, in the end, get them out of agriculture. The campaign for family agriculture is a global struggle for land, food sovereignty, democracy, and freedom. The plantation has no place in that process. But giant agriculture has to be defeated for that process to go anywhere.

The heart of such a struggle and strategy ought to include the distribution of land and traditional seeds to land-poor and landless peasants in the Third World and small family farmers in North America and Europe. Says the 1996 Southern African Charter on Land, Labour and Food Security, "Traditional systems of food production should be revived and strengthened. People must empower themselves and disempower the multinational corporations [MNCs]. Resist the imposition of the modern food systems, their environmentally destructive technologies, dietary food habits and consumerist values.... Land reform policy should break up the monopoly of land by landlords, commercial farmers and MNCs and give equal and secure ownership of land to those who live and work on it."[32]

Land and seeds empower the peasants to fight plantations and colonialism with their own knowledge, food, and resistance. And with their seeds planted for food and for conservation for the next growing season, the peasants become the custodians of their rich genetic agricultural traditions.

Hugh Iltis, the American expert on agricultural biological diversity, said correctly we ought to pay peasants to continue to do what they do so well—protecting the natural evolution of food seeds without which agriculture would not exist. If, for instance, we could help the peasants of Africa get back to the cultivation of their enormous variety of crops—which exist in the periphery of the continent—it would be humanity's greatest gift to the African people. Africans would have enough to eat, food security and food sovereignty would replace hunger, and the rest of us would know that those making the transition from cash cropping to sustainable farming could borrow seeds from Africa for expanding the narrow biological diversity of their agriculture.

Strong peasant / very small family farmer cultures bring the howling of the land to an end. Strong peasant / very small family farmer cultures bring democracy and food sovereignty to the world's countrysides. They are our best defense against predatory plantations.

The attractiveness of fighting giant agriculture—in the United States and Europe—is that the supporters of such struggle include (in the United States) the plantation-wounded black Americans with only a pitiful number of farmers still farming, the millions of white people (in both America and Europe) who lost their land and farms, the millions of Americans and Europeans who call themselves environmentalists, and the consumers of food—all in all, probably the vast majority of the American and European people.

In the end, the civil society and non-industrialized farmers must organize themselves and their supporters for a lengthy, protracted campaign at home and abroad. There's no way that democracy can live next to giant agriculture. Either one remains passive and eats the contaminated food of the plantation in an authoritarian and repressive political system—what the Greeks would call tyranny—or one chooses democracy and fights to end the poisoned food and dangerous power of giant agriculture. The outcome of this struggle will determine the nature of both agriculture and culture in North America, Europe, Latin America, Africa and Asia. In fact the fate of the earth depends on precisely this kind of struggle, a dramatic moment for Americans, Europeans and the rest of the people of the world to have their agricultural conversation with nature and the gods.

The Mad Horses of Glaucus Potnieus

In a surviving fragment of one of Aeschylus' tragedy, "Glaucus Potnieus," produced in Athens in 472 BCE, we learn that Glaucus, King of Corinth and son of Sisyphus, fed his racing horses flesh so that they would always win. Glaucus, however, paid with his life for such immoral act. During a chariot race at the funeral games of Pelias, King of Iolcus in Thessaly, Glaucus' horses lost the contest. Foaming at the mouth with madness, the horses turned against Glaucus. They tore him to pieces and devoured him.

Some 2,500 years later, the hubris of Glaucus was taken up by cattlemen who also want to win—in their case, more money and more power from the meat they "produce." So they started adding animal flesh and blood into animal meals, with the result that grass-eating animals eating other animals were struck by this most horrible ailment, almost a divine curse, described crudely as mad-cow disease.

Mad cow disease is an acute manifestation of the inhumanity and moral bankruptcy of the Western world's most prized possession—an agricultural system fueled by wrong science and operating within the straitjacket of a factory. The animals in that factory (poultry, hogs, and cattle primarily) are denied the dignity of being living species just like us—humans. Instead, they are treated like pieces of machinery for the manufacture of profits. Neither the scientists who legitimize the animal factories, nor the agribusinessmen who own and manage them, nor even those who eat the meat animal factories produce, have been disturbed by the habit—going back to the early 1900s at least—of cutting up thousands of wounded, crippled, or dead animals—rendering them—for meals to alive grass animals behind bars in the factory farm.

England suffered the most from such a barbaric habit. Scores of people died from eating the meat of ill cows, and thousands upon thousands of cattle were destroyed in order to put a break to the harrowing epidemic of animals dying with sponge-like brains. BSE or bovine spongiform encephalopathy or mad-cow disease is not an English disease but a deadly symptom of a systemic malady in the nature of industrialized agriculture. England and the European Union at least learned from that disaster and ended the practice of feeding animal protein to their farm animals. Yet in the United States it is still legal to feed cows other cows' blood and rendered pigs and horses. Animals ill with one of the transmissible spongiform encephalopathies can be fed to hogs and chickens. Every year more than a million cow brains are sold for food. Brains, of course, are at the very core of mad cow disease. They are the place in the animal where the fatal illness takes root and spreads to the nervous system and body. In the United States the cows for slaughter are first shot in the head with a stun gun. The blow of the gun is so severe that some of the cow's brain is pushed outside the cracked skull and into the animal's body. All this suggests that the United States is a possible candidate for a mad cow crisis of, theoretically, much larger proportions than that which wrecked England's livestock agriculture. Add to this the horror of what the mad-cow disease did to Europe, and the potential is real enough for Greek tragedy. Aeschylus would have probably written a play.

Aeschylus wrote his "Glaucus" tragedy like all his other plays, to remind the Greeks that the gods punish hubris most severely, sometimes with death. He turned to the Greek past for his stories—the epics of Homeros, the Persian Wars, or the case of the arrogant and mad Glaucus feeding his mares flesh. Aeschylus created tragic masterpieces from the explosion of human passion, the murder, for instance, of Klytemnestra, queen of Mycenae, by her son, Orestes, or the fearful fate of humans alone in the cosmos.

But now that we have banished the Greek gods from Western culture, we explain the Glaucus madness among our agribusinessmen as greed and, maybe, too much competition. Yet those who brought the harrowing mad cow disease to agriculture are guilty of hubris as well. Like Glaucus, they set aside their society's moral code and plunged into the abyss of nothingness. As a result, mad cows, like the horses of Glaucus, are tearing our rural culture to pieces—and eating us. They are nature's revenge. And the heart of the drama is that some of us know the revenge is coming, but we have barely begun to undo the factory farm.

Here's why from what I learned from a "hog summit." The Riverfront Park Convention Center in New Bern, North Carolina, was overflowing with people on January 11, 2001. Some 500 scientists, family farmers, environmentalists, public health experts, lawyers, state bureaucrats, animal welfare advocates, and politicians from all over the United States and Canada spent the day together trying to figure out what to do about this menace—huge number of hogs kept too close to each other in cement factories to be quickly fattened and slaughtered.

The scientists reported that hog factories mean pollution for rivers, disease and even death for the fish in the rivers, and contamination of the ground water, which, in many cases, is the only water available for countless thousands of rural Americans. A medical doctor spoke of the excessive amounts of tetracycline, penicillin, erythromycin and other antimicrobial drugs fed to the pigs not for curing disease but to force the animals to grow faster. In this dangerous fashion, for reasons that have nothing to do with therapeutic purposes, swine drink and eat about 10.3 million pounds of antimicrobials per year, cattle account for 3.7 million pounds, and poultry eat and drink 10.5 million pounds of antibiotic drugs per year.[33]

The videos we saw of the actual living conditions for the pigs in their factory homes brought to mind an inferno of violence made real behind thousands of concrete and iron bunkers imprisoning millions of hogs all over America. The image of the desperate sows biting the iron of their cages as they were trying to create a nest for giving birth to their young is still with me.

No less dramatic was the evidence of rural people caught in the range of offensive odors of the animal houses in their neighborhood. These smells are so bad they make living uncomfortable and, often, miserable. They violate human rights, and, with their persistence, they become an unbearable psychological torture violating norms of civilized behavior and living.

Robert Epting, a member of the Environmental Management Commission of North Carolina, summarized why animal farms have been an enemy of family farms—and not merely in his state. He spoke of the rivers of eastern North Carolina becoming red from the tides of hog feces. He wondered where did the owners of hogs bury the tens of thousands of drowned pigs during the hurricane Mitch disaster of 1999. He denounced the regulators of his state for doing nothing while the hog farms "were dumping their brimming lagoons directly into the rivers" during the spring and winter of the year 2000.

Robert Epting was merely one of several eloquent critics of hog factory farms. In fact the hog summit had nothing good to say about these animal factories save that they would be put out of business by lawsuits. This may well happen. The proliferating hog farm is spreading poisons, drugs, and huge amounts of waste in the nation's rivers and ground water. And it is wrecking rural communities in eastern North Carolina, Nebraska, Missouri, Iowa and all over America. Thousands of small family farmers have been put out of business. About 100 large hog factories control 40 percent of all pigs in the United States. In the 1990s, the largest hog companies put out of business something like 90 percent of family hog farmers. Thousands of small family farmers, in their desperation, have signed contracts with hog corporations that chain them to nearly voluntary servitude. For barely a living wage, often no more than $10,000 per year, they agree to be cogs in a vast corporate system searching for places to dump—wastes, slaughterhouses—and people to exploit. Most of the swine farms are in the communities of blacks and other powerless minorities.

Why not make America's corporate hog farms pay the costs—ecological and social—for producing pork? Make them treat the animal waste before dumping it onto the land and into rivers. Give federal and state subsidies to small family farmers who keep their pigs out of the hazardous confinement of the factory system. And label factory pork so the consumers have a choice to support family farmers who treat their animals humanely. That way family farmers would be able to survive and, possibly, replace this mechanical factory doing violence to both animals and agriculture in both the United States and the rest of the world.

While a Greek tragedy is cleansing and healing the soul by bringing us face to face with the most violent and abysmal in human nature, what is going to cleanse or even heal the agribusinessman wrecking agriculture and human culture with his animal factory madness? Outlawing feeding animals to other animals? Yes, but we need to go beyond treating the external sign of this calamity.

In the absence of the Greek theater, we need to immerse ourselves in the history of what we eat, and opt for food—including meat—that is grown without violence. This means condemning in the strongest moral terms, and doing away with, the feeding of cows flesh; abandoning the dangerous practice of spraying our food with toxins, and ending the shifting and splicing of genes from organism to organism. That is an experiment that even the Greek gods would be reluctant to carry out.

A well-informed citizenry is our best defense against the terrors of factory culture. An informed and caring citizen is likely to put his money where his health is. For example, I eat organic food. And to the degree I find organic coffee that is my preference both at home and at coffee shops. The Hop Brook Farm from New Salem, Massachusetts, sells organic coffee from Peru. "We only purchase beans from small farms and cooperatives," they say on the handsome packet they sell their 'Hazelnut Dream,' "largely made up of indigenous peoples working hard to maintain their culture and lifestyles in a hostile world. We do not buy beans from large 'estates' and 'plantations'. We've been there, and have seen the conditions of chronic poverty and malnutrition within which many of these farms produce those *other* coffees. Look in your kitchen—do you know where *your* beans come from?"

I would simply add: Do you know where *your food* comes from? Organic food makes it easier to answer such a question. Reliable food labeling would expand the frontiers of organic food and make the unambiguous connection between health and farming and food possible and, in addition, it may help each one of us to make the right moral choice. That way, the mad cow disease may fade into oblivion and, with it, the hazardous industrialized agriculture that gave it birth. Only then America's family farming has a chance to reclaim its territory and our moral, political, and economic support.

Finally, Platon and Aristoteles considered nature and agriculture (and all animals) nearly sacred—certainly indispensable for human existence and culture. Animal factories, like the remaking of crops and animals by genetic engineering, represent the worst form of industrialized agriculture. They break with that tradition. They change the world of traditional agriculture and culture into the terror of a brave new rural world. It's about time to dispense with such an error and return to democratic family farming and the core values of Greek and Western and indigenous civilization.

Notes

Preface

1   Vangelis Stoyannis and Paraskevi Dilana, eds., *The Odyssey of the Greek Agricultural Biodiversity* (Athens: Odyssey Network-Nea Ecologia, 2001).

Introduction

1   In 1966 an American presidential science advisory committee suggested that modernization demands that the "very fabric of traditional societies must be rewoven." The President's Science Advisory Committee, *The World Food Problem*, Vol. I (Washington, DC: US Government Printing Office, 1967), p. 5.

CHAPTER ONE

1   D. Christodoulou, *The Unpromised Land: Agrarian Reform and Conflict Worldwide* (London: Zed Books, 1990), p. xv. See also *The Struggle for Land and the Fate of the Forests*, edited by Marcus Colchester and Larry Lohmann (Penang, Malaysia: The World Rainforest Movement, 1995).

2   Quoted in William W. Goldsmith and Robert Wilson, "Poverty and Distorted Industrialization in the Brazilian Northeast," *World Development*, May 1991, p. 435.

3   Alan C. Mix and Lonnie G. Thompson, "Sensitivity of the Tropics to a Global Climate Warming: Evidence and Implications" (US Global Change Research Program, Capitol Hill Seminar, November 16, 1999).

4   Tomas Borge, "The Reality of Latin America," *Race and Class*, January-March 1992, p. 101.

5   Oscar Arias, "Export Goods, not People," *Washington Post*, July 17, 2005.

6   Oscar Ugarteche, "World Debt: Change the Rules or Refinancing Won't Help," *St. Louis Post-Dispatch*, November 1, 1999.

7   Nancy Scheper-Hughes, *Death Without Weeping: The Violence of Everyday Life in Brazil* (Berkeley: University of California Press, 1992), pp. x, 20.

8   Patrick Tierney, *Darkness in El Dorado: How Scientists and Journalists Devastated the Amazon* (New York: W.W. Norton, 2000), p. 30.

9   Tierney, *Darkness in El Dorado*, pp. 314-315.

CHAPTER TWO

1   Nick Middleton and David Thomas, eds., *World Atlas of Desertification* (second ed., London: Arnold for the United Nations Environment Programme, 1997), pp. 149, 154.

2   Ingar Palmlund, "Endocrine Disrupting Chemicals: From *Silent Spring* in 1962 to Policy Initiatives in 1997," *Human Environment*, Summer 1997, Vol. IV, No. 3.

3   Rachel Carson, *Silent Spring* (first published 1962, Boston: Houghton Mifflin,

1987), p. 297.

4   US Department of the Interior, Fish and Wildlife Service, *Fish, Wildlife and Pesticides* (Washington, DC: US Government Printing Office, 1966).

5   Emil M. Mrak, ed., *Report of the Secretary's Commission on Pesticides and their Relationship to Environmental Health* (Washington, DC: US Government Printing Office, December 1969), p. 25.

6   Carey McWilliams, *Factories in the Field: The Story of Migratory Farm Labor in California* (Boston: Little, Brown, 1939); Gerald O. Barney, ed., *The Global 2000 Report to the President: Entering the Twenty-First Century*, 2 Vols. (Washington, DC: US Government Printing Office, 1980); Marty Strange, ed., *It's Not All Sunshine and Fresh Air: Chronic Health Effects of Modern Farming Practices* (Walthill, Nebraska: Center for Rural Affairs, 1984); Angus Wright, *The Death of Ramon Gonzales: The Modern Agricultural Dilemma* (Austin: University of Texas Press, 1990); Douglas L. Murray, *Cultivating Crisis: The Human cost of Pesticides in Latin America* (Austin: University of Texas Press, 1994).

7   National Academy of Sciences, Board on Basic Biology, Commission on Life Sciences, "Research Briefing 1987" (Washington, DC, 1987).

8   National Research Council, *Alternative Agriculture* (Washington, DC: National Academy Press, 1989), p. 7.

9   John T. O'Connor and Sanford Lewis, "Shadow on the Land: A Special Report on America's Hazardous Harvest" (Boston: National Toxics Campaign, 1988), pp. 21-22.

10   Marty Strange, "Rural Economic Development and Sustainable Agriculture" (Walthill, NE: Center for Rural Affairs, August 1991), p. 4.

11   Jean Mayer, ed., *White House Conference on Food, Nutrition, and Health* (Washington, DC: US Government Printing Office, 1970), p. 1.

12   US Department of Agriculture, *A Time to Choose: Summary Report on the Structure of Agriculture* (Washington, DC: US Government Printing Office, 1981), pp. 1, 4-6.

13   US Department of Agriculture, *Report and Recommendations on Organic Farming* (Washington, DC: US Government Printing Office, 1980).

14   W. Van Dieren et al., *The Peasant Wedding Report: An Economic-Ecological Analysis of the Transition to Sustainable Agriculture in an Age of Globalisation* (Amsterdam: The Peasant Wedding Foundation, 2000), p. 1.

15   *Land of Plenty, Land of Want*, TV Documentary produced by Marilyn Weiner (Washington, DC: Screenscope, 1999). This documentary looks at the crisis of peasants / family farmers in Zimbabwe, France, China and the United States. Can they feed the world's population without destroying the environment?

16   World Wildlife Fund, *Resolving the DDT Dilemma: Protecting Biodiversity and Human Heath* (Washington, DC, June 1998) and *Hazards and Exposures Associated with DDT and Synthetic Pyrethroids Used for Vector Control* (Washington, DC, 1999).

17   Ronald Steenblik, "Agriculture and Sustainable Development" (Paris, OECD Secretariat, July 2000, com/agr/ca/env/epoc (99) 85/rev2), paragraphs 53-56.

18   Irakli Loladze, "Rising Atmospheric CO2 and Human Nutrition: Toward Globally Imbalanced Plant Stoichiometry?" *Trends in Ecology and Evolution*, Vol. 17, No. 10, October 2002, pp. 457-461.

19   Steenblik, "Agriculture and Sustainable Development," paragraph 128.

20   Coordination Paysanne Europeenne, "Press Release" (Rue de la Sablonniere 18-1000 Brussels, Belgium, September 2000).

21   Brian Halweil, "Where Have All the Farmers Gone?" *WorldWatch*, September / October 2000, pp. 12-28.

22   National Research Council, *Sustainable Agriculture and the Environment in the Humid Tropics* (Washington, DC: National Academy Press, 1993).

23   J.A. McNeely, "Human Influences on Biodiversity" in *Global Biodiversity Assessment*, edited by V.H. Heywood (Cambridge: Cambridge University Press for the United Nations Environment Programme, 1995), p. 744.

24   Paul Raeburn, *The Last Harvest: The Genetic Gamble that Threatens to Destroy American Agriculture* (Lincoln: University of Nebraska Press, 1996), p. 12; National Research Council, *Genetic Vulnerability of Major Crops* (Washington, DC: National Academy Press, 1972), pp. 6-15.

25   Cary Fowler and Pat Mooney, *Shattering: Food, Politics, and the Loss of Genetic Diversity* (Tucson: The University of Arizona Press, 1990), pp. ix, 54-89.

26   United Nations, International Conference on Nutrition, *World Declaration and Plan of Action for Nutrition* (Rome, Italy, December 1992).

27   Klaus Topfer, "Making Food Production Sustainable," *UNEP Industry and Environment*, April-September 1999, p. 3.

28   William Heffernan et al., "Consolidation in the Food and Agriculture System" (Report to the National Farmers Union, Department of Rural Sociology, University of Missouri, Columbia, Missouri, February 5, 1999), p.15. <http://www.nfu.org/Publications/Studies/Concentration/whstudy.html>

29   Dieren et al., *The Peasant Wedding Report*, p. iii.

30   Steenblik, "Agriculture and Sustainable Development," paragraph 106.

31   Coordination Paysanne Europeenne, "Press Release" (September 2000).

32   Jane Lubchenco, "Entering the Century of the Environment: A New Social Contract for Science," *Science*, Vol. 279, January 23, 1998, pp. 491-497.

33   Jules N. Pretty, *Regenerating Agriculture: Policies and Practice for Sustainability and Self-Reliance* (Washington, DC: Joseph Henry Press, 1995), p. 3.

34   Darrell Addison Posey, "The Science of the Mebengokre," *Orion*, Summer 1990, p. 21.

35   Robert Repetto and Sanjay Baliga, *Pesticides and the Immune System: The Public Health Risks* (Washington, DC: World Resources Institute, 1996); Frauke Jungbluth, *Crop Protection Policy in Thailand: Economic and Political Factors Influencing Pesticide Use* (Hannover, Germany: University of Hannover, Institute of Horticultural Economics, 1996).

36   Lori Ann Thrupp, ed., *New Partnerships for Sustainable Agriculture* (Washington, DC: World Resources Institute, 1996); Miguel Altieri et al., "The Potential of Agroecology to Combat Hunger in the Developing World," *Third World*

Resurgence, No. 118 / 119, June / July 2000, pp. 27-32.

37   Youyong Zhu et al., "Genetic Diversity and Disease Control in Rice," *Nature*, 406, August 17, 2000, pp. 718-722.

38   *The Ecologist*, January / February 1992.

CHAPTER THREE

1   Peter Montague, "Is Regulation Possible," *The Ecologist*, March / April 1998, pp. 59-61.

2   S.E. McGregor, *Insect Pollination of Cultivated Crop Plants* (US Department of Agriculture, Agricultural Research Service, Agriculture Handbook No. 496, Washington, DC: US Government Printing Office, 1976), p. 4.

3   Private communication, July 19, 1989.

4   Carl A. Johansen, "Pesticides and Pollinators," *Annual Review of Entomology*, 1977, 22: 178.

5   US Environmental Protection Agency, "Dioxin Strategy," August 15, 1983, Washington, DC, p. 4.

6   Paul Faeth, ed. *Agricultural Policy and Sustainability: Case Studies from India, Chile, the Philippines and the United States* (Washington, DC: World Resources Institute, September 1993), p. vii; Nick Middleton and David Thomas, eds., *World Atlas of Desertification*, 2nd ed. (London: Arnold and UN Environment Programme, 1997).

7   Ned H. Euliss, Jr. et al., "Wetlands of the Prairie Pothole Region: Invertebrate Species Composition, Ecology, and Management" in D.P. Batzer, R.B. Rader and S.A. Wissinger, eds., *Invertebrates in Freshwater Wetlands of North America* (New York: John Wiley, 1999), pp. 471-514.

8   Ted Williams, "Silent Scourge," *Audubon*, January-February 1997, pp. 28-35.

9   Cindi Deutschman-Ruiz, "Farm Chemicals Weaken Frog Immune Systems," *Great Lakes Radio Consortium*, July 15, 2002.

10   Warren P. Porter, James W. Jaeger and Ian H. Carlson, "Endocrine, Immune, and Behavioral Effects of Aldicarb (Carbamate), Atrazine (Triazine) and Nitrate (Fertilizer) Mixtures at Groundwater Concentrations," *Toxicology and Industrial Health*, (1999) 15 (1-2): 133-150.

11   Elizabeth A. Guillette et al., "An Anthropological Approach to the Evaluation of Preschool Children Exposed to Pesticides in Mexico," *Environmental Health Perspectives*, (June 1998) 106: 347-353.

12   George Hallberg, "Agricultural Chemicals and Groundwater Quality in Iowa" (Ames, Iowa: Cooperative Extension Service, Iowa State University, December 1984).

13   Daniel Grossman, "Curbing Nitrogen Pollution," *Great Lakes Radio Consortium*, July 15, 2002.

14   Peter M. Vitousek et al., "Human Alteration of the Global Nitrogen Cycle: Sources and Consequences," *Ecological Applications*, August 1997, pp. 737-750; William K. Stevens, "Too Much of a Good Thing Makes Benign Nitrogen a Triple Threat,"

New York Times, December 10, 1996, pp. C1, C8; Tom Horton and Heather Dewar, "Feeding the World, Poisoning the Planet," *Baltimore Sun*, September 24, 2000; "Cycle of Growth and Devastation," *Baltimore Sun*, September 25, 2000; "Sea Grasses Vanish, Marine Life in Peril," *Baltimore Sun*, September 26, 2000; Frank Langfitt and Heather Dewar, "China's Prosperity Turns Seas Toxic," *Baltimore Sun*, September 27, 2000; Heather Dewar and tom Horton, "Seeds of Solution to Nitrogen Glut," *Baltimore Sun*, September 28, 2000.

15   David Tilman et al., "Forecasting Agriculturally Driven Global Environmental Change," *Science*, April 13, 2001, pp. 281-284.

16   Mark Schaefer and Virginia Burkett, "Wetland Losses in the United States: Scope, Causes, Impacts, and Future Prospects" (US Global Change Research Program, Capitol Hill Seminar, July 7, 1997).

17   Nancy Rabalais and Donald Scavia, "Origin, Impact, and Implications of the 'Dead Zone' in the Gulf of Mexico" (US Global Change Research Program, Capitol Hill Seminar, July 19, 1999).

18   United Nations Food and Agriculture Organization, *Food for All: Success Stories in the Battle for Food Security* (Rome, 1997), p. 4.

19   James Liebman, "Rising Toxic Tide: Pesticide Use in California, 1991-1995" (San Francisco: Pesticide Action Network and Californians for Pesticide Reform, 1997).

20   Natural Resources Defense Council, *Harvest of Hope: the Potential of Alternative Agriculture to Reduce Pesticide Use* (New York, 1991).

21   Al Meyerhoff, "No More Pesticides for Dinner," *The New York Times*, March 9, 1993.

22   John Wargo, *Our Children's Toxic Legacy: How Science and Law Fail to Protect Us from Pesticides* (New Haven: Yale University Press, 1996); *Pesticides in the Diets of Infants and Children* by the National Research Council, National Academy of Sciences (Washington, DC: National Academy Press, 1993).

23   Paul Calabresi et al., *Cancer at the Crossroads: A Report to Congress for the Nation* (Bethesda, Maryland: National Cancer Institute, September 1994).

24   Ted Williams, "Hard News on 'Soft' Pesticides: A New Generation of EPA-Approved Pesticides is Killing Fish and Wildlife" *Audubon,* March/April 1993.

25   National Academy of Sciences, *Pesticide Resistance* (Washington, DC: National Academy Press, 1986); Robert M. May, "Resisting Resistance," *Nature*, February 18, 1993 pp. 593-594.

26   "A Tragic Mess," *The Ledger* (Lakeland, Florida), five-part series, Nov 15-19, 1992.

27   The Rachel Carson Council and the George Mason University sponsored a conference in Fairfax, Virginia, September 25-26, 1998 on pesticides. That conference brought up to date what we know of the effects of these chemicals on nature and human beings: "Wildlife, Pesticides and People: Conference Proceedings Book."

28   Emil M. Mrak, ed., *Report of the Secretary's Commission on Pesticides and their Relationship to Environmental Health* (Washington, DC: US Government

Printing Office, December 1969).

29   Robert van den Bosch died of a heart attack on Nov. 18, 1978: *Mother Earth News*, July/August 1979, pp. 17-20, 22.

30   Newsletter, College of Liberal Arts and Sciences, University of Illinois (Summer 1987).

31   *Environmental Health Perspectives*, Vol. 109, No. 9, September 2001, p. A420; Vol. 110 Supplement 1, February 2002, p. 27.

32   *Rachel's Hazardous Waste News*, #377, Feb 22, 1994 (Environmental Research Foundation, Annapolis, MD).

33   William S. Randall and Stephen D. Solomon, "54 Who Died," *Today Magazine*, (The Philadelphia Inquirer), October 26, 1975.

34   Charles Xintaras, Barry L. Johnson and Ido de Groot, eds., *Behavioral Toxicology: Early Detection of Occupational Hazards*, US Department of Health, Education, and Welfare, Public Health Service (Washington, DC: US Government Printing Office, 1974), pp. 294-95, 461.

35   Rachel Scott, *Muscle and Blood* (New York: Dutton, 1974), p. 3.

36   Paul Brodeur, Seminar, in *Lost in the Workplace: Is there an Occupational Disease Epidemic?* (Washington, DC, US Department of Labor, Sept. 13-14, 1979).

37   Colborn, "Listening to the Lakes," p. 8.

38   *Rachel's Hazardous Waste News*, #377, Feb. 22, 1994.

39   US Department of Agriculture, Economics, Statistics, and Cooperative Service, Agricultural Economic Report 438, *Structure Issues of American Agriculture* (Washington, DC: Government Printing Office, 1979), pp. 161-162.

40   Marty Strange, *Rural Economic Development and Sustainable Agriculture* (Walthill, NE: Center for Rural Affairs, Aug 1991); Laura DeLind, "Cheap Food" (Michigan State University, June 1992); Osha Gray Davidson, "Farming the System," *New York Times*, Jan. 4, 1993.

41   US Department of Agriculture, Economic Research Service, *Agricultural Outlook*, Jan-Feb. 2001, p. 47.

42   "Taking Control of Our Future," *Center for Rural Affairs Newsletter*, Walthill, Nebraska, Nov. 2000, p. 1.

43   US Department of Agriculture, *A Time to Choose: Summary Report on the Structure of Agriculture* (Washington, DC: Government Printing Office, 1981), p. 16.

44   USDA, *A Time to Choose*, p.16.

45   USDA, *A Time to Choose*, p. 129.

46   *Report of the Commissioner of Agriculture for the Year 1862* (Washington, DC: Government Printing Office, 1863), pp. 4-25.

47   Strange, *Rural Economic Development and Sustainable Agriculture*, p. 10.

48   E.G. Vallianatos, *Fear in the Countryside: The Control of Agricultural Resources in the Poor Countries by Nonpeasant Elites* (Cambridge, MA: Ballinger, 1976) and *Harvest of Devastation: The Industrialization of Agriculture and its Human and Environmental Consequences* (Goa, India: The Other India Press and New York: The Apex Press, 1994); Jack Ralph Kloppenburg, *First the Seed: The Political*

Economy of Plant Biotechnology, 1492-2000 (New York: Cambridge University Press, 1988); and Pat Roy Mooney, "The Parts of Life: Agricultural Biodiversity, Indigenous Knowledge, and the Role of the Third System," *Development Dialog*, December 1997.

49   Angus Wright, *The Death of Ramon Gonzalez: The Modern Agricultural Dilemma* (Austin, TX: University of Texas Press, 1990), pp. 184-185.

50   Stanley Wood, Kate Sebastian, and Sara J. Scherr, eds., *Pilot Analysis of Global Ecosystems: Agroecosystems* (Washington, DC: World Resources Institute, 2000), p. 6.

CHAPTER FOUR

1   Mark Lipson, *Searching for the "O-Word"* (Santa Cruz, CA: Organic Farming Research Foundation, 1998), p. 57.

2   Lord Northbourne, *Look to the Land* (London: Dent, 1940), pp. 96-97.

3   Pat Roy Mooney, "The Parts of Life: Agricultural Biodiversity, Indigenous Knowledge, and the Role of the Third System," *Development Dialog*, December 1997.

4   Michael W. Fox, *Beyond Evolution: The Genetically Altered Future of Plants, Animals, the Earth...and Humans* (New York: The Lyons Press, 1999); Andrew Kimbrell, *The Human Body Shop: The Cloning, Engineering, and Marketing of Life*, 2nd ed. (Washington, DC: Regnery Publishing, 1997); Barry Commoner, "Unraveling the DNA Myth: The Spurious Foundation of Genetic Engineering," *Harper's Magazine*, February 2002, pp. 39-47.

5   Michael Pollan, "Playing God," *The New York Times Magazine*, October 25, 1998, pp. 44-51, 62-63, 82, 92-93.

6   The Standing Senate Committee on Agriculture and Forestry, "Bovine Growth Hormone Evidence," Canada, Ottawa, Thursday, October 22, 1998, <http://natural-law.ca/genetic/SenateHearingsBGH.html>.

7   Russell Mokhiber and Robert Weissman, "Printer Shreds Ecologist's Monsanto Issue" (Environmental News Service, October 28, 1998, <http://ens-news.com/ens/oct98/1998-10-28-02.html>.

8   *The Ecologist*, September / October 1998, p. 251.

9   Michael Grunwald, "Monsanto Hid Decades of Pollution," *The Washington Post*, Jan. 1, 2002, pp. A1, A16-17.

10   The Standing Senate Committee on Agriculture and Forestry, "Bovine Growth Hormone Evidence"; James Baxter, "Scientists 'Pressured' to Approve Cattle Drug," *The Ottawa Citizen*, October 23, 1998.

11   Editorial, *Ottawa Citizen*, July 20, 2004.

12   Section 205.2 (Excluded methods), 65 *Federal Register* 80639, and section 205.105(f) and (g) (Allowed and prohibited substances, methods, and ingredients in organic production and handling), 65 *Federal Register* 80643 (December 21, 2000).

13   Barbara Kingsolver, *Small Wonder* (New York: HarperCollins, 2002), pp. 93-108.

14   Jeffrey M. Smith, *Seeds of Deception* (Fairfield, Iowa: Yes! Books, 2003), pp. 5-246.

15   Karen Charman, "Spinning Science into Gold," *Sierra*, July / August 2001, p. 44.

16   Barry Commoner, "Unraveling the DNA Myth: The Spurious Foundation of Genetic Engineering," *Harper's Magazine*, February 2002, pp. 46-47.

17   Rick Weiss, "Starved for Food, Zimbabwe Rejects U.S. Biotech Corn," *Washington Post*, July 31, 2002.

18   Opinion, "Poverty and Transgenic Crops," *Nature*, August 8, 2002, p. 418.

19   Clive James, "Global Review of Commercialized Transgenic Crops: 2001" (International Service for the Acquisition of Agri-biotech Applications, ISAAA Briefs, No 24 – 2001); "Ag Biotech Countdown" (ETC Group, June 2002, www.etcgroup.org).

20   Bill Freese, "Manufacturing Drugs and Chemicals in Crops: Biopharming Poses New Threats to Consumers, Farmers, Food Companies and the Environment" (Washington, DC: Genetically Engineered Food Alert, July 2002).

21   US National Research Council, *Environmental Effects of Transgenic Plants: The Scope and Adequacy of Regulation* (Washington, DC: National Academy Press, 2002), pp. 65-87.

22   Hembree Brandon, "Anti-biotech Radicals Turn Research into a War Zone," *Delta Farm Press*, August 30, 2002, p. 4.

23   Carson, *Silent Spring*, p. 297.

24   *Smithsonian*, July 2001, p. 15.

25   Marilyn Berlin Snell, "Against the Grain: Why Poor Nations Would Lose in a Biotech War on Hunger," *Sierra*, July / August 2001, pp. 30-33.

26   Mek Townsend, "Blair Urges Crackdown on Third World Profiteering," *The Observer*, Sept. 1, 2002.

27   Carmelo Ruiz Marrero, "Biotech Crops Invade Latin America," *Newspapertree*, April 28, 2005.

28   Hugh Pennington, "The English Disease," *London Review of Books*, December 14, 2000, pp. 3, 5-6.

29   Lord Phillips, June Bridgeman and Malcolm Ferguson-Smith, eds., *The BSE Inquiry*, 16 vols (London: Stationary Office, 2000), I, xvii.

30   Coordination Paysanne Europeenne / European Farmers Coordination, "Open Letter to the Ministers of Agriculture of the European Union" (Brussels, Belgium, December 1, 2000).

31   US Department of Agriculture, "State Fact Sheets: Population, Income, Education, and Employment" (Economic Research Service, September 6, 2005).

32   Michael Pollan, "How Organic Became a Marketing Niche and a Multibillion-Dollar Industry. Naturally," *The New York Times Magazine*, May 13, 2001, pp. 30-37, 57-58, 63-65.

33   *Sustainable Agriculture*, Fall 2001, p. 1 (Newsletter, University of California,

Davis).

34   Karen Klonsky and Kurt Richter, "Statistical Picture of California's Organic
      Agriculture" (University of California-Davis, 2005): www.aic.ucdavis.edu/
      events/cas_05/klonsky.pdf. Personal communication, Karen Klonsky, October
      12, 2005.

CHAPTER FIVE

1   Theodore Rosengarten, *All God's Dangers* (New York: Avon Books, 1975), p.
      316.
2   James Agee and Walker Evans, *Let Us Now Praise Famous Men: Three Tenant
      Families* (New York: Ballantine Books, 1976), pp. 124, 296.
3   *Transactions of California State Agricultural Society*, 1884, p. 285.
4   Quoted by Senator Gaylord Nelson in *Will the Family Farm Survive in America?*
      Joint Hearings Before the Select Committee on Small Business and the
      Committee on Interior and Insular Affairs, United States Senate, Ninety-Fourth
      Congress, First Session, Part 1A, Federal Reclamation Policy, July 17 and 22,
      1975 (Washington, DC: US Government Printing Office, 1976), p. 184.
5   David Lavender, *California: Land of New Beginnings* (Lincoln, Nebraska:
      University of Nebraska Press, 1987), p. 435.
6   Statement dated July 29, 1966 of Professor Paul S. Taylor, Berkeley, Calif. in *Will
      the Family Farm Survive in America?* p. 711.
7   John Steinbeck, *The Grapes of Wrath* (First published 1939, New York: Penguin
      Books, 1977), p. 36.
8   Letter of Governor William L. Guy to Senator Gaylord Nelson in *Role of Giant
      Corporations*, Hearings Before the Subcommittee on Monopoly of the Select
      Committee on Small Business, United States Senate, Ninety-Second Congress,
      First and Second Sessions, Part 3A, Corporate Secrecy: Agribusiness, November
      23 and December 1, 1971; March 1 and 2, 1972 (Washington, DC: US Government
      Printing Office, 1973), pp.4179-4180.
9   *Small Business and the Community: A Study in Central Valley of California
      on Effects of Scale of Farm Operations*, Report of the Special Committee to
      Study Problems of American Small Business, United States Senate, Seventy-
      Ninth Congress, Second Session, December 23, 1946 (Washington, DC: US
      Government Printing Office, 1946).
10   *Small Business and the Community* was reprinted in *Role of Giant Corporations*,
      Part 3A, pp. 4465-4648. Quotes from the introduction of Goldschmidt's study,
      pp. 4474-4477.
11   Victor Davis Hanson, *The Other Greeks: The Family Farm and the Agrarian
      Roots of Western Civilization* (New York: The Free Press, 1995), p. 27.
12   Victor Davis Hanson, *Fields Without Dreams: Defending the Agrarian Idea* (New
      York: The Free Press, 1996), p. xi.
13   Gene Logsdon, *At Nature's Pace: Farming and the American Dream* (New York:
      Pantheon Books, 1994), p. xi.

14   Walter Goldschmidt, "Research into the Effects of Corporate Farming on the Quality of Rural Community Life," *Role of Giant Corporations*, Hearings Before the Subcommittee on Monopoly of the Select Committee on Small Business, United States Senate, Ninety-Second Congress, First and Second Sessions, Part 3, Corporate Secrecy: Agribusiness, November 23 and December 1, 1971; March 1 and 2, 1972 (Washington, DC: US Government Printing Office, 1973), pp. 3925-3947.

15   Sophokles, *Philoktetes*, pp. 502-503.

16   Norman Borlaug, Nobel Lecture: "The Green Revolution, Peace, and Humanity," December 11, 1970 (www.nobel.se/peace/laureates/1970/borlaug-lecture.html).

17   Norman Borlaug, "Mankind and Civilization at Another Crossroad" (1971 McDougall Memorial Lecture, Conference, Sixteenth Session, UN Food and Agriculture Organization, Rome, 8 November 1971), pp. 36-70.

18   Timothy W. Jones, "Using Contemporary Archaeology and Applied Anthropology to Understand Food Loss in the American Food System" (Bureau of Applied Research in Anthropology, University of Arizona, Tucson, Arizona, 2004).

19   Henry W. Kindall and David Pimentel, "Constraints on the Expansion of the Global Food Supply," *Ambio*, Vol. 23, No. 3, May 1994.

20   Hembree Brandon, "Crop diversity vital to agriculture," *Delta Farm Press*, March 18, 2005.

21   Statement of Tony T. DeChant, president, National Farmers Union, Denver, Colo. in *Role of Giant Corporations*, Part 3A, p. 4181.

22   Statement of Ben H. Radcliffe, president, South Dakota Farmers Union, Huron, S. Dak., *Ibid.*, p. 4193.

23   US Department of Labor, *Migrant and Seasonal Farmworker Programs*, Employment and Training Administration, Office of National Programs (Washington, DC, 1978); Legal Services Corporation, *Special Legal Problems and Problems of Access to Legal Services of Veterans, Native Americans, People with Limited English-speaking Abilities, Migrant and Seasonal Farm Workers, Individuals in Sparsely Populated Areas*, A Report to Congress (2 vols., Washington, DC., 1979), II, 142-318.

24   House Select Committee to Investigate the Interstate Migration of Destitute Citizens, *Interstate Migration in Migrant and Seasonal Farmworker Powerlessness*, Hearings Before the Subcommittee on Migratory Labor of the Committee on Labor and Public Welfare, United States Senate, Ninety-First Congress, First and Second Sessions, Part 8-C: *Who is Responsible?* (Washington, DC: US Government Printing Office, 1971), p. 6042.

25   Robert LaFollette, "The Problem of Economic Democracy on the Land," *Congressional Record*, October 19, 1942, pp. 8318-8338, in *Ibid.*, p. 6255.

26   Quoted in *Ibid.*, p. 5972.

27   "What Harvest for the Reaper?" A Complete Transcript of National Educational Television's NET Journal, 1968, in *Migrant and Seasonal Farmworker Powerlessness*, Part 1: *Who are the Migrants?* p. 15.

28   "Migrant—An NBC White Paper," 1970 in *Migrant and Seasonal Farmworker*

Powerlessness, Part 8-C: *Who is Responsible?* p. 5972.

29   *Federal Environmental Pesticide Control Act of 1972*, Ninety-Second Congress, Second Session, Report No. 92-970, July 19, 1972 (Washington, DC: US Government Printing Office, 1972), p. 27.

30   The President's Commission on Mental Health, *Migrant and Seasonal Farmworkers*, A Report of the Task Panel on Migrant and Seasonal Farmworkers, February 15, 1978, p. 29.

31   Jack L. Runyan, *Profile of Hired Farmworkers, 1994 Annual Averages* (US Department of Agriculture, Economic Research Service, Agricultural Economic Report Number 748, Washington, DC, February 1997), p. iii.

32   US Department of Agriculture, *Yearbook of Agriculture 1936* (Washington, DC: Government Printing Office, 1936), p. 60.

33   Joseph A. Opala, *The Gullah: Rice, Slavery, and the Sierra Leone-American Connection* (Freetown, Sierra Leone: USIS, 1987).

34   Gary R. Grant, "Black Farmers not Taking Anything for Granted," Press Release, Black Farmers and Agriculturalists Association, Washington, DC, January 31, 1998.

35   Bill Mollison, "A Design Science with an Ethic," *Ceres*, November-December 1992, pp. 24-25.

36   Jan Rocha, "Jose Lutzenberger," *The Guardian*, May 16, 2002.

37   Duff Wilson, *Fateful Harvest: The True Story of a Small Town, a Global Industry, and a Toxic Secret* (New York: HarperCollins, 2001), p. 273.

38   Jerry Jost, "Looking to the Future," *Sustainable Farming News*. February 1992 (Kansas Rural Center, Whiting, Kansas).

39   Marty Strange, "An Open Letter to the Sustainable Agriculture Movement," *Center for Rural Affairs Newsletter*, December 1990 (Walthill, Nebraska).

40   United Nations Environment Programme, *Global Environment Outlook* (New York: Oxford University Press, 1997), p. 26.

41   Hugh Iltis, "Extinction is Forever," *Resurgence*, November/December 1997, pp. 18-22.

42   Luisa Maffi, "Linguistic Diversity" in Darrell Addison Posey, ed., *Cultural and Spiritual Values of Biodiversity: A Complementary Contribution to the Global Biodiversity Assessment* (London: Intermediate Technology Publications on behalf of the UN Environment Programme, 1999), pp. 21-35.

43   Hope Shand, *Human Nature: Agricultural Biodiversity and Farm-Based Food Security* (Ottawa, Canada: Rural Advancement Foundation International, December 1997), pp. 1-9. This report was prepared for the UN Food and Agriculture Organization.

44   Stewart Smith, "Farming - It's Declining in the U.S.," *Choices*, First Quarter 1992, p. 10.

45   Daniel Lee, "Progress of Agriculture in the United States," *Report of the Commissioner of Patents for the Year 1852*, Part II, *Agriculture*, Thirty-Second Congress, Second Session, House of Representatives, Ex. Doc. No. 65 (Washington, DC: Robert Armstrong, 1853), p. 1.

46   US Department of Agriculture, Economic Research Service, *Economic Indicators of the Farm Sector, National Finance Summary, 1987* (Washington, DC, 1987).

47   US Department of Agriculture, Economic Research Service, *Agricultural Resources and Environmental Indicators, 1996-97*, Agricultural Handbook Number 712 (Washington, DC, July 1997), p. 31.

48   Marty Strange, "Peace with the Land, Justice Among Ourselves," *Center for Rural Affairs Newsletter*, March 1997, p. 3.

49   Victor Davis Hanson, Personal Communication, February 21, 2000.

50   "The 400 Largest Private Companies in the U.S.," *Forbes*, Dec. 11, 1989, p. 220.

51   A.V. Krebs, *Heading Toward the Last Roundup: The Big Three's Prime Cut* (Des Moines, Iowa: PrairieFire Rural Action, June 1990), pp. 2-3. US Department of Agriculture, *Agricultural Statistics 1988*, p. 373. Krebs expanded *Heading Toward the Last Roundup* into *The Corporate Reapers: The Book of Agribusiness* (Washington, DC: Essential Books, 1992).

52   "Animal Waste Pollution in America: An Emerging National Problem, Environmental Risks of Livestock and Poultry Production" (Report Compiled by the Minority Staff of the United States Senate Committee on Agriculture, Nutrition, and Forestry for Senator Tom Harkin, December 1997).

53   Twiggs, Abrams, Strickland and Trehy, "Amended Complaint," State of North Carolina, Wake County, Neuse River Foundation, the Water Keeper Alliance v. Smithfield Foods, Inc., August 2000, paragraphs, 1-169.

54   "Animal Waste Pollution in America," p. 3.

55   Chuck Hassebrook, "Rural-friendly Livestock Industry Model Needed," *Center for Rural Affairs Newsletter*, Nov. 2001, p. 8; See also: Editorial, "The Curse of Factory Farms," *The New York Times*, Aug. 30, 2002.

56   John W. Helmuth, "Introduction," in Krebs, *Heading Toward the Last Roundup*, p. ix.

57   *Ibid.*, p. vi.

58   William Heffernan, Robert Gronski and Mary Hendrickson, "Concentration of Agricultural Markets—January 1999" (Department of Rural Sociology, University of Missouri, Columbia, Missouri, 1999). See also William Heffernan, "Confidence and Courage in the Next 50 Years," *Rural Sociology*, 1989, 54(2), 149-168; and "Agriculture and Monopoly Capital," *Monthly Review*, July / August 1998, pp. 46-59.

59   Eric Schlosser, *Fast Food Nation: The Dark Side of the All-American Meal* (Boston: Houghton Mifflin, 2001).

60   Upton Sinclair, *The Jungle* (first published in 1906, New York: Penguin Books, 1986), pp. 73-76.

61   Neal D. Barnard, "Throwing its Weight Around," *The Philadelphia Inquirer*, March 17, 2004, p. A15.

62   Jeff Cox and Ray Wolf, "Toward Mammoth Farms Run by Hirelings," *The New York Times*, March 6, 1977, p. E16.

63   National Academy of Sciences, Board on Basic Biology, Commission on Life

Sciences, *Research Briefing 1987: Report of the Research Panel on Biological Control in Managed Ecosystems* (Washington, DC: National Academy Press, 1987).

64 Vincent F. Garry et al., "Pesticide Appliers, Biocides, and Birth Defects in Rural Minnesota," *Environmental Health Perspectives*, April 1996, pp. 394-399.

65 National Academy of Sciences, National Research Council, *Alternative Agriculture* (Washington, DC: National Academy Press, 1989), p.7; Jane Houlihan and Richard Wiles, "Full Disclosure: What Ohioans Need to Know to Clean Up Their Rivers and Tap Water" (Washington, DC: Environmental Working Group, 1998); Velma M. Smith, "Protecting Groundwater from Pesticides: A Clean Water Action Guide" (Washington, DC: Friends of the Earth, 2000).

66 Gary Snyder, *Turtle Island* (New York: New Directions, 1974).

67 Warren P. Porter, "The Ecotoxicology Research Fund" in www.wisc.edu/zoology/faculty/fac/Por//Por.html.

68 Dan Fagin and Marianne Lavelle, *Toxic Deception: How the Chemical Industry Manipulates Science, Bends the Law, and Endangers Your Health* (Secaucus, NJ: Carol Publishing Group. 1996); Joshua Karliner with Alba Morales and Dana O'Rourke, "Lethal Injection: TriCal Inc. and the Poisonous Politics of Methyl Bromide" (San Francisco: Political Ecology Group and the Transnational Resource and Action Center, March 31, 1997); Charles Lewis, "Unreasonable Risk: The Politics of Pesticides" (Washington, DC: The Center for Public Integrity, 1998); Jeannine M. Kenney, Edward Groth and Charles M. Benbrook, "Worst First: High-Risk Insecticide Uses, Children's Foods and Safer Alternatives" (Washington, DC: Consumers Union of US, Sept. 1998).

69 Barry I. Castleman and Grace E. Ziem, "Corporate Influence on Threshold Limit Values," *American Journal of Industrial Medicine*, 13 (1988), p. 556.

70 A. W. Galston, "Defoliants," in *Chemical and Biological Warfare*, edited by Steven Rose (Boston: Beacon Press, 1969), pp. 62-75; Celia Kirby, *The Hormone Weedkillers* (London: BCPC Publications, 1980).

71 Kirby, *The Hormone Weedkillers*, p. 1.

72 "The Life Industry 1997: The Global Enterprises that Dominate Commercial Agriculture, Food and Health," *RAFI Communique*, November / December, 1997.

73 *Will the Family Farm Survive in America?* Joint Hearings Before the Select Committee on Small Business and the Committee on Interior and Insular Affairs, US Senate, 94th Congress, 1st Session, Part I: *Federal Reclamation Policy (Westlands Water District)*, July 17 and 22, 1975 (Washington, DC: US Government Printing Office, 1975), p. 74. See also: Peter Barnes, ed.. *The People's Land: A Reader on Land Reform in the United States* (Emmaus, PA: Rodale Press, 1975); Marc Reisner, *Cadillac Desert_* (New York: Penguin Books, 1987).

74 Donald Worster, *Rivers of Empire: Water, Aridity, and the Growth of the American West* (New York: Oxford University Press, 1985), pp. 3-15.

75 A.V. Krebs, *The Corporate Reapers: The Book of Agribusiness* (Washington,

DC: Essential Books, 1992), pp. 15-17.

76   Guillermo Delgado, "Indigenous People and UNCED", *The Independent Sector Network* (The Newsletter of the Centre for Our Common Future), Feb 1993, p. 3.

77   Angus Wright, "Taking Away a Heritage of Diversity," *Global Pesticide Campaigner,* Feb 1993, p. 8.

78   H. David Thurston, *Sustainable Practices for Plant Disease Management in Traditional Farming Systems* (Boulder, CO: Westview Press, 1992).

79   T.G.H. James, "Good Fellahs," *The Times Literary Supplement*, July 2, 1999, p. 4.

80   Leo Tolstoy, *Resurrection*, tr. by Rosemary Edmonds (Penguin Books, 1985), pp. 286-287.

81   Seabrook, pp. 113-114.

82   Matthias Uzo Igbozurike, "Against Monoculture", *The Professional Geographer,* Volume 23, No. 2, Apr 1971, pp. 113-117.

83   Cat Cox, *Chocolate Unwrapped: The Politics of Pleasure* (London: the Women's Environmental Network, 1993).

84   Chris McGreal, "Fears Grow for Children as Slave Ship Goes Missing," *The Guardian*, April 16, 2001; Alexandra Zavis, "African Child Labor or Slavery? Thousands Survive in Brutal Conditions on Plantation Fields," *Houston Chronicle*, May 5, 2001; Editorial, "Bitter Sweets," *The Philadelphia Inquirer*, June 27, 2001.

85   Joan Dye Gussow, "Breaking the Cycle of World Hunger and Poverty" (Remarks at Hunger Summit: Lessons from the Brazilian Experience, Aug 24, 1994) p. 4. See also: Susan George, *Ill Fares the Land* (London: Penguin Books, 1990).

86   "Women, Health and the Environment: Action for Cancer Prevention" (Consensus Statement drafted at the planning meeting convened by Greenpeace and WEDO in Austin, TX Feb 20-21, 1994; Women's Environment and Development Organization, New York, NY).

87   Thierry G. Verhelst, *No Life Without Roots: Culture and Development* (London, Zed Books, 1992), p.79.

88   William O. Douglas, "Revolution is Our Business" in *One Hundred Years of the Nation*, edited by Henry M. Christman (New York: Capricorn Books, 1972), pp. 290-294.

89   "The Cry for the Land," Joint Pastoral Letter by the Guatemalan Bishops' Conference, Nueva Guatemala de la Asuncion, Guatemala, February 29, 1988. Guatemalan Human Rights Commission, Washington, DC.

90   Elting E. Morison, *From Know-How to NoWhere: The Development of American Technology.* (New York: New American Library, 1977), p. 137.

91   Seabrook, p.111.

92   Hugh H. Iltis, "Freezing the Genetic Landscape," *Maize Genetics Cooperation News Letter, 1974* (Department of Botany, University of Illinois), pp. 199-200.

93   Hugh H. Iltis, "Shepherds Leading Sheep to Slaughter: The Biology Teacher and Man's Mad and Final War on Nature," *The American Biology Teacher*, Vol.

34, No. 3, March 1972, pp. 127-130, 137; "The Extinction of Species and the Destruction of Ecosystems," April 1972, pp. 201-205.

94   Gary Paul Nabhan, *Enduring Seeds: Native American Agriculture and Wild Plant Conservation* (San Francisco: North Point Press, 1989), pp. 49,193.

95   Lester M. Salamon, "The Time Dimension in Policy Evaluation: The Case of the New Deal Land-Reform Experiments," *Public Policy,* Spring 1979, pp. 129-141.

96   David Cecelski, "The Home Front's Dispossessed," *Southern Exposure*, Summer 1995, pp. 37-41.

97   Salamon, "The Time Dimension in Policy Evaluation," *Public Policy*, Spring 1979, pp. 141-183.

98   US Department of Agriculture, *Structure Issues of American Agriculture*, Economics, Statistics, and Cooperatives Service, Agricultural Economic Report 438 (Washington, DC: Government Printing Office, November 1979), pp. 80-81.

99   Patricia E. Funk and Jon M. Bailey, *Trampled Dreams: The Neglected Economy of the Rural Great Plains* (Walthill, NE: Center for Rural Affairs, 2000), pp. 1-7.

100   Interview with Calvin L. Beale, Senior Demographer, US Department of Agriculture, Washington, DC, Feb. 26, 2001. Beale has been a farm demographer with USDA for 47 years.

101   Edward M. Wolff, *The Rich Get Increasingly Richer* (Washington, DC: Economic Policy Institute, 1992), p.30.

102   John Pitney, "Will You Be Back?" *Christian Social Action*, Oct. 1994, p. 18.

CHAPTER SIX

1   Frank D. Alexander, "Cultural Reconnaissance Survey of Coahoma County, Mississippi" (Unpublished report, National Agricultural Library, Special Collection, US Department of Agriculture, Bureau of Agricultural Economics, December 1944), pp. 8, 13, 33.

2   Editorial, "Agricultural Racism," *Philadelphia Inquirer*, August 10, 2004.

CHAPTER SEVEN

1   Thierry A. Brun, "The Nutrition and Health Impact of Cash Cropping in West Africa: A Historical Perspective," *World Review of Nutrition and Dietetics*, Vol. 65, 1991, p. 152.

2   *Ibid.*, pp. 152-156.

3   Maxwell Owusu, "Agriculture and Rural Development Since 1935" in *UNESCO General History of Africa,* Vol. VIII: *Africa Since 1935*, edited by Ali A. Mazrui (Berkeley: University of California Press, 1993).

4   *Ibid.*, p. 350.

5   US Agency for International Development, "West Africa Regional Strategy: Concept Paper and Recommendations for Programmatic Action" (Bamako,

[Mali], Regional Strategy Team, October 26, 1998), pp. 10-13.

6   Eric Kashambuzi, "Critical Issues in African Development: Discussion Papers" (Unpublished monograph, New York, 1996). I had the good fortune to work with Eric Kashambuzi during 1995-1996 at the African Bureau of the UN Development Programme.

7   UN Food and Agriculture Organization, "Special Programme for Food Security" and "Investing in Food Security, a Worldwide Imperative" (TeleFood Fact Sheets, [October 1998].

8   *Ibid.*

9   UN Food and Agriculture Organization, "Water and Food Security" (World Food Summit, Rome, November 13-17, 1996.

10   Montague Yudelman, Anna Ratta and David Nygaard, *Pest Management and Food Production: Looking to the Future* (Washington, DC: International Food Policy Research Institute, Sept. 1998), p. 10.

11   Martin Meltzer and Philip Szmedra, "Pesticides and Productivity: Opportunities and Dilemmas in an Era of Agricultural Policy Reform in Africa" (Unpublished report, Bureau for Africa, US Agency for International Development, August 1996), pp. 21-22.

12   Meltzer and Szmedra, "Pesticides and Productivity," pp. 24-25.

13   Richard J. Tobin, *Bilateral Donor Agencies and the Environment: Pest and Pesticide Management* (Washington, DC: Bureau for Africa, US Agency for International Development, Technical Paper No. 42, December 1996), p. x.

14   Ken Saro-Wiwa, "We All Stand Before History," *New Solutions*, Spring 1996, p. 81.

15   Simeon T. Numbem, "Three Dimensional Use Framework for Resource Management: Application to Environmental Information System in the Humid Forest of the Congo Basin" (Unpublished draft paper, October 1998), p. 2.

16   UN Environment Programme, *Global Environment Outlook* (New York: Oxford University Press, 1997), p. 37.

17   UN Conference on Trade and Development, "Economic Development in Africa: Debt Sustainability, Oasis or Mirage?" (2004).

18   R.D. Mann, "Time Running Out," *The Ecologist*, March/April 1990, p. 53.

19   Ibid., p. 49.

20   United Nations Food and Agriculture Organization, "Water Development and Food Security" (Rome, 1996), p. 13.

21   J.H. Bernardin de Saint Pierre, *A Voyage to the Isle of France, the Isle of Bourbon, and the Cape of Good Hope; with Observations and Reflections Upon Nature and Mankind* (London: J. Cundee, 1800), pp. 119-120.

22   Allen Isaacman and Richard Roberts, eds., *Cotton, Colonialism, and Social History in Sub-Saharan Africa* (London: James Currey, 1995).

23   Cleophas Lado, "Female Labor Participation in Agricultural Production and the Implications for Nutrition and Health in Rural Africa," *Social Science and Medicine*, Vol. 34, No. 7, 1992, pp. 789-807.

24   Paul Richards, *Indigenous Agricultural Revolution: Ecology and Food Production*

in West Africa (Boulder: Westview Press, 1985), p. 162.

25   Laurence Roche, "Forestry and Famine: Arguments Against Growth Without Development," *The Ecologist*, Jan / Feb 1989, pp. 16-21.

26   Bill Rau, *From Feast to Famine: Official Cures and Grassroots Remedies to Africa's Food Crisis* (London: Zed Books, 1993), p. 147.

27   United Nations Food and Agriculture Organization, "Food, Agriculture and Food Security" (Rome, 1996), p. 11.

28   National Academy of Sciences, National Research Council, *Lost Crops of Africa* (Washington, DC: National Academy Press, 1996), p. 1.

29   Ibid., p. 15.

30   E.D. Morel, *The Black Man's Burden* (first published in 1920, reprint, New York: Monthly Review Press, 1969), pp. 128-132.

31   Chinua Achebe, *Things Fall Apart* (New York: Fawcett Crest, 1959), pp. 142-186.

32   Barbara Crossette, "U.N. Survey Finds World Rich-Poor Gap Widening," *New York Times*, July 15, 1996, p. A3.

33   Glenn Elert, ed., "Number of Billionaires" http://hypertextbook.com/facts/2005/MichelleLee.shtml; David Ludden, "A deadline for development," Frontline, April 13-26, 2002.

34   Aristoteles, *Politics* I ii, 1252b28-1253a2.

35   Xenophon, *Oikonomikos* 5.12-17.

36   Quoted in *Revolution: European Radicals from Hus to Lenin*, edited by Charles H. George (Glenview, Illinois: Scott, Foreman, 1971), p.134.

CHAPTER EIGHT

1   Edward Goldsmith, "Development as Colonialism," *The Ecologist*, March / April 1998, pp. 69-76.

2   Donald A. Brown, "American Shame: The Extraordinary Ethical Failure of the United States to Deal with Global Warming," Harvard Seminar on Environmental Values, Dec. 13, 2000.

3   UN Intergovernmental Panel on Climate Change, "Summary for Policymakers: Climate Change 2001: Impacts, Adaptation, and Vulnerability," Approved by IPCC Working Group II in Geneva, 13-16 February 2001.

4   "The International Research Partnership for Food Security and Sustainable Agriculture—Third System Review of the Consultative Group on International Agricultural Research" (Washington, DC: World Bank, September 30, 1998).

5   Octavio Paz, *The Labyrinth of Solitude*, tr. by Lysander Kemp, Yara Milos, and Rachel Philips Belash (New York: Grove Press, 1985), pp. 65-66.

6   Consultative Group on International Agricultural Research, "Toward Global Partnership in Agricultural Research" (Washington, DC, Document No: ICW/96/GF/07a, October 31, 1996).

7   Melaku Worede, "SOS/E: Working Towards Food Security," in *Voices from Africa: Sustainable Development*, edited by Leyla Alyanak (Geneva: UN Non-Governmental Liaison Service, August 1996), pp. 45-51.

8   Marguerite Feitlowitz, *A Lexicon of Terror: Argentina and the Legacies of Torture* (New York: Oxford University Press, 1998).

9   Cited in *No Life Without Roots: Culture and Development*, by Thierry G. Verhelst, tr. by Bob Cumming (London: Zed Books, 1992).

10 Joe Kane, "Moi Goes to Washington," *The New Yorker*, May 2, 1994, p. 74.

11 Laura Coppo, *The Color of Freedom*, ed. David H. Albert (Monroe, Maine: Common Courage Press, 2005), p. 210.

12 Philip Shenon, "Isolated Papua New Guineans Fall Prey to Foreign Bulldozers," *New York Times*, June 5, 1994, pp. 1, 14.

13 Wangari Maathai, "A New Partnership for Development: Agenda for Development, the Experience of the Green Belt Movement" (statement at the UN World Hearings on Development, New York, June 9, 1994).

14 Peter Raven, "Plants in Peril: What Should We Do?" (XVI International Botanical Congress, Missouri Botanical Garden, August 1-7, 1999, St. Louis, Missouri).

15 Quoted in Jeremy Seabrook, *Pioneers of Change: Experiments in Creating a Humane Society* (Philadelphia, PA: New Society Publishers, 1993), pp. 44, 46.

16 Noam Chomsky, *Hegemony or Survival: America's Quest for Global Dominance* (New York: Metropolitan Books, 2003).

17 Gabriel Garcia Marquez, *One Hundred Years of Solitude*, tr. by Gregory Rabassa (New York: Harper Perennial, 1991), pp. 234, 244.

18 Mark Vallianatos with Andrea Durbin, *License to Loot: The MAI and How to Stop it* (Washington, DC: Friends of the Earth, 1998).

19 Davison L. Budhoo, *Enough is Enough* (New York: New Horizons Press, 1990); Bruce Rich, *Mortgaging the Earth: The World Bank, Environmental Impoverishment, and the Crisis of Development* (Boston: Beacon Press, 1994).

20 Julie Delahanty, "Bracing for 'El Nuna': Andean Groups Hopping Mad About Popping-Bean Patent" (News Release, Rural Advancement Foundation International, March 20, 2001).

21 Darrell Addison Posey, "Maintaining the Mosaic" in *Cultural and Spiritual Values of Biodiversity*, p. 549.

22 Rich, *Mortgaging the Earth*, p. 149.

23 Environmental Defense Fund, "IMF Package Guts Environmental Protection in Brazil" (Washington, DC, Press Release, Nov. 25, 1998).

24 John Perkins, *Confessions of an Economic Hit Man* (San Francisco: Berrett-Koehler, 2004).

25 Hugh H. Iltis, "A Requiem for the Prairie," *Prairie Naturalist*, Vol. 1, No. 4, December 1969, p. 51.

26 Hugh H. Iltis, "Serendipity in the Exploration of Biodiversity: What Good are Weedy Tomatoes?" in *Biodiversity*, ed. E.O. Wilson (Washington, DC: National Academy Press, 1986), p. 99.

27 John DeMont, "Gunboat Diplomacy: Canada Fires the First Shots in What May Become an All-Out Fish War with Europe," *Maclean's*, March 20, 1995.

28 Sylvia A. Earle, "Human Health and the State of the Oceans: A Long, Deep View" (Washington, DC, Capitol Hill Briefing: Endangered Oceans: Threats to Human

Health, Center for Health and the Global Environment, Harvard Medical School, Dec. 7, 1998. The sponsors of the briefing, The Center for Health and the Global Environment of the Harvard Medical School, issued a report that summarizes the rise of marine-related diseases throughout the US Atlantic coast, Gulf of Mexico, and the Caribbean as well as the medical consequences of ocean pollution and climate change: Paul Epstein and others, *Marine Ecosystems: Emerging Diseases as Indicators of Change: Health of the Oceans From Labrador to Venezuela* (Year of the Ocean Special Report, Dec. 1998).

29   Institute for Agriculture and Trade Policy and World Hunger Year, "Proceedings from a Hunger Summit: Lessons from the Brazilian Experience," New York, August 24, 1994, pp. 4-7.

30   Bill Devall, ed., *Clearcut: The Tragedy of Industrial Forestry* (San Francisco: Sierra Club Books and Earth Island Press, 1993).

31   Paul R. Ehrlich and Anne H. Ehrlich, *Betrayal of Science and Reason: How Anti-Environmental Rhetoric Threatens Our Future* (Washington, DC: Island Press, 1996).

32   Dan Fagin and Marianne Lavelle, *Toxic Deception: How the Chemical Industry Manipulates Science, Bends the Law, and Endangers Your Health* (Secaucus, NJ: Carol Publishing Group, 1996).

33   Wilhelm C. Hueper, "Adventures of a Physician in Occupational Cancer: A Medical Cassandra's Tale" (Unpublished autobiography, 1976, pp. 300-302. Hueper Papers, National Library of Medicine).

34   Samuel S. Epstein and Liza Gross, "The High Stakes of Cancer Prevention," *Tikkun*, November 2000.

35   Samuel S. Epstein, "Losing the War Against Cancer: Who's to Blame and What to do about it" (The Fifth National Pesticide Forum, Washington, DC, March 20-23, 1987), pp. 1-7.

36   Hugh H. Iltis, "The Extinction of Life on Earth: Asking the Proper Questions" in "Threats to the Tropical Biota" (Symposium on the Biogeography of Mesoamerica, Merida, Yucatan, Mexico, 26-30 October 1984).

37   Robert U. Ayres and Udo E. Simonis, eds., *Industrial Metabolism: Restructuring for Sustainable Development* (Tokyo: United Nations University Press, 1994), p. xii. See also Robert N. Proctor, *Cancer Wars: How Politics Shapes What We Know and Don't Know About Cancer* (New York: BasicBooks, 1995; Samuel Epstein, "Winning the War Against Cancer? ... Are They Even Fighting it?" *The Ecologist*, March / April 1998, pp. 69-80.

38   John R. Krebs **et al.**, "The Second Silent Spring?" *Nature*, August 12, 1999, pp. 611-612.

39   UN Environment Programme, "Sustainable Agri-Food Production and Consumption Forum: Key Issues and Information Sources–Agri-Food Production and Biodiversity" [2001] <http://www.agrifood-forum.net/issues/production.htm>

40   World Wildlife Fund International, *Living Planet Report 2002* (Gland, Switzerland: WWF, 2002), pp. 3, 19.

41   International Joint Commission, *Ninth Biennial Report on Great Lakes Water*

Quality (Ottawa, Ontario, Canada, June 10, 1998), p. 10.

42   Niccolo Machiavelli, *The Prince*, trans. by George Bull (New York: Penguin Books, 1995), p. 56.

CONCLUSION

1   Dean MacCannell, "Agribusiness and the Small Community" (background paper to *Technology, Public Policy and the Changing Structure of American Agriculture*, US Office of Technology Assessment, US Congress, 1983).

2   Joel Schor, "Black Farmers / Farms: The Search for Equity" (USDA, unpublished paper, Spring 1995).

3   Ken Silverstein, "Meat Factories," *Sierra*, January / February 1999, pp. 28-35, 110-112.

4   Platon, *Gorgias* 479d-484c.

5   Carl B. Koford, "The Prairie Dog of the North American Plains and its Relations with Plants, Soil, and Land Use," *Symposium: Ecology and Management of Wild Grazing Animals in Temperate Zones* (Warsaw: International Union of Conservation of Nature, 1960), p. 340.

6   Douglas Tompkins, "Prologue" in *Fatal Harvest: The Tragedy of Industrial Agriculture*, ed. Andrew Kimbrell (Covelo, CA: Island Press, 2002), p. xi.

7   Via Campesina, "The Tlaxcala Declaration" (April 1996). The Secretariat of Via Campesina is in Tegucigalpa, Honduras.

8   Nick Middleton and David Thomas, eds., *World Atlas of Desertification*, p. 154.

9   Mary Jordan, "Unfamiliar Turf: Saving the Environment," *The Washington Post*, Dec. 28, 2001, pp. A1, A16.

10   Chad Kister, *Arctic Melting* (Monroe, Maine: Common Courage Press, 2005).

11   R.D. Hodges, "Agriculture and Horticulture; the Need for a More Biological Approach," *Biological Agriculture and Horticulture*, 1, 1982, pp. 1-13.

12   Leo Horrigan, Robert S. Lawrence, and Polly Walker, "How Sustainable Agriculture Can Address the Environmental and Human Health Harms of Industrial Agriculture," *Environmental Health Perspectives*, vol. 110, no. 5, May 2002, pp. 445-456.

13   Miguel A. Altieri, *Agroecology: The Science of Sustainable Agriculture* (Boulder, CO: Westview Press, 1995).

14   Paul Richards, "Casting Seed to the Four Winds: A Modest Proposal for Plant Genetic Diversity Management" in *Cultural and Spiritual Values of Biodiversity*, p. 316, also pp. 287-323, 381-382.

15   Jose Lutzenberger, "The Absurdity of Modern Agriculture–From Chemical Fertilizers and Agropoisons to Biotechnology" (Brazil, Fundacao Gaia, October 1998).

16   *Third World Resurgence*, December 1991.

17   Joan Martinez Alier, "The Ecological Interpretation of Socio-Economic History: Andean Examples," *Capitalism, Nature, Socialism*, June 1991, pp. 110-111.

18   Board on Science and Technology for International Development, National

Research Council, National Academy of Sciences, *Lost Crops of the Incas: Little-Known Plants of the Andes with Promise for Worldwide Cultivation* (Washington, DC: National Academy Press, 1989); Miguel A. Altiery, Peter Rosset, and Lori Ann Thrupp, "The Potential of Agroecology to Combat Hunger in the Developing World" (2020 Brief 55, Washington, DC: International Food Policy Research Institute, October 1998); United Nations Development Programme, *Agroecology: Creating the Synergism for a Sustainable Agriculture* (New York, 1995); Lori Ann Thrupp, *New Partnerships for Sustainable Agriculture* (Washington, DC: World Resources Institute, 1997); Lori Ann Thrupp, *Cultivating Diversity: Agrobiodiversity and Food Security* (Washington, DC: World Resources Institute, 1998).

19   Bernal Diaz, *The Conquest of New Spain*, tr. J.M. Cohen (Harmondsworth, England: Penguin Books, 1975), p. 231.

20   Michael Redclift, "'Raised Bed' Agriculture in Pre-Columbian Central and South America: A Traditional Solution to the Problem of 'Sustainable' Farming Systems?" *Biological Agriculture and Horticulture*, 1987(5), pp. 51-59.

21   Phil Gunson, "Honduran Villagers Survived Mitch with a Method as Old as the Hills," *The Guardian*, November 23, 1998.

22   Richard H. Grove, "Colonial Conservation, Ecological Hegemony and Popular Resistance: Towards a Global Synthesis," in John Mackenzie, ed., *Imperialism and the Natural World* (Manchester: Manchester University Press, 1990), pp. 15-50; Bron Raymond Taylor, ed., *Ecological Resistance Movements: The Global Emergence of Radical and Popular Environmentalism* (Albany: State University of New York Press, 1995).

23   Jonathan King and Doreen Stabinsky, "Biotechnology Under Globalisation: The Corporate Expropriation of Plant, Animal and Microbial Species," *Race and Class*, October 1998-March 1999, p. 86. One of the most sensitive interpretations of peasant behavior under the perpetual stress of scarcity is *The Moral Economy of the Peasant: Rebellion and Subsistence in Southeast Asia* by James C. Scott (New Haven: Yale University Press, 1976). James Scott is a professor of political science and directs a Program in Agrarian Studies at Yale University.

24   Silvia Ribeiro, "Seedy Squabble in Switzerland," *Rural Advancement Foundation International News Release*, November 20, 2000.

25   Rural Advancement Foundation International (RAFI), Press Release, March 23, 2001. RAFI changed its name to ETC in 2002 http://www.etcgroup.org. It remains an outstanding global civil society organization.

26   Julie Anton Dunn, "Organic Food and Fiber: An Analysis of 1994 Certified Production in the United States" (US Department of Agriculture, Agricultural Marketing Service, Transportation and Marketing Division, September 1995); Catherine Greene, *U.S. Organic Farming Emerges in the 1990s: Adoption of Certified Systems* (Washington, DC., US Department of Agriculture, Economic Research Service, Resource Economics Division, Agriculture Information Bulletin No. 770, June 2001).

27   E.G. Vallianatos, "Organic Farmers Would Be Better than One-crop Plantations," *St. Louis Post-Dispatch*, August 4, 1999.

28   Daniel Imhoff, "Beyond Organic: Farming with Salmon, Coyotes, and Wolves," *Sierra*, January / February 1999, pp. 24-26.

29   Catherine Greene and Thomas Dobbs, "Organic Wheat Production in the United States," *Wheat Yearbook/WHS-2001*, March 2001, pp. 31-37.

30   "French Farmers Damage Engineered Corn," *The Ram's Horn*, February 1998.

31   Agence France Presse, "Global Farmers' Body Calls for Solidarity Against Corporate Control" (Oct. 2, 2000).

32   "Southern African Charter on Land, Labour and Food Security" (Harare, Zimbabwe: International South Group Network, [1996]). Yash Tandon gave me a copy of this Charter supported by dozens of civil society organizations in South Africa, Zimbabwe, Angola, Tanzania, Mozambique, Botswana, Burkina Faso, Malawi, Swaziland, Lesotho, and Namibia.

33   Margaret Mellon, Charles Benbrook and Karen Lutz Benbrook, *Hogging It: Estimates of Antimicrobial Abuse in Livestock* (Cambridge, MA: Union of Concerned Scientists, 2001), pp. xi-xiii, 57.

Index

About the Author

E.G. Vallianatos is a passionate lover of nature and democratic family farming. He discovered the Cold War origins of US agricultural policy and corporate hijacking of American farming while an analyst with the US Envrionmental Protection Agency. The son of a Greek farmer, he is the author of *Fear in the Countryside* and *Harvest of Devastation*. He is also a humanist scholar with interest in Greek history and science, how Greek culture became the foundation of Western civilization. He is the author of From Graikos to Hellene. His articles have appeared in the *Christian Science Monitor*, the *Chicago Tribune*, the *St. Louis Post-Dispatch*, the *Philadelphia Inquirer*, the *Miami Herald*, the *Baltimore Sun*, the *Progressive Populist*, *Race and Class* and other publications.

6